DATE DUE

DEC 0 1 2009

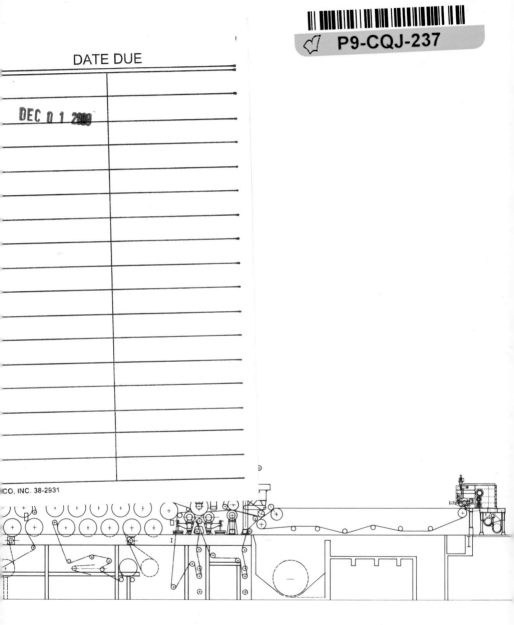

ETHYL

A *History of the Corporation*
and the People Who Made It

ETHYL

A History of the Corporation
and the People Who Made It

JOSEPH C. ROBERT

University Press of Virginia

Charlottesville

THE UNIVERSITY PRESS OF VIRGINIA
Copyright © 1983 by the Rector and Visitors
of the University of Virginia

Third printing 1984

Library of Congress Cataloging in Publication Data
Robert, Joseph C.
Ethyl : a history of the corporation and the people
who made it.

Includes index.
1. Ethyl Corporation—History.   2. Conglomerate
corporations—United States—History.   I.
Title.   HD9503.R62   1983   338.7′66′00973   83–6620
ISBN 0–8139–1001–3
ISBN 0–8139–1002–1 (pbk.)

*Front endpaper: Paper machine number three, Roanoke Rapids, N.C.
Basic drawings from Beloit Iron Works.*
Back endpaper: Main Building, Ethyl Headquarters, Richmond, Va.

Printed in the United States of America

Dedicated to
THE PEOPLE OF ETHYL
Past, Present, and Future

Contents

Illustrations

Preface

The plan of this book is to narrate the most significant events in the history of Ethyl Corporation and to describe those individuals who were central in its development. The emphasis is on people. Although the purpose is to tell of decisive circumstances, the following narrative makes no claim to being a complete history. To retain a manageable length, the author was forced to be highly selective in presenting both facts and people. It has been especially painful to abbreviate biographical facts extracted in interviews with many personable characters who contributed to corporate success. And the author does not expect all readers to agree with his choice of material to be included.

Furthermore, the author is well aware of that entrapment which may be entitled "the accident of evidence," for surely any historian in using what is at hand—as indeed he must—is tempted to identify the *available* as the *important*. And this equation is not always true. Thus in reporting what he has found, the author acknowledges that he leaves many heroes unsung because they have been recorded only fractionally or not at all.

This has been a cooperative venture; so numerous have been the people assisting that the book might well be defined as a joint enterprise. Choice bits of the narrative are drawn from the recollections of persons associated with Albemarle Paper Manufacturing Company and with Ethyl Corporation years ago. After checking memories against records of the times, the author has developed a new respect for the validity of mankind's ability to recall past events. As noted in the essay on sources, which follows the text, large segments of the narrative may be classified as "oral history." There were over 125 taped interviews that recorded the recollections of approximately 90 people, and there were numerous brief conversations and inquiries resulting in many dozens of memorandums. The narrative has especially benefited from the reminiscences of the late F. D. Gottwald as given in 27 taped interviews and a number of brief question-and-answer sessions.

Lawrence E. Blanchard, Jr., vice chairman of Ethyl Corporation, thought there was a story to be told and suggested the writing of this history because he was certain that the Gottwalds themselves would never seek such a volume. The gathering of material for the book was subsidized by the corporation. As for the resultant text, though Ethyl underwrote it, the author wrote it and assumes responsibility for the shortcomings in this often complex drama with its large cast of characters and scenes ranging all the way from the 1880s to the 1980s. His conclusion is that while mistakes have been made, Ethyl is a great and responsible corporation.

It is hoped that the recital of the careers of men who began in modest circumstances and then through energy and imagination achieved notably might explain to an often cynical generation something about America and its opportunities.

To understand the history of the present Ethyl Corporation, one must first of all remember that in 1962 Albemarle Paper Manufacturing Company, founded in Virginia in 1887, borrowed $200 million and purchased Ethyl Corporation (Delaware), which had been chartered in 1924. Albemarle Paper Manufacturing Company then changed its name to Ethyl Corporation (Virginia). Out of this essentially two-product organization as it existed at the time of the merger in 1962—paper from Albemarle and gasoline antiknock additives from Ethyl (Delaware)—has evolved the current company. To quote the company's most recent official statement as to its nature: "Ethyl Corporation is a diversified, high-technology producer of performance chemicals for the petroleum industry, specialty chemicals, plastics and aluminum products and has developing interests in oil, gas and coal. Ethyl also owns First Colony Life Insurance Company."

Worldwide in operation, the company employs approximately 14,500 people and reported annual sales of over $1.7 billion for 1981, the last full year for which statistics are available. Headquarters are in Richmond, Virginia, where the company occupies handsome office buildings along the James River and squarely on top of historic Gamble's Hill.

As indicated in the Ethyl seal, the corporate lifeline goes back to 1887. Thus as the first order of business the events of that important year must be reviewed.

Part One

ALBEMARLE

I

The Foundation Years
1887–1907

The Mood in Richmond, both Nostalgic and
Progressive

RICHMOND GREETED THE year 1887 with exuberant optimism. Journalists and civic leaders in this city of 75,000 boasted of its factories and mercantile establishments, and saw even greater prosperity ahead. The New Year's edition of the *Richmond Dispatch* displayed such headlines as "A Growing City" and "Manufacturers Busy."

In a cautious way Richmond was both innovative and international. The city's business community looked not only to the nation but to the world for its markets, an expansive view based on the traditional export of tobacco products and flour from the factories and mills along the James River. Indicative of a willingness to try new things was Richmond's welcome to the age of electricity. In February 1886 the city had been experimentally lighted by electricity, and before the end of the year 1887 it could boast of having the first electric street railway in the world.

No real Richmonder would be apologetic about Virginia's part in the Civil War, but he was willing to listen to the Centennial journalist who begged in poetic plea, "Give us back the ties of Yorktown. Perish all the modern hates!" The Boston post of the Grand Army of the Republic in 1886 was entertained by the R. E. Lee Camp, United Confederate Veterans. State officials were now with equal fervor dedicating monuments to heroes of

Murphy's Hotel, about 1889, from hotel billhead

the Old South and laying cornerstones of factories created by heroes of the New South. In prophetic phrases the editor of *The State* in its pages of January 1 wrote, "The year 1887 promises to mark a very important era in the history of our progress."

If anything else was needed to stir hope and to build confidence, such was abundantly provided by Henry W. Grady's immortal speech on "The New South" before the New England Society of New York on December 21, 1886, an intoxicating blend of love of the agrarian past and hope for an industrial future.

It was in this mellow climate of nostalgia and progressivism, of local pride and national reconciliation, that a handful of Virginians sought for opportunity in a new industrial venture and concluded that the time was ripe for the building of a paper manufacturing plant along the James River. True, there were already three paper mills in Richmond: Richmond Paper Manufacturing Company, Virginia Paper Company, and Old Dominion Paper Mill. However, the total annual output of these three, as reported late in the year 1886 and based on 1885 figures, was valued at only $285,000. Capitalization was listed as $176,000 and hands employed as 223. South of the river was the Manchester Paper Mill, specializing in paper twine, a relatively novel product.

At 9:15 on Friday evening, February 11, 1887, five businessmen—J. F. Chalmers, G. A. Cunningham, Thomas S. Flournoy, Jr., W. E. Dibrell, and E. B. Thaw—met at Murphy's Hotel, corner of Eighth and Broad, to consider the matter of forming a company for the manufacture of paper. One hopes that before the beginning of the business session the five dined bounteously on the oysters for which Murphy's was famous, because they had much to do between the hour of convening and bedtime. Chalmers was called to the chair, and Thaw acted as secretary. The group heard Thaw discuss the virtues of Richmond as the site of the proposed plant, authorized an application to the Circuit Court of the City of Richmond for a charter, created a board of directors and a slate of officers, named a committee to negotiate for real estate and for water rights, and favorably received a motion from one of the group, W. E. Dibrell, editor of the *Southern Tobacconist*, that the proposed corporation be entitled "Albemarle Paper Manufacturing Company." It was a good night's work by almost any standard.

The organizers were merchants or were closely allied to the mercantile community, sensitive to the quickening economic pulse of the Old Dominion. Three of the founding group deserve more particular comment: Thaw, the promoter; Chalmers, the first president; and, although of only momentary importance, Dibrell, who named the company.

At the time he gave his persuasive plea to the businessmen at Murphy's Hotel, Edward Bedell Thaw, a Richmonder by birth, was thirty years of age, an experienced bookkeeper and salesman, with little or no capital, and now looking for a major business connection. Needing a new alliance, he energetically pushed for the organization of a paper manufacturing concern in which he might have an active part. Neither wealthy enough to contribute accumulated capital nor old enough to have earned a Civil War record, he saw the chief titles go to others. He was made secretary and treasurer in the original petition; in a matter of weeks, however, he was put on the board of directors. By September he dropped his title of secretary and treasurer for that of manager, all the while drawing a salary of $60 a month.

James Fenelon Chalmers

The man who did assume the presidency of Albemarle Paper Manufacturing Company, and held that office for a full twenty years lacking one month, was James Fenelon Chalmers, at the time of the organization of the company legally a resident of Smithfield, Virginia. He was a bearded gentleman, fifty-four years old, a man of political as well as mercantile experience. Active in veterans' organizations, he answered to the name of "Captain Chalmers" all his adult life, for he had served as captain of Company E, 19th Battalion of Artillery, during the Civil War. As a merchant in Smithfield with conspicuous family connections, he had a large acquaintance over the county of Isle of Wight and for years was one of the commissioners of revenue. A one-hundred-percent Democrat, he entered local politics and in the fall of 1885 was elected by a large majority to the House of Delegates as representative from Isle of Wight County, attending the regular session, which lasted from December 2, 1885, to March 6, 1886, and the special session, which met from March 16, 1887, to May 24, 1887.

He conscientiously answered roll call at the meetings of the House of Delegates, voting along orthodox and predictable lines. In Richmond he liked what he saw; there was a vitality and communication in the capital city which Smithfield at that time simply did not have.

It was in the month before the beginning of the special session that Chalmers met with Thaw and others at Murphy's Hotel for the formation of the Albemarle Paper Manufacturing Company. He had the proper age, dignity, business experience, "connections," capital, and credit. When he agreed to be president, he knew that he would soon have to move to Richmond, as he did, first establishing himself on Grace Street in a manner proper for a man of his position. He drove a carriage with two horses and paid taxes on bonds and securities valued at $12,645. Albemarle was not enough for the expansive Chalmers; he also went into the coal and wood business. In 1903 Chalmers settled into a house of his own, buying the three-story residence at 1119 Grove Avenue for $9,000.

Dibrell, who chose Albemarle as the name for the company, had a manner and a background that made him feel comfortable in any Richmond gathering. As a consequence of his family connection with the tobacco export trade, he attended school in Germany, then settled in Richmond as a journalist and sometime dealer in tobacco. From reminiscences of his relatives and from extant documents, it appears that his family thought of him as somewhat indolent, perhaps even a black sheep. Though periodically lacking money, Dibrell was never short of wit and charm. He brought a light note to those early meetings of the board. Other than his urbane manner, his sole contribution to the new company seems to be the name he gave it. And nobody has ever presented a convincing reason as to why "Albemarle." So far as can be discovered, he had no connection with Albemarle County in Virginia, the Albemarle section of North Carolina, or that

portion of the Normandy coast of France that once went under
that label. Apparently the syllables simply pleased his ear, and
the other directors had no better alternative to offer.

At the meeting in Murphy's Hotel on February 11, 1887, J. H.
Dineen, a lawyer, partner in the firm of Spottswoods and Dineen
and present by proxy, was instructed to draw up the charter application. Under date of February 12, a petition was submitted
to the Honorable B. R. Wellford, Jr., judge of the Circuit Court
of the City of Richmond, for the creation of a joint-stock company, capital to be not less than $10,000 nor more than $200,000,
the shares to be subscribed on a basis of $100 per share. The
company's real estate was not to exceed 100 acres. The initial
officers are listed as: president, J. F. Chalmers; vice president,
G. A. Cunningham; secretary-treasurer, E. B. Thaw. Directors
were Chalmers, Cunningham, Flournoy, Dibrell, and Dineen.
The document was notarized on the fourteenth, and the corporation was authorized on the fifteenth by the creation of "a body
politic and corporate by the name of Albemarle Paper Manufacturing Company," as the action was recorded in the court minutes of that day.

From the records it is clear that the directors had not waited
until the issue of the charter to get affairs in motion. Indeed, in
some areas action had *preceded* the formal organizational meeting at Murphy's. The all-important lease of the land on Tredegar
Street between the James River and the Kanawha Canal chosen
for the location of the factory was negotiated earlier with the
Union Bank of Richmond, a savings institution closely allied
with the First National Bank. The date of the lease is February
11, 1887, and it is reasonable to assume that the arrangements
were completed in daylight hours, certainly not after the formal
meeting, which began at 9:15 P.M. The lease had a life span of
five years, with payment to be made at the rate of $400 per an-
num. The company reserved the option to purchase the property
at any time during the period of the lease at $25 per front foot,
meaning $10,000.

The organizers allotted among themselves the original issue of

220 shares at $100 per share: Flournoy took 75, Chalmers and Cunningham 50 each, Dibrell and Thaw 20 each, and Dineen 5. On this frail capital structure, nominally $22,000 but much in the form of promises to pay, people of hope began to translate an idea into brick buildings, iron machinery, and a working operation.

While the founders were men of vision, they were also men of practical experience, and they knew that even under the happiest of circumstances it would be about a year before production and sales could begin. There was, however, one thing they could do almost overnight: set up store and get into the paper business. Indeed, they thought that this wholesale paper business might be kept going alongside the manufacture and distribution of their own specialities; such an arrangement was being tried by other papermakers. Accordingly, company officers hired a few clerk-salesmen (including Captain Chalmers's son, W. F. Chalmers), rented warehouse space on Main Street near 13th Street, had a telephone and carpet installed, bought a papercutter and iron safe, stocked basic items that Richmond businesses needed, took out insurance on the stock, and proclaimed that they were in the business of selling paper. This immediate venture, which was under way by May 1887, came easily to both Chalmers and Thaw, each a salesman. In the long run the jobbing venture amounted to little, dying a natural death soon after manufacturing operations began early in 1888. Perhaps the main reason for the decline and disappearance of this particular business was the fact that major attention, quite properly, was being given to building the factory, purchasing and installing machinery, and getting production of paper under way.

The name Hollywood seemed appropriate, for the mill was near the eastern boundary of famed Hollywood Cemetery, separated only by the Kanawha Canal and its obsolete tow path, by that time a hard-packed foundation for the tracks of the Richmond and Alleghany Railroad. By its location the factory had easy access to the rail line and to the canal water needed in the manufacturing process and also as a source of power.

The first plans and specifications for Hollywood Mill were drawn by Ashley B. Tower of the architectural firm D. H. and A. B. Tower in Holyoke, Massachusetts, which advertised that paper mill designs were its specialty. Back home after a trip to Richmond for an on-site inspection of the land, Tower was dismayed to hear that Thaw was abandoning Tower's design and instead had drawn plans with some assistance from Peter J. White, a Richmond architect. (White was popular among Confederate veterans for his record as a teenage cavalryman under Fitzhugh Lee.) What features, if any, of Tower's plans and specifications surfaced in Thaw's own sketch, and exactly how much advice came by way of White, are factors which cannot be determined today. Thus responsibility for the design of the building should be divided in an unknown ratio among Tower, Thaw, and White. Hollywood's appearance was rescued from the shoe-box norm of nineteenth-century industrial architecture by its pleasant riparian setting and an elbow bend in the layout to accommodate land contours and the restrictions of a 400-foot frontage.

In the construction of the mill, three and four stories in height and approximately 40 feet by 300 feet in breadth and length, management hired individual workmen or firms to do the excavating, brickwork, and the like; there was no general contracting. The day labor was under the supervision of Thaw and of J. W. Stiles, a millwright with special knowledge of the waterpower chain, later superintendent of Manchester Paper Mill. Heavy equipment, of course, was put in place on the lower floors. The basic machine was an 88-inch Fourdrinier, bought in the summer of 1887 for $12,500.00. Other primary equipment included a rotary boiler 7 feet by 22 feet for $1,800.00, four 48-inch by 48-inch beating engines at $950.00 each, one "Jourdan" engine for $650.00, and a waterwheel for $544.25.

Though the waterwheel was the major source of power for preparing and refining the stock, from the very beginning there was a variable-speed steam engine for driving the paper machine which required more exact control than was possible with a take-

James Lishman

off from the waterwheel. The exhaust from the steam engine was used to operate the "can" dryers.

New Faces in Management and on the Board

The top management of Albemarle realized from the very beginning that country merchants, coal company clerks, and suburban lawyers, no matter how energetic and imaginative, were not qualified for the actual operation of a paper mill. All along the highest officers intended to employ a competent and experienced papermaker to assume oversight of the manufacturing process. The first superintendent was Lorenzo A. Sadler, who had served his apprenticeship with the McIlwaine Paper Mill in Petersburg and more recently had been associated with the Old Dominion Paper Mill in Richmond. He worked during March, April, May, and up to June 4. Then for reasons now unknown he left. At this point the directors were lucky enough, or smart enough, to employ a man who proved to be the best possible choice for management of operations. He was an Englishman, James Lishman, who, as much as any other man, was responsible for the success of Albemarle during the first twenty years of its existence.

Lishman was born March 3, 1852, in Cowan Head Village in Cumbria; he learned the business of making blotting paper, his specialty, under the tutelage of his father, superintendent of the

Postlip Mills in Gloucester County, northwest central England. In appearance James Lishman was compactly built, of medium height, of florid complexion, and with a prominent nose, a feature the family good-humoredly called "the Lishman nose." In motion he had a quick step and was slightly bent over, another trait the family thought characteristic of itself and labeled "the Lishman stoop." In manner he rarely raised his voice, but he soon let people know that he was a precise, no-nonsense manager who kept a sharp eye on costs.

As the winter of 1887–88 came and went, any astute observer of affairs at Albemarle Paper Manufacturing Company could see that Lishman was a man on the way up, Thaw a man on the way down and out. In November, Thaw found himself unable to meet the required payments on his stock subscription and thus had to forfeit his twenty shares. While it is true that after the beginning of the year 1888 Thaw's salary was raised from $60 a month to $100, the company was merely carrying out an earlier agreement. Thaw allowed his attention to become diverted from Albemarle to other affairs. For a brief period he assumed the presidency of a new firm, Virginia Printing and Lithographing Company (chartered March 19, 1888), this while retaining his position as manager of Albemarle. Then, spurred by restlessness and dissatisfaction, he grasped an opportunity a hundred miles or so farther up the James River: a paper manufacturing plant was being planned for Big Island in Bedford County, northwest of Lynchburg. This field looked greener to Thaw, and he severed connections with Albemarle as of April 1, 1888. The salary entry in Journal "A" of Albemarle Paper Manufacturing Company, March 1888, left no doubt that this was the last $100 to be paid Thaw: "E. B. Thaw for Salary for mo. of March in full to Apl lst at which time his connection with co. ends."

Tracing the story of Albemarle Paper Manufacturing Company does not require following in detail the personal fortunes and misfortunes of Edward B. Thaw after he left the company. He was indeed a wanderer, always confident that better opportunity lay elsewhere. After moving to Big Island he soon with-

Charles M. Boswell

drew from the company he had helped create (Allegheny Pulp
and Paper Company, chartered April 2, 1888, with many later
changes in name and ownership); managed the Big Island Land
and Improvement Company; departed for Lewisburg, West Virginia; returned to Richmond as a grocer on Main Street; went
into the building supply business; was an official of a building
and loan company; moved south of the river and became a traveling salesman. Then he moved to New York City and associated
himself with a manufacturer of pencils and fountain pens. In
summarizing the career of this restless man Edward B. Thaw, it
is only just to record the fact that he was an important, perhaps
even decisive, spirit in the creation of two major papermaking
companies along the James River: Albemarle in Richmond and
Allegheny at Big Island.

Though Thaw clearly deserves credit as promoter of Albemarle, his tenure was only a year plus a few weeks, and thus one
must look elsewhere to identify those key men who not only set
the company on a true course but manned it for a generally prosperous twenty years. The major responsibility rested on a three-
man partnership: Chalmers and Lishman, who have already been
described, and Charles M. Boswell, successively bookkeeper, assistant secretary-treasurer, secretary-treasurer, and eventually, beginning January 11, 1907, president for a few months. As early
as April 7, 1888, he was placed on the board of directors.

Boswell's employment began the first work day in January 1888,
which happened to fall on Monday, the second. Then thirty-one

years of age, he came well prepared in disposition and in experience for the demands that would be put on him. Born in Charlotte County, Virginia, the son of a country physician, Boswell had as his first job clerking in the store at Red Oak Grove run by "Marse" Albert Jeffress. (As Boswell later recalled, there were three barrels in the back of the store, one containing kerosene, one molasses, and the third whiskey, all selling for the same price per gallon!) After attending Eastman Business College in Poughkeepsie, New York, and working in a wholesale hardware firm in Danville, Virginia, he heard that a new paper mill was being built in Richmond along the James River and that there might be an opening for a bookkeeper. Boswell successfully applied for the position.

In Richmond, Boswell threw himself wholeheartedly into his new responsibilities, perhaps driving himself beyond normal limits at times. He was still a bachelor in those early days with Albemarle, not marrying until he was almost forty years of age. On December 17, 1895, he took as his bride his cousin Etta Lee Elam of Suffolk, Virginia.

Boswell was a big, handsome man with a ready wit. He was an excellent companion and a favorite raconteur, skilled in mimicry and dialect. He regaled his family and friends with stories about the ragpickers, who removed buttons and pins from the rags and found remarkable trinkets in the pockets of discarded garments: $50 gold pieces, watches, and jewelry.

In addition to being a competent bookkeeper, with careful additions and a fine Spencerian hand, Boswell was willing to go on the road to buy rags, to collect moneys due, and to obtain new orders. He maintained amiable relations with Lishman and, according to family tradition, lent a helping hand in the creation of "World" blotting paper and the special design "Vienna Moire." Like any other honest man, Boswell sometimes could be charged with misplaced faith, and at least once suffered from having advanced money to one of the traveling salesmen, and a relative at that. Incidentally, the directors, obviously feeling that Boswell was not entirely at fault in this particular error, covered the first

$100 of the loss. Over the years the directors increasingly realized Boswell's talents and treated him handsomely. Though he began with a salary of $40 a month, in less than a year and a half he was making as much as the president, $150, and by May 1902 had been raised to $350.

Perhaps Boswell's most distinctive contribution was the development of an early system of cost accounting that permitted management to see how the expense involved in the creation of a pound of paper was distributed among the various cost elements: raw materials, labor, power, rent, and so on. Yet policymakers seemed disinterested in, or ignorant of, the concept of depreciation and replacement. "Surplus" became a sort of grab bag from which dividends and extraordinary expenses might be extracted.

Beginning in October 1891 Boswell had at his elbow an amiable and efficient aide, a nephew, Arthur F. Robertson, whose career was to span not only the Chalmers-Lishman-Boswell era but was to extend another decade.

In the earliest months of the company's organization there was the inevitable shakedown period of misunderstanding, false hopes, and cautious second thoughts by the fainthearted. Outright inability to carry through on promises to pay for stock subscriptions had a screening effect on the original list of entrepreneurs. Captain Chalmers offered to serve as president for the first year without a salary, but Colonel Cunningham, who had been chosen vice president, thought this nonsense. However, he would be willing to work for only $1,500 per annum. His fellow directors declined this offer and the colonel resigned both office and stock subscription. Furthermore, Dineen and Dibrell, unwilling or unable to take up the stock for which they had originally subscribed, were ruled ineligible as directors. Thaw's similar demotion has already been noted.

Before the end of the year 1887 support and guidance came from a new group of stockholders and directors, a group in which the names Ellerson and Davenport were prominent. There were two Ellerson brothers, John H. and James R. The first named,

Isaac Davenport, Jr.

familiarly called "Jock," was a tall and congenial life insurance
agent who became a director and substantial stockholder. James
R. Ellerson, formerly a tobacco commission merchant, joined
Albemarle management in September 1887 as secretary-treasurer.
Although the Ellerson brothers themselves soon disappeared from
the Albemarle scene, John H. dying in 1891 and James R. resigning in 1893 to enter the real estate business in Washington,
D.C., the Ellerson name was kept before Albemarle management because of the considerable stock held by Ida Watkins Ellerson, widow of John H. Ellerson.

It was late in the year 1887 when Isaac Davenport, Jr., probably the most important financial leader in Richmond at the time,
became interested in Albemarle Paper Manufacturing Company
as both stockholder and director. Davenport was called the elder
statesman of Main Street; the term *merchant prince* was often
used by journalists in referring to this enterprising gentleman who
was not only president of the First National Bank and the Union

Savings Bank but also head of Davenport and Company, stockbrokers and insurance agents, and a senior partner of Davenport and Morris, importers, wholesale grocers, and commission merchants.

He suffered a paralytic stroke in April 1891 and died October 23, 1896. His stock was divided among his four children: Mary Heath Davenport (Mrs. Virginius Newton), who died in 1899; Gideon A. Davenport; Alice Hathaway Davenport (Mrs. Charles V. Williams); and Charles Davenport.

The Davenport group had potential if not actual dominance of Albemarle at the policymaking level for several years. Perhaps the most powerful of those enjoying the Davenport legacy was Virginius Newton, the son-in-law, a gentleman with a waxed moustache who promptly assumed Davenport's role as head of Davenport and Company and, after an interval, 1897–1904, followed in the footsteps of Isaac Davenport, Jr., as president of the two banks, First National and Union Savings.

To measure the Davenport influence, note for example the board meeting of December 14, 1899, held in the offices of Davenport, Morris and Company. Two directors were absent, six were present. Two of the six were Chalmers and Boswell, who might be classified as management. The four remaining were Charles Davenport, son of Isaac Davenport, Jr.; Charles V. Williams, son-in-law of Isaac Davenport, Jr.; Frank A. Davenport, grandson of Isaac Davenport, Jr.; and Junius A. Morris, longtime partner of Isaac Davenport, Jr., in the firm of Davenport and Morris. Within the year Isaac Davenport, grandson of Isaac Davenport, Jr., was elected director. Not only at the directors' meetings but at the stockholders' meetings the Davenport connection made a formidable array, especially when Virginius Newton appeared representing stock in the name of his late wife.

With oversimplification one might say that during the first twenty years policy power was divided among four overlapping and usually cooperative elements: (1) the Davenports. (2) Closely entwined with the Davenports, but not always identical in interest, was the First National Bank itself, which became the authorized depository of company funds. (3) Gustavus Millhiser, president of the Richmond Cedar Works, shared in the ownership of several other businesses in Richmond, wholesale dry goods, notions, and clothing. The second largest stockholder, he became a director in 1893. (4) Management was represented on the board by Chalmers and by Boswell with a lesser stake. As already indicated, Chalmers brought capital with him when he moved from Smithfield to Richmond. Just how much capital it is impossible to say. At one time he had enough money at hand to lend Thomas F. Flournoy, Jr., one of the original Murphy's Hotel group of organizers, $9,500, which Flournoy presumably used in the purchase of Albemarle stock. By friendship and by financial arrangements Chalmers became closely identified with the First National Bank, which lent him money, money well protected by Albemarle stock.

Thus the financial group largely replaced the promoting group; to put the matter in a more specific way, the Thaws, the Cunninghams, and the Dibrells were out, the Morrises and Millhisers were in. The new powers had money, or at least access to money. Before the year 1887 had ended, the number of shares was increased to 725, thus raising capitalization to $72,500. When additional financing was needed in 1889, the directors simply assessed all the stockholders for a loan equal to 20 percent of the face value of the stock held. In 1891 it seemed logical to the directors to round out the number of shares to an even 750 by issuing 25 to be sold for no less than $140 per share. To insure against invasion by unpredictable outsiders, the directors restricted the sale of these new shares to those individuals or companies already owning stock. Davenport and Morris promptly acquired all 25 new shares.

The directors wisely left day-to-day operations to the officers. Though Chalmers had the superior title, in practice Boswell was directly responsible for accounting and sales, and Lishman gave detailed supervision to papermaking.

The Albemarle office, it might be said here, had a wandering address for the first few years of the company's existence. A cu-

bicle was rented at the office of *The Whig* on Main Street at
$8.16 a month. Then other space on Main Street and on Cary
Street was temporarily acquired.

An office building adjacent to the mill was discussed as early
as 1893 and completed two or three years later. On April 9, 1896,
it was recorded that the president had announced to the stockholders "that a comfortable office building had been erected near
the western line of the company's property & adjoining the city's
'old pump house' property & that same was being occupied with
much comfort & satisfaction."

Years of Prosperity: "World" Blotting Paper

A key decision was to concentrate on the making of blotting paper. Indeed, this may have been the reason for employing Lishman, who, as explained earlier, had become skilled in this
specialized art under the tutelage of his father in England. Five
years after operations had begun, Albemarle Paper Manufacturing Company had the reputation of making and selling more
blotting paper than any other plant in the world. Its premium
product was "World" brand, put on the market in 1889 and, as
permitted by a later Act of Congress, identified and protected by
the United States Patent Office as Trade-Mark No. 72,402. It is
said that for a brief period newsprint and manila were produced,
but the basic product even in the earliest years was blotting paper
for the penman. Specialty items soon evolved. There was "Photo
Finish World," which the company described as "the perfect
photographic blotting." Among the brands less expensive than
"World" was "Vienna Moire," this a distinctive product with a
rippling, watery finish. But the "World" brand, highly absorptive, was the company's main claim to distinction.

Boswell's most important ally in sales was Austin Smith, who
joined the company in its first year of operation and soon had an
office in New York City. He earned the satisfaction of seeing his
name on the company stationery, alongside those of Chalmers,
Boswell, and Lishman.

From the beginning Albemarle had something of an international flavor. Lishman applied to the new plant along the James the techniques learned in England; most of the rags were imported from Europe; the paper was sold abroad as well as at home.

As already suggested, foreign trade came naturally to the Richmonders, accustomed to seeing their major exports, tobacco and flour, go to many distant lands. During the first critical years the board of directors had the advice of Isaac Davenport, Jr., who was well adjusted to international market operations. In addition to other overseas interests, he owned for a while a line of ships sailing between Virginia and South American ports. The most important of the foreign markets in the early days were Canada and Australia. At the end of the twenty-year period under discussion, foreign sales represented about 25 percent of the total output of the paper mill.

The company learned to cope with the unexpected. At one time stories of the plague in Mediterranean areas from which rags came caused a temporary shift to other sources. There were crises arising from domestic wind and flood as well as from foreign disease. In October 1896 a violent storm ripped off the corrugated metal roof of the Hollywood Mill. Management then turned to the more permanent slate; with inevitable replacements, it is still there. It was the nature of the business to be dependent on the flow from the Kanawha Canal for power and for water needed in the making of pulp. Occasionally, muddy water caused the suspension of manufacturing operations.

The company classified its labor force into "day" and "hour" groups. Payrolls for the early 1890s show an average of between thirty and forty people employed, most of the day labor being men. A register for the week November 26, 1892, shows nineteen day laborers, seventeen men and two women, making from 70¢ per day to $3.00 per day; thirteen hourly, all women, making 15¢ per hour. Sample weeks a year later, November 25, 1893, and two years later, November 24, 1894, reflect almost the same labor force and wage scales. The hours worked per week by the day laborers cannot be determined from available records.

As had been anticipated, the company took advantage of its option to purchase the land on which the factory had been built, and changed from the original leasing arrangement to ownership on February 11, 1892, paying $10,000 for the property, one-third cash, one-third in nine months, and one-third in eighteen months.

From the first year of operation the paper mill made a profit, and soon the so-called surplus seemed to warrant the payment of dividends. It will be remembered that by 1891 the capital stock outstanding totaled 750 shares, meaning a nominal capitalization of $75,000. By the time the company celebrated the twentieth anniversary of its founding, the stockholders had received in dividends a total of $483,750, which may be translated into $645 per original share. On May 8, 1902, the directors voted a 100 percent stock dividend that resulted in a capitalization of $150,000 with 1,500 shares outstanding.

During these years the directors had no set policy as to either the timing of the dividends or their amount. In practice the directors simply looked at the books on an average of four or five times during the year and then somebody would move that dividends be declared. The first dividend, equal to $10 per share, was paid in 1891. On a calendar year basis the dividends per share were as follows:

1891	1892	1893	1894	1895	1896
$10	$30	$0	$10	$35	$35

1897	1898	1899	1900	1901	1902
$30	$45	$45	$55	$70	$50

1903	1904	1905	1906	1907
$60	$60	$40	$50	$50

(For the sake of uniformity and comparison during the 1891–1907 period, the dividends per share are given on the basis of the 750 shares outstanding in 1891.)

Since the accounting practices of the time failed to make adequate provision for depreciation and renewal, it is difficult to state the real profits each year. In what was essentially cash book-

Machine Room, Hollywood Mill, about 1900. The machine is the 88-inch Fourdrinier bought in 1887. The man is a "back tend" The women are "sorters" and "counters."

keeping, the overpowering temptation was to take a short-term view of the buildings and equipment.

The End of an Era, 1907–8

Coincident with the twentieth anniversary of the chartering of Albemarle Paper Manufacturing Company there occurred a series of developments that meant the end of one era and the be-

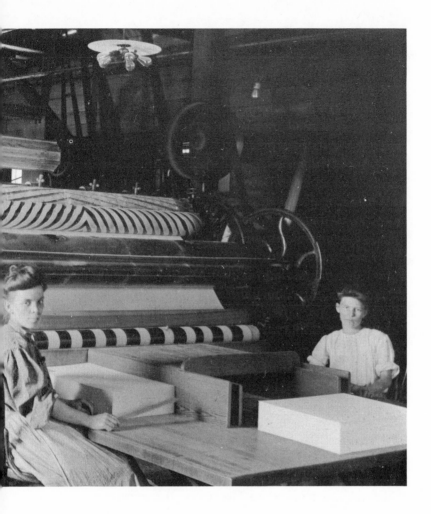

ginning of another. In the span of eighteen months, January 1907 to June 1908, major changes in personnel took place. As for the presidency: Chalmers died; Boswell, his successor, had a nervous breakdown and resigned; and H. Watkins Ellerson took over as chief officer. Three important staff people farther down the line resigned: in the spring of 1907 both John Gibson, Jr., secretary, and Austin Smith, top-flight salesman, left Albemarle to join a competing firm; in June 1908 Lishman, master of the factory, returned to his native England. Contributing to the uncertainties in this period was the well-advertised Panic of 1907. As already suggested, there was an equally ominous, though not quite so

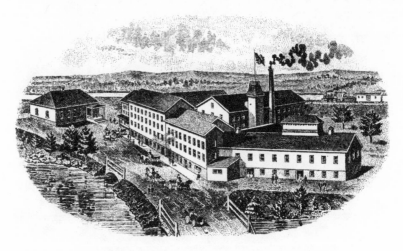

Hollywood Mill about 1907, from company letterhead

obvious, fact that the plant was now in need of repairs and renovation. These critical events of 1907 and 1908 require detailed
examination.

After an illness of several months, James F. Chalmers, the first
president of Albemarle, died on January 7, 1907, with subsequent burial in Hollywood Cemetery, the records of which list
the cause of his death at age seventy-four as angina pectoris. Any
assessment of Chalmers must begin with the acknowledgment
that he was something less than a full-time president of Albemarle, giving considerable attention to his wood and coal business at the corner of Broad and Laurel that over the years went
under a variety of titles, one being simply J. F. Chalmers and
Co. His greatest contribution to Albemarle was his role in choosing, then in advancing, the two men who actually ran the company, Lishman in the mill and Boswell in the office. Chalmers
had been for many years the largest single stockholder, a fact that
made his influence more important than would have been the
case had he appeared at board meetings merely as titular chief

executive. The fact that he owned 27 percent of the stock made his holograph will, drawn July 22, 1906, of special significance in the history of the company.

He wrote out a specific request as to the handling of his Albemarle stock, which was being held by the First National Bank as collateral. If there was pressure for payment, every effort should be made to borrow from other sources rather than sell. "My object in doing this is to save, if possible, intact to my estate this said above named stock." And he appointed his friend John M. Miller, Jr., then cashier and vice president of the First National Bank, executor. Through this circumstance Miller first became an important force in the management of Albemarle.

A native of Lynchburg, Virginia, Miller had come to Richmond in 1902 as cashier of the First National Bank, an institution he was to serve as vice president, president, and chairman. Miller made an emphatic entrance on the Albemarle scene in the spring of 1907. He first showed up at the stockholders' meeting on April 9, 1908, as executor of the estate of Captain Chalmers, thereby voting the 400 shares in Chalmers's name, the largest single block of stock outstanding.

He called attention to the fact that Chalmers's estate had not been given proper notice of the last meeting of stockholders, a point conceded by Boswell, and then with a combination of basic firmness and courteous generosity successfully moved to make legitimate the decisions of that otherwise nonlegal meeting. The contrite directors in conclave later in the day elected him a fellow member of the board, a position he held for three years. At a later date he was to return to the board in his own right, and there he exercised an often decisive and an always conservative influence.

If anything in the history of Albemarle was predictable, it was that on the death of Chalmers, Boswell would be made president. He had been the key man in the front office for many years, a situation the directors had recognized by giving him the highest salary in the company, even a bit above that paid the president. And Boswell's single-minded devotion to the business was a gratifying response to this faith. Yet this very devotion was to prove his undoing.

On January 11, 1907, four days after Chalmers's death, Boswell was named president; John Gibson, Jr., clerk and occasional inventor, was made secretary. In a matter of weeks Boswell's new responsibilities, added to weariness from previous labors, left him completely exhausted.

Then came a double blow: the company lost to a competitor, the Wrenn Paper Company of Middletown, Ohio, the new secretary, John Gibson, Jr., and the senior salesman, Arthur Smith. These men departed with a thorough knowledge of Albemarle's business practices and with a full list of its customers. Something was salvaged when Gibson on receipt of $400 surrendered to Albemarle all his rights in the brand "Vienna Moire," which he had presumably invented. Gibson contracted never to design or to manufacture a similar paper.

It was just about this time that Boswell's illness became even more acute. After April he ceased coming to board meetings, seeking improved health in Chase City, where he had built a home for his mother. On October 31, 1907, he sadly wrote a letter to the board resigning as president and director. "I have tried hard to get well, but continued ill-health and weakness unfit me for the duties of the position." His family in subsequent years labeled his condition a nervous breakdown. This illness was soon followed by a paralytic stroke that left him without full use of his right side. Eventually he overcame his difficulties to the point that he could write with his left hand, shoot from his left shoulder, and mount a horse, though from the "wrong side." Confined to a wheelchair late in life, he revealed in a conversation with his son his own explanation of his breakdown in 1907: it was because of his persistent attempts to make *this* month beat *last* month, a reference to his struggle to earn good profits for Albemarle. He warned his son *not* to do likewise.

Except to his family he rarely spoke of his early years with Albemarle. He considered his kinsman Arthur F. Robertson, whom he had brought into the company, in a special category. Boswell had a personal code phrase when talking to Robertson: "How about my Sundays?"—meaning when do the stockholders get a dividend or a stock split? In those rare moments of reminiscing, Chalmers was not often mentioned, but when Boswell spoke of Lishman it was with appreciation. In his words Lishman was a real *wheelhorse.*

On receipt of Boswell's letter of resignation, the directors chose as their new president Henry Watkins Ellerson, who was to head the company for a third of a century. He was the son of John H. Ellerson, director and stockholder, who died in 1891, and nephew of James R. Ellerson, secretary of the company from 1887 to 1893. As already indicated, the Ellerson family had retained an interest in Albemarle by way of the stock in the name of John H. Ellerson's widow, Ida Watkins Ellerson.

About six months after Ellerson became president, Lishman, master of the factory, tendered his resignation. Lishman's decision to return to his native country was influenced by developments both domestic and professional. According to family tradition, Lishman's second wife was never completely reconciled to her new home in America. According to office tradition, Lishman was never completely reconciled to his new president, who probably chafed at the information that Lishman's salary was somewhat higher than his and that Lishman had a very special place in the hearts of the directors. At the time of his resignation in 1908 Lishman's salary was $333 per month; the new president, Ellerson, was paid $300.

Ellerson seems to have made it quite plain that he, Ellerson, was now the boss, and should Lishman be told to put railroad ties into beaters, this should be done without question or argument. If an open break occurred, it was patched over by the decencies of the moment, by the inherent courtesies of the two men. When Lishman's resignation was delivered to the board of directors, Ellerson was authorized to present Lishman with a suitable gift, the gift to cost no more than a hundred dollars. It was characteristic of Ellerson that he carried out his assignment in elegant fashion. He selected a silver bowl appropriately engraved, a souvenir Lishman descendants in England treasure and exhibit to this day. The engraving reads: "Presented to James Lishman, May 14, 1908, by the Albemarle Paper Manufacturing Company, Richmond, Virginia, U.S.A. In testimony of his long and faithful services."

On May 17, 1908, three days after the presentation, Lishman sold his house, and next month returned to the land of his birth. Lishman died in 1932 at the age of eighty, spending his last years at Exmouth in Devon.

II

The Ellerson Era
1907–41

The Man Ellerson

H. WATKINS ELLERSON, who came to the presidency of Albemarle on December 1, 1907, at the age of 32, brought youth and vigor to the paper company. In the judgment of all who knew him, he was a superb salesman and a most spirited individual. Contemporaries said he was "high strung" under ordinary circumstances and "a lion" when angry. And yet in his paradoxical way Ellerson at times was forgiving beyond the tolerance of the average person. For example, Douglas Fleet, who began as an office boy and eventually became a vice president and member of the board of directors, tells the story of an erroneous report he himself made to Ellerson, who on this basis thoroughly dressed down a complaining customer. Then on Fleet's fearful correction, Ellerson said not a word of rebuke, but merely called the customer to explain with some apology that he, Ellerson, had based his earlier statement on erroneous information.

In appearance Ellerson was stocky, with blue eyes and an excellent carriage, always well groomed. Repeatedly he fancied himself on the verge of a serious illness, which he attempted to ward off by a battery of nose sprays. According to family tradition he learned that a world-famous heart specialist was in Richmond and, convinced that he had coronary problems more serious than local physicians had discovered, Ellerson sought and obtained a full examination by the visiting dignitary, only to receive a bitter-

H. Watkins Ellerson

sweet report that confirmed what his local medical men had told him all along: there was nothing wrong with his heart. When the bill came Ellerson almost had a real heart attack! But his wife would not let him complain, saying the experience was worth every penny of it if Ellerson would only cease his imaginings.

More dominant than those complaints was a zest for living; he enjoyed good company and was a famous host. He frankly relished associating with celebrities. In politics he was comrade and supporter of Harry Byrd. As Richmond "society" was structured at that time, Ellerson was awarded the most elevated posts, leading the Richmond German and the Deep Run Hunt Club. Of course he enjoyed membership in the usual social clubs.

He attended the Second Presbyterian Church, which he served for many years as a deacon. His philanthropy was concentrated on the Crippled Children's Hospital, then under the special care of his friend Dr. William Tate Graham. Ellerson ordered his own children *not* to break any bones (instructions they only fractionally obeyed) because Dr. Graham absolutely refused to send him a bill, and it was *so hard* to find a compensating present.

Ellerson was a man of strong convictions, at times self-confident to the point of being overbearing. In quotable exaggeration it was said that half of Richmond dearly loved him, and half cordially hated him.

At Albemarle his strength was more in salesmanship than in administration, a trait that might have been anticipated, for his background was in the meat-selling and life insurance businesses, activities that honed a natural instinct for persuasive words. Although from time to time Ellerson dutifully walked the few feet from office to factory with blotting paper samples in hand, he never felt thoroughly at home alongside the workingmen from Oregon Hill and elsewhere tending the machines and shifting the stock.

In the Albemarle office, as a gesture of control he developed the habit of opening every letter himself, although after slitting the envelopes he often did not examine the contents. As an entrepreneur he was venturesome to the point of daring, characteristically wanting to expand in the belief that better times would come. In the eyes of a friendly critic, Ellerson's greatest weakness was a too liberal attitude toward friends, who took advantage of this generosity. On balance, Ellerson was a much better than average businessman in his fundamental ideas.

Once Albemarle was well on its way under his new leadership, Ellerson gave attention to other enterprises. One of his truest friends and an associate in sundry business ventures was Julian H. Hill, then president of State Planters Bank and Trust Company. In 1916 the two men founded Universal Motor Company, a Ford dealership, with Ellerson as president and Hill secretary-treasurer. Neither had time nor inclination to give detailed supervision, but old-timers at the Ford showroom recall that Ellerson frequently visited the offices, glancing first at the sales information posted on a board. Often he depended on the employees to drive him to Washington or elsewhere. According to whimsical family tradition, even when Ellerson might find it difficult to buy shoes for the household he could always supply Model T Fords!

In addition to being a director of Universal Motor Company and Albemarle, Ellerson served on the boards of the State Planters Bank and Trust Company and the Richmond Cedar Works.

Transition and Boom Times, 1907–29

Though Ellerson's early days as president could properly be called a time of change, several key employees already in the office adapted to his ways and provided a helpful continuity. The most important of these were Arthur F. Robertson and Basil W. Coale, both meticulous and hardworking. As already mentioned, Robertson joined the company in October 1891. Treasurer in the old regime, he was given the title of secretary-treasurer after the departure of Gibson for Ohio. A benign and friendly individual, brimful of anecdotes and good will, he showed a uniform calmness that was a useful counterbalance to Ellerson's pyrotechnics. Arthur Robertson's hobby was Ginter Park Presbyterian Church, on whose governing boards he served with relish and dedication. He had a strength of character far beyond the ordinary.

In 1907 Robertson had employed a young man from Maryland named Basil Coale whose introduction to the Albemarle group came about in a novel way. He was living in Richmond with his uncle, Dr. Basil Dennis Spalding, one of the first nose-and-throat specialists in the city. "Doc" Spalding and Arthur Robertson played cards every Friday night and Basil Coale was invited to keep score. According to tradition in the Coale family, "Mr. Robertson liked the way he handled his figures, so he offered him a job." At any rate Coale joined the company, serving first as shipping clerk and later as cashier, bookkeeper, treasurer, secretary, and vice president. The special esprit de corps in the office is suggested by the fact that the congratulatory telegram to Coale on his marriage in 1910 was signed by the whole office

Basil W. Coale

force, including the janitor. When Basil Coale was married, his salary was raised from $35 to $60 per month. In philosophy he was a devotee of the work ethic. In manner he was genteel, in appearance distinguished by full face and large brown eyes and, later in life, by thick, silver hair. He was a fair fisherman and an impossible golfer, explaining that he was mediocre with the clubs because he was too busy teaching his wife, who became the city women's champion.

When Ellerson began as president on December 1, 1907, he faced an uncertain business climate and a certain need for plant repairs and improvements. It was precisely at this moment that the national economy was severely shaken by the panic on Wall Street, brought on by speculative excesses and tightened credit. The subsequent recession lasted well into the following year. Albemarle was peculiarly sensitive to general economic conditions because, as Ellerson noted, "our product is principally used in advertising." (Perhaps a generation unfamiliar with pen-and-ink techniques needs to be reminded that a favorite form of business advertising was the imprint on small blotters distributed by the tens of thousands.) The company reported a 13 percent decline in sales for the fiscal year ending March 31, 1908.

At the conclusion of the first full fiscal year in his own administration, March 31, 1909, Ellerson reported that there had been much delay and inconvenience caused by extraordinary repairs to machines and building, efforts that required the cessation of operations for twenty-seven days. There had been a small decrease in sales, 3.25 percent, a decrease of about 10 percent in foreign business. In Ellerson's report there was a hint of innovation; the president pointed out that late in the year 1908 the mill had operated from one to two nights a week and that during the year there had been experiments to produce specialty papers though without complete success.

The company soon entered a new era of prosperity. By 1912 Ellerson could boast to a correspondent that business was the best ever; the capacity of the mill had been "very materially increased," and "we are considered about the best blotting paper manufacturer in the world."

Based on continued high earnings, the liberal dividend policy was maintained. In the dozen calendar years 1908–19, inclusive, annual dividends, now computed on the basis of the shares outstanding since 1902, averaged over $30 per share, never dropping below $20, and in the banner year 1917 going as high as $55.

During World War I, contracts with the government for blotting paper proved especially profitable. There were many votes of thanks to Ellerson, words made more meaningful by handsome bonuses and outright salary increases. In 1917 he received a presidential bonus of $19,000, and his salary increased to $10,000 per year; next year a vacation at company expense and a salary increased to $13,000 per year.

Expansion of plant and equipment was modest during these first dozen years, although the officers picked up a bargain in machinery here and there. At the end of World War I, Ellerson was ready for bigger things. Thus he was receptive when the opportunity to buy Dixie Paper Mills on nearby Brown's Island was dangled before his eyes. There is still some debate as to whether in this deal the great salesman met an even greater salesman. The mill, though young in terms of the location in Richmond, was equipped with ancient and nearly worn-out machinery.

On December 15, 1919, the board of directors authorized the purchase of Dixie Mills at a price not to exceed $112,000, a sum to cover only machinery and equipment, not the building and grounds, for they had been leased from the Virginia Railway and Power Company, a corporation that eventually became Virginia Electric and Power Company. Albemarle later bought the land and the building. While Hollywood was mainly making blotting and allied papers, Brown's Island was soon devoted exclusively to producing kraft—heavy, strong paper.

If one visited the Hollywood and Brown's Island mills in these years after World War I, he found individuals who were busy and colorful. The best blotting paper was made from rags, which were shipped in from all parts of the world. In the words of Frederick P. Wilmer, who became Albemarle's chief engineer in 1926: "The rag room was something to behold. The old crones who were in there were *something*. They were characters, no teeth, no hair, just good old ragpickers. And Egyptian rags were dirty—ye gods."

One cannot affirm with certainty that benevolence character-ized the plant, but evidence warrants the statement that there were at least some elements of a familylike atmosphere. For ex-ample, note an exchange of letters between Ellerson and a black man, William Hewlett, being retired after thirty-two years of ser-vice to the company.

Ellerson's letter to Hewlett, dated December 4, 1919, offered many congratulatory words, made Hewlett a pensioner, and added that if his pension proved insufficient for his support, Hewlett could call on Ellerson personally for help. In the letter of ac-knowledgment from Hewlett's wife and children there was an emotional comparison between the present answer to Hewlett's prayers for comfort in his declining years and the answer, fifty years earlier, to his prayers for freedom in the land.

Former employees "in need of some money to buy a few things,"

Brown's Island Mill about 1920

as one petitioner phrased it, would often address "Dear friend and old Pal—Mr. Coale" for help, and usually received aid.

This was the day when men still professed to love their tools. When Robert Edward Lee Chiles, a deaf man, died on February 26, 1934, he was counted the oldest employee in the company from the point of view of service. By resolution of the board the old Seybold Cutter, which Chiles used when he first came to the mill, was to be preserved in the finishing room as a monument to him.

Albemarle was not exempt from the typical hazards of paper manufacturing in those days. Office secretaries doubled as nurses and gave first aid when minor accidents occurred in the plant, the most characteristic being the nicks and cuts from the table knife in the rag room used in removing metal hooks, buttons, and other attachments. For many years a generous application of turpentine was considered good therapy. One hears of major tragedies involving loss of life and limb. Old-time employees tell of the mangling of hands or arms when a workman was threading

the paper through the calendar stacks. This particular danger was eliminated when the machine tender began using sticks instead of his hands in the threading process.

Some of the mellowest recollections of these days center on the lunch hour, when the office staff was served "a real dinner." The midday meal for company officers and secretaries had been initiated many years earlier, primarily because of the isolated situation of the Hollywood mill. There was a succession of good cooks, perhaps the most memorable one being Emma, whose biscuits are remembered even to this day by a clear-minded lady of ninety-two who worked in Ellerson's office during the first half-dozen years of his presidency. A secretary planned the meals, which included roasts, pork chops, other meats, and a variety of vegetables. Conveniently located was a large five-gallon jug of drinking water. Ellerson carried both seniority and domestic habits into the company dining room. His custom was to say the blessing, though old-timers recall that often he would neglect this ritual until the middle of the meal when people had food in their mouths. Since the staff worked five and a half days, the Saturday lunch was in a special category, many times featuring Smithfield ham sandwiches. One group hurried through the dinner to sit on the heavy rolls of paper and enjoy a game of pinochle before returning to work.

Once the Brown's Island plant had been purchased, Ellerson decided that the charter needed amendments to enlarge the powers of the corporation and to make possible a new issue of common and preferred stock to produce capital for still further expansion. After appropriate resolutions by the board of directors on December 31, 1919, and by the stockholders on January 30, 1920, charter revisions were duly granted by the Corporation Commission. New powers included the right to purchase standing timber and the privilege of increasing the common stock from the basic 1,500 shares to 10,000 shares. After the charter was amended, the directors resolved that only 1,500 of the newly authorized additional shares would be issued: 1,000 to current stockholders and 500 to company officers. The 1,000 shares specified for the stockholders were subdivided in this manner: 300 represented a 20 percent stock dividend, and 700 were to be sold at par (meaning $100 per share) to stockholders in proportion to their holdings. The 500 shares designated for officials and employees were awarded 330 to Ellerson, 120 to Robertson, and 50 to John S. Mowry, the superintendent who succeeded Lishman. In a curious pattern of concession and control, the directors specified that these three grantees should pay for their stock at the rate of $200 per share, $100 in cash, the second $100 payment to be in the form of promissory notes. All of these notes were eventually canceled. The proposed preferred stock was not put on the market at that time.

Almost immediately after the granting of these special shares to the three management people, Arthur F. Robertson, secretary-treasurer, died. His death came on November 10, 1920. As already noted, at Robertson's elbow for more than a decade was Basil Coale, who on Robertson's death was appointed treasurer. W. L. Saunders, a salesman brought in from New York, was made secretary. His tenure was marred by illness, made more likely because of exposure to poison gas during World War I. However, his office and pay were maintained until his death. His duties and title eventually were inherited by Floyd Dewey Gottwald.

In the light of the subsequent history of Albemarle, the employment in the middle of November 1918 of a twenty-year-old clerk named F. D. Gottwald was of major significance. He resigned his position as assistant paymaster with the Richmond, Fredericksburg and Potomac Railroad Company to work in a firm that promised more advancement. Gottwald always said that he was going to be president of any company for which he worked. In this case he was absolutely right.

Young Gottwald had the superficial tools of his trade; he was an expert typist and a competent writer of shorthand. But these were not his main assets. He showed a single-mindedness that absorbed most of his waking hours. He was determined to master the paper business and talked about it at all hours, to all people, even at times boring a few of his relatives who, concentrating on the card game, setback, were not quite that interested in paper. Soon his major responsibility centered on the export trade, where for a season he assisted an unusual character named Louis Szanto, a Hungarian, who readily spoke several languages, including Italian, French, and Spanish. Szanto left Albemarle to enter the tobacco business, but he persuaded Gottwald in his spare time to aid a bit in what became a very specialized African trade.

With the departure of Szanto, Gottwald took over the export division and in a few years built it up to where the paper shipped abroad was about 40 percent of total production. As linguist and aide he later on had at his side a somewhat eccentric woman translator named Rosa Pascual, Spanish-born and well versed in various European tongues. By working with her and earlier with Szanto, and by thumbing through dictionaries, Gottwald himself developed sufficient skill to handle French, Spanish, and Italian correspondence. Curiously enough he never learned German, although his father could speak it fluently. One Gottwald-watcher over the years is quite sure that Gottwald's original basis of power

in the company was his competence in the export business. Gottwald himself clearly recalled trade with Cuba, Argentina, Japan,
and India.

At the paper company Gottwald was alert to all new opportunities. In the communal lunch room he paid particular attention
to hints about the business. He was fond of Robertson, who habitually ate biscuits between meals, this for the sake of his stom-
ach ulcer. But the office mice often got the biscuits first. Gottwald
endeared himself to Robertson by presenting him with a mouse-
proof biscuit box! As already indicated, Robertson died two years
after Gottwald arrived on the Albemarle scene.

Gottwald first appeared in the permanent records of the company by virtue of his having purchased five shares of Albemarle's
stock in 1923. He was present at virtually all stockholders' meetings, and, either on his own initiative, or more probably on Ellerson's invitation, made a few routine motions. In 1928 Gottwald
was made assistant secretary.

Concern for the quality of the goods exported under his responsibility, both blotting and kraft, led Gottwald into close association with the manufacturing process. His fellow workers
remember that he spent endless hours standing by the machines
(and incidentally he could suffer the industrial heat better than
most because of his consistently low blood pressure).

As for the board of directors, Ellerson had a group that typi-
cally gave him enthusiastic support, though there were instances
when he was curbed in his more venturesome proposals. Prominent people came to and went off that board for many years,
and for a while, to quote a contemporary who watched the matter closely, "they damned near ran Richmond."

Certain continuities were maintained. The traditional influence of the Davenports and the Millhisers could clearly be seen.
In 1920 the board was strengthened by the election of J. Scott
Parrish to membership. Treasurer of the Richmond Cedar Works
and later president of the Richmond Foundry and Manufacturing Company, he was recognized as one of the great leaders of
Virginia business. The banking interests were well represented

on the Albemarle board. A notable addition to the list of directors was John M. Miller, Jr., who had returned to the board on
October 18, 1923. It will be remembered that he held membership on the board from 1907 to 1910. The Chalmers inheri-
tance, first represented by Miller, was subsequently evidenced in
the person of William Ferguson Chalmers, who, as already noted,
was a clerk-salesman in the wholesale paper business of 1887-88.
After W. F. Chalmers left the board, the Chalmers interests reap-
peared in the person of T. Croxton Gordon, who in 1913 had
married Mary Fenelon Chalmers, the daughter of W. F. Chalmers. According to one observer, "Mary Chalmers was one of
the most beautiful sights that ever lived." Gordon was a director
from 1921 to 1961.

In 1924 James P. Massie, Ellerson's young nephew, became a
member of the board. His family discouraged him from undertaking a medical career toward which he himself was inclined.
Those who were devoted to him often remarked that Jimmy Massie
had a scholarly rather than a business instinct and that he seemed
ideal as a candidate for a professorship or for the legal or medical
profession. He was uncomfortable in the role of a hail-fellow-
well-met and felt uncertain in the rough-and-tumble of factory
and marketplace.

Royal E. Cabell was Albemarle's counsel during the 1920s,
1930s, and 1940s. Commissioner of revenue under William
Howard Taft, Cabell was prominent in the Republican party at a
time when such an affiliation raised both eyebrows and suspi-
cion. By any yardstick he was a tax lawyer of distinction. As for
physical appearance, he had a somewhat large head with a small
round nose and a high forehead, and very small feet, which
troubled him late in life when he had a weight problem. In his
later years he suffered from an arthritic condition aggravated by
an automobile accident. He had a reputation for an explosive
temper. Some of this was generated for effect; much was genuine
anger.

Now, Cabell's client, Ellerson, had a temper himself, and the
two fast friends would sometimes blast each other over the tele-

phone, alarming members of the younger generation who happened to be within earshot. Especially was there shouting when Ellerson suggested some ventures that provoked Cabell into his usual cry that if Ellerson carried out his plans he would certainly bankrupt the company or put all officers and directors in jail! Cabell was categorical in his judgments. Joseph M. Lowry, controller and later senior vice president and a member of the board, recalls an emphatic conversation: "I said, 'Mr. Cabell, as a practical matter couldn't we do this?' And he said, 'Young man, there's no such thing as a practical matter in law. It's either legal or it's illegal.'"

In 1921 the management of Albemarle became involved with the Chesapeake Corporation of West Point, Virginia. Chartered in 1913, the original Chesapeake mill at West Point, a town at the confluence of the Mattaponi and Pamunkey rivers and a superb shipping point for the steamers of that time, was built by the Fox Paper Company of Cincinnati, presumably to supply pulp for its own operation. The mill did not prosper and fell into the hands of an international financier, Christoffer Hannevig. Then a controlling interest was obtained by William Joseph Fallon in New York, who is freely described as a man knowing nothing about the business. In the meantime there had appeared on the scene in West Point an aggressive Swede, Elis Olsson, who never completely conquered the English language and its full scale of intonations but with considerable finesse mastered the art of making pulp and paper, a craft he had learned as a young man in the old country. He and Ellerson became acquaintances and then friends. Ellerson developed an enthusiasm for the Chesapeake mill as a complement to Albemarle and had visions of still further enlarging the paper operations in Richmond.

In 1921 Ellerson attempted to move Albemarle as a corporate body into the ownership of stock in the Chesapeake Corporation. After initial encouragement, the directors in effect told Ellerson that current business conditions did not warrant the Chesapeake venture. But Ellerson would not be denied and initiated on a personal basis what for all practical purposes took the form of a partnership between Albemarle and Chesapeake.

After a firm negative from the Albemarle board, Ellerson proceeded to conclude negotiations that left him and a group of friends, including five of the Albemarle directors—Parrish, Gordon, Coale, Isaac and Charles Davenport—owning 2,400 of the outstanding 2,970 shares of Chesapeake. The Ellerson group buying into Chesapeake at this time included not only Ellerson himself and his five fellow Albemarle directors but Ellerson's mother, Mrs. Ida Watkins Ellerson, a longtime owner of Albemarle stock. Ellerson with 720 shares was the largest single stockholder. There was a prompt restructuring of Chesapeake management: Ellerson became president and Elis Olsson vice president.

The alliance between Albemarle and Chesapeake in one form or another, visible and invisible, overt or covert, lasted for many years. Some of this relationship was by way of directors and stockholders in common. Some was in extremely complicated purchase agreements. As will be noted below, one phase of this association took the form of joint ownership of a third company known as Albemarle-Chesapeake Corporation, and a short-time cooperation in setting up the Chesapeake-Camp venture.

There are two schools of thought as to these arrangements between Albemarle and Chesapeake. One school contends that the clever management at Chesapeake helped support Albemarle; another school, quite as vigorous, is certain that Chesapeake nearly ruined Albemarle. The kraft paper being made at Brown's Island required as raw material the great laps of pulp that were produced at Chesapeake or imported from the Scandinavian countries. The two corporations headed by Ellerson developed contracts that created a series of arguments over price. As though disagreements were expected, important contracts provided for competent arbitrators.

Concentrating on affairs other than Chesapeake, Ellerson and his board during the year 1924 seriously considered, but then rejected, a chance to buy the Wrenn Paper Company of Middletown, Ohio, and turned their expansionist ideas inward. They improved the Brown's Island operations and erected a new structure, Riverside, on a landfill between Hollywood Mill and the James River. This new mill, completed in 1925, was equipped with a 94-inch machine and made colored specialties and cover stock.

In 1924, a time of planning and change, Ellerson gave particular thought to obtaining more capital for carrying out his plans for growth. The charter was changed to permit the issuing of additional common and preferred stock, the last under a pattern of elaborate restrictions. After much planning and discussion during the years 1924–26, the common stock was increased from 3,000 to 7,500 shares, and there were issued 6,000 shares of 7 percent preferred at $100 per share.

These were boom times. Common stock dividends remained substantial, never less than 10 percent, although Ellerson had announced a new policy of more moderate dividends in order to insure against too great a dependence on borrowed money. Salaries went up, bonuses were increased, a grand gesture was made to poor Saunders, now critically ill.

The proposal for a new kraft paper manufacturing company to be named Albemarle-Chesapeake and built adjacent to the Chesapeake plant in West Point was studied by the Albemarle board of directors in July and August 1928 and then approved by directors and stockholders. At the outset of this joint enterprise, Albemarle and Chesapeake each would subscribe to 2,500 shares of common at $100 per share and 2,500 shares of preferred at $100 per share. There was an agreement that Chesapeake would sell pulp to the jointly owned corporation, that Albemarle would be sales agent for the finished product, kraft paper, and that in case of disagreement as to price paid for pulp or as to commission to be paid Albemarle, an arbiter would be called on.

The officers of the Chesapeake Corporation were the officers of the new company. However, in recognition of the special efforts exerted by Olsson in the creation of the Albemarle-

Chesapeake Corporation, Ellerson in January 1929 resigned the presidency of Chesapeake in favor of Olsson and thus Olsson became the chief executive officer of both West Point corporations.

Ellerson now felt that he could indulge himself in the matter of more elegant living quarters. His new home, Glen Roy, a bigger-than-life Westover-style mansion, was built on River Road west of Richmond. Designed by Duncan Lee, known as one of the more expensive architects in Richmond, it was a magnificent structure characterized by beautiful hand-carved woodwork, executed, it is said, by itinerant Italian craftsmen. To quote Gottwald, "The china closets in the dining room are the most exquisite and beautiful things that you've ever seen." Ellerson later admitted that the structure was not justified by his resources at the time, but he contended that the building of Glen Roy was based on affection and concern for his family.

The Great Depression, 1930–37

Then came the crash, the beginning of the Great Depression. For Albemarle, this meant a season of severe retrenchment. Ellerson reduced inventories and cut costs in many ways. Both preferred and common dividends were omitted, much to the embarrassment of Ellerson. Yet he felt he had learned some lessons. As he wrote to his friend and cousin William T. Reed: "However, the experience of 1930 has been to a considerable extent a blessing in disguise. It has taught me at least more about manufacturing economics than all I have ever learned in past years." Even Ellerson's restrained optimism proved mistaken; 1932 was a disastrous year.

When the workers were told that salaries as well as wages were being cut, protests were minimal, or at least open complaints were few. Ellerson's temper, always abbreviated, was shortened still further by the dismal economic situation, and legend has it that at one staff meeting he testily announced a salary reduction and added that if anybody didn't like it he could just get out and not come back. The most severe reductions took place during the year 1933. This was the time when Douglas Fleet, by then an experienced salesman, returned from Ohio, where he had been selling "tire wrap" to the rubber companies, only to be greeted by an extremely depressed state of affairs. As he recalls the situation, "We were just about busted."

Albemarle was finding its joint venture with Chesapeake something of a burden. Start-up problems had been severe, and for three years, 1930–33, Albemarle and Chesapeake were under promise each to lend annually $100,000 to the new mill. The great sales opportunity that seemed offered by Albemarle-Chesapeake disappeared when the new mill discontinued the production of kraft, which Albemarle was going to market under exclusive sales rights, and concentrated on paper board, which Chesapeake was to sell. Whereupon Albemarle renegotiated the fees it was supposed to pay for the rights to sell the kraft. Whether justified or not, many Albemarle people began to think that money and energy were being directed at West Point that might better be kept in Richmond.

There was improvement in the general situation by the time of the annual meeting of the Albemarle stockholders in the spring of 1935; Ellerson was in cheerful and expansive spirits. The 2,500 shares of Albemarle-Chesapeake preferred stock, for which Albemarle had subscribed at the time of the incorporation of the joint enterprise in 1928, had been sold and with the proceeds all bank indebtedness had been cleared away. There were no outstanding obligations of any consequence save for default on the Albemarle preferred stock. It was at this moment that Ellerson went on record as to the changing nature of Albemarle. As he explained to the stockholders, Albemarle was now thought of primarily as a manufacturer of kraft, which was more important than either blotting paper or specialty items, such as cover stock. The shift of emphasis was well timed; in a few years the ballpoint pen virtually destroyed the market for high-quality blotting paper.

Convivial and friendly with his peers, Ellerson became quite popular in the national kraft trade groups, many members of which were trying to cure their ailing business by cut-throat competition. Ellerson attempted to calm the warring brethren and thereby earned for himself Olsson's admiring compliment that Ellerson was a first-class conciliator. Federal authorities took a different view, and before the decade was out, indicted for anti-trust violations the leading kraft manufacturing companies, including Albemarle and its two key officers, Ellerson and Blair Stringfellow, who was in charge of sales.

Ellerson protested that he had never done anything illegal. It was the considered opinion of his colleagues that he simply was one of the many who declared in meetings that low prices were suicidal and had to be set more realistically. On advice of counsel, however, the company and the individuals accepted a plea of *nolo contendere.*

To the employees, the clouds seemed to be lifting when the directors granted a handsome Christmas bonus in December 1935. Ellerson thought this a proper season for catching up on those preferred stock dividends, first in default on January 1, 1931. The sum of $156,313.53 was needed to satisfy the claims of the preferred stockholders. Ellerson's plan was to borrow $150,000 from banks and to take care of the rest from earnings. Of the $150,000 borrowed, $100,000 came from First and Merchants and $50,000 from State Planters. It might be added here that in just a little over a year after the borrowing of the $150,000, the notes were paid off.

Because of their interests in all three operations, Albemarle, Chesapeake, and Albemarle-Chesapeake, Ellerson and some of his coinvestors at times thought of the three as subdivisions of an unincorporated holding company. One discovers a meeting of the Chesapeake board of directors in the Albemarle offices, and a meeting of the Albemarle directors in the Chesapeake offices. Eventually, on January 23, 1936, there was a proposal in the Albemarle board that a committee be appointed to consider the advisability of merging the three corporations into one, but nothing formal came of this move.

Apparently not everybody was happy about this close relationship. Yet the highest officials were in such close alliance that
Albemarle and Chesapeake joined in still another venture. On
August 19, 1936, Ellerson informed the Albemarle board that
he and Olsson had been negotiating with the Camp Manufacturing Company of Franklin, Virginia, for the joint construction
of a 150-ton kraft pulp and board mill in the Franklin area. In
subsequent discussions the board was told that the cost would be
about $3,400,000, that the new company at Franklin was to be
called Chesapeake-Camp Corporation, and that Albemarle would
subscribe one-eighth of the common stock ($100,000) and one-
eighth of the preferred. The three companies, Chesapeake, Camp,
and Albemarle, would guarantee interest on bonds that were to
be issued.

Emergence of F. D. Gottwald as Ellerson's Senior Aide, 1937–41

Curiously enough, it was at the very moment when Albemarle
management was arranging for commitments to the Franklin
venture that Ellerson turned the attention of the directors to a
problem that in itself would involve major appropriations of capital and eventually a liquidation of those company investments
made jointly with Chesapeake. Albemarle would proceed in a
new direction because of the pulp needed for the Brown's Island
plant.

To quote from Ellerson's statement to the Albemarle board,
"For six years the company has relied almost entirely on Scan-
dinavia for its pulp supply." In Ellerson's judgment such a restricted source constituted an extremely hazardous situation. The
beginning of a European war would simply shut down Brown's
Island, which was the real source of profit to the company. Also,
Ellerson recognized the possibility that an American import duty
might be levied on foreign pulp. He emphatically concluded that
a domestic source of supply must promptly be developed. By

Historical marker, Roanoke Rapids, N.C.

now he regretted not having built a pulp mill at the time the Albemarle-Chesapeake plant was erected.

Albemarle could build or it could buy a plant already in existence. Ellerson had in mind the Halifax mill at Roanoke Rapids, North Carolina, a pulp and paper operation that could be acquired for about $400,000.

The words of Ellerson resulted from vigorous debate within the Albemarle family, a debate in which the younger officers won out over a conservative group led by cautious directors. In the reminiscing words of Gottwald, "The directors were against this move; the key officers were against this move. But we had a sort of rebellion of the palace guards, and the secondary officials were pretty determined that this acquisition was the salvation of the company at the time." He referred to the "rebellious group of which I was one." Ellerson was persuaded; the directors yielded to the "small fry" and proceeded to purchase the Halifax pulp and paper mill at Roanoke Rapids.

The Halifax plant, immediately south of the boundary line between North Carolina and Virginia, had had close ties with the Richmond area since its beginning. It was founded in 1906 under the title Roanoke Rapids Manufacturing Company and began operations in the following year. Of considerable importance to historians of the paper industry is the fact that on February 26, 1909, this mill became the first in the United States to produce kraft pulp using in the sulphate process the wood called southern loblolly pine.

A man named Ernest A. Kendler had an option on the purchase of Halifax, and there were some voices proposing a delay because at the expiration of Kendler's option the property might possibly be purchased at a lower price. The owners of Halifax were Richmond men, A. D. Williams and William T. Reed, the latter, as already noted, a close friend and kinsman of Ellerson. Those insisting that the company move ahead promptly were led by F. D. Gottwald, who, having won the initial point, now fought successfully against a delay. The deal was completed early in 1937. This determination to "integrate backwards," to control the company's own supply of pulp, in the long run may have been the most important single business decision Gottwald ever made. The development of Halifax, more than any other single factor, provides the clue to the eventual prosperity of Albemarle.

Without doubt, Gottwald's position was on the rise. On April 15, 1937, soon after the purchase of Halifax, he was made a vice president and director. A listing of salaries at that time shows that he and Coale were the highest-paid employees, Ellerson excepted.

At a later date Gottwald referred to the anxiety and the difficulty in working out purchase arrangements. As already indicated, the price asked for Halifax was approximately $400,000 or, as it was phrased more exactly, $380,000 plus whatever profit had been earned by the firm since September 1936. The device of financing was to put a lien on the Halifax property, and then Scott and Stringfellow, Richmond stockbrokers, would sell $400,000 worth of serial notes. The purpose of subsequent financing was to increase the productivity of the newly acquired pulp plant to about seventy-five tons per day.

The year 1937, which started as though it were to be "the great year," ended in near disaster. The recession of 1937–39 struck the kraft paper industry with peculiar force, and on November 1 the construction of the new facilities at Roanoke Rapids, now about four-fifths completed, was stopped. The management of

Albemarle complained of excessive construction costs, of the difficulty in obtaining money from banks, and of defective practices in the industry, by the last complaint really meaning that price-cutting was beyond reason. The directors voted $1.00 per share common stock dividend on October 26, 1937. This was the last such for nearly nineteen years; that is, until September 5, 1956.

Although there could be some sort of delay in the great changes planned for the Halifax enterprise, there simply had to be substantial expenditures at Brown's Island because contracts with Virginia Electric and Power Company with regard to steam supply had expired and it was necessary for Albemarle to install its own boiler.

In this recession Gottwald painfully learned the hard fact that one should not depend on short-term loans for capital expenditures. He had to plead with the bankers in order to avoid drastic measures. As he recalled the circumstances, "I, for one, passed amongst the creditors, asking them to hold up for a little while. And they did, and saved the company from bankruptcy."

Ellerson never gave way to outright panic. According to all evidence he preserved his aplomb. He was called in by the presidents of First and Merchants and State Planters banks and told that a creditors' committee would have to be formed. Ellerson was assured that he was to continue operating the company, although important financial decisions would be made by the creditors' committee. According to tradition in the Richmond financial community, Ellerson agreed and said he believed that if one is going to have financial troubles he ought to have them big enough so that the banks wouldn't carve up the business. If one were of proper size, he would be indispensable and would continue to run the business.

As the months wore on, the situation improved and new financing was arranged, notably with the Reconstruction Finance Corporation in 1938. Of the $1,200,000 needed, the RFC took $850,000 and the rest was lent by the First and Merchants Bank. At about the same time Albemarle negotiated with Chesapeake for a full release from direct involvement with the Albemarle-

Chesapeake mill at West Point, exchanging the Albemarle-
Chesapeake common stock for 12,343 shares of Chesapeake, with
a market value of about $470,000.

Ellerson began to have long bouts of illness, which meant absence from many board meetings. He did make a very strong
statement in September 1939, reviewing his early pressure for
the development of the company's own supply of pulp. By coin-
cidence, on September 1, 1939, the day World War II started in
Poland, the renovated Halifax plant began producing. This event
marked the completion of the first expansion program; 100 tons
could be produced in a twenty-four-hour period. Even when the
Halifax plant was running at full capacity there was still the necessity of getting from twelve to fifteen hundred tons of foreign
pulp annually. Thus Ellerson, never timid, suggested that additional expansion should be undertaken. Most of the pulp produced at Roanoke Rapids, and it was entirely sulfate kraft pulp,
was sent to Richmond, shipped in "wet laps," which were one-
third of an inch thick, 18 inches wide, and three feet long.

Business was going fairly well in the summer of 1940. Then
there occurred one of the greatest floods in the history of the
Roanoke valley. The normally tame Roanoke River went on a
rampage and threatened disaster to the whole Halifax operation,
which was built alongside the river at the fall line. The Roanoke
rose to unprecedented heights. Not satisfied to bend with the
banks, the raging waters cut across the Halifax properties, floating away many cords of wood, breaking up buildings, and damaging machinery. Early estimates of loss ran as high as $200,000.

Gottwald, as vice president and general manager, assumed prime
responsibility for repairs. He clearly recalled the flood:

> We had just gotten the plant in a good profitable condition.
> We had $96,000 cash in the bank, I particularly remember
> that, and the flood came. And I'll tell you it was a flood. The
> mill was on a point in the river, so as the river rose it cut a
> tremendous ditch right through the property. I rode over to see
> what damage there was, and the boat that I was in struck the

top of the box cars that were in the yard. So you can get an idea of how high the water was in the pulp and paper mill. Two of the men stayed in the pulp mill, which was up above the water line. They were tall buildings and they, the two men, spent their time catching the livestock, roping the livestock as it rode down the river.

There was a tremendous job of cleaning up the damage, of drying out motors in a nearby brickyard, of obtaining additional digesters made by the Richmond Engineering Company. Ninety percent of the wood that had floated away was recovered.

Did he go down and personally supervise? "Oh yes, I stayed down there. Ate more collards than I had ever eaten in my life, good collards too, and some things I hadn't gotten since I was a kid. And salsify. Did you ever hear of salsify?" (To city dwellers it might be explained that salsify, sometimes called oyster plant, has roots which, boiled and seasoned, are considered by some a choice dish.)

Pessimists were confounded; in a matter of weeks production was resumed. The flood occurred August 16, 17, and 18, and Gottwald could report that by September 11 pulp was again being made.

On September 14, 1940, less than a month after the flood, the Albemarle board of directors granted Ellerson a leave of absence and made Gottwald executive vice president. Ellerson was in a sad state of decline. In these circumstances, of course, Gottwald as senior of the active officials moved into day-by-day command.

With the death of Ellerson on May 6, 1941, there was an interval that left the Albemarle and Halifax communities gossip-ridden and uneasy. Some thought that Overton Dennis, a newly elected director and a talented man with a reputation of being a prime troubleshooter, might be chosen president. It is well known that elements in the Ellerson family had felt that James Massie was being trained for the job. Apparently Ellerson had never undertaken the painful task of informing Massie that he was not slated for the presidency; rather Ellerson had let the situation remain in uncertainty. Since no action had been taken by the board for several weeks after Ellerson's death, Gottwald went to two key individuals, Parrish and Miller, and explained that the board had to make up its mind. And if he, Gottwald, were not going to receive the office that went along with the responsibilities he had been carrying, he might as well go somewhere else. He received from both Parrish and Miller assurances that this attitude was understandable. At the same time Gottwald had a very strong supporter in Walter S. Robertson, later assistant secretary of state for far eastern affairs (1953–59), then an important partner in Scott and Stringfellow. At any rate, at the board meeting on July 21, 1941, Parrish moved and Miller seconded the motion that Gottwald be made president. Though the precise terms of the motion had to follow charter provisions requiring that officers be elected to serve from one annual meeting to the next, the acceptance of Parrish's motion by the board was in fact a permanent laying-on-of-hands.

Before that July 21 meeting, one or more of the directors, knowing that Mary Ellerson Jamerson had been very close to her father and talked business with him many times, called her in Washington, D.C., where she was living to ask her what her father had said about Gottwald. She emphatically stated that her father relied on him more than on any other person and that there was every indication that Ellerson had wanted Gottwald to succeed him.

III

The Presidency of
F. D. Gottwald
1941–1962

A Season of Frustration

THE FIRST HALF-DOZEN years of Gottwald's presidency can only be described as a season of frustration. There were inhibiting wartime regulations, a major industrial accident, and exhausting differences between management and important directors.

The style of Gottwald's administration was quite different from Ellerson's. Ellerson was a club man, socially inclined, instinctively a salesman. Gottwald was straight-forward, a no-nonsense sort of person who simply disliked small talk and chitchat. In communication he went directly to the point without beating around the bush. Furthermore, as already noted, there was a residual unhappiness in one segment of the Ellerson family at the destruction of the family-legacy concept in passing over Massie and choosing Gottwald as president. In fairness to Massie's memory, it should be reported that Gottwald described Massie as uniformly cooperative and always honest.

More troublesome than any disappointment Massie might have felt was the mood of ultraconservatism in the board of directors inherited by Gottwald. The dominant group was not as bold and imaginative as was the new president. And initially the board exercised oversight that was almost embarrassing. A three-man supervisory committee, appointed before Ellerson's death to assist Gottwald, was continued for a season after Gottwald became president.

Gottwald was scarcely settled into his new title when the United States entered World War II. As a patriotic citizen he proposed that the shops be devoted to armament. Nothing came of this offer. There were new laws to tax and to regulate, to allot and to restrain. In December 1941, searching for information about new taxation, Gottwald approached Senator Harry Flood Byrd, who had been Ellerson's close friend. Byrd warned that the excess-profits tax would be heavy.

The financial results were mixed during the war years in the face of a scarcity of needed materials and an abundance of restrictive and sometimes contradictory federal regulations. The worst year was fiscal 1943, when sales dropped from the high point of $5.2 million in the previous year to $3.8 million, and net income changed from a profit of $656,599 to a loss of $114,558.

In the middle of the war years Albemarle suffered the greatest human disaster in the history of the company. A rotary rag digester, or boiler, a twenty-five-foot cylindrical vessel six feet in diameter, exploded on the third floor of the Hollywood Mill at 4:24 P.M. on Tuesday, April 20, 1943, resulting in the death of nine men and the injury of more than a dozen. Part of the boiler went thirty feet through the wall of the Hollywood Mill, the original building constructed in 1887, crossed a twenty-eight-foot alley, and buried itself in the brick wall of the Riverside Mill, which, as already noted, had been operating since 1925. Among those killed in the blast was Lynton B. Knighton, assistant superintendent of the plant, a thirty-seven-year-old graduate of Oglethorpe University. A few minutes before the blast, word of trouble at Hollywood had gotten out and James Inge, a supervisor at Brown's Island, headed for Hollywood to investigate. He ran into Knighton, familiarly called "Skeeter," who told Inge, "You go on home and I'll go up there." Inge added, in recalling that event, "That boy that got killed took my place."

It was a terrifying sight, with charred flesh hanging from the dead and wounded as they were carried away. Contemporary

newspaper pictures showed the two damaged buildings, the lit-
tered alley, piled-up timber, twisted pipes, rags draped from shat-
tered walls, and, conspicuously, the boiler jammed into the side
of the Riverside Mill. Policemen, firemen, civil defense personnel, ambulance crews, as well as Albemarle workers cooperated
in the removal of debris while searching for victims of the blast.

The exact cause of the explosion is unknown. There had been
a general boiler inspection by insurance representatives two months
previous to the explosion. The most convincing theory is that a
leak occurred at one of the rivet heads, and the action that pre-
cipitated the explosion was the tragically mistaken belief by one
of the workmen that he could hurry along the rag-digesting process by increasing the pressure in the digester beyond the usual
limits. On the other hand, it has been said that the safety valve
somehow or other might have been fouled by the rags. As Gottwald recalled the event, the black man who was the operator of
the equipment "had been asked to open the valve and let the
pressure go up a little bit, and in some way or other—I have no
idea what he did—but anyhow, the pressure ran away with him."

The whole community was shocked by the disaster at the
Hollywood Mill, and the management of Albemarle was tempted
to radical readjustments in the structure of the corporation. In
reporting to his board of directors on April 27, 1943, a week after
the explosion, Gottwald stated that the accident would shut down
Hollywood for about six months, and "he considered liquidation
to be [in] the best interest of the Albemarle Paper Manufacturing
Company." There was general discussion of the possibility of the
sale of assets to other companies engaged in similar manufacturing. Subsequent records make clear that the main, if not the
only, point of Gottwald's statement was the suggestion that the
blotting paper business might be sold. There were in fact serious
negotiations with Standard Paper in June and early July. Standard's offer was too low to suit Gottwald. Finally, on July 12,
1943, the board decided to notify Standard Paper that Albemarle
had determined to continue manufacturing blotting and its traditional line of absorptive papers. For a few months the manu-

facturing of blotting was shifted to the small machine at Brown's Island. Early in 1944 this specialty was returned to a repaired Hollywood Mill.

Particularly galling to Gottwald was the fact that during and immediately after World War II larger business decisions had to be made within boundaries outlined by board members who, scorched by the Great Depression, wanted no bold new ventures. On the other hand, Gottwald was expansion-minded. He sought more modern equipment, and he was not at all frightened at the thought of borrowing large sums of money. True, there was something akin to formal applause by the board from time to time, as indeed there should have been in the light of achievement under adverse circumstances. Except for the aforementioned loss during the fiscal year 1942–43, the company was in the black. But the board was simply unwilling to accept Gottwald's plans in their entirety. Gottwald was straining at the leash. He became restless at the failure of the directors to take affirmative action on his proposed program of postwar renovation, and at the board meeting on December 9, 1943, he said that the time had now arrived for management to know the minds of the directors. The board reacted in piecemeal fashion during the next several months. Gottwald's frustration is obvious even in the formal records. At the board meeting of September 30, 1944, he again made the point that he ought to have specific instructions from the directors as to whether he should continue with postwar planning, which involved rather large additions to the plant.

The most severe jolt given Gottwald by his directors was their refusal to agree with him in the proposed Hummel-Ross acquisition. Gottwald had worked out preliminary plans for the merger and control of the Hummel-Ross Fibre Company of Hopewell, Virginia, which manufactured kraft pulp and paper. The two leaders in opposition were T. Croxton Gordon and John M. Miller, Jr., good friends but ultraconservative. "These two sort of killed it," said Gottwald. He probably had well over half of the directors on his side, but, as he said, "You can't go along with a thing of that kind with [simply] a *majority* of directors. You have to come pretty close to having a unanimous decision." He never forgot the anguish of the moment of rejection, and for the rest of his life a mere glance at the room in the Commonwealth Club where that gathering was held evoked renewed pain. Some months after Gottwald gave up on the Hummel-Ross deal, he saw to his great discomfort the acquisition of the Hopewell firm by Continental Can Company.

The board gradually came around to accepting a number of Gottwald's projects and by 1946 agreed to a large-scale reorganization and refinancing proposal that had as its core the borrowing of $3.5 million from the Reconstruction Finance Corporation. Before the end of the year Miller, leader of the conservatives, resigned from the board, removing himself entirely from the debate over reorganization and refinancing. Two years later he was dead. An editorial in the *Times-Dispatch* in which his death was noted called him "the dean of Virginia bankers and one of the most distinguished banking executives in the South."

To Gottwald's mortification, by the time the board became reconciled to his major points of view, new adversaries appeared in the shape of a group of preferred stockholders. Upset by the nonpayment of dividends on their stock, they were unwilling to consent to a first lien on the physical properties as required by the Reconstruction Finance Corporation before it would make the major loan for which Gottwald was applying.

Strong feelings developed on all sides. As the lines were drawn, Gottwald was heartened by expressions of support from friends old and new. John Green Hayes, the onetime manager of the Mayo tobacco plant where Gottwald worked as a youth, owned 500 shares of preferred and promised Gottwald his votes in a planned showdown. The most eloquent testimony to the intensity of feeling is the codicil attached to the will of an Albemarle staff member, O. J. McSwain, then in terminal illness. In a document dated October 5, 1943, McSwain specified that if he died before the proposed meeting he wanted his widow to vote in support of Gottwald's reorganization and refinancing plan.

This particular program never came to a vote, however, for on final analysis Gottwald and his board saw that too much opposition remained; the Reconstruction Finance Corporation negotiations should be dropped, at least for a time.

Gottwald now decided that there was only one way out. He would personally obtain controlling interest in the company, and at the same time he would get rid of the 7 percent preferred with its accumulated dividends, the owners of which, in a sense, were now holding the company in bondage. It is hardly short of miraculous that with no fanfare he substantially accomplished these objectives before the end of the fiscal year 1947.

The most significant blocks Gottwald acquired were two. First there was a total of 1,051 shares from the old Millhiser holdings. Some of these Millhiser shares came in a roundabout way from banks that had acquired the stock when the Richmond Cedar Works went into receivership; part came directly from Mrs. Regina V. Millhiser of New York City, widow of Clarence Millhiser, brother of Gustavus Millhiser. Gottwald said with reference to Mrs. Millhiser, "When she sold her Albemarle Paper Company stock I bought it, and I bought it without knowing how I was going to finance it or anything." The outcome was a visit to the Central National Bank, which lent him the money. The second major unit was a block of 1,510 shares obtained from the estate of O. J. McSwain, the friend who prepared the codicil mentioned above. Gottwald consolidated his borrowings by arranging a major loan from the Raleigh branch of the Wachovia Bank and Trust Company, which was aware of the real equity in the stock Gottwald put up as collateral.

To wipe the slate clean of arrearages on the old 7 percent preferred, Gottwald in the years 1947–48 was able to eliminate virtually all of that class of stock in an exchange arrangement whereby the owners received new 6 percent preferred on a 1.67 basis plus a small amount of cash.

Although a 45 percent ownership might be considered effective control by most businessmen, Gottwald did not feel absolutely secure until the company developed a pattern of voting and nonvoting stock, and he and his family had acquired well over 50 percent of the voting variety. In recalling those days, Gottwald said, "I finally got the directors going my way by weight of the voting stock."

Gottwald Takes Full Command

Immediately after Gottwald's acquisition of a controlling percentage of stock, a series of bold new financial operations took place, bringing to the company from various sources about three million dollars used principally for modernization of plants.

The first phases of the new financing included the retirement of the old 7 percent preferred stock, a maneuver already mentioned, and the carrying out of plant improvements, especially at Roanoke Rapids. In that watershed year 1947, a million dollars came from Knox Glass Associates of Knox, Pennsylvania, which in return received a new issue of common stock called Common B with limited voting rights, and a favorable contract for the supply of paperboard to Knox by Albemarle. (Incidentally this block of stock was eventually obtained by the Lacy family, boxmakers who were doing business with Knox Glass Associates.)

Next, by way of Scott and Stringfellow, Albemarle turned to four Richmond-based life insurance companies for financing: the Life Insurance Company of Virginia, Atlantic Life Insurance Company, Home Beneficial Life Insurance Company, and Union Life Insurance Company. Before the calendar year 1947 had ended, Albemarle borrowed $600,000 from those four companies, and two years later expanded the indebtedness to $950,000. In the meantime Albemarle became disenchanted with the Knox supply contracts and bought itself free through the payment of $75,000.

By 1948 Gottwald spoke cheerfully of the $200,000 expansion and improvement program then in process. His mood was thoroughly justified; sales and profits were on the upswing.

Much of management's attention was now directed to the Halifax subsidiary in Roanoke Rapids, North Carolina, which received the major benefit of the new financing. The papermaking machine from the Riverside Mill in Richmond was moved to Roanoke Rapids in 1948.

Efforts were made to improve the living conditions of both the management personnel and workers in the Roanoke Rapids area. During World War II, when building materials were scarce, the company constructed several houses which it rented, and ultimately sold, to employees of the company. A block on which these dwellings were located was called, appropriately, Paper Mill Hill!

In an attempt to take care of the health situation, the Halifax Mill in partnership with a local textile company constructed a medical clinic and in effect operated it. Employees paid 50¢ a week for doctors' care and 50¢ a week for hospital care. The sponsoring companies underwrote the deficiencies in the cost of looking after the employees.

Improvements in the Halifax Mill were not sufficient to overcome the effects of a recession, and the mill suffered serious operating losses for the first seven months of 1949. Officials in Richmond were determined to apply a cost-cutting formula to all plants, including that at Roanoke Rapids. Monthly employees at both Albemarle and Halifax were subjected to a 10 percent cut in salaries. And the time had come for negotiating a new labor contract with Local 697, United Paper Workers of America, CIO, at the Halifax Mill. The company asked the union to accept a four-cents-per-hour reduction in wages and the elimination of time-and-a-half pay for Sunday work. The union refused, and the company had a strike on its hands, beginning at 7:00 A.M. on Monday, August 1, 1949. The work stoppage was to last for twenty-three long and tense days.

During the first part of the strike the company failed to receive from law enforcement officers protection of the right to enter and leave the plant. Thus, contrary to original plans to keep the mill going with a skeleton crew of laborers and supervisory personnel, operations ceased.

There were fist fights, the damaging of cars, threats, and harassment. One crisis was averted when Kirkwood Adams, manager of operations at Roanoke Rapids, failed in his attempt to start a truck, which he planned to use in gaining entry to the plant by smashing through the picket lines. The rough tactics of some of the strikers were displayed so clearly in a court trial that public opinion became less sympathetic toward the pickets.

There would have been even more violence if the company had not restrained the wood haulers, tough men who did not like the way the strikers were interfering with the delivery of pulpwood. Some of the wood haulers said they could easily open a way in for everybody: they would sharpen their axes and come in swinging. According to rumor, a group of wood haulers and one striker found themselves together in a roadside joint featuring bootleg whiskey, and the striker decided to take to the woods.

Joseph Lowry recalls the periodic meetings to determine the proper course of action. "There would be strategy sessions at the Crescent Restaurant about five miles or so south of Petersburg. Kirkwood Adams would come up to the restaurant and we would go over what had happened. There was a big fireplace, with two fans, one on each side of the hearth, so warm air would be blown from behind the fireplace."

Company policy was clearly formulated on August 4, Thursday, the fourth day of the strike, at a meeting of four officers: Gottwald and Lowry, who came down from Richmond, and Kirkwood Adams and H. Watkins Ellerson, Jr., son of the late president, officers at the Roanoke Rapids plant. The plan was to keep the mill shut down, let the situation become quiet. And despite urgings from some tough Roanoke Rapids industrialists to the contrary, the company in substance maintained its position as intermediary in the payment of fees to insure hospital and medical services for the workers.

Two circumstances gave a new complexion to the strike. Seaboard Railway officials, on finding that their tracks were being blocked by strikers, took the first steps to obtain an injunction. Then key state officials visited Roanoke Rapids and cleared up whatever misunderstanding had tied the hands of the local police force.

Furthermore the workers were embarrassed by unpaid bills and the failure of the union leaders fully to carry out assurances of strike benefits. There is a story to the effect that oil rags were thrown into the fireboxes under the boilers, thus creating so much smoke that the strikers believed that the mill had started without them.

The strike was over by 7 A.M., Wednesday, August 24. In the end the employees returned to work under the same wage conditions they had refused before going on strike, though apparently the company now permitted a checkoff of dues. Before many months had passed, the company restored the pay cuts and even improved the wage scale. Major wage raises came only after the building of famous Machine Number Three, itself a result of the all-important loan from the Reconstruction Finance Corporation.

The management of Albemarle now revived the request for a major loan from the RFC, an application that had once been checked by uncooperative preferred stockholders. It is generally agreed that the proposed RFC loan could not have been effected without giving the federal agency convincing evidence that there existed a genuinely *balanced* paper operation, meaning a pulp mill with an assured supply of pulpwood. From time to time there were set up revolving funds for the purchase of wood-hauling trucks and also for buying land that could be used for timber cutting. But the most impressive move in the direction of an adequate supply of pulpwood was contracting with the North Carolina Forestry Foundation for rights in the Hofmann Forest, over 82,000 acres of timberland in Jones and Onslow counties, North Carolina. The lease was negotiated for a term of ninety-nine years.

The Hofmann Forest was and is a phenomenon itself, a saucer-shaped area with special drainage problems and with a certain amount of hardpan a few feet down. The swampy land formation, termed *pocosin*, was a challenge to the wood haulers, but no more so than were a few nearby small farmers and bear hunt-ers, who were careless with fire and occasionally forgot that the Hofmann Forest was a regulated area.

As far as the written records go, it appears that on December 19, 1949, Gottwald first presented to the Albemarle directors the idea of a new multimillion dollar loan to be used primarily for the purchase and erection of a new paper machine at Roanoke Rapids. Back of this proposal was Gottwald's well-founded belief that, within commonsense limits, the bigger the machine, the cheaper the cost per pound of paper. Thus the proposal for a 200-inch-plus machine would make the Albemarle-Halifax operations more competitive in what Gottwald was sure would be a highly competitive market in the 1950s.

Gottwald prepared well for this new venture in financing. It should be recalled that the RFC was set up to make loans to worthy enterprises, that, in light of the economic conditions in the country, could not obtain those loans from the usual sources. Gottwald made a point to get acquainted with the proper individuals, those who would give him a hearing. In particular it was necessary to obtain the goodwill and understanding of the administrator in the RFC who had charge of paper and other forestry products. This key man was W. C. Ribenack, assistant chief of the Reconstruction Finance Corporation, described as having a good background, a fine education, and a charming wife. As for his extracurricular interests, to quote Douglas Fleet, "he loved to play bridge, so you would fish all day and then play bridge with him half the night."

In recalling those days, Gottwald spoke in detail and with appreciation of his acquaintance with Ribenack. "We asked him if he would consider it undue influence if we took him to enjoy a week or ten days with us at Virginia Beach, and he said he had never had a nicer thing offered before in his life. And since the loan was all over with, he certainly couldn't see any harm in it. This was in the month of October at Virginia Beach, the most beautiful [time] for swimming and fishing you can possibly imagine." The businessmen-sportsmen were successful in fishing for drum in the Chesapeake Bay up toward the Eastern Shore and for blues out in the ocean.

When Ribenack was rowed to some special fishing grounds just below Virginia Beach, he made a wager. As Gottwald recalled, "Before he got out there he said, 'I'll bet a dollar I'll catch the first fish, the biggest fish, and the most fish.'" Gottwald made quite a story out of this challenge from Ribenack by explaining that son Bruce, then a teenager, said, "If Daddy will pay the bill I will bet you." Of course Bruce, who was conditioned to that kind of fishing, caught the first fish, and wound up catching the biggest fish and the most fish. Whereupon Gottwald in mock exaggeration said to Bruce, "You ruined us." To end his reminiscing Gottwald added, "The old guy took a liking to Bruce, so everything came out all right."

It was useful if not essential to obtain senatorial endorsement of the project. First Gottwald went to Senator Harry F. Byrd, with whom Ellerson had been very close as allies in Virginia politics. Byrd would not endorse the application, saying that people should take care of themselves; they should not call on the government.

Next Gottwald appealed to Senator Frank Porter Graham, former president of the University of North Carolina. As Gottwald recalled these circumstances: "He told me to write a letter, giving the background of the company, and what we wanted to do. That turned out to be a four-page letter. And that man took that letter, looked at it, turned to the next page, looked at it and turned the next page. And he talked to me in intimate detail as to what was in that letter. It was the most amazing experience I've ever had." As a result of this interview, Graham backed Gottwald on the proposition.

In figuring how much he wanted to borrow, Gottwald estimated that a 200-inch machine would cost about $4.5 million. He wanted money above the cost of the machine for auxiliary expenses and to pay off the outstanding loan from the insurance companies.

Albemarle's first application in 1950 to the Reconstruction Finance Corporation was for $6,050,000. It was turned down on June 8, 1950. Then there was a compromise, ultimately taking the form of a loan of $5,800,000 with an extra million dollars required to be raised by the issuing of 10,000 shares of second preferred Albemarle stock. To provide security for its $5,800,000 loan, the RFC accepted a lien on the plants in Richmond and in Roanoke Rapids, the rights under the Hofmann Forest lease, the capital stock of Seaboard Manufacturing Company, and insurance on Gottwald's life of not less than $270,000. There was precise allocation of the borrowed money, a matter of some concern to the Albemarle management, which would have desired more freedom.

Recollections indicate that in carrying out the terms of the loan there was continuous auditing by the RFC. With regard to the work at Halifax and the installation of Machine Number Three, Hugh H. Baird, who was then auditor, refers to government auditors "who were in our hair all the time." Gottwald said, "The RFC was a little bit exacting, I think, but anyhow with the Beloit Iron Works cooperation we got the paper machine in." Taking an overall view, Gottwald conceded that the RFC officials "were intelligently understanding." The RFC loan was an excellent, even decisive, move. The consequent construction of Machine Number Three could rank along with the Ethyl acquisition in any listing of important events in the company's history. The machine produced its first paper January 23, 1953. The acquisition of this machine was the turning point in the development of the company. After its installation statistics showed a reduction in man-hours per ton and an increase of company profits.

Forward Integration and General Expansion in the 1950s

Although it is appropriate to designate the 1950s as a time of forward integration and general expansion, these basic ideas had been with F. D. Gottwald from the beginning of his presidency. ("Forward integration" means going into the business of converting the paper into a finished product such as shopping bags or fertilizer sacks.) In the 1940s Gottwald had succeeded in a modest effort to integrate forward. The impulse to get into the converting business was encouraged, even required, by the example of competitors. Such integration forward made for more economical production, diverted middlemen profits into the company treasury, and tended to iron out the characteristic ups and downs that existed in a nonintegrated paper business. Perhaps the most immediate imperative in the major purchases of converting plants was to preserve a market for the kraft paper that might be lost if the convertor was purchased by a competing paper manufacturer.

As early as 1942 Gottwald bought nine machines for the manufacture of self-opening bags and two presses for their proper bundling. A complicated deal was worked out with the Morgan Brothers and Seaboard Bag Company of Richmond for the manufacture of multiwalled sacks using paper produced by Albemarle. In 1943 Albemarle management agreed to lease part of the first and fourth floors of the Riverside Mill to Seaboard Manufacturing Company. Gottwald was to have charge of the manufacturing operations so long as the arrangement was agreeable to Albemarle, to Seaboard, and to Gottwald himself.

The new financing developed in 1947 after Gottwald's large stock purchases included $300,000 for the acquisition of Seaboard stock. On April 1, 1950, the directors agreed to purchase the remaining one-third of the stock of the Seaboard Manufacturing Corporation, thereby making Seaboard a wholly owned subsidiary.

A new era of integration forward began in 1955. At the board meeting on September 9, 1955, Gottwald, according to the minutes, "discussed again the desire of the management for acquiring and operating a bag company." Gottwald decided that Albemarle would purchase Raymond Bag Company of Middletown, Ohio, which made multiwalled paper-shipping sacks used in the bulk packaging of agricultural and food products, building materials, chemicals, drugs, dyes, and minerals. The company employed about 350 persons in a 150,000-square-foot plant and used, when running at capacity, 30,000 tons of kraft paper a year. On November 11, 1955, the directors gave formal approval of the Raymond purchase, which was concluded before the end of the month.

When announcing to the newspapers the acquisition of Raymond Bag Company, Gottwald said, "This is a large step toward integration of all operations, from the tree seed to the final paper product." And he added that the purchase "will allow conversion of a much greater proportion of our kraft paper into our own paper products."

The second major acquisition in the converting areas was Interstate Bag Company of Walden, New York. Albemarle management described Interstate as the "leading producer in this country of 'single handle' shopping bags." Negotiations between Albemarle and Interstate lasted for over a year. Although Albemarle's management complained of the price, it reluctantly concluded that it simply must go ahead with the transaction as a measure of self-protection. The basic agreement, dated September 9, 1957, called for Albemarle stock and later cash for inventories. The Interstate chief executive officer, H. Kirk Steen, was soon elected to the Albemarle board of directors.

As part of a plan to make folding boxes on a large scale, Albemarle on April 13, 1959, concluded the purchase of the Randolph Paper Box Corporation in Richmond, an old firm founded in 1832. The acquisition of fixed properties of Randolph was financed on a sale-and-lease-back basis with Atlantic Life Insurance Company. The operations at Randolph Paper Box were expanded by the purchase on February 29, 1960, of the folding box business of Consolidated Paper Box Company, which was then moved into the Randolph plant. Equipment and organizational changes were made at the Randolph Paper Box division in a frustrated attempt to improve profits. Albemarle management in 1962 decided to close the plant, a development allied to a plan to buy a substantial interest in the New Haven Box and Carton Company, a move to which more specific reference will be made below.

Turning its attention to the corrugated box business, the management of Albemarle acquired two companies: the Richmond Container Corporation in September 1959, which was made a division of Seaboard, and the Armstrong Container Corporation in Baltimore in October 1960. The Armstrong plant was renamed Albemarle Container Corporation.

The organization of converting operations was modified late in 1961 when Albemarle Container Corporation, Raymond Bag Corporation, and Seaboard Manufacturing Corporation were merged into Halifax Paper Company, Inc., a wholly owned subsidiary of Albemarle.

Gottwald now determined to get into the manufacture of folding box board for use in Albemarle's converting plants. In the background was his belief that in the long run Brown's Island was not going to be competitive in kraft paper. One advantage in the manufacture of folding box board was that scrap paper and ground wood could be used; thus the expensive haul of pulp from Roanoke Rapids might be avoided.

The first stage in Gottwald's plan was to obtain suitable land for the proposed manufacturing plant. To quote Gottwald: "We were going to build a box plant down here in the Tredegar Iron Works. In fact Tredegar was bought with that in mind." The Tredegar property—about twenty-two acres between the James River and the Kanawha Canal, acres that closed the gap between the Hollywood and Riverside mills on the one hand and Brown's Island properties on the other—was acquired by the maneuver of a merger, a drawn-out process. The Tredegar Company, as historians will recall, had a long record of iron manufacturing and arms production before, during, and after the Civil War. Tredegar rolled the plate for the famous ironclad the *Merrimack*, sometimes called the *Virginia*. The company continued in the armament business; it was manufacturing practice shells on the original site until shortly before the merger with Albemarle.

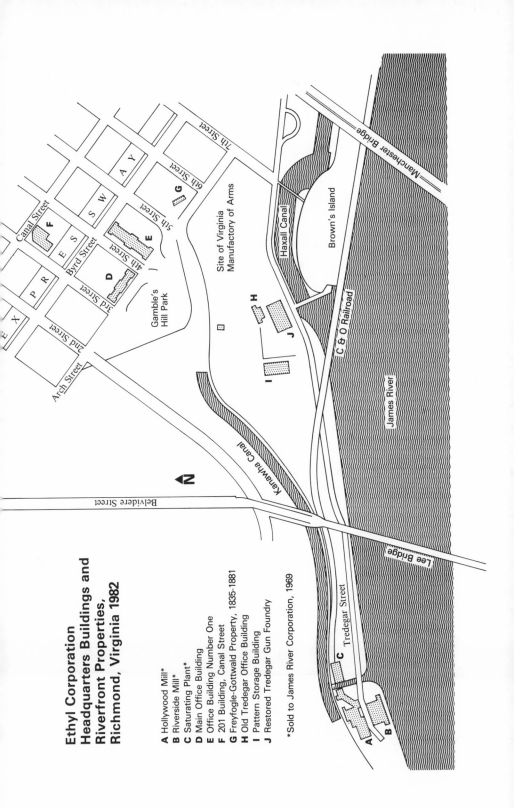

Ethyl Corporation
Headquarters Buildings and
Riverfront Properties,
Richmond, Virginia 1982

A Hollywood Mill*
B Riverside Mill*
C Saturating Plant*
D Main Office Building
E Office Building Number One
F 201 Building, Canal Street
G Freyfogle-Gottwald Property, 1835-1881
H Old Tredegar Office Building
I Pattern Storage Building
J Restored Tredegar Gun Foundry

*Sold to James River Corporation, 1969

According to the terms of the merger, officially consummated February 25, 1958, the stockholders of Tredegar were given a new issue of class B stock and cumulative preferred 6 percent series B.

Less easily solved than the problem of a real estate base for the proposed new folding box board was the need for a more efficient method of manufacture. There were experiments and some progress was made toward that goal. To quote Gottwald, "And then instead of developing that business ourselves, we arranged [for] and I think it was a 33.33 percent interest in the New Haven Box and Carton Company, controlled by William W. Fitzhugh, Inc." The company operated a mill in New Haven and one in Baltimore. The latter obviously would soon be shut down because its effluent ran through a major park. The plan was to close the Baltimore mill and to build one on the Tredegar tract.

But Gottwald's imagination ran ahead of several rough realities. Entranced by the history of the new acreage, he planned a factory designed along the lines of the so-called armory, the Virginia Manufactory of Arms, which had been destroyed in the fire of April 1865 when Richmond fell.

In the meantime the Albemarle research people confronted the problem of reducing the amount of effluent from the paper board process and refined the technique to the point that there was only a 5 percent residual in the water that had to be disposed of. There were difficult negotiations with the city for the disposal of this remnant waste.

Then the principal figure in the New Haven firm, William Fitzhugh, became incapacitated by illness. Fitzhugh's decline meant the disappearance from the arrangement of a very interested party. Meanwhile on April 18, 1962, after study by independent consultants, Albemarle purchased a controlling interest in exchange for Albemarle stock.

The failure to reach an understanding with city authorities in the matter of the effluent and the decline of William Fitzhugh meant abandonment of the plans for the reconstruction of the old armory as a factory building and for coordination with the

New Haven plant. A quantity of folding box board was made on a machine at Brown's Island, but Gottwald's dream of developing this product was never realized. In 1963 the board of the new Ethyl Corporation authorized the disposal of all its interest in the New Haven plant.

While large-scale integration forward by way of acquiring converting plants was the most novel of the developments in that momentous decade of the 1950s, the basic and decisive growth was in other areas: in papermaking itself; the manufacture of pulp for those papermaking machines; the guarantee of adequate supplies of pulpwood by purchase or by longtime lease of timberlands; and the scientific treatment of forestry resources. Thus there was a strong pattern of complete integration: backward to the trees as well as forward to the finished product ready to be used by the citizen consumer. The observer could notice bigger and better pulp and paper machines, more modern chemical recovery units, more efficient labor-saving devices for material handling. Furthermore, the company scientists and engineers in the course of time were assigned not only to quality control but to research and development of new and improved products.

The intensive research at Albemarle, which was quite evident in the late 1950s, centered in three areas: the development of a pilot plant for the manufacture of polyethylene; attempts to create a new process of cast coating that would be used for folding cartons; and, unrelated to either plastics or paper, the production of a unique material by the "arc process," a procedure that involved the introduction of silica between electrodes, the end result being the creation of extremely small silica particles as filler material. The polyethylene venture proved too costly for commercial production; the cast coating experiments in the course of time matured into important production; the arc process was eventually abandoned.

In this period the research and development group was headed by Brenton S. Halsey, a Virginian by birth, who joined Albemarle in 1955. When he left in 1966 to head an Albemarle subsidiary, Interstate Bag Company, as president and general manager, he was succeeded by Robert C. Williams, a native of Illinois, who had been with Albemarle since 1959. Both Halsey and Williams were professionally trained at the Institute of Paper Chemistry in Appleton, Wisconsin, as was their co-worker in research, Richard C. Erickson, native of Illinois, who had joined Albemarle in 1960.

By 1962 the pulp mill at Roanoke Rapids required about 1,400 cords of wood per day, most of which came from private owners of wood lots, though the company owned outright or held under long-term lease over 200,000 acres of woodlands within acceptable hauling distance of Roanoke Rapids. In the mid-1940s Halifax had begun hiring professional foresters to develop its own acres and to encourage private owners in its area of procurement to become better managers, to think of trees as a crop rather than as a onetime windfall. There were successful experiments with cross pollination, and the company distributed millions of seedlings to private landowners, 4-H clubs, and FFA clubs.

The prime objective of the pulpmakers was to keep up with the needs of the papermaking machines. Pulp production and the pulp requirements of the paper machines eventually were in rule-of-thumb balance. Refinements in the pulp mill at the Halifax plant included elaborate recovery units, conspicuously the new lime-burning and continuous causticizing system, which reduced lime consumption in the manufacture of pulp by about 90 percent. Also there was the development of a process for using sawmill waste in the form of chips. Of equal importance was the introduction of procedures whereby hardwood could be used along with pine, an innovation of almost revolutionary significance. New equipment and modernization of processes were immediately costly but profitable in the long run. About $7 million were put into pulpmaking at Roanoke Rapids during the 1950s, and production of pulp rose from approximately 225 tons per day in 1950 to 850 tons per day by 1962.

In papermaking the most dramatic single event was the installation in 1959 of the "Dixie Queen," the great Number Four Machine at Roanoke Rapids, sister to Number Three, which has already been described. The new equipment was a Beloit Four-drinier with a wire width of 246 inches and capable of producing a continuous sheet of paper nineteen feet across. The Dixie Queen was primarily a producer of heavyweight paper and board; Machine Number Three was manufacturing a lightweight paper.

James H. Scott of Scott and Stringfellow was tremendously impressed by Gottwald's ingenuity and courage in installing the second big machine at Roanoke Rapids in a season when everybody else was quite frightened at business conditions. Indeed, Gottwald took advantage of the downswing by making an especially good deal with the Beloit people, who had very little to do at this particular time.

In operation on June 8, 1959, the Dixie Queen soon exceeded its rated capacity of 300 tons per day. The installation of the Dixie Queen permitted innovations in operating the four small units originally scheduled to be shut down with the coming of the new 246-inch Fourdrinier. One of the machines was adapted to the production of Clupak, a stretchable paper Albemarle was now licensed to make.

The financing of the Dixie Queen in 1958, the high point of money-raising by Albemarle in the 1950s, had both traditional and innovative features. By way of background it should be noted that as of January 1, 1951, all of the old 7 percent cumulative preferred called in by the recapitalization plan of 1947 had been retired, replaced by a less punitive 6 percent preferred. In 1950 Albemarle had issued a 5 percent second preferred to help finance expansion at Halifax. As for the common, the pattern of A, voting, and B, restricted voting, as developed in 1947 was continued and expanded in the recapitalization of 1953, which saw additional A and B shares offered by J. C. Wheat and Company and associated brokerage firms. There were further issues of common B and new layers of preferred to finance acquisitions and improvements.

Of special importance was the disappearance of the RFC and the appearance of Northwestern Mutual as a willing creditor. In this period the major source of large-scale and long-term loans was Northwestern Mutual, which sometimes acted jointly with New England Mutual. In 1954 a loan of $5.0 million at 4.50 percent for twenty years was negotiated with Northwestern Mutual, this to retire that part of the indebtedness of Albemarle to the RFC that remained at the time and to provide additional working capital. There were periodic rearrangements and increases in the amount Northwestern lent to Albemarle. In 1956 a new agreement provided for a total of $8.5 million at 4.75 percent.

This association between a Minnesota insurance company and a Virginia paper company was primarily personal communication between Joseph Lowry of Albemarle and Peter Langmuir of Northwestern. Such was the faith each had in the other that millions of dollars were negotiated with a telephone call. As Lowry says, "In the case of Langmuir, he'd give you an answer then: 'Yes, we will do it. Go on back home and tell your people.'"

By way of strengthening the posture of the company, Gottwald wanted a resumption of dividends on the common stock. At the board meeting of December 10, 1955, Gottwald "reminded the directors that the corporation during recent years had eliminated all arrearages on its first preferred stock, and that arrearages on the second preferred stock would be eliminated on the first of January 1956." The management of Albemarle felt justified in declaring on September 5, 1956, a quarterly dividend of 12.5¢ on the common stock both A and B. This policy of an annual dividend of 50¢ per share continued until after the merger of 1962, when increases were in order. Stock dividends became frequent though irregular in timing and amount: 1953, 100 percent; 1956, 100 percent; 1958, 5 percent; 1959, 5 percent; 1960, 25 percent; 1962, 5 percent.

The borrowing in 1958 of the $6.5 million needed for the purchase and installation of the Dixie Queen in Roanoke Rapids was important not only because the financing made possible a more economical operation but also because this transaction developed new friends useful four years later in the purchase of

Ethyl. There were three basic elements in the borrowing in 1958. First, Northwestern Mutual and New England Mutual jointly agreed to take $10.5 million in first mortgage bonds. Of that $10.5 million $8.5 million were to be used in refunding bonds then current; $2.0 million might be called new money. Second, from First and Merchants Bank and from Wachovia Bank and Trust Company $1.0 million were borrowed. Third, there were $3.5 million of subordinated convertible debentures, carrying a rate of 5.5 percent and due in 1978. In the distribution of these debentures certain preemptive subscription rights were granted to holders of A and B common stock. Northwestern Mutual and New England Mutual together were allowed to buy $1.5 million worth; the rest was handled by underwriters headed by Scott and Stringfellow.

All who subscribed to the subordinated convertible debentures came out well. Issued at $100, these debentures immediately rose in price. The range was as follows for the next several years:

	1958	1959	1960	1961
High	$175	$238	$187	$155
Low	$109	$160	$121	$140

The explanation of course is that the convertible feature provided that common B could be bought from August 31, 1958, to July 1, 1963, at $16.775 per share. Then at $18.29 up to July 1, 1968. Of special significance in light of later events was the fact that Blyth and Company, New York investment bankers, had a good experience in selling the debentures to their clients. And also note that the New York legal firm of Debevoise was called in to represent Northwestern, and there developed personal friendships with Albemarle's counsel remembered in 1962.

No one argued the fact that during the period of expansion summarized above, F. D. Gottwald was "boss man" in the company. Those responsible for management tactics had as their assignment the blending of day-to-day procedures with Gottwald's announced goal of venturesome research, careful economy, and steady growth. Gottwald could look about him and see a panel of senior officers who had been carried over from the earlier regime with his approval, or whom he had hired.

Albemarle was indeed blessed with an adept management team. Blyth and Company in 1958 published a brochure entitled "A Study for Investors on Albemarle Paper Manufacturing Company" describing the corporation and listing with biographical notes eight corporate officers: F. D. Gottwald, 60, president; S. D. Fleet, 51, vice president and sales manager; B. W. Coale, 75, vice president; K. F. Adams, 55, vice president and general manage of Halifax Paper Company; F. D. Gottwald, Jr., 36, vice president and secretary; C. H. Robertson, 48, vice president and director of industrial and public relations; J. M. Lowry, 50, treasurer; C. R. Hailey, 36, controller. Their average age was 51. The company was applauded for its "management in depth" with "each key executive now 'back-stopped' by one or more junior officers fully capable of assuming responsibility."

The list is a useful identification of key personnel. Other than Gottwald himself and Coale, whose retention after retirement age was a matter of special ruling, the senior member of management in terms of length of tenure was S. Douglas Fleet, whose earliest years with the company have already been mentioned. He became head of sales after the resignation of Blair Stringfellow in 1944. At the annual stockholders meeting on May 27, 1948, Fleet was elected vice president and a director. Fleet's special importance can be appreciated only when one understands that Gottwald was primarily a man of finance and production; he was not a salesman in the ordinary sense of the word and accordingly left the selling to others.

Fleet's connection with Albemarle began in 1925, when on completing his courses at John Marshall High School in Richmond, he answered a newspaper advertisement run by Albemarle, was interviewed by Basil Coale, and immediately became an office boy. For two years he sandwiched his work at Albemarle between terms of study at the College of William and Mary in Williamsburg, but finally ended his academic training to accept full-time and regular employment at Albemarle, concentrating on sales.

Fleet, outgoing and personable, had a special talent for ingratiating himself with customers, a knack of turning a business encounter into a personal friendship. When the great Machine Number Three was in operation, on many a Friday he telephoned his favorite customers with the plea that there just *had* to be some orders to keep the machine busy over the weekend.

Basil W. Coale's early career already has been sketched. During his tenure with Albemarle he served as shipping clerk, cashier, bookkeeper, assistant secretary, secretary, treasurer, vice president, and director.

Kirkwood Adams is one of those Virginians by nurture and by education who must explain that they were born elsewhere. This elsewhere was Greenville, Tennessee, and the date of his birth was 1904. His family moved to Richmond when Kirkwood was three or four years of age. After attending McGuire's School, he enrolled in Virginia Military Institute. At the end of his second year he transferred to the University of Virginia, graduating in 1925 with a major in business and the sciences. For a season he undertook clerical officework with the Chesapeake and Ohio Railroad and then in the year 1927 began working at Albemarle as an office boy, succeeding Douglas Fleet in that springboard position. He rose through the ranks to become production manager about the time Gottwald was elected president.

As manager of the plant in Roanoke Rapids, he made notable contributions in both performance and philosophy. He was an articulate person whose ideas on management and on the importance of timber as a renewable source of energy spread far beyond the Richmond and Roanoke Rapids bases.

In a sense Charles H. Robertson was a legacy from an earlier generation. It was his father, Arthur F. Robertson, secretary-treasurer of the company and Kellogg's friend, who provided Gottwald with his original reception at Albemarle. After graduating from Hampden-Sydney College, Charles Robertson entered his father's firm and eventually achieved a vice presidency and membership on the board of directors. His most conspicuous successes were in the area of labor relations; when negotiating, he was noted for his coolness and good humor. These qualities and an expansive friendliness earned for him recognition by various professional and trade associations. He was an amusing raconteur and is credited with inventing several famous tall tales in the duck blinds. Occasionally he confounded the skeptics by bringing in game compatible with his boasts. His employment with the company was interrupted by service in the navy during World War II. To reconcile his Calvinistic heritage with his desire to be at church with his wife, the distinguished pianist Florence Richardson, Charles was one of the very few people claiming membership in both Episcopal and Presbyterian churches.

As already noted, Joseph M. Lowry, imaginative financial officer, spearheaded the sometimes novel borrowings in this period. A Richmonder by birth, Lowry became a public accountant and held office in several corporations before coming to Albemarle in 1947. Lowry was initiated into the paper business through his services with Leach, Caulkins, and Scott as auditor at the Halifax Plant in Roanoke Rapids, at Chesapeake Corporation, and at Camp Manufacturing.

Fleet played an important part in obtaining for Albemarle Lowry's services. When Gottwald saw Coale approaching normal retirement age, he sought to strengthen the financial staff. Fleet suggested to Gottwald that Lowry would be a good addition. The key interview between Fleet and Lowry occurred while they lunched in the ballroom of the Hotel Jefferson. After a few months Lowry did come to Albemarle as controller, this in the year 1947. He was elected a director on May 24, 1951. A year later he was given the title of treasurer.

Although C. Raymond Hailey's most conspicuous services to the company were in the Ethyl era, his earlier responsibilities gave him a broad experience that prepared him for decisive judgments. A native of Toano, Virginia, he enrolled in the College of William and Mary in 1939. On the death of his father late in 1940, he withdrew from college and came to Richmond to look for a job. The fact that he had completed a year and a half of college chemistry persuaded him that he was a qualified professional. Thus he took employment with Albemarle as a paper tester, this at about the time that the company presidency was assumed by F. D. Gottwald. In World War II he was in the European Theater with a tank corps. When peace came he returned to Albemarle, this time in the accounting department, pursuing his academic studies at night at the University of Richmond. The year 1956 was a time of celebration for Hailey; within that twelve-month period he received his college degree, passed his CPA examination, and was appointed controller of the company.

Important in the management team in the years before the acquisition of Ethyl of Delaware by Albemarle were F. D. Gottwald's two sons, Floyd D. ("Bill") Gottwald, Jr., and Bruce C. Gottwald. The senior Gottwald was careful to see that they worked hard and were exposed to a variety of company experiences. Remembering that he himself greatly benefited by his own services as corporate secretary, Gottwald insisted that each of his sons, at least for a season, serve as secretary of Albemarle Paper Manufacturing Company.

Although their early years and special interests will be reviewed in a later chapter, it should be noted here that Floyd D. Gottwald, Jr., in 1956 was appointed secretary of the corporation, vice president, and director. Bruce Gottwald was elected assistant secretary in 1960, secretary, vice president, and director in 1962.

Albemarle had the benefit of what can only be described as brilliant legal assistance in these years of bold growth. The company employed no staff lawyer but depended on general outside counsel. Conspicuous was the talent of Lewis F. Powell, Jr. With the death of Royal E. Cabell in 1950, Gottwald approached Powell of the law firm then known as Hunton, Williams, Anderson, Gay and Moore and asked Powell if he would succeed Cabell as general counsel. Powell was one of the few Virginia lawyers well prepared in interpreting Securities and Exchange Commission rules. Although he had been previously associated with Cabell

Lewis F. Powell, Jr.

in the deal with Knox Glass Associates, his important relationship with Albemarle had been in a technically adversary category
when representing Scott and Stringfellow. Thus Powell was quite
surprised at Gottwald's invitation. Powell, who had earlier concluded that Gottwald was one of the most alert and shrewd businessmen in the region, decided to accept the offer.

As the years went by, Powell's role became more than legal
advisor. Indeed, he was an intimate member of the business family, enjoying the confidence of the Gottwalds and sharing in the
discussion of important plans and decisions. In 1953 he was elected
a director. As for his legal activities, Powell worked under the
team concept. B. Warwick Davenport was Powell's number one
aide on the Albemarle account until 1959, when he went on the
board of Chesapeake. Before that time he was actively involved
in much of the forward and backward integration developed by
Albemarle. Also at Powell's elbow during most of this period of

Lawrence E. Blanchard, Jr.

Albemarle's expansion was Lawrence E. Blanchard, Jr., who eventually joined Ethyl of Virginia as a senior officer. Thus Blanchard's early career deserves attention.

In his characteristic way, Blanchard always has insisted that he is just a North Carolina farm boy. The halfway excuse for this exaggeration is the fact that his father for a brief period was a farm demonstration agent, presumably the first in the state of North Carolina, before marrying Anna Neal Fuller and managing for two years the farm owned by her father outside Lumberton. This was the period in which Blanchard was born, March 7, 1921. The family moved about a bit, going to Florida in the boom-bust times and then settling in Raleigh, where Blanchard grew up. Following the Trinity College–Duke tradition in his family, he attended the university at Durham, where he was a leader, being president of the student body, of his class, and of almost everything else. He solemnly declares that his career has been downhill ever since those days! Graduated in 1942, he spent four years as an officer in the navy, serving in the latter part of the war in the Pacific. During his navy years he married Frances Hallum of Rockingham, North Carolina. Out of the navy in March 1946, he entered an accelerated program at Columbia Law School, and on graduation in June 1948 headed south to look for a job, defying all the customs of the period by neglecting to apply to a single New York law firm.

One of his Columbia professors told him of Hunton, Williams, Anderson, Gay and Moore in Richmond, a firm of which heretofore he had never heard, and he presented himself to Powell, who was putting on his coat to fly to California and could only glance at Blanchard's credentials. Powell referred Blanchard to Thomas B. Gay, a senior partner. Gay was impressed, but said Blanchard was late. The interview was on a Friday and Gay had to let the other applicants know by Monday morning. However, he offered Blanchard a job if Blanchard would take it immediately. Blanchard protested that he couldn't even buy a necktie without Frances's permission, and Gay allowed him until Sunday morning to make up his mind. Blanchard accepted, and started work on July 1, 1948, working with Wirt Marks for four and one-half years. And then, on the withdrawal of Marks from the firm in March 1953, Blanchard was offered a partnership and was assigned to work with Powell in corporate financing. Note that when working with Marks, Blanchard had been engaged in trial practice, handling the Richmond, Fredericksburg, and Potomac Railroad account and doing some bank work. It was as a member of Powell's team that Blanchard first became acquainted with the Albemarle account. When Warwick Davenport went to the Chesapeake board in 1959, Blanchard became Powell's senior cohort on the team.

As for the directors, the pattern of membership on the board was, of course, the fruition of Gottwald's deliberate plan after his frustration in the 1941–47 period. In Gottwald's own words, "So finally we had directors of management choice." In reminiscing, he gave a cheerful and unapologetic mea culpa. The directors now were men who clearly recognized Gottwald's talents, were willing to accept his leadership, and applauded the growth of the company. Gottwald in turn showed respect for the group by giving a full briefing before asking for an endorsement in major decisions.

A relic of the old regime was T. Croxton Gordon, with a tenure dating from 1921, who resigned his directorship in 1961, explaining that he was leaving both the Albemarle and Chesapeake boards because their competitive character made "my position in both camps clearly untenable." It was after Gordon's resignation that Bruce Gottwald was elected to the board. By mid-1962 the board consisted of K. F. Adams, B. W. Coale, H. W. Ellerson, Jr., S. D. Fleet, B. C. Gottwald, F. D. Gottwald, F. D. Gottwald, Jr., J. M. Lowry, R. T. Marsh, Jr., L. F. Powell, Jr., C. H. Robertson, S. B. Scott, and H. K. Steen. The three most recently elected were Robert T. Marsh, Jr., of First and Merchants Bank, elected April 7, 1959; Sidney Buford Scott of Scott and Stringfellow, elected May 28, 1959; and, as already indicated, Bruce C. Gottwald, elected May 24, 1962, from management.

In the 1950s everyone realized that the office space for Albemarle was totally inadequate. As early as March 20, 1953, Gottwald spoke to his directors of the office space then available as

Albemarle's "incredibly bad" old office building

"badly congested." As Douglas Fleet recalls the conversations about the "incredibly bad" offices, "Gottwald said, 'If you will stop complaining about the offices I promise you we will have a fine office in X years.' So I sort of shut up on the thing. Gottwald was always a man of his word."

By June 1957 Gottwald had been successful in either buying or obtaining options on all the property in the key block on Gamble's Hill between Third and Fourth, and Arch and Byrd, except for a certain lot owned by the Second Presbyterian Church, which eventually was obtained. The board voted a general approval of his idea.

Gamble's Hill offered a superb view of the river and the city and was a place of considerable historic significance. The name was given because here was the residence of Colonel Robert Gamble, who in 1799 bought the almost completed house being built by Colonel John Harvie. The residence was a famous one,

New office building (Main Building)

designed by Benjamin H. Latrobe, often described as the first professional architect in the United States. Gamble entertained in Grey Castle many notables, including his friend John Marshall. Gamble and his two sons were prominent in the business history of Richmond; later the two sons established a name for themselves in Florida. Grey Castle was famous also for its association with two of Gamble's sons-in-law, William H. Cabell, who became governor of Virginia and judge on the state Court of Appeals, and William Wirt, who was well known as an author, orator, and for twelve years attorney general of the United States.

As the years had gone by, houses crowded into the space around Grey Castle and the building lost much of its grandeur. It was occupied from 1877 to 1888 by the McGuire University School, but was torn down in 1888 or 1889.

The style of the Albemarle building was along the lines desired by F. D. Gottwald, who had become interested in Colonial Williamsburg. In exterior appearance it was a good copy of the Williamsburg Inn. One board member at first was startled by the design, claiming, "Well I don't particularly like it. It looks like a girl's finishing school to me." At the November 16, 1960, meeting of the board Gottwald pointed out that the "design had been selected by management primarily for two reasons, namely, first it was felt that this type of architecture was particularly well suited for a building located on Gamble's Hill, where it would be readily visible to traffic approaching Richmond on the Lee Bridge from the south, and would in the opinion of management have significant advertising value; and two, management preferred the Georgian design to modern or contemporary designs which are now more customarily used in office buildings, and architects advised that no significant additional expense would result from this preference." Although the president's office and the board room were designed with paneled walls, the remainder of the offices were simple and economical. Carneal and Johnston, architects, attested that no one could fairly criticize the design as extravagant or incompatible with requirements of modern office buildings. Bids were received in 1961 and the architects recommended Virginia Engineering Company, whose bid of $1,007,000 was accepted.

Some preservationists protested the tearing down of Pratt's Castle, an architectural oddity on Arch Street, to clear the way for the erection of the new building. Albemarle management felt that there was no strong case for preserving that deteriorating Gothic structure and thereby upsetting basic plans for the new Albemarle offices. Pratt's Castle was constructed partly of stone, mostly of wood covered with sheet metal painted to resemble stone. It was in a run-down condition at the time of its demolition in the fall of 1957. Perhaps it might be pointed out here that the company proved to be sensitive to the history of Gamble's Hill and other areas of Richmond. It had already made a rather handsome gesture toward preservation of a historic site on Church Hill and soon would adopt restoration of the Tredegar Foundry as a special project.

Albemarle's new office building utilized temporary financing, but soon after completion the building was taken over by the Albemarle pension trust fund and was rented to the company under long-term lease.

New Pressures and Larger Plans

By the late 1950s Gottwald quite naturally had developed a self-confidence rooted in the considerable achievements of the previous dozen years. Then, almost overnight, his business was threatened by novel materials, particularly by polyethylene film, which virtually annihilated the market for several established paper products. As Gottwald recalled the situation, "The polyethylene bag replaced the double-walled water-proofed bag that we used to make." He felt that soon the time would come when the single-walled water-proofed bag would also be replaced. "When it would come nobody knew, but you could see it coming anyway."

He added, "And then we decided that it would be a doggone good thing for us to make the bags ourselves." Looking in the other direction, he recalled how unprofitable the Albemarle business had been until it began to integrate backward, and he asked himself what would be the sense of buying polyethylene film and then making it into those bags. Rather, "we ought to make the polyethylene ourselves." In the laboratory Albemarle started the experimental work in making polyethylene, but found the laboratory-made product more expensive than what could be purchased.

Despite his general opposition to joint enterprises, F. D. Gottwald and his management team began to seek a company to go partners with in a polyethylene film venture. To quote Gottwald when recounting these events, "We decided to accelerate our efforts to join in a plastic venture." In inquiring about companies that had some position in the area of this interest, he heard of Ethyl. Gottwald arranged to see several of the Ethyl people in Baton Rouge, Louisiana, the first visit taking place on May 14, 1958, the second on June 2. The meeting at the City Club in

Baton Rouge on May 14 is in a sense the beginning of what became the Ethyl purchase. In a moment of public whimsy Gottwald said that if somehow the table around which the representatives of Ethyl and Albemarle gathered that day were a college or university, he would like to endow it!

It was on the flight back to Richmond after either the first or second conversation with Ethyl representatives in Baton Rouge that Floyd D. Gottwald, Jr., first heard his father say something about purchasing Ethyl. "I remember very distinctly sitting on that plane flying back to Richmond when Pop said, 'Wouldn't it be a nice thing if we could buy Ethyl?' It was not until that moment that the idea had been expressed at all." The younger Gottwald's answer to his father was to the effect that the idea was *great*, but he wondered how in the world they would be able to raise the money.

Shortly after Gottwald's visit to Baton Rouge, Ethyl representatives came to Richmond, and over doughnuts and coffee at the Hotel Jefferson reviewed with Gottwald his various ideas. Eventually the negotiations broke down because the proposed operation—even when bolstered by the plan of acquiring or cooperating with Lamex, a plastic bag manufacturer near Atlanta—seemed to Ethyl too small for profitable development. Probably more important in the ending of these conversations was the increasing determination of the owners of Ethyl to restrict further development of products not directly related to the manufacture of tetraethyl lead, the antiknock additive to gasoline that was Ethyl's prized product.

In recalling the initial conversations, F. D. Gottwald himself noted that he had wished for Ethyl ever since these early talks. It is quite certain, however, that this particular ambition was only one of many dreams floating around in his active mind.

What was the nature of this company called Ethyl for which Gottwald hungered?

Part Two

ETHYL
OF
DELAWARE

IV

Epochal Discoveries:
Kettering and the
Creation of Ethyl
1916–1926

Boss Ket's "Playhouse" and the Players 1916–21

ETHYL GASOLINE CORPORATION, chartered in Delaware in 1924, originated in the research efforts of Charles F. Kettering and the team of scientists he organized. Kettering, who created about as many proverbs as inventions, claimed that the price of progress is *trouble*, and that almost invariably every useful new product must survive a "shirt-losing" period. The early Ethyl story provides full confirmation of these maxims. In this particular case, however, the frustrations were countered by a pattern of lively fraternity and good cheer, reaching in times of triumph the height of frenzied elation. Indeed, there is a large element of validity in Kettering's whimsical description of the research establishment he organized in 1916 as his "playhouse" and in his contention that he and his staff went about their investigations as other men played golf, though with somewhat less profanity.

Kettering's research group, first called the Dayton Research Laboratories Company, grew out of a long conversation between Kettering and Thomas Midgley, Jr., one Saturday afternoon in

The 1912 Cadillac that knocked

the fall of 1916. The subject was engine knock, a phenomenon that had irritated Kettering for several years.

Kettering's feud with the knock may be dated from the misbehavior of a 1912 model Cadillac. His rivals, the magneto makers, claimed that engine knock was caused by a Kettering innovation, battery ignition, an accusation Kettering knew to be false, but no one had discovered the exact nature of this pounding, which beat on the eardrum and made impossible high-compression and therefore high-powered engines.

Kettering had an additional grievance when his Delco-Light engine, a farm power unit, was required by the fire underwriters to use kerosene, a fuel which knocked so severely that Kettering unhappily was forced to reduce the compression and thus the power of the engine. Kettering was not the sort of man quietly to accept such. His whole life was a life of inquiry.

The staff Kettering put together sustained a high degree of enthusiasm and imagination. Although there were important supporting individuals, including the technical director Dr. F. D. Clements, who first came into Kettering's life as his laboratory instructor at Ohio State University, the major personalities contributing to the amazing success of the Kettering research laboratory were three: (1) Charles F. Kettering himself, who established, encouraged, and supported; (2) Thomas Midgley, Jr., engineer turned chemist, first member of the technical staff and one of the most brilliant chemists of his generation, a man to whom the word *genius* is habitually applied; and (3) Thomas A. Boyd, diligent worker and careful chronicler, whose sound achievements were somewhat obscured by the forceful charm and showmanship of his senior co-workers, Kettering and Midgley.

Appraisals of Kettering's relationship with Ethyl rest comfortably on superlatives. "Ethyl Corporation is a monument to his pioneering," said the Ethyl directors in 1959 soon after his death. On his seventy-fifth birthday his association with Ethyl Gasoline was described in these words: "He conceived its need, supervised its destiny. He even chose the name and wrote its first advertising."

Born on a farm near Loudonville, Ohio, Kettering went through the typical experiences of his era and vicinity; and all his life he enjoyed telling of his barefoot days and his attendance at the one-room country school that went under the name of Big Run. At high school in Loudonville he excelled in mathematics and physics. Characteristic of this tall, gangling teenager was his reaction to a failure which he (and every member of his class) suffered from an unexpected test in Latin grammar. To be better prepared next time, he tied his book with binding string to his plow handle and mastered the balky rules as he walked along the furrows. Graduating from high school at the age of nineteen, he took charge for a year at Bunker Hill School, quite similar to the one-room school he himself had first attended. At Bunker Hill his warm personality and his bold variations from the cut-and-dried textbook approach made him beloved by his pupils, though a local clergyman became upset when Kettering encouraged attendance at an exhibit featuring an X-ray machine, which the minister felt was the work of the devil. The year ended peacefully and Kettering, to prepare for the ministry in accordance with his parents' wishes, enrolled in the summer session at Wooster College for the study of Greek.

At Wooster he happened upon a catalogue from Ohio State University and was fascinated by the description of the engineering course since it included blacksmithing. At about the same

Charles F. Kettering

time he developed very serious eye trouble that forced him to leave Wooster before the end of the summer. Improvement in his vision was slow, and indeed he continued to have difficulties with his eyes for much of his life. He was well enough by the middle of the school year to resume his teaching, this time in a two-room school in the village of Mifflin, Ohio, about ten miles from the Kettering farm. Here he taught the upper grades of the elementary school, where he continued the relaxed and informal methods he had developed earlier. The twenty-year-old was long remembered as strict but full of fun as he stood before his class and emphatically gestured with a small pointer in his right hand while he hooked a thumb in his left pants pocket.

In the fall of 1898 he entered Ohio State, enrolling in the electrical engineering course. Despite financial and visual problems he maintained a good average his freshman year. At the beginning of the sophomore year there was such a breakdown in his eyesight, attended by severe headaches, that he had to return home, a downhearted young man.

Then came a significant turn. Thinking that outdoor activities might improve his health, he began working with a crew of men who were setting poles for a telephone circuit. It was action to his liking and soon he became foreman of the tough line gang. The men appreciated Kettering's good humor and his remarkably strong muscles in a slender body. He was moderately successful in teaching the members of the line gang to take pride in their work; the men in the gang were even more successful in teaching him an advanced course in swearing. From this time forth, on proper occasions he had available this verbal leverage for moving men and materials. (In later years he claimed with mock pride that he was the only man who could swear as Edison did, this to explain why he was made president of the Thomas A. Edison Foundation!)

After additional experience with the telephone system, including switchboard installations, he returned to Ohio State University for the completion of his engineering courses, though he received special faculty permission for class substitutions less trying on his eyes than the specified mechanical drawing.

When testing telephone equipment, he had become acquainted with a young lady in his neighborhood named Olive Williams. Thus it happened that, like F. D. Gottwald a few years later, Kettering courted and married the organist of a neighboring church. Olive's talents were complementary to his; she provided a charming home for entertainment of his business associates; and she saw to it that his wardrobe, which he always considered of third-rate importance, benefited from a new suit every now and then. Concentrating on weightier matters, even when a very wealthy man he often neglected to carry enough currency in his pockets to take care of his needs and had to borrow from his traveling companions.

As to physical appearance, to quote T. A. Boyd, who worked with him for many years and was his biographer, "He was a tall, gangling fellow. He was a farmer and walked like a farmer." Others offered the fact of his bad eyesight to explain Kettering's shambling, somewhat uncertain gait. Again to quote Boyd, this in his oral statement to the present author concerning Kettering, "His hair stayed black, although in later years he was bald." *Fortune* magazine rather flippantly described Kettering as "tall and gangling, a little bit reminiscent of Abraham Lincoln and a little bit of Ichabod Crane."

The trait that lifted Kettering out of the ordinary was an overpowering curiosity. He was dominated by the spirit of inquiry. He wanted to know the *whyness* of natural phenomena. Robert Kehoe, an outstanding toxicologist who was associated with Kettering for a long time, speaks of Kettering and his "very considerable curiosity about what was going on. His whole career, beginning with his own personal life, was an inquiry into what he was doing and what it meant. He would have been a plowboy the rest of his life if it hadn't been for this spirit of inquiry that he had. And he turned out to be a very great man with a humble beginning."

Furthermore, Kettering had a sustained and contagious enthusiasm. This was good because his role was to excite others to experimentation. To balance his fervor was a professional patience.

Gregarious by nature, Kettering was no closet scientist. He was a frank showman; he loved the dramatic portrayal possible in public lectures. When before an audience he drew on all the talents, both natural and studied, which he had developed since he first stood before his pupils in the little country school in Ohio. He methodically put his hearers through their paces. He shocked by oversimplification: "We don't know anything about anything." He dismayed by questioning the obvious: "What is magnetism?" "Why is the grass green?" He amused by puncturing the pompous; he mesmerized by illustration and anecdote; he inspired by proving that great things remained to be done and could be done with perseverance. His major theme was that the world was still there to be conquered. He claimed that research was simply a high-hat word for "nothing but a state of mind—a friendly, welcoming attitude toward change." He was not only a great showman but a public speaker who unhesitatingly advocated the ancient virtues. At scientific and professional gatherings his anecdotes might have been used before, but his audiences enjoyed hearing them again. He retained his platform vigor into old age. T. A. Boyd heard one of Kettering's last speeches, an address in Cleveland, and counted the laughs during the twenty-five-minute presentation. There were exactly twenty-five, one per minute—not giggles says Boyd—but laughter that forced Kettering to stop his remarks while the audience settled down.

While in this present study it is appropriate to concentrate on Kettering's role in the discovery of tetraethyl lead as an antiknock, there were many other inventions and developments to his credit, including the electric cash register, a battery ignition system for automobiles, and a small, thirty-two-volt farm lighting system. Kettering's development of the first practical electric self-starter permitted the American woman to achieve an emancipating mobility; she was no longer kept at home because of the forbidding handcrank on the front of the automobile.

After more powerful engines were possible because of higher octane gasoline, Kettering turned his attention to improving the diesel engine. He bought a yacht for the purpose, though he explained his purchase at the time by saying that when a man reached a certain age he either got a new wife or bought a yacht, and he thought he would do the latter. And this he did, naming it "Olive K" for his wife.

Kettering dearly loved to call himself a "monkey-wrench engineer," a tinkerer. He poked into machines often enough, even in later life, to get grease on himself sufficient to upset Olive and to give superficial confirmation of his self-imposed label. In fact, Kettering was at one and the same time both speculative and practical, blending research for understanding with research for progress.

Added to his other qualities was that more dynamic form of patience called persistence; he did not easily give up; as already said, he was reconciled to a "shirt-losing" period in any worthwhile new economic adventure. He also had a considerable amount of persuasive power. All of these traits plus his strong position as a major stockholder in General Motors made him a powerful ally of the research people in the laboratories.

And yet, as one of his discriminating contemporaries has said, there were theoretical scientists and people in the research laboratories who, "surprisingly enough, were not inspired by Ket." They did not like the fact that he was such a good showman, and the signs in his laboratory, such as "Aero-dynamically a bumble bee can't fly," taunted rather than inspired some of the theorists. He would put problems in ultrasimplistic ways. Some churlish critic thought he invented, or reinvented, the platitude.

Kettering's foremost lieutenant was Midgley, who though formally trained as an engineer became one of the leading chemists of his generation, winning the four top awards of the profession and eventually holding simultaneously the presidency and chairmanship of the American Chemical Society. Coming from a family of inventors, even as a youth he showed his aptitude for practical innovation by developing, with the help of a teammate, a so-

Thomas Midgley, Jr.

phisticated version of the old spitball by using the juice from the inner bark of the slippery elm. And the ball, it might be said here, behaved in most unexpected ways. At Betts Academy in Stamford, Connecticut, he accumulated, among other pieces of intellectual baggage, knowledge and appreciation of the periodic table of the elements. But he was unwilling to accept the theological approach to the subject as advocated by his teacher, one Professor Henry M. Robert, Jr., son of the Robert of *Robert's Rules of Order,* eventually professor of mathematics at the U.S. Naval Academy. About fifteen years after his first encounter with the periodic table of the elements, Midgley was to return to that table with sensational results.

Five years after receiving from Cornell University a degree in mechanical engineering, a specialty he had adopted to please his father, Midgley took a job at the Dayton Engineering Laboratories Company, which had been set up by Kettering, and thus began an enduring personal and professional relationship. Kettering regarded Midgley with brotherly affection. It was a mutual feeling. In introducing Kettering at a meeting of the American Chemical Society, Midgley said, "Everything worthwhile I have ever accomplished has been done under the magic spell of his inspiration."

Richard Scales, who worked alongside Midgley for many years, summarized the cooperative effort: "In this relationship between the two of them Kettering was the fellow who had already pinpointed certain things which he believed were great opportunities for improvement and great opportunities for solving basic problems. So he came to Midge—saying, 'Here is a problem, here is what I think could be the approach to it. You take the job over.' Now this didn't mean that from then on they didn't talk together, but what happened was that Kettering would say, 'What do you know now, Midge? What progress have you made on such?' And then he, Kettering, would comment on that, and they'd work together."

Kettering said he never knew of anybody who could come to such logical conclusions from so few data as did Midgley. According to Kettering, Midgley had the ability to invent, then to reduce the invention to practical usefulness, and then to sell the public on the advantages of the invention. Thus Midgley was a crusader as well as a scientist. No doubt about it, Midgley was brilliant. James Boudreau, eventually vice president and director of public relations of Ethyl of Virginia, went so far as to say, "He was one of the great geniuses on earth."

While Midgley's most important achievement was his share in the development of tetraethyl lead as a practical antiknock compound, he was almost as triumphant in the field of refrigerants, discovering dichlorodifluoromethane (Freon), a nontoxic, nonflammable compound suitable for household appliances. Like Kettering in being something of an exhibitionist, he amazed audiences by inhaling the Freon vapor, then slowly exhaling it to extinguish a lighted candle.

He was intensely social and rejoiced in his professional societies, particularly in the fraternal gatherings that accompanied the formal meetings. At a convention of the American Chemical Society, Midgley sponsored a facetious "Hydriadiatic Instipoop." Its motto was "Temperance Despite Prohibition"; its presiding official the Chief Ninkompoop.

As Julian Frey, later vice president in charge of sales, said when discussing Midgley, "He was an amazing fellow, great fun to be with, and if you did any talking with him you knew that he was quite a poet. And he used to say, 'The more we drink, the smarter we get.'" Tradition has it that Midgley could entertain scientific friends all night with discussion of scientific matters and then, come morning, do a full day's work.

As a wide-eyed young member of Midgley's household for a year, Richard Scales was present at several fabulous sessions in Detroit with Kettering and Midgley. To begin the evening, Kettering would find a bottle of gin, order a pitcher of orange juice, and create his own version of what later was called a screwdriver. According to Scales, "They began the discussion on the basis of getting really into the fundamentals of chemistry, way beyond what was being discussed in those days, and some of it was conjecture." One of the tools which both of them used as much as anything else in the field of chemistry was the international critical tables. "This was recreational drinking as well as thinking for them. And for me it was lessons that I had never learned from [other] sources."

Because Thomas A. Boyd so often blended into the background of retorts and test machines and because he characteristically wrote large the exploits of his two comrades in research, his own contributions to the research group are not always fully understood and appreciated.

Originally destined for the ministry, Boyd felt uncomfortable with those among his collegemates making similar declarations of theological intent and accordingly shifted his attention to the natural sciences. At Ohio State in 1918 he completed his bachelor's degree in chemical engineering. He was recommended to

Kettering, who promptly and profitably put him to work with the research group in Dayton, by that time known as the Dayton Metal Products Company.

When Kettering seriously undertook research for an adequate antiknock compound, he was operating under the team concept. The principals were not only Kettering, Midgley, and Boyd, but other scientists including Clements, a helpful administrator, and Graham Edgar, the author of the octane scale, who came a bit later. On the periphery of production research but squarely in the middle of investigating the toxic qualities of antiknock additives was the decisive Dr. Robert A. Kehoe.

There is a discernible line of continuity in Kettering's major contributions to American economic life. His realization that a sudden surge of electrical current through a small motor could result in a surprising amount of power led first to production of an electric cash register then, as mentioned above, to the first practical automobile self-starter. The knock in the 1912 Cadillac and its successor models and the knocking in the little engine running the thirty-two-volt Delco home lighting system heightened both his curiosity and his irritation.

In oversimplification it might be said that the work of the research team in the antiknock investigation was essentially threefold: (1) to determine what the so-called knock really was and what caused it; (2) to discover a satisfactory antiknock additive; (3) to develop a feasible way to manufacture or to procure the ingredients in the antiknock formula.

The first antiknock agent was discovered even before the researchers developed a clear understanding of the nature of the knock. The discovery resulted from an odd combination of a mistaken theory and a semiaccident. Concentrating on kerosene, which knocked worse than gasoline, Kettering and Midgley assumed that some of the fuel persisted in droplet form during the normal combustion period, and then the tardy fuel ignited in delayed action, thus producing that traumatic knock. How could one hurry that very unrighteous remnant? Remembering that the rusty-colored leaves of the trailing arbutus bloom in the spring

even while the snow is still on the ground, the scientists specu-
lated that if the fuel were dyed a similar color, it would absorb
more radiant energy and thus vaporize early enough to prevent
the knock.

In the search for a proper dye the semiaccident occurred. When
Midgley one day in December 1916 went to H. R. Wolf's chemical laboratory at Delco, he could find no oil-soluble dye. But
Fred L. Chase, the only one in the chemical laboratory at the
time, discovered a bottle of iodine and suggested that it might
give the desired color to the fuel. The iodine did give a reddish
color to kerosene, and the fuel thus dyed performed beautifully
without so much as a single knock.

Subsequent experiments proved that coloration had nothing to
do with developing antiknock properties in the fuel, and thus the
romantic thesis of the trailing arbutus went into the researchers'
trash heap. But because the iodine stopped the pounding in the
engine, it is properly considered the first antiknock compound to
be discovered. The researchers now knew that there was something that could subdue the knock. Yet iodine was not the answer; it was scarce, expensive, and quite corrosive. The search
had to continue.

For pragmatic reasons, during the year 1917 the Dayton Research Laboratories Company changed its name to the Research
Division of the Dayton Metal Products Company, another Kettering operation. World War I had started, supplies were difficult
to obtain, and the Dayton Metal Products Company, producing
military goods exclusively, had a high priority rating in the buying of materials. Soon the favored classification was fully justified
by the search for a more nearly knock-free airplane fuel. This
effort, with the backing of the War Department, began about
October 1, 1917.

Among the many mixtures tested by the cooperative team from
the Dayton group and the Bureau of Mines was one submitted
by Henry Ford under the emphatic label "H. Ford's Knock-
knocker." In performance it was less memorable than its title.
The basic object of the wartime research was to increase power

by boosting engine compression. The major result was a special aviation fuel made with cyclohexane and benzene named "Hecter," which allowed a boost in the compression ratios of airplane engines from about 5.1:1 to 8:1. With the end of the war the project for large-scale production was dropped.

As plans for the commercial manufacture of Hecter were abandoned, the researchers returned to their old objectives and after a brief period of very low spirits, a new vigor came to the project with the discovery on January 30, 1919, by Boyd, then a new member of the staff, of a second real antiknock compound, aniline. Aniline had sundry limitations, including a bad smell; thus neither it nor iodine was practical.

The Research Division of the Dayton Metal Products Company was purchased from Kettering and associates by General Motors Corporation early in 1920. Along with the purchase was an arrangement whereby Kettering himself would direct for General Motors a research team organized around the laboratory that he had founded in 1916.

There was a temporary connection with the Dayton-Wright Division of General Motors, and then the laboratory was given autonomy under the title of General Motors Research Corporation (GMRC), the charter dated June 11, 1920. A few weeks before this incorporation, the laboratory was moved to Moraine, near Dayton, and set up in a large building that had been occupied during the war by Dayton-Wright Airplane Company.

For a season the objectives of the General Motors Research Corporation were broadened to include the making of motor fuels from vegetation, since Midgley was predicting the immediate decline of petroleum as an energy source. It is good that Midgley was better with a test tube than with a crystal ball. And the GMRC scientists, pessimistic about the chance of finding an antiknock more effective than aniline, began trying to develop a more economical method of application, to reduce its disagreeable odor, and to minimize gumming. Indeed plans were being made to work with DuPont in an effort to market an aniline injector. However, the problems with aniline soon seemed insurmountable, especially the terrible smell. There was also concern about the toxicity of aniline and its corrosive effect on metals.

Then on April 6, 1921, the Kettering group of researchers discovered that a compound of selenium oxychloride was a more effective antiknock than anything hitherto discovered. Selenium, which the press called a "universal solvent," was a by-product of copper, lead, and silver smelters.

Because of selenium oxychloride's extremely corrosive nature, better compounds of selenium were sought. In the search, a compound of the similar element tellurium, diethyl telluride, was made. When tested by Boyd, diethyl telluride was found to be several times as effective as selenium oxychloride. With allied discoveries, the whole tone of the endeavor changed. There was the problem of supply, however, and then there was the odor!

As Boyd tells the story, the great news of selenium and tellurium was spread around a meeting of the American Chemical Society in Rochester not only by the spoken word but by the "satanic garlic smell" that clung to the bodies of those working with volatile compounds of selenium and tellurium, especially tellurium. To quote Midgley, "There was no getting rid of it. It was so powerful that a change of clothes and a bath at the end of the day did not reduce your ability as a tellurium broadcasting station. Nor did the odor grow much weaker when several days were passed in absence from the laboratory." Fellow workers in the laboratory and the familly became accustomed to it. "Going out at night, however, was a problem, although I found one best solution. When we went to the movies, I would look around until I found a man of Mediterranean extraction, and we would sit down beside him. Presently people would scowl at him from all directions as they got my perfume, but we were secure and comfortable."

It was no wonder that the Chevrolet test car, which during the summer of 1921 had its compression raised to 7:1 from 4.1:1, was called "The Goat." Its mountain-climbing ability was only part of the explanation; the smell out of the exhaust pipe was memorable.

Up until the time of the discovery of the antiknock effects of selenium and tellurium, there had been a somewhat random selection of compounds to test. It was, to quote Boyd, "the Edisonian method of 'cut and try.'" Now an analysis of data already obtained from the testing of both knock-inducing compounds and a consideration of the periodic arrangement of the elements suggested that the desired antiknock characteristic just might be a period function. The chart used was entitled "A Periodic System Based on the Langmuir Theory of Atomic Structure and an Arrangement by R. E. Wilson" with one box entitled "Number of Electrons in Outer Shell" and the second "Number of Vacant Spaces in Outer Shell." Plotting known characteristics on the table gave more than a hint as to where the search would end, and there ensued what Midgley termed a systematic "fox hunt."

Now there were not only orderly plans for testing additional compounds but new equipment for the more accurate measurement of knock, notably the so-called bouncing-pin indicator, which Boyd and Midgley developed in the summer of 1921. Under more controlled conditions a retesting of various materials already considered resulted in the discovery that there was "a periodic function of the elements with respect to effect upon knock, and that degree of effectiveness increased as the bottom of each column was approached." As the research moved ahead, there was almost frenzied excitement. The discovery that tetraethyl tin possessed antiknock qualities suggested that lead, immediately below tin in the carbon group, would probably be a powerful antiknock element.

The historic engine test occurred on December 9, 1921, when Boyd, in the presence of Midgley and Carroll A. Hochwalt, who had prepared the tetraethyl lead, used a solution of one percent tetraethyl lead in kerosene fed into the test Delco-Light engine. The results were immediately apparent; the solution was so free from knock that it could not be compared with the aniline solutions that had been established as reference fuels. The tetraethyl lead solution was then weakened and the investigators discovered

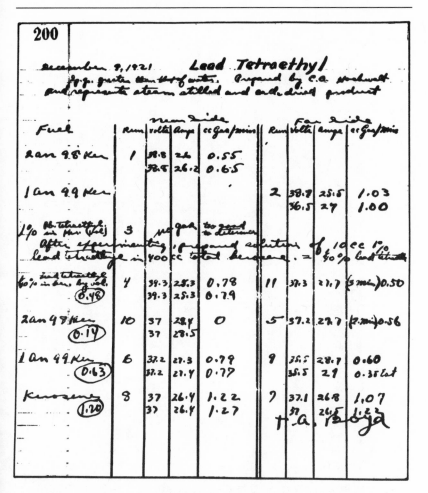

Laboratory record of first engine test of tetraethyl lead antiknock

that one-fortieth of 1 percent tetraethyl lead was equivalent to 1.3 percent aniline in kerosene.

It is appropriate to reflect for a moment on the significance of the discovery on December 9, 1921. Obviously the innovation was the force that created a profitable business, but this is not the main point. Tetraethyl lead made possible the early development of the modern high-compression, high-powered internal com-

Thomas A. Boyd and the Delco-Light engine in whi

bustion engine. A new character was given to the automobile, the tractor, and the bus. Williams Haynes, in his monumental

tetraethyl lead was first tested

American Chemical Industry, develops the thesis that tetraethyl lead not only improved the performance of gasoline but had a stimulating effect on the oil refiners, who became "definitely chemically minded" by the late 1920s. "Tetraethyl lead, perfected by General Motors and produced by DuPont, not only improved the performance of gasoline, but it focused attention upon the chemical constitution of the oil refiners' most important product." And Haynes adds with reference to tetraethyl lead's broader influence, "It served also as a powerful mental catalytic agent, stimulating physical and chemical inquiries into the internal combustion engine and its fuel."

Midgley took the news of the tetraethyl lead discovery to the meeting of the Society of Automotive Engineers at White Sulphur Springs, West Virginia, in June 1922. The report in a trade journal carried a picture of a group gathered around Midgley, one person kneeling. The caption read: "This is not a crap game, but a group of engineers observing the cremation of tetraethyl lead, the new fuel dope which Midgley exhibited."

Following this demonstration Midgley was asked to present a paper before the American Chemical Society at its September meeting in Pittsburgh. The paper, prepared under the joint authorship of Midgley and Boyd, is significant as the first scholarly essay dealing with the antiknock qualities of tetraethyl lead.

In Pittsburgh the president of the Carnegie Institute registered shock at the first announcement that a Delco-Light engine would go through its paces from knocking to purring on the same stage where Madame Schumann-Heink sang and Fritz Kreisler fiddled. Permission was granted, however, and despite a near tragedy when the engine in its warm-up blew a cylinder head gasket, the performance went off well. The paper was indeed a landmark, though it had suffered partial mutilation at the hands of the patent section of General Motors, which wanted no public statement as to the correlation of antiknock effectiveness with the periodic arrangement of the elements.

The paper, repeated before other groups, not only led to Midgley's earning the William H. Nichols Medal from the New York section of the American Chemical Society, but was largely responsible for the sober, unhysterical reaction of the scientific community to the tragic deaths in Bayway, New Jersey, and elsewhere in 1924 and 1925 to be explained later.

Much remained to be done before the new discovery could be satisfactorily presented to the American motoring public. Still needed were economical and efficient methods of manufacturing the tetraethyl lead; a satisfactory "scrubber," or "scavenger," to clean out residual material in the cylinder; a proper system of distribution; and adequate safety measures. Yet the winter of 1921–22 was a great season; the breakthrough had been made. Incidentally, it was to be five years before any profit could be seen in the venture, and it was a good thing that Kettering had disciplined himself to expect a "shirt-losing" period in the development of any useful new product.

Factors in the Formation of Ethyl Gasoline Corporation, 1921–24

The researchers found that tetraethyl lead left in the engine a deposit of oxide of lead, grayish-yellow in color, which in time eroded spark plugs and burned valves. The problem was handed to Boyd, who by the summer of 1922 concluded that as a corrective agent bromine added to the gasoline along with tetraethyl lead was the most effective chemical available; chlorine was next.

The demand for bromine as a scrubber, or scavenger, outstripped the quantity available at the major if not sole domestic supplier, the Dow Chemical Company of Midland, Michigan, which extracted the needed chemical from the strong brine pumped from salt wells. After venturesome trips abroad, including a notable investigation by Kettering of the possibilities in North Africa, those responsible for the production of a usable corrective to accompany the tetraethyl lead in gasoline decided that there must be created an adequate domestic supply of bromine and that seawater appeared to be the best source for the quantities needed.

DuPont was called on to build a pilot plant based on techniques of seawater extraction developed by the Midgley research

group and then to erect a full plant on a cargo ship acquired for the purpose.

Under the name of the S.S. *Ethyl* the ship made one voyage, this in the spring of 1925. There was only limited success, the problems stemming in part from the fact that many of the chemists and engineers aboard were too seasick properly to attend their duties. Yet scientists had learned enough to be sure that the sea could become a good source for the bromine. News of the achievements aboard the *Ethyl* was overshadowed by violent debate about lead as a health hazard. Almost simultaneously with the *Ethyl's* docking, the production of tetraethyl lead was suspended while investigations were going on. In the 1930s the effort to procure bromine was to take the form of the Ethyl-Dow plant at Kure Beach, North Carolina, to be discussed more particularly below.

Soon after the discovery that tetraethyl lead had powerful antiknock qualities, officials of General Motors contracted with DuPont for the manufacture of the new gasoline additive. The formal arrangement of 1922 seemed a natural development. DuPont owned a large block of General Motors stock, 38 percent by 1920. Even before the tetraethyl lead discovery, DuPont had been called on for assistance in minor research.

The fraternal nature of the relationship between the two corporations is suggested by the contract of 1922 between General Motors and DuPont for the manufacture of tetraethyl lead, signed by two brothers, Pierre S. du Pont, president and chairman of the board of General Motors, and Irénée du Pont, president of DuPont. The method of manufacture used by DuPont in these early days was basically the ethyl bromide process, which the Kettering-Midgley-Boyd group had developed by the time of the contract.

Kettering was in a hurry to make available to the public what he himself named "Ethyl" gasoline. He pushed for marketing before research had developed a suitable answer to the lead oxide deposits in the engine. He explained that despite its limitations many people wanted the new mixture and that its deficiencies would be remedied more quickly if it were on the market and customer reactions were observed.

The first public sale of Ethyl gasoline was made by the Refiners Oil Company station at Sixth and Main streets, Dayton, Ohio, on February 1, 1923. Less than four months later Kettering and Midgley persuaded several of the drivers in the Indianapolis Memorial Day race to use Ethyl fluid in their gasoline. The first three places in the 500-mile race were won by drivers using the Ethyl antiknock compound, a fact well publicized.

It was Boyd who in May 1923 recommended that Ethyl Gasoline be dyed to distinguish it from ordinary fuel. The original red dye was labeled "Sudan IV," which Standard Oil Company of Indiana imaginatively advertised as "a wine color."

The first major sales contract was an agreement between Standard Oil of Indiana and the General Motors Chemical Company in September 1923. This arrangement was unique in the history of the sales of Ethyl gasoline in that Standard of Indiana was given an exclusive dealership in its area for a period of five years. The contract with Indiana Standard grew out of the long personal friendship and mutual respect which R. E. Wilson and Midgley had for each other.

A Pennsylvanian by birth, Wilson brought a broad background of academic training to his eventual concentration on chemical

*Service station where the first public sale of Ethyl Gasoline
was made, February 1, 1923*

engineering. He earned the Ph.B., magna cum laude, from the
College of Wooster in Ohio, then a B.S. in chemical engineering from Massachusetts Institute of Technology (MIT). After research experience with various institutions, he became associate
professor of chemical engineering at MIT and director of the
Research Laboratory of Applied Chemistry in that institution
during the years 1919–22. Then he accepted an invitation to
become assistant director of research at Standard Oil of Indiana.

It may be remembered that Midgley was a great man for
professional societies, and at these meetings Midgley and Wilson
spent long hours discussing the research carried on by Midgley
and his group in their "scientific fox hunt." And it was Wilson's

version of the periodic table of elements that prompted Midgley to turn aside from the Edisonian cut-and-try technique for a more systematic series of experiments with the elements, a procedure which, as already noted, eventually led to the sensational tetra-ethyl lead discovery.

In making arrangements for the large-scale distribution of Ethyl gasoline, Sloan, Kettering, and others sponsored the founding of the General Motors Chemical Company on April 23, 1923, as a Delaware corporation. The director's were: Charles F. Kettering, Thomas Midgley, Jr., Charles F. Smart, Alfred P. Sloan, Jr., and Earle W. Webb. Kettering was president, Midgley was vice president. Note particularly that Webb, general attorney for General Motors, was on the board.

A paper on antiknocks written by Kettering in 1919 greatly impressed an independent patent attorney, Frank A. Howard, who persuaded the executives of Standard Oil of New Jersey to establish a free-ranging research and development organization along lines drawn by Kettering and managed by Howard himself. Such was the confidence of Howard in his own earliest research that at one time he claimed the Jersey company was one jump ahead of Kettering. Howard, who was to become a major character in the history of Ethyl, was born in Illinois and trained in both engineering and law. In the course of time Howard was chosen president of the Standard Oil Development Company and vice president of the parent company, Standard Oil of New Jersey.

Under Howard's prodding the Jersey research people now concentrated on developing economical methods of producing tetraethyl lead. A Jersey consultant, Professor Charles A. Kraus, then at Clark University, an authority on metallo-organic compounds, discovered in the first months of 1924 a manufacturing process cheaper and more efficient than the ethyl bromine process that had evolved in the General Motors laboratory and then been adopted by DuPont. Professor Kraus was aided by Conrad C. Callis, and thus the new method, the ethyl chloride modifi-

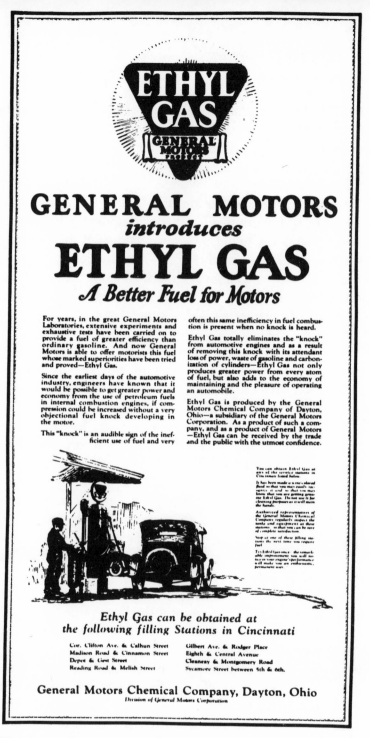

First newspaper advertisement of Ethyl Gasoline, published in the papers of Cincinnati in the summer of 1923

cation of the sodium lead process, became known as the Kraus-Callis procedure.

Thus while General Motors had the basic patents for the introduction of tetraethyl lead into gasoline as an antiknock additive, Standard now possessed manufacturing technique far superior to any other method. The obvious solution was to join forces.

In August 1924 General Motors and Standard Oil of New Jersey created Ethyl Gasoline Corporation. (Later, on April 9, 1942, the name was changed to Ethyl Corporation.) The new corporation was given all the patent rights held by the two companies in the antiknock field and all the assets of the General Motors Chemical Company.

The directors of the new corporation were: from General Motors, Donaldson Brown, Charles F. Kettering, Alfred P. Sloan, Jr., and John Thomas Smith; from Standard Oil of New Jersey, E. M. Clark, Frank A. Howard, Arch M. Maxwell, James A. Moffett, Jr., and Walter C. Teagle. The executives were Charles F. Kettering, president; Frank A. Howard, first vice president; Thomas Midgley, Jr., second vice president and general manager; A. M. Maxwell, third vice president and sales manager; Donaldson Brown, secretary and treasurer; Chester O. Swain, general counsel. The corporation established its offices in the Cunard Building, 25 Broadway, New York City.

DuPont officials looked on the creation of the new company with a measure of concern since the Jersey negotiators were adamant in their insistence that Jersey should be allowed to produce at least *some* tetraethyl lead. As a compromise Jersey was permitted one small plant at Bayway, a "semiworks," a crumb from the table. Apologetically, Sloan, new president of General Motors, explained to his DuPont friends that this minute gesture was necessary to placate Jersey but that the production allowed was inconsequential.

This Bayway plant operated by Jersey soon closed and under the most tragic circumstances. The process of manufacturing tetraethyl lead as then carried on was discovered to be a hazardous operation that required new and stringent safety regulations.

Tragedy and Trial, 1924–26

If ever a company started its corporate life under bleak circumstances, it was Ethyl Gasoline Corporation, which had to learn the hard way that it was dealing with a chemical compound that in concentrated form was lethal far beyond original estimates. As then prepared, the compound to be mixed with gasoline readily exploded. One of Kettering's friends, who for a season kept a gift bottle on his desk, congratulated Kettering on having invented a bomb, fragments of the bottle on disintegration barely missing the friend's eye. Knowing that tetraethyl lead should be classified as a poison, workers in the laboratory thought they were taking proper precautions.

Under date of December 20, 1922, there were words of warning from Dr. Hugh S. Cumming, United States surgeon general, who was alarmed by what he had heard at the New York section of the American Chemical Society a few weeks earlier. By the time of the statement from Cumming, Midgley had already started correspondence with the Bureau of Mines to arrange an investigation of the toxicity of tetraethyl lead.

Further evidence of danger did not await such studies. Early in February 1923 Midgley himself went to Florida for a month of rest and recuperation. He was trying to rid himself of the effects of too much exposure during the previous several months when he was experimenting with various methods of manufacturing tetraethyl lead. On March 15 he was back home but still complaining that his temperature had not become normal.

Several months later—the formal contract was signed October 19, 1923—Midgley completed his arrangements with the Bureau of Mines, which, using the chamber built to measure possible fumes in the Harlem Tunnel, immediately began testing exhaust emissions from automobiles using Ethyl gasoline. As stated later by the officials of the Bureau of Mines, they interpreted their responsibilities to be "to make an exhaustive and impartial experimental investigation on the possibility of poisoning from the lead in automobile exhaust gases from gasoline containing lead tetraethyl, and to make the results public, regardless of what they might be."

There were tentative though incomplete negotiations for a research contract with the Harvard Medical School, and the actual signing of a research contract with Columbia University. In all of these negotiations with research elements in universities, Midgley was sensitive to the code of proper academic behavior. For example, in his preliminary communications with Dean David L. Edsall of the Harvard Medical School, Midgley wrote, "We would of course render this assistance without any strings attached whatever to the full understanding it is for the purpose of increasing the total of human knowledge and with no ulterior motive in mind whatever. Freedom to publish all results and everything also would of course be quite the same as in other pieces of academic research work."

Almost coincident with its formation, Ethyl was threatened with extinction because of a series of fatalities in experimental laboratories and in plants manufacturing tetraethyl lead. The deaths, which occurred in 1924 and 1925, totaled fifteen insofar as can be determined today.

The tragedies were centered in three locations: the experimental manufacturing by Ethyl at Dayton; the Bayway "semiworks" (the small plant Standard Oil of New Jersey had insisted on its right to operate); and in DuPont's Deepwater, New Jersey, plant. The deaths at Dayton were the most painful to the original developers of the tetraethyl lead additive; the fatalities at Bayway caused the most sensational publicity; the loss of life at DuPont's Deepwater plant, according to critical observers, came nearest to being muffled by management.

The first known deaths occurred in the summer of 1924 at Dayton, where workers were under the close direction of Midgley, who became tremendously upset. An outgoing and fraternal sort, Midgley himself had employed these people, had enjoyed social hours with them, and was depressed to the point of considering giving up the whole tetraethyl lead program.

Kettering's calmer approach was to inquire first as to what caused these deaths and then to see whether ultrasafe procedures could be developed that would permit the continued production of the additive. In looking for someone to head the company's inquiry, Kettering discovered Robert A. Kehoe, M.D., the assistant professor of physiology at the College of Medicine, University of Cincinnati. Eventually he became one of the world's leading authorities on the toxic nature of tetraethyl lead and on methods to avoid contamination.

Quite as remarkable as the scientific achievements of this man was his reputation for professional honesty. High officials in the companies owning Ethyl had supreme faith in Kehoe. Sloan, who succeeded Pierre du Pont as president of General Motors, told Kehoe that if in his judgment the toxic qualities of tetraethyl lead could not be controlled—if it were impossible to make the operation safe—he, Sloan, would take the responsibility of closing the whole tetraethyl lead business.

As a result of the Dayton fatalities, a supplemental agreement was formally concluded with the Bureau of Mines on October 2, 1924. In contrast to the earlier experiments that concentrated on exhaust fumes, the major purpose now was to discover the effects of exposure to the liquid itself and to its vapors. As early as July 8, 1924, at a conference with representatives of the Bureau of Mines, Kehoe had indicated his belief that the real problem was not with the public's exposure to toxic matter but rather with the manufacturing process. Subsequent investigations confirmed his judgment.

On October 25, 1924, at the "semiworks" in Bayway, New Jersey, where tetraethyl lead was being produced by Jersey, an accident resulted in the illness of about forty workers. Of that number, five died. Some of those fatally ill became insane and had to be placed in straight jackets before their deaths. These tragedies provided the journalists covering the event an excuse for coining the phrase "looney gas," which for a long time clung to gasoline containing the new additive.

Newspapers in the United States and abroad gave sensational publicity to the Bayway story, picturing in lurid detail the agonies of the ill and dying. Several jurisdictions, including the cities of New York and Philadelphia, suspended the marketing of gasoline containing tetraethyl lead. Total sales headed downward and distributors pleaded with Ethyl officials to assure them that the treated gasoline they were selling was harmless to their workers and to their customers.

The management of Ethyl sought to meet the situation on several fronts. Repeatedly it underscored the fact that the Bayway fatalities had occurred in an experimental manufacturing plant and that with ordinary precautions the gasoline containing the very small quantity of tetraethyl lead was harmless. It publicized the first results of the experiments being carried on by the Bureau of Mines, data which led to the conclusion that exhaust gases from engines using Ethyl gasoline appeared to be harmless to humans. (The full report, entitled "Experimental Studies on the Effect of Ethyl Gasoline and Its Combustion Products," by R. R. Sayers, A. C. Fieldner, W. P. Yant, and B. G. H. Thomas, was not published until 1927.) Midgley, who thoroughly recovered his aplomb, appeared in New York and in an interview on October 30, 1924, at the offices of Standard Oil Company rubbed some of the tetraethyl lead on his hands to prove that the material was not dangerous in small quantities. He met the issue head-on at a meeting of the Industrial and Engineering Division at the American Chemical Society in Baltimore. His paper, entitled "Poison Hazards in the Manufacture and Use of Tetraethyl Lead," reminded the audience that "the actual hazard involved in the general program of treating gasoline with tetraethyl has been found to exist only in the manufacture and handling of the concentrated material."

The company was learning the hard way that it had to develop, and quite soon, an affirmative program of public relations. On December 11, 1925, the board of directors authorized the creation of a general publicity and advertising department and the immediate employment of James T. Grady, journalist at Columbia University, to prepare articles for the newspapers.

Grady, who for many years served Ethyl on a part-time consulting basis, is known as a pioneer in the "behind-the-scenes" type of public relations counseling. Whenever his name is mentioned by those who knew him, the word *integrity* always appears. Even the cynical writers of the 1930s, bent on exposing what they considered the puffery of "P.R. people," allowed that Jim Grady was an exception. Grady's special gift was to present technical matters in terms understood by the ordinary reader. His exact role during 1926 and thereafter is not clear, but his friendship with Midgley was so sustained that it was mentioned in Grady's obituary notice. Incidentally, Grady, when approached by Ethyl, did not fully realize his own bargaining power. The Ethyl directors authorized officers of the corporation to go as high as $7,500 for the year if necessary in employing Grady. He came for $4,500.

The surgeon general, Hugh S. Cumming, felt that definitive answers to the questions being raised as to tetraethyl lead must be found and called for a conference to meet on May 20, 1925, for consideration of the matter. Ethyl Gasoline Corporation promised full cooperation, and at the same time it continued its own special investigation under the direction of Dr. Kehoe.

About a month before the convening of the surgeon general's conference, there was an abrupt change in the management of Ethyl. On April 21, 1925, Kettering was replaced as president by Earle W. Webb, who had been serving as general attorney at General Motors. It will be recalled that Webb was one of the directors of the General Motors Chemical Company, which had preceded the formation of Ethyl.

Kettering's reported statement in later years that he had been fired to create a position for a man who would make more money is a jocular oversimplification of a complex problem. When Kettering's reminiscences are added to those of others, it seems clear that at one and the same time Sloan figured that Kettering's genius was in the area of science and invention, rather than administration, and that the times called for a leader with some aptitude in law and business. In the transition Midgley retired from the board to make way for Webb. Kettering stayed on the board.

Apparently neither Kettering nor Midgley was upset by the shift in command, and each continued to give the company the benefit of his ingenuity. Webb certainly proved that Sloan was right in his choice of a successor to Kettering.

One of Webb's first acts was to announce, on May 5, a general suspension of sales until the matter of public health hazards would be settled once and for all. Webb came out in full support of the conference and of whatever subsequent investigation would be promoted by the surgeon general. Some contemporaries looked at the suspension of sales as a bowing to public opinion; company spokesmen tended to report it as a self-denying rule. Events proved that it was a wise piece of strategy.

The surgeon general's conference of May 20, 1925, was attended by scientists and others of diversified views. There was a lively exchange of opinion both on and off the floor.

Boyd's account of one episode deserves quoting: "It was during an intermission at this conference [that] Dr. Alice Hamilton, assistant professor of industrial medicine at Harvard Medical School and a vociferous opponent of putting lead in gasoline, went up to Mr. Kettering and with fire in her eye told him that he was nothing but a murderer. 'Why, there are thousands of things better than lead to put into gasoline,' she said.

"'I will give you twice your salary,' Mr. Kettering offered, 'if you will name just one such material.'

"'Oh, I wouldn't work for you!' was her weak and unprofessional response."

In justice to Dr. Hamilton it should be said here that subsequently she made a judicious survey of safety procedures developed in the manufacture of the tetraethyl lead additive and had good things to say about precautionary measures adopted by the industry.

Reports of research into the nature of tetraethyl lead were made by representatives of the Bureau of Mines, the Department of Industrial Hygiene of Columbia University, and Ethyl Gasoline Corporation. The Ethyl report was given by Dr. Kehoe. The key resolution of the conference read:

It is the sense of this conference that the Surgeon General of the United States Public Health Service appoint a committee of seven recognized authorities in clinical medicine, physiology, and industrial hygiene to present to him, if possible by January 1 next, a statement as to the health hazard involved in the retail distribution and general use of tetraethyl lead gasoline motor fluid; and that this conference endorses as wise the decision of the Ethyl Gasoline Corporation to discontinue temporarily the sale of ethyl gasoline; that the investigation shall be paid for exclusively out of public funds; and that the results of this investigation shall be reported back to a public conference called for the purpose by the United States Public Health Service, at which labor shall be represented.

The investigating committee appointed by the surgeon general did consist of seven recognized authorities in clinical medicine, physiology, and industrial hygiene.* Dr. William H. Howell, professor of physiology, School of Medicine and Public Health, Johns Hopkins University, was chosen as chairman.

Webb and his people wanted to cooperate, but they also knew that they had to keep an arm's length from the investigation. The preliminary report from the Bureau of Mines was being dis-

---

*A. J. Chelsey, M.D., St. Paul, executive health officer, Minnesota State Board of Health; David L. Edsall, M.D., Boston, dean of the Medical School and of the School of Public Health, Harvard University, formerly professor of clinical medicine at the University of Pennsylvania and at Harvard; William H. Howell, Ph.D., M.D., Baltimore, professor of physiology, School of Hygiene and Public Health, Johns Hopkins University, formerly professor of physiology at the University of Michigan and at Johns Hopkins Medical School; Reid Hunt, M.D., Boston, professor of pharmacology, Medical School, Harvard University, formerly professor of pharmacology at the Hygienic Laboratory, United States Public Health Service; Walter S. Leathers, M.D., Nashville, professor of preventive medicine, Vanderbilt University, formerly executive health officer, Mississippi State Board of Health; Julius Stieglitz, Ph.D., Chicago, professor of chemistry, University of Chicago; Charles-Edward Amory Winslow, M.S., New Haven, professor of public health, Medical School, Yale University, president, American Public Health Association.

counted by critics who reminded one and all that Ethyl Gasoline Corporation was financing the study. It was difficult to avoid involvement with the surgeon general's committee, especially when members of the investigating groups complained of inadequate funds and wanted advice from the Ethyl officials even in such matters as where to find room and board when visiting in the Midwest.

The report of the surgeon general's committee, which was printed as *Public Health Bulletin No. 163*, published in 1926 and entitled "The Use of Tetraethyl Lead and Its Relation to Public Health," had as its basic conclusion that insofar as the committee could see there was no health hazard to the public. "In view of these conclusions the committee begs to report that in their opinion there are at present no good grounds for prohibiting the use of ethyl gasoline with a composition specified as a motor fuel, provided that its distribution and use are controlled by proper regulation." The public interpretation of the report is best illustrated by the headlines in the *Literary Digest* for February 6, 1926: "A Bill of Health for Looney Gas."

Encouraged by the report of the surgeon general's commission and by sustaining evidence in the other research programs, Ethyl decided to put its antiknock addditive back on the market. This it did beginning May 1, 1926, just one year after sales had been suspended. The company issued stringent new safety regulations applicable to the manufacture and distribution of the additive.

V

The Era of Earle Webb

1925–1947

Webb and the Ethyl People

EARLE W. WEBB was president of Ethyl from 1925 to 1947, and he remained on the board of directors for another ten years. More than any other single man he determined the shape and the policies of a corporation which, teetering on the edge of disaster when he became president, was among the most prosperous of its size in America when he retired from the presidency. If in trying to identify personalities in the complex story of early Ethyl one calls Kettering the founder and Midgley the prime inventor, then Webb can appropriately be labeled the good husbandman who nurtured the business into a landmark American institution.

Earle Wayne Webb was born in Morehead City, North Carolina, February 9, 1883, son of Alexander Haywood Webb and his wife, Harriet Evelyn Wade, a lady who habitually went under the familiar name of "Hattie." Earle was the middle child, sixth of eleven children. His father was the local telegraph operator and express agent. A favorite niece, Mrs. Grace Taylor, recalls, "He didn't make a lot of money. Way back then nobody had any money down in this section." Nevertheless, in September 1898 Earle was sent to Trinity College in Durham. These were happy days, and Earle showed his gregarious nature by bringing classmates to Morehead City in vacation periods where they teased the girls in good sophomoric fashion and filled family living rooms

Earle W. Webb

with light chatter and heavy tocacco smoke. At the end of his junior year he transferred to the University of Michigan, from which he graduated in 1902 with a bachelor of arts degree. He then settled in New York City, studied at New York University Law School, was admitted to the bar, and engaged in independent practice for seventeen years, 1904–21. In 1911 he married Eva Arnold, daughter of Mr. and Mrs. Everett D. Arnold of New York.

Webb was employed by General Motors as general attorney 1921–25, in this office attracting the favorable attention of Alfred P. Sloan, Jr., officer of that corporation. With the purchase of the Kettering laboratory and the development of tetraethyl lead, Webb was, as already indicated, put on the board of the General Motors Chemical Corporation. Then, in the middle of the furor over the toxic character of the new additive, he was made president of Ethyl Gasoline Corporation, replacing Kettering. Webb's legal training seemed to be needed at this stage in the history of the company. Furthermore, Webb's temperament was ideally suited to the occasion; he gave diplomatic and calm cooperation to investigating authorities.

What sort of man was Webb, who more than any other person created the original Ethyl mystique? Those who knew him present an avalanche of superlatives. He was great; he was a man with the highest ethical standards; he was a man whose interest was in people; he was the only "mister" in the whole outfit.

Webb's physique was a prophecy of his personality. An admiring lady says he looked just as a man *should* look! He was of full stature with a massive head and a warm smile. Both men and women comment on his eyes, and one person who observed him from close range for many years speaks of his "great piercing blue eyes with a touch of sadness in them." A discriminating friend observes that Earle Webb was *monumental* but not *pompous*. There is abundant testimony to the effect that his dignity never eclipsed a compassionate sense of social democracy.

Indeed, the first characteristic remembered by those who worked with him is his courteous attention to people both great and small. On the waterfront he got along well with the simplest fishermen. When he visited the factory he was never too busy to speak to the youngest engineer or to the sweeper. Webb's care for the staff and his sympathetic understanding of their problems were abundantly shared by his wife, Eva Arnold. Carolina neighbors recall the warmth with which Webb greeted children when he entered the home of acquaintances. His old-fashioned gallantry was such that friends and neighbors learned to be cautious in the admiration of some bric-a-brac, or else it would show up on their doorsteps. There was nothing artificial about Webb. His smile was genuine, and *forthright* was one of his favorite words. A congenial man, he dearly loved the role of raconteur.

Webb's life was marred by several family tragedies, the earliest being the loss of his son, Earle, Jr., a student at Duke University, who suddenly died of a severe lung infection on December 23, 1932. Webb's own character is illuminated with peculiar clarity in his communication with Dean W. H. Wannamaker of Duke University after the death of Earle Webb, Jr. A calendar of characteristics which Webb credited to his son reflects Webb's own ideals. Earle, Jr., according to his father, was the personification of courtesy, consideration, and sympathy for others. In memory of his son, Webb established the Earle Wayne Webb, Jr., Memorial Library and Civic Center in Morehead City, this being the birthplace which Webb loved and to which he came as often as he could.

During these periods of escape from business, Webb, his first wife, and small children stayed at the old Atlantic Hotel. In 1928 Webb built a fine residence west of the town among the water oaks along Bogue Sound, an estate later called Oak Bluffs. This eleven-bedroom house, used for long vacations, was planned primarily as a retirement home. Despite living on the waterfront, Webb was much more of a hunter than a fisherman. He enjoyed going after duck or geese, and to maintain his marksmanship often shot clay pigeons.

Having divided his undergraduate training between Trinity College, around which Duke University was organized, and Michigan, Webb professed allegiance to both, but ties personal and geographical directed his major affection and support toward the North Carolina institution. First elected a Duke trustee in June 1933, he served for many years, enjoying the friendship of administrators whom he first knew as his professors. Webb managed to create an Ethyl-Dow fellowship at Duke and an equivalent award at the University of North Carolina. He assumed a sponsorship role in Duke's awarding an honorary doctorate to

Alfred P. Sloan, Jr. Such was Webb's intimacy with Duke that he felt free to call to the attention of university officials what he felt were Marxist tendencies in a text on economic principles. Apparently the text was not being used at Duke, but he feared that it might be. The Trinity-Duke tradition of academic independence went through this event unscathed; certainly no attempt was made to tell the professors what they ought or ought not to do about the text in question.

When Webb first assumed the presidency of Ethyl, he inherited the original 1924 board except for the replacement of John Thomas by Irénée du Pont and of Midgley by Webb himself. There were relatively few changes in the board until the last years of Webb's presidency. Seven of these men—Brown, Clark, Howard, Kettering, Sloan, Teagle, and Webb—were still serving at the end of the year 1942. This continuity in the directorate permitted a consistency of policy during the Webb regime. And one of Webb's prime policies was to employ the best people available to serve Ethyl.

In carrying out Webb's ideas, officials at Ethyl recruited a dynamic group of young men to engage in research, technical services, and sales, these areas constituting the company's total program for its first dozen or so years.

The Ethyl men in the laboratories and out in the field were characteristically enthusiastic, and hours meant nothing to them. Their zeal was of a missionary quality; they were promoting a product that they felt the country needed. In the earliest days only single men seem to have been employed for field work, since their assignments often took them away from home for weeks and even months at a time.

If one may believe company tradition, these recruits not only worked hard but they played hard. Certainly in the whole organization there was a broad spectrum of humor, stretching from Webb's anecdotes of the Carolina coast and Midgley's satirical "Instipoop" to spontaneous verbal quips in office and laboratory. For example, the distinguished scientist Dr. Graham Edgar, creator of the octane scale and at the time vice president of Ethyl, told the following on himself: He was inflicting minor gallantries on a personable young lady in the laboratory when she more than held up her side of the repartee by exclaiming, "Oh, you are nothing but a wolf in veep's clothing!" All in all, the company in the Webb era never lost that lightness of spirit which characterized Boss Ket's "playhouse."

It has wisely been said that the most distinctive characteristic of Ethyl in those springtime days was the zealous combination of technical expertise and warm salesmanship. The hallmark of the Ethyl man was this very formula of training and aptitude in both science and human relations. The common experiences and similar background made for a conspicuous homogeneity leading to the avowedly exaggerated contention that "you could recognize an Ethyl man as soon as you saw him." Such was the fraternal feeling that the sales and technical conferences were likened to a college reunion.

In its search for college talent, Ethyl gave special consideration to the engineers and chemists who were in the top 10 percent of the graduating class. Ethyl's attractiveness was based in part on the fact that the company was owned jointly by two great and prestigious firms, in part on the fact that some room was given for imagination in those early days, and partly because its wages, once the company left the "shirt-losing" period, were bolstered by a most attractive bonus system.

Within the corporate family Webb contended that the fact of risk was reason enough for the generous salary and bonus formula. When Frank Howard, a director representing the Jersey interest, questioned the schedules of remuneration, Webb explained that his policy dated from the earliest years of the company and was based on a confessed recognition of the somewhat hazardous nature of the business. The late James E. Boudreau, who eventually became director of public relations, thanked Webb for the bonus received at the end of his first year of service. Whereupon Webb replied, according to Boudreau: "You know why we are paying you this bonus? We don't know how long the company will exist." The bonus system, which had been initiated in 1929, provided that the total amount of the bonuses was not to exceed 10 percent of the company's earnings. Half of the bonus was given in General Motors stock and half in Jersey stock.

Ethyl's attitude towards its employees was a blending of the contrasting philosophies of its two owners, described in these words drawn from the minutes of a special meeting of the executive committee, December 11, 1940: "There appeared to be two schools of thought with respect to the general subject of the bonus; namely, that of the Jersey company which stresses security rather than incentive, and that of General Motors which places considerably more emphasis on incentive and leaves security largely to the individual."

As for the risk factor, some of the older staff members say that Webb was brought into the company to close it down. The point is denied by others, including the careful historian of early Ethyl, T. A. Boyd. Whether or not Sloan ever had in the back of his mind liquidation as an assignment for Webb, it is certain that there were many painful and threatening factors facing Webb when he took office.

One of Webb's chief aides was John H. Schaefer, born in Buffalo, New York, in 1898, and educated at the University of Delaware, which awarded him the B.S. degree in 1924, and at the Massachusetts Institute of Technology, which granted him the M.S. degree in 1925. His academic concentration was in chemical engineering. He began working for Ethyl in 1926 as head of the control laboratory at Deepwater, New Jersey, and advanced in responsibilities as the company expanded. After only one year with Ethyl he was made manager of manufacturing and transportation. He was named vice president in charge of manufacturing and traffic in 1943 and a member of the board from 1946 until the time of his retirement in 1958. His responsibilities were extensive; at one time over 80 percent of the company's employees were in his department. At the end of World War II Schaefer was in charge of the multi-million-dollar expansion program. Such was his competence that repeatedly he was sent to Europe to advise in the construction of the new plants licensed there.

Webb himself gave Schaefer high marks, by report saying that without the three key men—Bartholomew, Kehoe, and Schaefer—Ethyl simply could not have done what it did.

Some of Webb's personality rubbed off on Schaefer, who was both knowledgable and affable, inviting direct communication from the workers. Webb and his first wife were intimately concerned with the well-being of Schaefer and his family. One guesses that Schaefer was never quite as happy in his work after Webb retired from the presidency.

Research and Service

To give aid and comfort, most of the giant personalities of the early days were still around. Kettering, Boyd, Kehoe, and Edgar lived out the Webb administration; Midgley died in 1944. At all levels there was a strong group of scientists guiding research activities. The first generation was strengthened by the coming of new and creative research people.

While not among the "founding fathers," Earl Bartholomew entered the research laboratories in 1926, soon after the formation of Ethyl. He was a native of Oklahoma. While holding an instructorship at the Harvard School of Mechanical Engineering, he decided he was going to leave his academic career and go into industry. Although from the standpoint of permanent security a connection with one of the established automobile companies seemed desirable, he saw the possibility of enormous economic benefits to the nation because of the increase in compression ratio permitted by a new antiknock compound. In his own words, "The prospect was so interesting that throwing assured security to the winds, I staked a future on the mutual adaptation of engines and fuels."

The heart of his thinking was the necessity for this mutual adaptation of automotive engines and fuel. In speaking of the need for redesigning the engines, he explained that the potentialities of gasoline having higher antiknock quality could be realized only when gas pressure at the end of the compression stroke

Earl Bartholomew

was increased to the limit permitted by the fuels. Engines of that period were not very satisfactory for capitalizing on the benefits from the better fuels. He was in complete agreement with the wording on the plaque once exhibited in the lobby of the Detroit research laboratories: "The problems of engines, fuels and lubricants are inseparable." (Weary laboratory technicians sometimes read this as "the problems of engines, fuels and lubricants are *insufferable.*")

His most solid contribution in the Webb era was the development of an effective and economical "scavenger." Bartholomew's greatest achievement in the search for the ideal scavenger was a triumphant mixture of bromine and chlorine so important that patent applications were placed under a cloak of secrecy during World War II. The so-called Application No. 543,993 was accepted April 9, 1946, as U.S. Patent No. 2,398,281. To quote

Ethyl Corporation, Research Laboratories, Detroit, Michigan, Report No. GA-46 dated November 2, 1951, "When the termination agreement was made between Ethyl and du Pont in 1947, this single Ethyl patent was offset against all du Pont's tetraethyl lead manufacturing patents, including those covering the manufacture of sodium." Eventually Bartholomew's special achievement was to leave his normal laboratory assignment and to develop an engine that could use tetraethyl lead and yet remain well within any commonsense clean air regulations, a subject to be reviewed in a later chapter.

An important addition to the research staff was Harold J. Gibson, born on a farm about 25 miles from Detroit. After graduating from the University of Michigan with a B.S. degree in mechanical engineering in 1929 and the M.S. degree in mechanical engineering in 1930, he joined Ethyl's Detroit research laboratories as a mechanical engineer. According to him he began working for Ethyl for two very good reasons. "In the first place it was the only job available in the year 1930, and in the second place the professor that I worked for said that this was a sound investment and the company just couldn't help but grow." Gibson here is referring to Professor Walter Lay, whom he further describes as the "best teacher I ever had." He adds that "this guy could make automobiles come alive." Gibson developed equipment and methods for a better evaluation of motor fuels and engaged in a variety of other research activities. His many contributions to technical literature have been principally in the closely related fields of fuels, lubricants, and engines. Various promotions were capped by his appointment as technical director of the laboratories in 1959 and manager of the laboratories in 1963.

A distinctive figure in the laboratories was Dr. George Calingaert, who eventually became director of chemical research. Born in Belgium, he migrated to MIT, which was his connection at the time he was employed by Ethyl. His special contribution was to establish basic principles for the proper mixture of tetraethyl lead with the scavengers, bromine and chlorine. Calingaert coined the name triptane (chemical designation, triethylbutane), first produced in America in 1926 by Ethyl and by others later, as high performance aviation fuel. Speaking French, Flemish, Dutch, German, and Italian, he was called on during World War II to serve as operations analyst for the U.S. Strategic Bombing Survey.

The research laboratories led a wandering existence. In January 1926 there was a movement from Moraine, Ohio, to Yonkers, New York, where the research group operated in a converted garage. Research activities logically gravitated to the vicinity of the motor car manufacturers. In November 1927 there was a beginning of a shift to Detroit, where the original location was 723 East Milwaukee Avenue. Ten years later there began a move to the present location on West Eight Mile Road. The Eight Mile Road laboratory evolved in stages; first came a chemical research pilot plant, and then the engineering research organization.

In 1935 several Detroit people migrated to San Bernardino, California. The trek from Detroit to the new location is still referred to as the "California Caravan." Advancements in engine design had outrun the testing methods available in Detroit; the newer cars could no longer be given strenuous and breakdown tests in the few miles available for such in the General Motors proving ground. San Bernadino was chosen because in a drive of an hour or so from that location one might cover an area where almost all kinds of road conditions and climate in the country could be duplicated.

While the investigations seeking the best methods of manufacturing tetraethyl lead had now been turned over to DuPont, research activities in a variety of areas continued at Ethyl. Many of the investigations were in close alliance with the sales, services, and safety divisions. There were continuous experiments to determine the proper mix in gasoline and, in association with metallurgists, cooperation with the automobile manufacturers to discover the proper composition of valves and pistons in those engines using the new additive. Beyond these immediately functional and control endeavors was a pattern of defensive research.

By virtue of its patents in the manufacture of tetraethyl lead and in the process of injecting it into the gasoline, Ethyl Corporation had a legal monopoly, but for a limited period only. Of major concern throughout the years was the danger that some competitor would find an antiknock superior to tetraethyl lead. Thus, a large part of Ethyl's research effort was of a defensive nature. If an antiknock better than tetraethyl lead was to be discovered, Ethyl wanted to be the discoverer.

During the first years of its existence Ethyl gave special attention to iron carbonyl as a possible alternative to tetraethyl lead. In their investigations the researchers at Ethyl found it necessary to negotiate with Badische, Anilin, and Soda-Fabrik (BASF), the German chemical firm that had pioneered in iron carbonyl research. German research had been stimulated particularly by Dr. Carl Bosch's visit to the American laboratories in 1923. Bosch charmed his hosts by impromptu and erudite lectures on the Grand Canyon and other natural phenomena, and earned a special place in the heart of Walter C. Teagle, president of Standard Oil of New Jersey, by successfully prescribing for Teagle's favorite and ailing pointer.

Jasper E. Crane, European manager for DuPont, in 1924 heard about the iron carbonyl discovery from a director of the Badische company and Crane passed the word to Kettering. Kettering and Crane together went to Ludwigshafen, Germany, on a two-day visit November 28–29, 1924, talking to Dr. Bosch and others and witnessing a demonstration of the antiknock qualities of the solution under examination. Kettering correctly guessed the substance but was not so informed by the Germans. The iron carbonyl was relatively cheap, being created in quantity as a by-product of the manufacture of ammonia and methyl alcohol.

After obtaining samples, American scientists complained that the iron oxide (jeweler's rouge, as it is sometimes called) left in the cylinders resulted in extreme wear; in addition, this oxide was an electric conductor that tended to foul the spark plugs.

Treasured at Ethyl is a narrative of Teutonic provincialism. In April 1925 Dr. Mueller-Conradi of the Badische company and a colleague traveled to America to examine the Ethyl laboratory. Apparently Dr. Mueller-Conradi's stay in the United States was less than completely happy, not only because of the limited success of iron carbonyl when tested but because of his limited understanding of higher education and higher research in America.

As the story is told, when Dr. Mueller-Conradi met Dr. Graham Edgar, director of the Ethyl research laboratory, he asked Dr. Edgar the dates of his study in Germany. When Edgar explained that he had never been in Germany, Mueller-Conradi expressed astonishment. On hearing that the doctor's degree had been granted by Yale University, he said, "Why I did not know that doctors' degrees were given anywhere except in Germany."

There was an intermediate and obviously temporary gentleman's agreement between Badische and DuPont dated February 22, 1925, providing for the division of the world market. "As regards to the division of the world's markets, it seems to be advisable to adopt the plan that certain districts shall be supplied with fuel containing American iron carbonyl, and others with fuel containing German iron carbonyl." A direct agreement in 1926 between Ethyl and Badische is referred to in company documents as similar to the 1925 understanding between DuPont and Badische, though there is no document available to the present researcher in which the world division between Ethyl and Badische is written out. The understanding was never of commercial importance.

The Ethyl-Badische arrangement blended with the larger concern of Jersey as personified by Frank Howard for research contracts with the Germans in order for American interests to benefit from the intensive German research efforts in such areas as hydrogenation to create gasoline from coal and the creation of synthetic rubber. The Jersey contract was signed in 1927, and subsequent agreements became a matter of great controversy later. In the suit against Standard Oil instituted by the federal government in 1941, the Ethyl agreement sometimes appeared in the argument.

Mostly because of spark plug fouling, iron carbonyl eventually disappeared from the European market. In the United States, Midgley was reluctant to give up the investigation of iron carbonyl. He wanted to push the research because iron was cheaper and less toxic than lead and could more easily be put into a chemical compound. In 1927 a contract was made with the Moto Meter Company for research to correct spark plug difficulties when iron carbonyl was used. Results were unfavorable. Next Midgley went to Cornell University, found and employed a young chemistry student, Richard Scales, giving him the primary responsibility of finding out whether iron carbonyl could be made a successful antiknock compound. Scales eventually became general manager of the Detroit research laboratories.

The hiring of Scales by Midgley is a classical example of urgency and persuasion. "You don't have to make up your mind until tonight," said Midgley and asked Scales to dine with him at the Ithaca Inn. The dinner was good; Scales accepted. He finished his work at Cornell and then began working on iron carbonyl. The research conducted by Scales was mostly a painstaking examination of the residue in cylinders after a multitude of different scavengers had been added, all in the hope that the character of iron oxide had been modified to the point that spark plugs would no longer be damaged. Then came the dreadful day when Scales felt that he had to recommend to Midgley abandonment of the iron carbonyl project.

The decision of Scales to "pull up his socks," as he phrased it, and recommend to Midgley the dropping of the iron carbonyl investigation was not the ending of Ethyl's defensive research. In a sense such research was the heart of the laboratory program. Howard H. Hesselberg, who later became a vice president of Ethyl (Virginia), says that the assignment was broadly based research to explore the fundamentals of combustion, this to determine the mechanism of knock, and in the process to learn how lead alkyls controlled that knock, all to the purpose of applying "that knowledge to the search for another antiknock compound." He adds that "at the same time we were trying to figure what aspects of fuel made tetraethyl lead better or worse." Hesselberg also notes that a major project dealt with the antagonism of sulphur to lead.

An important product of the Ethyl laboratories in this period was the octane number scale, now used worldwide to measure the antiknock value in gasoline. The creator of the octane scale was Graham Edgar, director of research for Ethyl. Kentucky-born, Edgar received his doctorate in chemistry from Yale University and held important academic posts including a professorship at the University of Virginia before coming to Dayton the first part of 1924 to work with the General Motors Chemical Company, soon to become Ethyl Gasoline Corporation.

When Edgar joined the tetraethyl lead firm, the basic "Ethyl standard" against which fuel could be tested was gasoline from a refinery in Lima, Ohio, to which three cubic centimeters of tetraethyl lead per gallon were added. A bundle of folklore collected around the "Ethyl standard," which, said gossips, was a can of fluid kept in a New York vault, and one which was seasoned with a bit more tetraethyl lead whenever the market was slow and extra sales to the refiners were needed.

To tell the truth, the gossips were right in their contention that the "Ethyl standard" varied from time to time. To the dismay of Ethyl officials, new quantities of gasoline from that Lima refinery proved different from the original test batch. It was imperative that a stable and measurable reference fuel be developed, and this objective broadened into a plan to create a scale of antiknock value.

The result of intensive and imaginative research was to establish a zero-to-100 scale. The lower base zero was pure normal heptane, the distillation of the sap of the Jeffrey pine that grows in the High Sierras. The number 100 was assigned to a newly developed iso-octane prepared by treating tertiary butyl alcohol with sulfuric acid and then hydrogenating it. The story of the octane scale was announced in a paper read before the American Chemical Society in Philadelphia in September 1926.

A landmark acceptance of the octane scale came in 1930 when the measuring procedure was approved by the joint committee

of the Society of Automotive Engineers and American Petroleum Institute, which functioned with the cooperation of the
Bureau of Standards. It ought to be observed here that Edgar's
study of the branched chain paraffins in his creation of the octane scale also greatly helped in the making of the first 100-octane
aviation fuel.

Vast quantities of bromine were required in the manufacturing
process. The search for an adequate supply of bromine became
an enduring assignment of Ethyl officials. Mention has already
been made of the voyage of the S.S. *Ethyl*, which proved beyond
a doubt that bromine could be extracted from seawater. Eventually there was worked out a joint agreement with Dow Chemical
and the erection of facilities at Kure Beach in North Carolina,
operations beginning in 1934.

The process used at Kure Beach was a Dow invention, an
improvement over the early procedure developed by Ethyl and
DuPont. A new era in harvesting from the sea began on January
10, 1934, when the flood gates were opened at the newly constructed plant operated by Ethyl-Dow. As pointed out two years
later by C. C. Furnas, associate professor of chemical engineering at Yale University, in his *The Next Hundred Years: The Un-
finished Business of Science*: "From the beginning of terrestrial
time down to that day no one had ever put into operation for
commercial production a plant for the bona fide chemical extraction of any one of the elements from the boundless reservoir."
Though admitting the extraction of low-grade salt by solar evap-
oration and seaweed harvesting and burning, Furnas dismisses
these enterprises as no more chemical than is fishing.

Naturally the Ethyl-Dow operation excited the midas-minded
science-fiction breed ready to suspect bars of gold in foot lockers
at Kure Beach. All of this provided much merriment in Ethyl
headquarters, where a great ceremony announced the recovery
of a speck of the precious metal.

The "Remo" adventure, a dismal failure, deserves classification as a minor research and development enterprise. About 1930,
under persuasive pressure from Kettering, a sort of "quick fix" for

the removal of carbon from the cylinder of the internal combustion engine was created and named "Remo." This came about because Kettering repeatedly was asking Midgley, "How are you getting along with getting rid of the deposits?" The Remo project was a natural outgrowth of the concern about cylinder deposits in the iron carbonyl experiments. Scales was put on the Remo assignment immediately after he had given up the iron carbonyl research.

Scales poked around service stations and dealer showrooms, buying discarded pistons at the rate of about 10 for $3.00, much to the amusement of the attendants, who said, "The kid's nuts," and were happy to dispose of scrap in that way. Scales then had the laboratory shop cut each piston in six pie-shaped segments which he then tested for carbon removal. Eventually he discovered an excellent carbon remover, a combination of xylene and furfural alcohol.

A subsidiary company was established, Scales heading the manufacturing part and Julian Frey sales. An injection device for getting the material into the automobile intake was created.

Under perfect conditions the carbon remover worked beautifully. But when instructions were not followed to the letter, the concoction simply gummed up the engine as though asphalt had been poured into the cylinders, and the car owner was left with a repair bill of several hundred dollars. The developers of Remo sadly came to the conclusion that the cure was worse than the disease. The Remo business was a fiasco, a small-scale disaster unless learning that a large percentage of the public will *not* follow directions can be classified as an important discovery. Midgley was quite philosophical. To quote Scales, "And Midge just kind of grinned about it and said, 'Well your career here in manufacturing didn't get very far, did it?'"

Although Kettering and Midgley, the sponsors of Remo, were almost above criticism, several of the board members about this time decided there was a line beyond which researchers could not go if they were counting on outright production. As early as 1940, the research group received a signal to the effect that the company was going to stay within the gasoline additive field, that there was to be very little diversification. The occasion was a reminder from Dr. George Calingaert to the coordination committee of heavy chemical elements and a request for the committee's reaction to a plan for the manufacture and distribution of heavy carbons, referring no doubt to carbon 14, useful as a tracer in medical diagnosis and research. Webb's reaction was to pronounce a policy which, in general, was to circumscribe the research and development groups down to the time Ethyl was sold to Albemarle. To quote from the minutes of the coordination committee, "Mr. Webb stated that such a venture could only be justified if the products had a relation to problems in our business." And everyone knew what "our business" was. Webb was to repeat his words of caution within the next several years.

The question of directed research versus free-ranging research surfaced when officials were considering relations with institutions of higher learning. After some discussion the general verdict of the company was in favor of full freedom of research in those colleges and universities receiving assistance from the corporation. The point was made clear in 1939 when the coordination committee made a grant for the assistance of graduate students in the Yale Sheffield Scientific School.

The spirit of free inquiry suggested by the scholarship and fellowship programs was reflected in liberal tendencies in the Ethyl laboratories, where researchers were given a fraction of their time to follow their own notions. The leaders of the research group developed a rule of thumb which permitted the young scientists to spend about 15 percent of their time following up their own ideas. It was felt that this concession was a good investment in building up the spirit of the young researcher.

Much of the research was of an interdisciplinary nature, bringing together engineering and chemistry. To paraphrase the famous plaque, the problems of engines, fuels, and lubricants were indeed inseparable. Not only was there a coordination of several different fields in the natural sciences, but many of these laboratory people developed an aptitude in the social sciences: public relations and human relations in management and economics. Obviously, the research activities were closely allied with service to the refiners and to the automobile manufacturers.

The hallmark of old Ethyl was intensive service; this fact was an emphatic plus when patents expired and competition appeared.

As understood by members of his staff, Webb's philosophy was "give 'em a fair price and then kill 'em with service." There was a group called "technical services," the members of which explained how best to overcome any problems that might appear in connection with the Ethyl additive, either in the petroleum or the automotive industry.

In the earliest days of Ethyl there was a complaint from manufacturers, mechanics, and the general public that the new additive hastened the deterioration of engine metal, especially attacking spark plugs and valves. As already mentioned, openly critical were various elements of the General Motors oganization, a fact noted again and again by the Ethyl executive committee in 1926. Underlying these complaints was a philosophy in the Buick and Pontiac divisions of General Motors favoring low-compression low-speed engines based on the belief that such meant durability.

In truth, in the mid-1920s the deterioration of spark plugs and exhaust valves was a real problem. Most of the engines were not designed to operate on leaded fuel. The Ethyl people saw their technical job as twofold: first, to improve the bromine compounds the better to clean out the combustion chamber; and second, to persuade the automobile manufacturers to put better metal in their engines. As Boyd says, "The steel used for exhaust valves in the early days of Ethyl gasoline was not resistant enough to oxidation to withstand even the effects of burning the regular gasoline for very long. Therefore, valves, spark plugs and electrodes had to be developed that would not be attacked."

Thus it was absolutely necessary to work closely with the automobile manufacturers. One of the problems was to overcome the old NIH prejudice ("not invented here"). In a sense it is a miracle that manufacturers could be persuaded in a relatively brief period of time to convert to the new order. Although there was much trouble in 1927 and in 1928, by 1929 the situation was markedly improved. Two factors help explain this apparent miracle of conversion. In the first place there was the personality of Kettering and his key position in the automobile industry. His influence spread far beyond the bounds of General Motors. Second, there developed a real desire by most of the manufacturers to move ahead toward high compression. They realized that they had to meet the new situation, so obvious were the advantages of high compression.

The increasing compatibility of tetraethyl lead with the automobile engine came not only because of improved metals used by the manufacturers but because of improved formulas developed by Ethyl that increased the use of bromine instead of chlorine. Especially significant was the work of Earl Bartholomew in this area.

Much of the earliest cooperative work was done with Chrysler Corporation, which was the first of the major manufacturers to put out high-compression engines, notably the famous "Red Head" of 1927, painted red to indicate that red-colored gasoline, Ethyl, was to be used. General Motors yielded in stages; in February 1927 the Cadillac service manual approved the Ethyl additive. The missionary work with manufacturers had to be repeated in those foreign countries toward which the sales people directed their efforts.

Ethyl officials, wounded by memories of what they considered yellow journalism in 1924, continued to be greatly concerned about the attitude of the public toward their major product. Records of the corporation show that the public relations efforts of 1924 and 1925 were redefined and enlarged. In 1926, Batten, Barton, Durstine and Osborn were employed as an agency, a relationship that endured for many years. As is well known, Bruce Barton earned fame as a popular writer, his books including the bestsellers, *The Man Nobody Knows* (1925) and *The Book Nobody Knows* (1926). The appropriations for advertising moved steadily upwards save for a downswing during the latter part of the depression and during World War II. The advertising budget for 1926 was $350,000; for 1929, $1,000,000. It rose to $1,175,000 in 1932 and then averaged about $1,200,000 per year for the period 1944–48.

Among the special campaigns before the beginning of World War II was that entitled "What's in a Name?" There were advertisements in periodicals and a booklet, all explaining the original meaning of 700 names, both masculine and feminine. Decorated with attractive cartoons was such information as that David means "beloved," William means "defender," etc. And of course appended was the commercial proclaiming that "Ethyl is a trademark name" for an additive put into gasoline to prevent knocking.

There are company employees who first became acquainted with Ethyl in their search for a name to be given a newborn child. James H. Kirby, later vice president, accounting, says: "Right after my first daughter was born we were considering a name. Some friends of ours in Detroit suggested a listing in a little pamphlet called 'What's in a Name' by the Ethyl Corporation. That was the first time I ever heard of the Ethyl Corporation."

As early as the mid-1930s Ethyl had earned a secure place in the American scene. Witness the free advertising in the burlesque journal entitled "Bawl Street Journal" put out by the Bond Club of New York. Here "Ethel" was a featured roadside sign, backdrop for a young man thoroughly slapped by a lady putting on roller skates.

A memorable feature of Webb's rule was to sell the antiknock additive at exactly the same price no matter whether the customer was large or small. This policy of uniform pricing irritated several of the great refiners, but endeared the Ethyl people to the small producers, who simply could not have manufactured high octane gasoline without this concession. This uniformity of sales price included delivery, a formula that certainly was thought of at the time as being antimonopolistic. It is somewhat ironic that this uniform pricing has recently been cited by the government as a possible antitrust violation.

Quit, Fueling Around — Fill Up With Ethel And Make A Moll A Minute

20 MILES TO THE GAL.   **20 GALS TO THE MILE**

Webb became such a favorite with so many of the refiners that in an unprecedented gesture, although he was not a refiner, he was made a member of the board of directors of the American Petroleum Institute, controlled by the "little boys," some of whom eventually became "big boys."

On the very last morning at annual meetings of the API, Ethyl often gave a champagne breakfast, something the members talked about for a long time. One of the Ethyl veterans noted, with a twinkle in his eye, that the general membership might not have realized it, but the champagne breakfast was more economical than a whiskey cocktail hour in the evening!

Although the Ethyl people went to the general public, to service station operators, and to automobile dealers explaining the virtues of Ethyl gasoline, the major sales objective was to persuade the oil companies to use the additive. This decision by the refiners was a matter of such importance that ordinarily the question was referred to the company boards. After all, in the typical company the purchase of the tetraethyl lead compound was a major expenditure, second only to crude oil. In the colorful narrative of sales manager Malcolm P. Murdock, "Old San Wagner, who was my immediate predecessor, summed it up, I think, so very well. He said: 'This business is just like shooting elephants. You hide in the bushes until the big ones come by. And you only got one shot. You damn well better be right.' So that 364 days of the year you conducted yourself so that the decision made on that last day would be in your favor."

Even in those years of what might be described as a legal monopoly, Webb reduced prices, this often to the consternation of young staff members. He was thinking about a later day. Sloan was in full agreement with Webb's pricing policy. His analysis of the matter is important enough for quotation. In a letter of June 30, 1939, he wrote to Webb agreeing with his point of view: "I do not think we should hesitate to sacrifice profits providing we get, in return, greater stability, looking toward the future. I believe that we should discourage competitive methods of improving the quality of gasoline from the antiknock standpoint, by price reductions rather than to encourage them by price maintenance."

Though Sloan was willing to take a lower profit in exchange for longtime security, the price reductions at this stage in the history of the corporation do not appear to have hurt the income of Ethyl. The "shirt-losing" period prophesied by Kettering for innovative developments came to an end in the year 1928. The losses during the calendar years 1924, 1925, 1926, and 1927 were, respectively, $72,524, $1,348,253, $1,211,927, and $99,425. After these four years of deficits, the earnings were good. The company started paying dividends in 1929 and maintained an excellent return on investment down to the end of its corporate existence, though, as will be indicated later, the profits declined in the several years immediately before the sale to Albemarle.

Expanding Markets, Domestic and Foreign

An important element in the expanding domestic sales of tetraethyl lead was the decision in 1933 to permit the mixing of tetraethyl lead with regular gasoline, the resultant product being called the Q Brand. Up until this time the policy of Ethyl in the domestic market had been to restrict the sale of tetraethyl lead to use in premium grades clearly indicated as such at the pump. However, the threat of a general decline in sales—plus the marketing of a refinery-created higher octane regular gasoline by Shell—induced Ethyl's management to permit this injection of a limited quantity of its additive into regular grades. Ethyl's more liberal policy had been anticipated in the Canadian market two years earlier.

Now, the introduction of tetraethyl lead into regular gasoline initiated a series of events, some of which were most embarrassing to Ethyl management. The rapid increase in demand for tetraethyl resulted in acute shortage of ethylene dibromide, a situation the company tried to meet by simply reducing the proportion of ethylene dibromide added to the mixture and substituting chlorine for that bromide. It was discovered that the resultant mixture caused a degradation of quality.

Thus, Bartholomew and his fellow workers were challenged to develop a composition of fluid which would be as good as that used immediately before June 1, 1933, and no more expensive than that currently sold. The remedial program was successful and a new formula was worked out. This eventually was covered by U.S. Patent No. 2,398,241, already mentioned as one of Bartholomew's several claims to fame.

An important element in the expanding consumption of high-octane gasoline in the 1930s was the modernization of the farm tractor, its change from a low-compression, kerosene-burning unit to a high-compression gasoline-powered piece of machinery. A key individual in the promotion of the modern tractor, one that made efficient use of the tetraethyl lead additive, was Carl George Krieger, Jr., born in Portsmouth, Virginia, in 1905. From Virginia Polytechnic Institute in Blacksburg, he received a degree in agricultural engineering. His formal study in the two fields of agriculture and engineering, and his subsequent on-the-job training in the oil industry, made him what one trade journal described as "probably the only one of the kind in the entire country."

He joined Ethyl in 1929 as an agricultural engineer. Five years later in Kane County, Illinois, Krieger initiated something of a farm revolution by converting Clarence L. Dauberman's tractor into a high-compression gasoline-burning unit. Before the year 1934 was out, Krieger was riding on a wave of optimism. He wrote home on October 24 to "Dear Pap" of great changes coming to the agricultural industry. "The trend is in the right direction—that is—toward high compression engines and Ethyl treated gasoline."

A gregarious soul, fond of both man and beast (he was quite a dog lover), he poured forth both whimsy and honest platitudes. His philosophy is best summarized in the first sentence of an essay entitled "The Farm Engine Fuel Situation" that appeared in the June 1932 issue of *Agricultural Engineering*. He begins with this basic thought: "Power is, and always has been, the cornerstone of the great agricultural structure." After retiring, Krieger wrote that his forty-four years with Ethyl revolved around the basic and multifaceted theme of "The Conservation of Natural Resources," including energy.

More dramatic if not more important than the increase of power on the farm was the improvement of engine performance in the air by the Ethyl scientists. The Ethyl Gasoline Corporation and its predecessor research organization created efficient airplane fuels, highly valued by both military and civilian users. It will be recalled that during World War I an experimental fuel, Hecter, was developed by the Kettering-Midgley-Boyd group for the United States government.

The reconciliation of the air-cooled airplane engine and high octane fuel was in considerable part the work of one man, Sam D. Heron, who for eleven years served the Ethyl Corporation. Sam D. (D is for Daiziel) Heron was born in Newcastle upon Tyne, England, on May 18, 1891, the son of an itinerant actor. Although Heron was a student at Alleyn's School in Dulwich, London, and attended several classes at London University, he was essentially a self-educated man. In personality Heron was forthright to the point of bluntness. He did not suffer fools gladly. Yet among his intimates he was known as a kind and considerate man.

After creative work at Wright Air Field, Heron in the year 1934 came to Ethyl as director of aeronautical research. In the course of his professional career he invented the sodium-cooled valve (thus making the exhaust live with the high concentration of lead that was necessary in aviation fuel). Heron turned his hand to writing and published two monographs, one entitled "Development of Aviation Fuels," a section of a book *Development of Aircraft Engines and Fuels*, published by the Harvard Graduate School of Business Administration (1950), the other a *History of the Aircraft Piston Engine: A Brief Outline* published by Ethyl Corporation (1961). Heron retired in 1945 but continued to serve for a season as consultant. He died July 10, 1963. In those days before jet airplane fuel, which requires no tetraethyl lead, Heron was of importance in bringing gasoline of proper quality to the airplane, a move that obviously served to expand the market for Ethyl.

From the earliest days of his presidency, Webb attempted to establish overseas sales. In 1927 he directed his attention to the British market. A precipitating event was an inquiry from the Anglo-American Oil Company seeking an exclusive contract for the sale of Ethyl gasoline in Great Britain. There had been other inquiries from that quarter. Webb feared that a rival antiknock might preempt the British market and was anxious to obtain a foothold before competition appeared. Furthermore, he thought this an excellent time to obtain approval by the British health authorities of the sale of Ethyl gasoline. Then he made the happy discovery that Drs. Graham Edgar and Robert Kehoe were ripe for a sea voyage and a vacation. As he explained to his executive committee on March 28, 1927, for the foregoing reasons he had made reservations on the S.S. *Adriatic* sailing May 14 for Dr. Kehoe, Dr. Edgar, and himself.

This business-pleasure journey led to a one-year exclusive

contract with the Anglo-American Oil Company and to favorable talks with the health authorities in Great Britain. After their own investigation they issued a report on tetraethyl lead paralleling the go-ahead verdict of the American Surgeon General's Committee. The Anglo-American Oil Company began marketing a premium-grade leaded petrol under the label of Pratts Ethyl. Furthermore, about this time there was an advantageous agreement with the British Air Ministry for the use of tetraethyl lead.

To promote foreign sales, Ethyl Corporation on October 20, 1930, organized a wholly owned subsidiary, Ethyl Export Corporation. The officers in the London branch, where active administration was carried on, were two extremely able Englishmen who had become acquainted with tetraethyl lead while they were employed by Anglo-American. There was T. R. A. ("Ray") Bevan, general manager, a Welshman by birth, educated at Cambridge, where he was awarded the B.A. degree in engineering. Bevan had a cool head and was the guiding hand in Ethyl Export and its successor organizations, Associated Ethyl and Associated Octel. He developed a great friendship with Webb, a fact that was quite apparent in later years when Bevan contrasted what he considered the ill-treatment to which Associated was then subjected with the intelligent cooperation received during the Webb regime.

The technical manager of Ethyl Export, F. R. ("Rod") Banks, tells his story in a readable autobiography entitled *I Kept No Diary* (1978). Abandoning formal education at the age of fourteen, he became internationally famous as an expert on fuels and engines and eventually was given national honors and awarded the rank of air commodore. As he himself says, "I was also one of the first in the UK to try tetraethyl lead."

He was laboring with a pounding Stromboli single-cylinder unit when he first experimented with the new antiknock additive. After injecting tetraethyl lead into the gasoline, he heard no more knocking and became about as excited as the early American experimenters. Banks also discovered some increase in engine power. Subsequently he joined Anglo-American and was consistently an enthusiastic proponent of the new additive.

Ray Bevan, then manager of the Export Division of Ethyl, offered Banks a job. Banks accepted and in November 1930 joined Ray Bevan and Ethyl Gasoline Corporation. By all evidence it was a happy combination. Such was Banks's enthusiasm and his ability to explore the possibilities of the new fuel that in 1934 he addressed the Royal Aeronautical Society explaining Ethyl Gasoline and for this paper was awarded the Taylor Gold Medal.

Banks, who had the knack of conditioning himself to strange places and circumstances, encouraged the use of Ethyl fluid in both England and on the Continent. Equipped with a one-liter can of Ethyl fluid and wearing rubber surgical gloves, he assisted test pilots in demonstration flights before possible customers. His performances, in fact, were elaborate versions of the old demonstration by Midgley and others in which a few drops of tetraethyl lead fluid in a test engine would cause sensational improvement.

All in all, however, there was not a great deal of tetraethyl lead used in Europe before the outbreak of World War II. Banks concentrated his efforts on explaining the advantages of tetraethyl lead in aviation fuel and encouraging the manufacturers of airplane engines to develop engines capable of taking advantage of the additive. The result was that for Europe in general there was an appreciable increase in the use of leaded gasoline in airplanes, but the development was much slower in the automobile market.

A special difficulty in the distribution of Ethyl gasoline in Europe was the fact that rival fluids were often under government monopoly, and it was sometimes difficult to compete. Excess alcohol from the vineyards and expendable benzol from the steel plants, both government monopolies in the major European countries, were added to gasoline to raise the octane numbers.

The Ethyl organization, either directly through the Ethyl American office or through the London managers of Ethyl Export, licensed plants abroad for the manufacture of antiknock in the period 1936 to 1940. Under shared ownership arrangements the construction of factories for the making of antiknock fluid took place in Germany, France, and England. The German plant was built in 1936, the French in 1938, and the British in 1940, though authorized in 1936. Also, plants for the extraction of bromine from seawater were completed in France and in the United Kingdom to permit the manufacture of ethylene dibromide.

The relations between Ethyl Corporation and Ethyl Export Corporation, on the one hand, and the Germans, on the other, during the 1930s were in part conditioned by the always complex and sometimes debatable agreements between Standard Oil of New Jersey and the German chemical trust I. G. Farben. An inevitable principal in negotiations was Frank A. Howard, who was head of Standard Oil Development Corporation and also an officer of both Standard of New Jersey and Ethyl Corporation.

It is well known now, but it was less well known then, that in 1929 there was an understanding between Farben and Jersey for exchange of patent information. Frank Howard had long been interested in German experiments in the hydrogenation of coal and then especially in the development of synthetic rubber. He, Walter Clark Teagle, president of Jersey, and other Jersey officials always maintained that American industry and the American nation stood to gain from knowledge of advanced German technology. In the suit against Jersey during World War II, however, the Department of Justice, particularly in the person of Thurman Arnold, took a contrary point of view.

With the assistance of Banks of Ethyl Export Corporation, in 1931 Lufthansa began a series of tests using the Ethyl additive. In their flights to China in 1933 the German pilots carried liter cans of tetraethyl lead that had been imported through Ethyl Export of London. The German flight crews blended the tetraethyl lead at the Gobi Desert stop. The German nation imported only 12 tons of tetraethyl lead fuel in 1934, 104 tons in 1935. In 1936 there was a drop-off to 4.65 tons because in that year the German tetraethyl plant began operating.

Negotiations for this plant had begun in the winter of 1934–

35. At the request of the German Ministry of Aviation, I. G. Farben communicated with Ethyl Gasoline Corporation about the possibility of constructing such a plant. Frank Howard, traveling in Europe in the last months of 1934, became interested, even agitated, over the German situation. Fearing that efforts would be made by European competitors to counter Ethyl, in a series of cables he urged the authorization of a joint enterprise, part German and part American. Howard's point of view is best summarized in a message cabled under date of December 7, 1934, from which the following sentences are drawn: "The problem is to out-maneuver the benzol people who may if they have time to do so try to stir public opposition by campaign poison propaganda Stop Also probably Royal Dutch Shell will oppose if possible Stop."

DuPont officials now issued to Ethyl a warning, whether from economic or patriotic considerations one can only guess. The proposed plant, said DuPont officials, would be commercially valuable, but it also would furnish the German war machine with technical knowledge it had not as yet obtained. Ethyl's London office tended to oppose the creation of the German plant. Banks writes: "When the Germans indicated that they wished to build a lead manufacturing plant in their own country, this was at first resisted by us as uneconomic. Eventually, we had to agree to a joint manufacturing company formed between ourselves and I. G. Farben." Webb felt that he should go along with the Howard point of view.

The company, called Ethyl G.m.b.H., was owned 50 percent by I. G. Farben and 25 percent each by subsidiaries of General Motors and Jersey. The stock owned by the subsidiaries of General Motors and Jersey was soon transferred to Ethyl Export Corporation. After agreement had been reached between Ethyl and I. G. Farben, the German chemists went to DuPont and Ethyl for training. The plant was built at Gatel, about fifty miles west of Berlin. By April 1936 the Gatel plant was supplying tetraethyl lead for use in aviation gasoline. The second plant in Germany was built in 1939 at Frose, this theoretically without Ethyl's knowledge or permission. The London office had heard rumors of an unauthorized plant and through one of those marvelous mailing mix-ups that plague all businesses obtained first-hand information. Through mistake the Germans put, in a packet of mail addressed to Ethyl Export, an envelope directed to the plant at Frose. Banks promptly steamed open the letter within the packet, read all about this unauthorized plant, resealed the letter and returned it to the Germans, who had been telephoning frantically for the return of this particular piece of mail. Banks notified the proper British officials, who in this way knew exactly where the second plant was located.

Over the years there has been much complaint about Ethyl's authorization of the Gatel plant in Nazi Germany. Critics quote the words of the German August Knieviem: "Without tetraethyl lead the present method of warfare would have been impossible. The fact that since the beginning of the war we could produce tetraethyl lead is entirely due to the circumstances that shortly before the war Americans presented us with the production plans, complete with their know-how." The statement was made during the war, and it was a defensive declaration by a man fearing an unfavorable review of the fuel situation by the Nazi government.

In all fairness it should be noted that the deal between the Americans and the Germans was not entirely one-sided. While in the complex negotiations between the Jersey and I. G. Farben interests Howard did not get the full and prompt disclosure of German techniques in the production of synthetic rubber, apparently the United States did get something from German know-how. Even the critical Joseph Borkin in his book *The Crime and Punishment of I. G. Farben* quotes Robert T. Haslam of Standard Oil to the effect that American technical warfare would have been less effective if I. G. Farben had not supplied Standard with valuable information before the war.

Defenders of Jersey and of Ethyl might say that, first of all, it is hardly fair to assume that Howard, Teagle, Webb, and others could foresee the coming of World War II. Secondly, and this is more important, critics either fail to mention or fail to emphasize the fact that Ethyl licensed not only tetraethyl lead plants in Germany but in France and Great Britain as well.

Permission for the construction of a tetraethyl lead plant in France apparently evolved from a clause in a supply contract dated August 24, 1935, "between the Minister of War acting in the name and on behalf of the French government represented by Mr. Blanchard, military engineer and chief director of explosives of the one part" and Ethyl Export Corporation on the other. Section IV was entitled "Possible Construction of Plant."

The definitive contract was concluded April 3, 1937, almost two years later, when Ethyl agreed that a plant would be constructed. According to the document, the date of the completion was to be no later than July 1938. The firm of Kuhlmann was to build a plant for Ethyl's account and under the supervision of Ethyl Export Corporation on the basis of a 5 percent commission. The completed plant was to be owned by a manufacturing company, the stock in which would be issued 4 percent to the French government, 46 percent to Kuhlmann, and 50 percent to Ethyl Export. The French government would have veto power in matters concerning national defense. Ethyl was to organize a sales company wholly owned by Ethyl Export.

The plant was duly constructed at Nazaire, France. Apparently it was about the size of the first German tetraethyl lead operation. The accompanying bromine plant was built under license from Dow Chemical and was operated by Ethyl Kuhlmann.

The question of a lead manufacturing plant in the United Kingdom was being discussed by Ethyl Export and the Air Ministry as early as 1935. It was decided that the lead plant would not be built at that time, but plans would be drawn and an agreement made that could be carried out in times of emergency. To insure smooth operation in this anticipated crisis, British Ethyl Corporation was formed on May 9, 1936, owned 50 percent by Ethyl Export and 50 percent by Imperial Chemical Industries (ICI). The basic technology was to come from Ethyl Export and the operating staff from ICI. To cope with whatever demands might develop before actual construction and operation of the proposed plant, large stocks of Ethyl aviation antiknock fluid were imported. Eventually both the tetraethyl lead plant and the bromine plant were owned by the Air Ministry and leased to British Ethyl Corporation. Both were operated during the war by the Alkali Division of ICI on behalf of British Ethyl Corporation.

Though profits would eventually come from special licenses for the erection of overseas plants, direct overseas sales of the Ethyl fluid were disappointingly low in the 1930s. Furthermore, the specter of additional European plants not authorized by Ethyl haunted company officials. Bevan was troubled by the lack of interest in lead on the part of the great international refineries; Shell Oil in particular was unenthusiastic about tetraethyl lead and purchased it only when aviation customers so demanded. It was learned that one reason for Shell's resistance was the fact that Ethyl was half-owned by Jersey, a competitor.

Bevan determined on a radical innovation to entice Shell and other reluctant customers. He would create a new organization in which ownership would be shared by the great oil companies, and profits would be shared by those companies roughly in proportion to their purchases of tetraethyl lead. Ethyl management, hoping the proposed new organization would open a new market, agreed to the idea. The creation of what became Associated Ethyl Company was a tedious, and at times a most disheartening, project.

The new company was domiciled in England and operated under English law. The stockholders of Associated were the major oil companies of the world (including Standard Oil of New Jersey) plus General Motors, which came in by way of its part ownership of the Ethyl Corporation. Though Associated Ethyl took corporate form July 16, 1938, the agreement with Ethyl became effective about ten months later. There was formal notice to the industry that on May 1, 1939, the business of Ethyl Export would be taken over by Associated Ethyl, and its address would be Adelphi, London WC 2. The heart of the agreement was the purchase by Associated of all the assets of Ethyl Export and the use of the Ethyl name and all antiknock patent rights of Ethyl Corporation throughout the world except for the continent of North America, which was reserved for Ethyl itself. Thus Associated Ethyl had the sole rights of sale and manufacture of tetraethyl lead under the Ethyl patent in the area specified. The special licenses and permits already granted in Germany, France, and England were acknowledged, though whatever share Ethyl Export had in these corporations was passed along to Associated Ethyl as part of Associated Ethyl's new assets. For these concessions Ethyl received $1,200,000 and the belief that Associated would open up hitherto restricted markets.

The records are clear as to which companies put up the money and how much each paid:

Anglo-Saxon	£126,426 =	$591,994.15
Anglo-Iranian	61,628 =	288,573.68
Socony	3,805 =	158,293.61
Texas	24,934 =	116,755.86
California	9,478 =	44,382.70
Total	256,271 =	1,200,000.00

Associated Ethyl had the right to purchase fluid from Ethyl at less than the domestic U.S. selling price. Any sale of Ethyl fluid by Ethyl to countries covered by the above-mentioned license to Associated Ethyl required that a commission be paid to Associated. Although Jersey kept membership in the new group for a brief period, neither of Ethyl's owners remained a permanent partner in Associated Ethyl.

Certainly to the amusement and possibly the discomfort of some of the principals in the formation of Associated Ethyl, Julian Frey, in analyzing the system of allowing the customers to share in the profits, openly proclaimed that this was something like a farmers' cooperative with patronage dividends.

The arrangement promised an important new market, but when the war came the problem was not obtaining new customers but rather the allocation of a material in great demand. One of the several embarrassing features in the agreement was the wide-open promise of supplying all that Associated wanted.

As has already been indicated, Canada was considered within the Ethyl province and not within the area reserved for Associated Ethyl. For several years after the formation of Ethyl Gasoline Corporation, Canadian sales were thought of as a convenient and uncomplicated extension of the United States market. The first public sales in Canada took place not long after the resumption of the distribution of Ethyl gasoline in 1926. Reportedly, the first shipment to Canada occurred August 5, 1926, and was directed to the Imperial Oil Company, which had been granted the exclusive right of distribution for a limited time, reportedly about thirty months. J. Coard Taylor was Ethyl's first Canadian representative, having been assigned to service the Imperial Oil Company account. When in November 1927 he was transferred to New York, he was succeeded by J. N. Fitzgerald. The efforts of Taylor and Fitzgerald and their staff were supplemented by an energetic program of magazine advertising initiated in the spring of 1927 paralleling new and bold publicity efforts in the United States. There was an additional spurt of consumption when in 1931 Imperial was permitted to add tetraethyl lead to its regular gasoline.

A special staff serviced the Canadian oil companies, among the staff members being C. J. McFarland in the western provinces with his headquarters in Calgary. In 1937 he gave conspicuous aid in the fruitless search for a Russian four-engine plane, which was downed somewhere in the Arctic. McFarland joined Sir Hubert Wilkins to supervise the blending of Ethyl fluid with the regular aviation gasoline to improve combustion in the cold. His efforts earned him membership in the Explorers Club on recommendation of Sir Hubert and the Russians.

In this period Ethyl was supplying all, or virtually all, of the tetraethyl lead used in Mexico. Old Ethyl employees emphatically assert that there was a very fine relationship between the Ethyl representatives and the Mexicans. The explanation of the elevated character of the business is that negotiations were carried on with the highest officers. Small presents were indeed exchanged in the $40 or $50 category, but this was all.

The Mexicans, in negotiating contracts with Ethyl, insisted that the arrangements for supplies and services be exactly like the contracts with refineries in the United States. This was agreed to by Ethyl, but in the long run it probably would have been more advantageous to the Mexicans if the situation had been handled otherwise, because for a time the world price for tetraethyl lead was lower than the domestic price, which controlled the Mexican contract.

Competition and Federal Restraints

In paradoxical fashion the story of the relationship between Ethyl and DuPont has been confused by the blinding light focused on, and variant interpretations of, the facts brought out in the federal suit that eventually forced DuPont to give up its part-ownership of General Motors. It must be remembered that General Motors itself was half owner of Ethyl Corporation for most of the 1924–62 period.

As already noted, Ethyl Gasoline Corporation, after organization, left the manufacture of tetraethyl lead to DuPont. Jersey's small efforts at Bayway had collapsed in the wake of the fatalities at that plant.

Sloan was inclined to favor DuPont all along. As he wrote Irénée du Pont in December 1925, "DuPont will always be the manufacturing agent of Ethyl Gasoline Corporation whether we make tetraethyl lead or whatever we make, now or in the future. I am sure of that." And yet Ethyl administrators felt that DuPont was somewhat demanding. When the sale of Ethyl fluid was suspended in 1925 and 1926 while the surgeon general's investigation was going on, DuPont insisted on completing its supply contract. An adjustment that almost, but not quite, yielded to DuPont's demand eventually was effected.

And yet Webb had a mind of his own. In the year following his election as president of Ethyl he made an overt though unsuccessful attempt to develop a second source of supply, one that would be competitive with DuPont. Though Webb was legally responsible to the Ethyl stockholders, meaning Jersey and General Motors, he quickly developed a pride in and a prime loyalty to the organization created by Jersey and General Motors. Thus Webb was troubled as he looked down the road toward the time when Ethyl's patents would expire. He saw important omissions in the wording of supply contracts with DuPont. These contracts did not require DuPont to reveal its evolving know-how to Ethyl. Webb could readily envisage Ethyl's eventual competition with DuPont, which would by that time have all the advantages of a score of years of improvement.

After five years of corporate life Ethyl was able to force an adjusted contract that required DuPont by 1938 to disclose all its technical information relative to manufactured lead. This new contract, which was signed in 1930, represented a highly successful tactic for Webb, not a complete victory. He had attempted to insert in the 1930 contract a promise from DuPont that it would restrict its sale of tetraethyl lead to Ethyl when the patents expired, at least for a time; but this concession was not acceptable to DuPont.

There is a strange chapter in the complex relations among General Motors, Jersey, and Ethyl, an episode during which General Motors shared its half ownership of Ethyl with DuPont. While economic historians cannot doubt the strong influence of DuPont in determining Ethyl's policies, they do not have to accept the contention by the government's lawyers in the divestiture case that "DuPont was in fact an equal partner with General Motors and Standard Oil." General Motors passed on to DuPont only 50 of its 7,500 shares, and this divided ownership lasted only about three years. At the annual stockholders meetings of 1936 and 1937 the following apportionment of shares was recorded.

Names	No. of shares
E. I. du Pont de Nemours & Co.	50
General Motors Corporation	7,450
Standard Oil Company (New Jersey)	7,500
Total	15,000

The listing of the directors in the *Ethyl News* for November 1934 follows:

Donaldson Brown
General Motors Corp.

E. M. Clark (Retired)
Standard Oil Co., N.J.

Irénée du Pont
E. I. du Pont de Nemours & Co.

W. S. Farish
Standard Oil Co., N.J.

Frank A. Howard
Standard Oil Co., N.J.

Charles F. Kettering
General Motors Corp.

C. G. Sheffield (Resigned)
Standard Oil Co., N.J.

Alfred P. Sloan, Jr.
General Motors Corp.

W. C. Teagle
Standard Oil Co., N.J.

Earle W. Webb
Ethyl Gasoline Corp.

The sharing of stock was a short-lived venture. By the time of the annual meeting in 1938, the usual 50–50 General Motors and Jersey allocation of shares was resumed. Though the background discussions are not clear, there was a new bylaw to the effect that "no stockholder shall have the right to sell, assign or transfer all or any of its shares of the capital stock of this corporation (including stock warrants and stock rights) without first offering in writing said share or shares of stock for sale to the other stockholders of this corporation."

Then there began an intricate series of moves eventually resulting in Ethyl's assuming the role of manufacturer, the most important immediate reason being the unwillingness of DuPont to expand to the degree that Ethyl officials thought proper. By 1937 the DuPont production of tetraethyl lead was about 65 million pounds annually, near the DuPont capacity. This apparent need for new facilities encouraged DuPont and Ethyl to come to a new understanding as to physical facilities and their operation.

Ethyl and DuPont in 1936 agreed that DuPont would build at Baton Rouge for Ethyl a lead-manufacturing plant about the same size as the DuPont plant at Deepwater, New Jersey. Technically, in 1938 Ethyl became a manufacturer. Its production at first was

Baton Rouge plant in 1937

by proxy. Ethyl worked out a manufacturing agreement with DuPont whereby DuPont as Ethyl's agent was to operate both Ethyl's new Baton Rouge plant and DuPont's own New Jersey plant, which it was leasing to Ethyl. This manufacturing-service agreement, originally planned to last seven years, was extended to ten years. Critics claim that the formula's compensation meant that the DuPont company was to receive about the same profits that it had obtained under the pre-1938 arrangement.

The coming, if not the current, adversary position of DuPont became so obvious that Irénée du Pont felt he should resign from the Ethyl board, giving as his reason a possible conflict of interest. His letter of resignation was dated December 10, 1937.

By the end of 1947, the 1938 agreements as amended would expire, as would Ethyl's key patents. To clear the air, DuPont in 1946 had announced that it was going to manufacture and market tetraethyl lead on its own account beginning in 1948.

According to later declarations by the U.S. Department of Jus-

tice, these developments resulted in no real competition, a conclusion with which the Ethyl salesmen would certainly have argued
since they were under orders to "slug it out" with DuPont.

To insure the safety and stability of its business, Ethyl Gasoline
Corporation developed a system of distribution whereby refiners
were licensed and they, in turn, were permitted to sell only to
those jobbers licensed by Ethyl. Both refiners and jobbers were
subjected to detailed health and safety regulations. Ethyl reserved the right to cancel the licenses of jobbers when it saw fit,
and there were investigations by Ethyl representatives to guard
against what Ethyl Gasoline Corporation described as violation
of "business ethics," a phrase conceded to include price cutting.

The federal government brought suit against the corporation,
accusing it of violating the Sherman Anti-Trust Act in its licensing system, which the government said went beyond the privileges given in patent rights. The case in the District Court of the
United States for the Southern District of New York went against
Ethyl Gasoline Corporation. On an agreed statement of facts the
case was appealed to the United States Supreme Court, where it
was argued March 1 and 4, 1940, and decided March 25, 1940.
The leading lawyer for the company was Dean G. Acheson; the
government's case was advanced primarily by Thurman W. Arnold, assistant attorney general; the Court's reasoning was given
by Mr. Justice Stone, who found for the government.

The verdict meant no major change in the system of distribution and sales. Indeed, in the trial it was clearly shown that Ethyl
Gasoline Corporation was not absolute in its control over the
price structure.

In the midst of the negativism in the Court's opinion there
were two or three statements from which Ethyl Gasoline Corporation could draw a measure of satisfaction. No one doubted
that tetraethyl lead improved the efficiency of high-compression
engines. Mr. Justice Stone referred to tetraethyl lead, "which when
added to gasoline used as a motor fuel, increases the efficiency
of high pressure combustion engines in which the fuel is con-

sumed." Furthermore, the opinion stated: "There is no authentic instance of injury resulting from the handling of lead-treated gasoline, after its manufacture, attributable to its lead content."

The suit revealed to the public the all-pervasive character of the company at that time. According to testimony, 85 percent of all the gasoline of a high-octane rating was treated with Ethyl fluid; 70 percent of all the gasoline manufactured and sold in the United States was treated with the Ethyl fluid; of the 147 major refiners, all but one had entered into license agreements with Ethyl. Of the 12,000 jobbers in the United States, 10,000 were licensed by Ethyl.

World War II and Immediately Thereafter

With the coming of World War II many employees entered the armed forces or joined government agencies. Such was the demand for tetraethyl lead that sales were no longer a problem but allocation was. When Julian Frey in 1944 became sales manager, he was teased by his friends, since there was nothing that needed selling. He and others were really getting ready for the time when DuPont was going to sell in competition.

Kettering, recalling the "dramatic part" tetraethyl lead played in World War II, quoted the British as saying that "if it had not been for tetraethyl lead they would have lost the Battle of Britain. Similar expressions of its value can be had from many important people in many important positions."

On July 25, 1943, a German submarine fired five shells at the Ethyl-Dow plant at Kure Beach, North Carolina, but all of the shots landed in the Cape Fear River without damaging the structure. Yet this firing on the bromine-extraction operation indicated the importance with which the enemy considered tetraethyl lead. Incidentally, the Nazi submarine was sunk the next day by an American patrol plane.

The company on April 9, 1942, became Ethyl Corporation instead of Ethyl Gasoline Corporation, the change occurring because some products not directly related to the antiknock compound might be marketed in the future. This move for a broader identification leads to the curious story of "Ethyl Cleaner," a topic still a matter of discussion, not to say debate, among the old-time Ethyl people.

Ethyl Cleaner was born in a test-marketing venture in 1944, and it died when Ethyl ceased distributing the product in 1948. The subsidiary corporation in charge of the project was called Ethyl Specialties Company. Ethyl Cleaner was created primarily in the attempt to strengthen the legal position of the Ethyl trademark, which the company did not want restricted to the anti-knock fluid. The major proponents of the venture were in public relations, not research and development. Ethyl Cleaner was related to Ethyl's main business only in a roundabout way; the soapy detergent in a water mix was good for washing automobiles.

For a while orders rolled in, and then the cleaner project simply fell apart. The disaster signal went up when on September 16, 1946, the board of directors was told that the cleaner operation was running at a loss of from $400,000 to $500,000 per year. However, the disaster was not quite so great as the figures suggest at first glance. This was the season of the excess-profits tax and the write-off eased the pain of the liquidation. About this time it was hard to find anybody in the company willing to say that he had sponsored that venture.

Looking back on the history of the Ethyl Cleaner, those involved in the attempt to get into the direct-to-customer business list several reasons for failure and also several lessons that were learned. The product had been test-marketed in a time when there was a soap shortage and almost anything soapy would sell. The consignment system used gave a false feeling of great sales for a while, but when the no-sales returns started showing up, the disaster seemed threefold. At the end of the war vigorous competition came from companies conditioned to this sort of selling and offering a line of allied products. Ethyl was trying to sell the same product in two markets, one the grocery store with a small mark-up and the other the service station or hardware store. Furthermore, the word *Ethyl,* while excellent in the automobile market, was a bit frightening in the grocery stores, and some people feared that lead might be in the cleaner. Another embarrassing feature was the fact that the cleaner was in competition with some products being made by refiners who were customers for the tetraethyl lead.

All in all, Ethyl found that it was simply not prepared for retail sales; in that area Ethyl had no experience. Some people at Ethyl thought that the cleaner experience was a warning to be more careful of test-marketing. "I think it hurt our pride more than anything else," says Robert Herzog, chief chemist in the cleaner project and one of the several individuals who claimed that they learned a lesson from the Ethyl Cleaner venture. Herzog adds, "It was not a product based on profound research results," and "it helps to prove we were not able to just branch out wherever we wanted."

Herzog, who eventually rose to become executive vice president and member of the board, was born in Brooklyn and attended the Cooper Union Institute of Technology in New York City, from which he received his B.S. degree in chemistry. Then he enrolled in the University of Michigan, where he earned his master's degree in chemistry. He entered the employment of Ethyl in the year 1940, this being his first and only full-time job. After the cleaner project he licked his wounds, and they were rather small wounds, then went back to Baton Rouge in 1947, rejoining the research group.

Another man who learned something from the cleaner experience was Malcolm P. Murdock, who became sales manager, then general manager of Ethyl Specialties, the corporate name for the production of Ethyl Cleaner. Murdock was born in Melrose, Massachusetts, December 9, 1905, and grew up in the western part of New York State. He graduated from Cornell University with a B.A. degree in economics in 1928 and held various jobs for brief periods including work with an investment firm, a business that practically disappeared in the 1929 crash. Then, in

Robert Herzog

his words, he "ended up in Buffalo, New York, as the the best-dressed gasoline pumper" at $18 per week and thought he was rather lucky at that. In 1933 he started working for Ethyl Corporation as a field representative out of the New York office and later headed one of Ethyl's motor clinics. By his own statement one learns that Murdock's experiences with engineering were not particularly inspiring. "I found out that the piston went up and down instead of the cylinder." This revelation and his social instincts led him into sales. He came to the position of assistant general sales manager after a chaotic two-year period with Ethyl Cleaner. Interestingly enough, he remains enthusiastic about the cleaner, claiming it to be a good product; in his garage he still keeps samples that work just fine. Back in the main line of business he continued to move ahead in the sales department, and in 1952 was elected vice president in charge of sales and also a member of the board of directors.

During World War II, antitrust action by the Department of

Justice brought on heart-breaking experiences for certain Jersey officials, who, under pressure from their attorneys and coworkers, accepted a *nolo contendere* plea to permit the company to go ahead with full concentration on its wartime work. Such is the thesis advanced by careful historians exploring this phase of the story of Standard Oil of New Jersey.

Sympathetic observers say that Teagle of Standard Oil died right there in the courtroom as his patriotism and integrity were assailed and hitherto private agreements with the Germans, a topic already mentioned, were exposed. These events signaled a new era in the interpretation and enforcement of the antitrust acts, and the counsel for Ethyl reexamined various agreements, especially that with Associated Ethyl made May 11, 1939.

At its meeting on January 11, 1943, the board approved an arrangement to cancel the sales agreement of 1939. The definitive cancellation did not take place until 1945, when Ethyl contracted to pay Associated Ethyl $1,700,000; in return Associated Ethyl released its exclusive right to market tetraethyl lead in certain areas of the world. Furthermore, Ethyl gave to Associated a license to manufacture and sell Ethyl fluid. In addition there was a new supply contract in which Ethyl committed itself to furnishing Associated with its needs at a fixed price. Although at this time Ethyl did not reobtain its trademark, Ethyl eventually managed to buy back its exclusive right to the Ethyl name and emblem. These negotiations will be noted in a later chapter.

As Webb was approaching the mandatory retirement age of sixty-five, he began to have serious circulatory problems, and about the time he gave up the presidency suffered the loss of a leg. To outsiders he seemed to be accepting with grace what could not be helped. No doubt he remembered the example of Earle, Jr. There is convincing evidence, however, that the wound never fully healed and that he failed to handle his false leg effectively. In 1941 his first wife died. Three years later he married Lille Adelaide Milderberger, who traced her ancestry to the early Dutch settlers. Widow of Walter J. Berbecker, she had a business of her own in New York City and never quite developed the affection for Morehead City that had characterized the first Mrs. Webb.

Webb's remaining son, Arnold, died in a boating accident on the Neuse River in North Carolina in 1944. As might have been expected, with illness and age Webb occasionally became a bit testy. There is a revealing episode of temper and subsequent contrition which occurred late in his tenure as president. Ethyl had a savings plan, and this plan included certain rights to withdraw money when the depositor needed such. A new employee, Walter Cosgrove, who calls himself just a "whippersnapper" at the time, was unfortunate enough to be in charge when Webb sent down a request to withdraw some money. As fate would have it, Cosgrove had been auditing the books and noted that Webb had overdrawn his account. The practice heretofore had been to advance Webb money whenever he wanted it. Cosgrove, however, felt that these overdrafts were not right and said he was not going to let Webb have the money. At the moment, in Cosgrove's words, "he blew high, wide, and handsome and he got the vice president of finance in here and got everybody in. But he didn't get his money and he really let me have it." Webb made the chilling observation that he was disappointed in Cosgrove. Then Cosgrove adds, "About a week later he came down to my office and apologized because he was upset. He had a need for that money and he was counting on it and realized afterwards, when he calmed down, I was right." Cosgrove feels that it was rather big of the man to come down and apologize, for as Cosgrove says, "I was just a young kid at the time." He stayed with the company, and eventually became assistant director of employee relations.

Webb retired from the presidency August 9, 1947, being succeeded by Edward L. Shea. The office of chairman of the board was held by Webb from the date of his retirement as president until February 9, 1948, when he stepped down as chairman but remained on the board for another nine years. In the year 1954 the directors authorized the painting of Webb's portrait, which was placed in the board room.

In his retirement years Webb spent more and more time at his residence in Palm Beach. His home on the outskirts of Morehead City was destroyed by fire, and as already noted, the second Mrs. Webb was not overenthusiastic about the Carolina coast lands. Webb died in 1965 at the age of eighty-two while vacationing at Baden-Baden, Germany.

VI

Shea and Turner Head
a New Kind of Ethyl
1948–1962

New Leaders and the Beginning of Competition

THE YEARS 1947 and 1948 marked a turning point in the history of the original Ethyl Corporation. The disappearance of basic patent rights at home and of cartel arrangements in the world market initiated an era of competition everywhere. Furthermore, Ethyl took over the manufacture of all the tetraethyl lead it was marketing; thus the once research, sales-and-service company became a manufacturing, research, sales-and-service corporation.

As manufacturing contracts with DuPont expired in 1947, that corporation announced it was going into production of tetraethyl lead for its own use and would put its product on the market by January 1948. It would then be selling the tetraethyl lead from the Deepwater plant, which since 1938 had been operated on Ethyl's behalf.

By way of its part ownership of General Motors, DuPont had a continuing and even embarrassing interest in the Ethyl Corporation. As is well known, in 1957 this connection between DuPont and General Motors was severed by court decree. Despite hints to the contrary, there seems to have been real competition between Ethyl and DuPont in the marketplace.

Edward L. Shea

Brought up in the days of protection by patents, some members of the Ethyl sales organization simply could not perform well in a competitive market, and there were numerous early retirements. As Murdock says, "One of the toughest jobs I ever had to do was get rid of about one-third of the sales force." In this open-market period, Ethyl had a great advantage because of its fair treatment in the earlier days of small as well as large companies. When considering the market for the antiknock additive, one should recall that the competition came not only from rival chemical firms but from refining processes used by the oil companies, processes that would step up the octane numbers.

The total tetraethyl lead market became sluggish. Depressing factors included the coming of smaller cars that offered better mileage and jet or turbojet planes that had no need for leaded gasoline. Thus the chief executives who followed Webb had on their hands an uncertain market and a very certain competition.

The board of directors in choosing the first chief executive officer in the new era went outside Ethyl Corporation and picked a so-called organization man, one accustomed to large enterprises. Edward L. Shea, New Hampshire–born, followed the Ivy League tradition by attending Phillips Exeter and enrolling in Princeton, from which he graduated in 1916. He served as a naval aviator in World War I. For more than a score of years he was associated with the oil industry, subsequently heading a large utilities system; this was his occupation when in 1947 he was chosen president of Ethyl.

Employees and staff members, accustomed to Webb's somewhat easygoing manner, privately termed Shea "a cold fish." In truth Shea faced a situation quite different from that of an earlier time, and he developed an administrative style new to Ethyl. Budget control and efficiency were uppermost in his mind. He prided himself on being a "tough guy," an executive with close oversight of all operations. To confront the new problems, Shea assumed a hard-nosed, tight-reined posture and developed cost-cutting techniques. One of his earliest and longest-remembered economies was to do away with the linen towels in the New York office and substitute paper. It was a prophetic and symbolic gesture. Shea was convinced that Ethyl had to get lean and hungry. In a word, he was a strong personality. He kept people busy.

In extemporaneous analysis Murdock says: "Of course Shea was another great guy. That rascal! I was very fond of him. Tough to work for, kept your neck in the collar, nothing but your best efforts would satisfy him. I tried so hard to put a report on his desk and avoid that damn red pencil that he had, and I never succeeded. If there was a chink in the armor, that man could find it. He put up this very tough exterior, and yet he was an easy touch. I remember when one of the elevator operators in the building—wife had a miscarriage or something—and this poor kid was financially in trouble. I didn't know [about] it until quite a bit later. Very quietly, Mr. Shea took care of everything for this boy, just an employee in the building. He was a great guy." Independently wealthy, Shea maintained a magnificent establishment on Skunk's Misery Road, Long Island.

Shea became obsessed with the concept of relaxation and employed an expert to give a course in relaxation for executives.

Paul Cahill, whose work as a specialist in taxes will be mentioned below, had the bad luck to be subjected to Shea's instructions for curing a stiff neck, which Shea said came about because Cahill did not relax. (Cahill knew it was because he had slept in a draft.)

Shea was far from being relaxed when witnessing a challenge offered by two of his employees to one of Ethyl's owners. The story, which is of the Jack-the-Giant-Killer variety, deserves telling. In the early 1950s there was debate as to the proper price to be paid for ethylene that Ethyl was buying from Jersey. It should be remembered that ethylene was one of the essential ingredients in the manufacture of tetraethyl lead. Affairs came to a head in 1952. In the immediate background was a project run by Dr. Harry O'Connell and E. Malcolm Harvey to determine the cost if Ethyl were to develop its own supply of ethylene by cracking an ethane-propane fuel stock.

In figuring the cost, Harvey came up with the figure of two and one-quarter cents per pound as compared with the seven to seven and one-quarter cents per pound being paid by Ethyl to Jersey. Furthermore the ethylene being produced under the experimental conditions was of a concentrated rather than dilute variety and, if the technique were applied on a large scale, smaller and less expensive equipment could be used.

The Jersey people at the Baton Rouge plant had checked and rechecked Harvey's figures and uphappily for them could find nothing wrong with the numbers. Shea was uncomfortable at the thought of confrontation with Jersey representatives on the board of directors. To quote Harvey, "The then chief executive officer for Ethyl, Mr. Ed Shea, said my numbers better be right or I would look for another job." His numbers proved to be right and the contract was renegotiated. These experiments and subsequent negotiations in the Houston, Texas, plant effectively broke the Gulf Coast ethylene price for fifteen years.

While the shift from Webb to Shea meant noticeable changes in spirit and program, there was basic continuity of policy during all those dozen or so years constituting the Shea-Turner era. The

B. Bynum Turner

transition from Shea to B. Bynum Turner was somewhat gradual and free-flowing, inasmuch as Turner had worked under Shea, and even after Turner became president Shea was kept on as chief executive officer for about a year and a half.

Bynum Turner, a giant of a man with a booming voice, was born in Angleton, Texas. In 1933 he graduated in chemical engineering from Rice Institute. Before coming to Ethyl, Turner was associated with the research program of Humble Oil and Refining Company, and during the war years made an impressive record as manager of the butadiene plant and then was head of one section of the Washington-based Rubber Reserve Company producing synthetic rubber from petroleum. He joined Ethyl in 1946, not long before Webb was to retire as chief executive officer. Thus Turner had about a decade of experience under Shea before being made president. In the manufacturing department from 1946 to 1951, He directed much of the expansion of Ethyl in those early days of the Shea administration. Turner was elected vice president in charge of research and engineering in 1951, executive vice president in 1955, and president in 1956. On January 1, 1958, Ethyl made Turner chief executive officer. Those years in which he presumably was being groomed for the presidency might be described as the most productive in Turner's professional life. He had the reputation for being direct, dynamic, intelligent, and energetic. As Stephen B. Rodi, now vice president and director of employee relations, clearly recalls, "You could get a decision in two or three minutes and then he let you do your job."

There is much testimony to the effect that when the company went out to hire new employees, it aimed at the people of highest quality. James M. Gill, later manager of several manufacturing operations and eventually a senior vice president and member of the board of Ethyl of Virginia, recruited for the company for several years. He says the policy could be phrased this way, "We do not hire the average; we don't plan to be average. We want the very best."

One clue to the superiority of the people in old Ethyl was the fact that its owners did not use Ethyl as a dumping ground for their incompetents. A conspicuous exception was a Belgian bon vivant who did not fit in with Standard of Jersey and thus was passed on to Ethyl, which suffered his wanderings for a few years.

With the retirement of Webb, an experienced lawyer, there was need for a new pattern of legal assistance. An important figure was William R. Perdue, Jr., who was born June 24, 1913, in Macon, Georgia. He attended Emory University, graduating in 1934 with an A.B. degree in history. He entered the Duke University Law School and graduated in 1937, after which he joined the firm eventually known as Cahill, Gordon, Reindel and Ohl in New York City. He left the Cahill, Gordon group to serve in the army from June 1941 to August 1945, achieving the rank of lieutenant colonel. Back in private practice with the same firm, he was lent to Cahill, Gordon's client, the Ethyl Corporation. His service as temporary general counsel ended in 1950 when he joined Ethyl as "permanent" general counsel. Perdue came well versed in corporate affairs because of his earlier experience with several Wall Street firms that were clients of Cahill, Gordon. Soon he was made vice president of Ethyl. In 1955, he became vice president of finance and a member of the board of directors. In this position he supervised most of the staff activities of the company and assumed special responsibilities for Canadian operations.

When Perdue was made vice president of finance, the position of general counsel was filled by another attorney from the Cahill, Gordon firm, Frederick P. Warne. Born in Yonkers, Warne completed his undergraduate work at Dartmouth College and then attended Harvard Law School. At Harvard he had the good fortune to study under some of the "greats," including Samuel Williston, authority on contracts. During World War II, Warne served with the navy, an experience that confirmed his basic love of the sea. His personality and broad interests characteristically moved his responsibilities beyond any narrow confines of the legal office.

Among other officials who should be mentioned is Joseph A. Costello, elected vice president in 1949, a director in 1952. Born in Scranton, Pennsylvania, in 1900, he graduated from Pennsylvania State University with a B.S. degree in engineering in 1925. He began working for Ethyl three years later as a field representative, sales. Costello played the difficult but useful role of devil's advocate and thereby stimulated the free and sometimes forceful exchange of ideas in upper management.

Charles H. Zeanah, Ethyl's director of corporate community relations, tells with enthusiasm of Maj. Gen. Stephen G. Henry, who became manager of community relations in Baton Rouge in 1947. General Henry's position was sensitive and important because the readjustment of personnel to civilian life after World War II and various episodes of labor unrest called for reestablishing Ethyl's favorable image in the community. Zeanah says that Henry was the man who recommended sponsorship of football broadcasting in 1949, and this fact is of significance in the career of Zeanah himself.

A goodly number of company officials had the great talent of persuading without using stern language. Notable in this respect was Glenn O. Hayes, plant manager at Houston, briefly vice president in charge of employee relations, then vice president, manufacturing, with Schaefer's retirement in 1957. Hayes had the light touch, but he could be very firm when firmness was needed. Benjamin D. Harrison, who was special assistant to Hayes when Hayes served as vice president, manufacturing, says, "He didn't heckle the pants off you, but you darn well did your job or Mr. Hayes would work you over. He was a delightful fellow to work for."

Harrison had a broad experience with the company that well prepared him for his later responsibilities as corporate budget director of Ethyl of Virginia. A Kentuckian by birth, he graduated from the University of Kentucky, served as field representative in the Ethyl sales department, became a major in the U.S. Army during World War II, headed industrial engineering at Baton Rouge, and served as director of cost control before becoming special assistant to Hayes.

Hayes shared in redirecting the company's labor policy in the 1950s. More permanent in this area was Stephen B. Rodi, who became director, corporate employee relations, in 1958, filling the gap created by the shift of Hayes to vice president, manufacturing. Rodi, a native of New Orleans, after earning both B.A. and LL.B. degrees from Loyola University of that city, served with the federal internal revenue service and the state department of revenue before coming to Ethyl as attorney in 1951. By gradual stages he moved into the area of labor relations.

By way of background for the changes in labor relations beginning in the early 1950s, note that when Ethyl was in a monopoly position because of its patents and was making handsome profits, the general attitude of management was to buy itself out of any labor problems. In the words of James M. Gill, "Ethyl had a rather benign type of relationship with the unions. I think they did everything they could to not take a strike." As wise observers realized, this extravagant policy would eventually create a tough situation.

A modification came about when competition forced cost cutting and required reexamination of labor relations. The company gradually assumed a position that it was not afraid to take a strike. The new attitude was clearly discernible about 1952.

Rodi's theory was to move to the courts or arbitration panels if the company was being put in an unfair position. He insisted on litigation in the "portal-to-portal" controversy, the question being: should the company be responsible for the time required in suiting up in safety clothes? There was a series of these cases in the parish courts of Louisiana beginning in 1952, all of which were decided in favor of the company.

Perhaps the most critical period in labor relations was the year 1957, when there were minor and major strikes at the tetraethyl lead plant in Baton Rouge. At the time Wallace F. Armstrong was manager of the plant, Hayes was vice president, employee relations, and Shea chief executive officer. First there was a strike of some four or five days quite significant in terms of what the foremen learned while operating the facility. It was a period of economic stringency, and management, after probing and analyzing all reports by the supervisory personnel operating the plant during the brief strike, saw that further mechanization could reduce labor requirements by one-third.

Company officials went ahead with such a plan. In July the union walked out, the company insisted on keeping operations going, and there was a rough time for forty-seven days. Violence was a sad novelty in the history of Ethyl, and some in management pined for those good old days when happiness was created in such circumstances by hiring more people. The strike ended with management having made its point and reasserted its prerogatives. Labor accepted the new situation and a long period of labor peace and increased efficiency dates from the ending of the tetraethyl lead plant strike of 1957.

In reviewing supervisory personnel, one is reminded of a comment made by the late George F. Kirby, who served Ethyl in important capacities including the presidency. "It was the best group of management a company that size ever had." The basis for his superlative becomes more evident as the story of the competitive era unfolds.

Attracting the Public Eye and Ear

The maintenance and improvement of profits, which characterize the first phase of the fifteen years under review, were based in part on a vigorous advertising and public relations program. The advertising budget finally reached over $2 million per year. Officials of the company were determined to make the Ethyl trademark more visible, its message more audible. The professionals in the company made effective use of the traditional printed message and the newer media, radio and television. Cleverness in print, an association with sports, and a championing of the "American Way of Life" were hallmarks in this era.

In 1947 Russell B. Weston was appointed director of advertising. Weston made a lasting impression on his contemporaries. He was a stately gentleman, gray haired, a man fastidious in appearance who always wore black shoes and a three-piece suit normally dark in color. Very precise and proper in behavior, he was somewhat paradoxical inasmuch as at the beginning of a conversation he might be quite firm, almost dogmatic, but he kept such an open mind that he was ready to be convinced if arguments contrary to his original ideas appeared. To quote Gordon E. Saxon, currently director of advertising and sales promotion: "He was one of the few people I have known in my own career who could start off a conversation by saying no, that he was wrong, and you were right, which made working with him really a lot of fun." Saxon adds: "He was a man who could look at a piece of copy, an ad concept, and almost intuitively tell you whether or not it would have the desired result. He was, I think, as strict with himself as he was with others."

The Ethyl advertising department achieved extraordinary publicity in a series of campaigns to make the motorist aware of the special properties of Ethyl gasoline. Particularly noteworthy was the "trademarks series" of 1949, featured in various magazines such as *Life*, *Look*, and *Time*. Displayed to the reader were the real differences between animals allied in appearance, such as the chimpanzee and other apes; and the sea lion and the seal, the clues to the distinction being special "trademarks" that distinguish one from the other. Then, of course, there was the trademark of Ethyl Corporation, identifying an additive that conspicuously improved gasoline.

In a variety of presentations the "two equals three" campaign demonstrated the fact that two gallons of "Ethyl" gasoline in a modern automobile or tractor did the same or better work than did three gallons of ordinary gasoline twenty-five years earlier. The most conspicuous demonstration was probably at the official opening of the New Jersey Turnpike in 1951.

In the mid-1950s the most prominent themes were two: first, "Drive More—It Gets Cheaper by the Mile" and then the memorable "road bird" series containing the highway safety messages that in 1956 won the National Safety Council's public interest award. In the cast of characters the villain was the "darting road runner," who recklessly weaves in and out of traffic. And then, to fit in with a special appeal to the "Keep America Beautiful" theme, there were such careless birds as the "uncouth coot" and "wild flicker," who put their garbage on the highways. Probably the most extensive was the "Magic Circle" campaign, which dominated advertising budgets for several years beginning in 1958. The main point of the "Magic Circle" message was that within a reasonably short distance from home there were notable places to visit and things to do. The Magic Circle campaign in print and on television plus other efforts by Ethyl Corporation netted an award from the Freedoms Foundation of Valley Forge, Pennsylvania, for promoting interest in American history and for appreciation of the American way of life.

In the 1950s Ethyl made a special attempt to capture the attention of the great body of Americans devoted to sports, especially the spectator variety, baseball and football. Probably the first significant move in this direction was the sponsorship in 1949 of a play-by-play broadcast over the radio of the entire football schedule of Louisiana State University. It was a gesture that brought plaudits from the Chamber of Commerce and other groups.

Charles H. Zeanah, born and brought up in Tuscaloosa, Alabama, began working with Ethyl in 1951 as an announcer for these games, living in a dormitory with the football team and commuting to Alabama. After this trial period he entered Ethyl public relations and was put in Houston as General Henry's counterpart there. He returned to Baton Rouge in 1952 and in 1954 went to New York as assistant director of public relations. In 1959 he again moved to Baton Rouge succeeding General Henry. He later became director of corporate public relations and then director of corporate community relations.

In the 1950s television was adopted as a major vehicle for advertising, and this move was intimately allied with the athletic theme. In 1952 Ethyl arranged for a series of telecasts presented by such prominent sports commentators as Bill Stern, Ted Husing, and Red Barber. So important were these television programs that they were filmed and shown in moving picture houses and drive-in theaters. A variation in 1952 was the weekly telecast under the title "Ask Me Another." The sports commentators answered questions presented by a panel of celebrities. Ethyl's reward in 1953 was a commendation from the National Baseball Hall of Fame.

In that same year there appeared on television the most famous of all the Ethyl athletic programs, "The Big Playback," this on twenty-five stations and the National Broadcasting Company network. The main feature was the presentation of Bill Stern, who, using film strips, recalled memorable athletic events of the past. Later Jimmy Powers succeeded Bill Stern in the role of narrator.

Very special projects were aimed directly at the oil industry. Under the head of trivia was the distribution of large buttons reading "90 YOOP," conversation pieces interpreted as saying "90 years of oil progress." This button was called a hit on the 1949 Oil Progress Week, October 16–22, which celebrated the ninetieth anniversary of the oil industry in the United States.

To mark the one hundredth anniversary of the drilling of the Drake Well at Titusville, Pennsylvania, Ethyl publicly displayed for the first time representative items from its collection of Petroleum Americana, consisting of rare books, documents, advertising cards, and allied memorabilia relating to the early days of the industry. The exhibit at Allegheny College, Meadville, Pennsylvania, January 23–25, 1959, included such treasures as Lewis Evans's "A General Map of the Middle British Colonies in America" drawn in 1755, displaying the word *petroleum* in that part of "Pensilvania" near the present Oil City.

As a service to the refiners Ethyl sponsored the production in 1952 at Sloan Laboratory, Massachusetts Institute of Technology, of a film entitled *Fundamentals of Fuel Knock*. Among the various programs developed to aid the oil companies was one called *Fire Power*, a dramatic presentation to underscore the necessity of safety in the handling of gasoline. Such was the popularity of the show that at one time there were five road companies playing all over the country. Ethyl was particularly generous in its relations with that group of smaller oil companies organized as the National Petroleum Association (NPA). These refiners had developed a warm affection for Ethyl Corporation during the Webb regime. At their meeting in Atlantic City in September 1952, which was the NPA's Golden Anniversary Convention, Ethyl sponsored special entertainments that strengthened already strong ties with the group.

Repeatedly Ethyl programs and publications received recognition from the Freedoms Foundation of Valley Forge, Pennsylvania, as contributing to a better understanding of the American way of life. One such program was a training course prepared by Ethyl employees themselves and entitled, "The American Economic System."

Kettering in his last years contributed to the publications distributed by the Ethyl Corporation, reassuring his readers of the validity of the ancient maxims and giving practical examples of the success of the free enterprise system. On one memorable occasion, an unplanned incident at the opening of a new manufacturing unit in Houston, he made a dramatic appearance offering a sort of olympian prophecy as to the primacy of solar energy in any picture of the future.

By continuing and strengthening a fellowship program, Ethyl enhanced its reputation with institutions of higher learning at a level quite different from that achieved by the sports broadcasts that have been mentioned. The selection of fellowship recipients was always made by representatives of the college faculties and administration, not by Ethyl.

New Plants and the Search for Larger Markets

As already indicated, by 1948 Ethyl had to rely exclusively on its own manufacturing resources in coping with the new market divided between itself and DuPont. While this era meant competition and a resultant loss of a fraction of the tetraethyl market, it also meant relief from the heavy cost of the DuPont contracts. Thus net earnings appreciably increased, reaching a peak in 1957, Shea's last year as chief executive officer.

The capacity of the Baton Rouge plant in 1948 seemed insufficient for the market Ethyl hoped to retain. Therefore in the following years Ethyl officials decided to expand production facilities at Baton Rouge and also to build plants in Texas, California, and Canada.

In Baton Rouge a $40-million improvement program was completed by November 1949 in time for the festivities accompanying the city's 100th anniversary as capital of Louisiana. The modernization and enlargement of the Baton Rouge plant validated the label of Baton Rouge as "Antiknock City U.S.A." The expanded operation in Baton Rouge made that industrial complex the world's largest manufacturer of tetraethyl lead and also the largest producer of sodium and of ethyl chloride.

In 1952 the company completed and put in operation a new plant at Pasadena, Texas, on a 400-acre site south of the Houston Ship Channel. Self-contained and independent of Baton Rouge, the plant was convenient to sea lanes and to major rail lines.

Freeport, just fifty miles from the tetraethyl plant near Houston, was the Ethyl-Dow installation, which had been in operation since 1941, producing ethylene dibromide, an important ingredient in the formula for the antiknock compound. In the making of ethylene dibromide, ethylene was combined with bromine. Bromine was extracted from seawater in an elaborate process involving huge evaporating towers and giant fans, all to obtain those minute fractions in the seawater. A million parts of seawater were required to produce 67 parts of bromine.

In 1952 an $8 million expansion program at Freeport resulted in about a 25 percent increase in ethylene dibromide capacity. The efficiency of the Freeport operation and its adjacency to the main tetraethyl lead manufacturing plants made unnecessary the Kure Beach plant, which had been maintained on a standby basis since 1942.

Almost coincident with the considerable expansion of operations at Freeport, Ethyl acquired a plant in Orangeburg, South Carolina, the Wannamaker Chemical Company, which was distinctive in both operation and administration. The firm had been founded in 1937 by T. E. Wannamaker, a man of endless ideas and strong opinions, a native of Orangeburg, who had graduated from the Citadel and then from Cornell University, where he earned a Ph.D. degree in chemical engineering. Still an "unreconstructed Southerner," as he describes his mood at the time, he suffered two more years away from home working with Eastman in Rochester, New York. Then he returned to Orangeburg and, with the help of friends, constructed a small laboratory on his father's farm on the edge of town. To quote Wannamaker, "We built the building with our own hammers and saws." The shoestring operation which first concentrated on a dye intermediate, developed into an important wartime producer of a booster for high explosives. Looking ahead Wannamaker saw that he must diversify for economic self-protection and thus he moved into broader areas. Ethyl was one of several larger companies that contracted with Wannamaker for the production of special chemicals. In 1953 Ethyl bought the plant and arranged for

Wannamaker, now under the corporate title of T. E. Wanna-maker, to continue managing the operation for Ethyl. The total Orangeburg production was soon going to the new owners.

The multipurpose plant at Orangeburg was built to be flexible. The equipment, much of it glass-lined and stainless steel, was not restricted to the making of a single product but could be readily shifted from one project to another. In the course of time the Orangeburg plant, with improvements in process and expansion of equipment, not only retained its experimental character but became a resource for smaller batches of special chemicals, and, if need be, an auxiliary supplier of basic products.

The better to serve the West Coast, Ethyl early established sales and research facilities in that region, notably an office-auditorium building in Los Angeles. The original office-auditorium building occupied in 1938 was razed because of the construction of a freeway, and a new one was occupied in 1951. As already noted, a testing and research laboratory was established in San Bernadino in 1935.

It was not until the 1950s that Ethyl decided to build a tetra-ethyl lead plant in California. The new plant, on a seventy-five-acre tract about halfway between Pittsburg and Antioch along the San Joaquin River, was opened in 1958. Its first manager was James M. Gill, who had been with Ethyl for about ten years. Gill is a native of Ruston, Louisiana, where he spent his youth working at a newsstand and delivering papers as all American boys are supposed to do. He attended Louisiana Tech, graduating with a B.S. degree in chemical engineering. After approximately a year with Armour and Company's pilot plant at the Chicago Stockyards and service in the navy during World War II, he took postgraduate training at Louisiana State University, earning the M.S. degree in chemical engineering. He says the simple reason that he came to work with Ethyl is that he married a girl from Norwood, Louisiana, and wanted to stay in that part of the country.

At Ethyl he was attached to the research and development department, benefiting by a rotational management program. From research and development he moved directly to head the maintenance organization. Later he served as manager of various chemical operations and in the fall of 1956, about the time the decision was made to build the plant in California, he was chosen to attend the Harvard advanced management program. Subsequently he went to California to supervise the construction of the antiknock plant and to manage operations, remaining there from 1957 to the closing of the plant in 1964.

By way of review it may be recalled that with the beginning of operations in California, Ethyl had chemical plants in the United States at five locations: near Pittsburg, California; in Baton Rouge, Louisiana; in the vicinity of Houston, Texas; in Freeport, Texas, for the extraction of bromine from seawater; and in Orangeburg, South Carolina, the versatile plant acquired in 1953. These production units served customers and each other more effectively because of improvements in the methods of delivering their products and bringing in raw materials. Storage facilities were dramatically increased, and new cleaning processes provided a more rapid turnaround of containers. While there were considerable advances in the methods of land delivery, there were revolutionary changes in the system of delivery by sea.

After the first experimental years, the pattern of delivery by land was a combination of drums, tank trucks, and railway tank cars. In 1930 Ethyl put in service the first of what became a large fleet of company-owned tank cars. The number was increased from time to time, by 1950 totaling 365, by 1960 almost 750. Most were in the 6,000-gallon category. All were built to insure maximum safety. They were easily recognized by their code letters EBAX, standing for "Ethyl Brand Antiknock," plus the letter X, the designation in railroad vocabulary for "privately owned." The first of the special cars put in service was the EBAX 300, which was retired at the expiration of thirty years of accident-free service. After criss-crossing the country many dozens of times and taking antiknock fluid to both Canada and Mexico, one of its last adventures was to deliver Ethyl fluid via ship to the Shell refinery in Cuba.

The Cuban mission of EBAX 300 was one small part of a series of innovations in the delivery to overseas markets. Beginning in January 1957, tank cars filled with tetraethyl lead were put on special ferries and shipped to Cuba, where they were hoisted by cranes, put on railway tracks and moved a short distance to the Shell Oil Company refinery near Havana. Next year, 1958, there was a further innovation through development of the sea-land service in which 2,200-gallon tanks were loaded on C-2 ships.

In late 1960 or early in 1961 a Texan, A. B. Horn, Jr., and his coworkers concluded that an improvement should be made in the methods of shipping tetraethyl lead overseas. Horn, who eventually achieved an important role in the export business, was born in Corsicana, Texas, on March 4, 1923. After completing public school he attended Virginia Military Institute, enrolling in September 1940. He left the institute to enter the armed services early in the spring of 1943, spending three years and nine months in the army. He was discharged in August 1946, entering the University of Texas the following month. After two academic years he received a bachelor's degree in chemical engineering. He was awarded a master's degree in 1949. He is very frank in saying that he came to Ethyl because the only other good job offered him was dominated by a man he didn't like.

In a rare and unexpected moment of self-revelation, Horn explained that whatever drive he possesses originated in a little Texas town dominated by the newly rich, who had provoked in him that aggressiveness.

When Horn and those working with him concluded that a better method of overseas delivery was needed, they sought for a new kind of vessel. Eventually, with the approval of the Ethyl Coordinating Committee, Horn developed the idea of a small specialty chemical tanker equipped to haul only antiknock compound. The first ship chosen was a dry cargo vessel of approximately 2,000 tons that was converted into a specialty tanker and then called the *Chemical Trader*.

Horn says that because of the earlier mistakes of another company, it was "a bloody nightmare" to get the *Chemical Trader* approved by the U.S. Coast Guard and by the British Ministry of Transport. The *Chemical Trader*, a chartered vessel, was owned in Nassau and registered in London. Foreign registration and ownership made possible a competitive operation; as is well known, such would not have been possible if the vessel were flying the American flag.

Improved methods of transportation had much to do with an

invigoration of foreign trade in this period. It might be added here that Horn, as project manager reporting to the vice president in charge of sales, aided in developing several significant contracts in the Latin American area, one of the earliest being with Daniel K. Ludwig, described by Horn as the "last of the U.S. billionaires." According to Horn he, Horn, "negotiated most of that deal riding from Battery Place up to my hotel on Park Avenue in the back of his [Ludwig's] Rolls Royce."

A great deal of thought was given to foreign trade in this period. As already suggested, technological as well as competitive changes at home prompted a search for new markets wherever they could be found. Someone has said that every time a jet airplane, which burned kerosene and needed no tetraethyl lead, was put into service, this was equivalent to taking 1,000 automobiles off the road. Ethyl officials sought to compensate by developing overseas trade.

Ethyl had no European market of any consequence in the early 1950s, in part because of a combination of common market restrictions and protective devices, such as tariffs in those countries having tetraethyl lead plants. In the late 1950s, however, Ethyl did obtain a fair amount of business in Europe, the decisive item being tetramethyl lead, which, as will be noted more particularly later, Ethyl was the first of the antiknock companies to manufacture. There was a technical distinction between tetraethyl and tetramethyl. When used with certain base stocks, the tetramethyl, even though more expensive on a pound-for-pound basis, was more economical in the long run. Associated Ethyl in Great Britain, which developed into something of a lusty and competitive stepchild, did attempt to get into tetramethyl and eventually succeeded, but not until after Ethyl had obtained a favorable though modest foothold in Europe.

Thus, over the years a competitive situation evolved not only at home but abroad as the 1945 revocation of the exclusive license agreements with Associated took full effect. Officials at Ethyl privately estimated that in 1960 Ethyl took away from Associated Ethyl (soon renamed Associated Octel) about 5 million pounds of antiknock business; in 1961, 12 million; in 1965 about 5 million. Much of this was tetramethyl lead going to four Esso refineries in Europe, to Caltex in Holland, and to Stanvac in Australia and Indonesia.

Associated Ethyl, now in the role of competitor, on July 1, 1961, changed its name to Associated Octel Company. In that same year Ethyl bought back from Octel the Ethyl trademark for $15,000. Officials at Octel were very reasonable about the whole thing, although, according to Julian Frey, "They had us over a barrel."

As a competitor Associated Ethyl/Octel could hardly be called benevolent, and yet by all reports this onetime ally of Ethyl observed the decencies of the situation. It not only released to Ethyl the tradename "Ethyl" but refrained from litigation to force Ethyl to carry out the supply agreement during a period of scarcity and allocation.

As has already been suggested, Associated, by the very location of its plants, enjoyed advantages over Ethyl in the European market. Not long after the end of World War II, Associated Ethyl took over the operation of the tetraethyl plant built in Great Britain in 1939. During the war both the tetraethyl lead plant and the bromine plant constructed in the United Kingdom had been owned by the Air Ministry. In 1945 British Ethyl Corporation, by then wholly owned by Associated, bought the British tetraethyl lead and bromine plants. Operations were soon taken over by Associated.

Although England, France, and Italy had active manufacturing plants in this period, West Germany did not. The factories at Gatel and Frose had been dismantled. Between the end of World War II and the spring of 1949 high octane gasoline needed in West Germany had been imported already leaded. Beginning late in 1949 a small quantity of tetraethyl lead came into West Germany from America, but the lead import business was dominated by non-Americans during the 1950s.

However, as a result of conversations with Julian Frey in the export sales department of Ethyl Corporation, Oscar Tiemann of

Hamburg obtained in 1962 a regional distributorship of Ethyl's petroleum additives. At the moment there were no large plans for energetic movement into the European markets; Tiemann apparently concentrated on antioxidants and similar additives.

Vigorous competition took place in those Latin American areas once reserved for Associated Ethyl. There were sharp differences in the supply and service techniques as carried out by the two companies, and Associated experienced a measure of unhappiness as Ethyl varied from the pattern of somewhat limited service which Associated had developed in the period of its dominance in the Latin American areas.

The story of Ethyl in Canada and Mexico has a measure of continuity, because these countries were never included in that territory designated for Associated Ethyl in those years before the supply contract was canceled in 1945.

In Canada a distribution and service system that had been severely upset by World War II was reestablished and improved in 1949 through the formation of Ethyl Antiknock, capitalized at $50,000, a wholly owned subsidiary of Ethyl Corporation. The principal Canadian office was in Toronto, a city that had been the headquarters of Ethyl representatives since they first entered the Canadian market. The purpose of the newly formed corporation was to furnish Canadian oil companies with essentially the same products and services the parent company had been supplying to the petroleum industry in the United States. The general sales manager and the vice president of the new organization was William M. Turnley.

When considered simply on the basis of the $50,000 capitalization, dividends returned to the parent company in the four years 1950–53 appear quite adequate; they ranged from $100,000 to $190,000. But Shea felt that these returns in no wise reflected the full potential of the Canadian market.

On August 10, 1954, the Ethyl board approved the construction of a new plant in the area of Sarnia, Ontario, at an estimated cost of $14 million and with a capacity of 20 million pounds of tetraethyl lead per year.

To produce and market antiknocks in Canada, a new company, Ethyl Corporation of Canada, was established under the laws of the Province of Ontario in 1955. Ethyl Antiknock was dissolved and its assets were taken over by the new company. Ground was broken the same year, 1955, and the plant, located in the area called Chemical Valley near Sarnia, was completed in 1956. This was the first authorized tetraethyl lead plant on the continent of North America outside of the United States, and it was the first of its kind in Canada. The formal dedication of the plant on June 5, 1957, featured an address by the Canadian minister of trade and commerce, C. D. Howe.

As indicated in an earlier chapter, there had been for years favorable and comfortable contracts with the Mexicans. And yet until about 1950, Ethyl gasoline could be purchased only in the area of Mexico City. Then the oil administration of the Mexican government provided for more general distribution of this premium-grade motor fuel. By the late 1950s, however, Pemex, the Mexican government's petroleum administration, decided that it wanted an antiknock plant within its own borders. A major problem in the extensive negotiations between Ethyl and Pemex was a Mexican law that limited the outside partner to 49 percent of ownership, an arrangement unsatisfactory to Ethyl's owners, especially to General Motors, which was against any involvement that left Ethyl in a minority position. Pemex preferred Ethyl over all other candidates for partnership, but neither side would yield on the matter of the 49 percent. Then Pemex turned to DuPont, which was willing to accept the Mexican terms. This change in the Mexican market meant a loss in sales for Ethyl of about 10 million pounds of tetraethyl lead per year. These developments in Mexico constituted one phrase of the uncomfortable situation facing Ethyl management at the end of the decade of the 1950s.

The Japanese trade was almost as old as tetraethyl lead antiknock itself. As early as 1927 Ethyl made a shipment to Japan through Assano Busam, later called the Totsu Company. The business grew, and by the mid 1930s the Japanese market was considered an important outlet. During World War II Japan attempted to manufacture its own tetraethyl lead and, in terms of pounds produced, succeeded in a small way, but in the process reportedly killed 16 or more operators. At one time over 40 percent of the workers in the tetraethyl lead enterprise were suffering from lead poisoning.

After the war Ethyl developed a close association with the Japanese oil industry, first helping to dispose of a widely dispersed quantity of contaminated tetraethyl lead. Ethyl soon succeeded in reestablishing its position as a leading supplier of tetraethyl lead and by 1961 was contributing over 60 percent of all the tetraethyl lead used in Japan. Ethyl Corporation gave technical assistance to the Japanese petroleum industry and even brought some of the technicians to this country for training.

An important element in the postwar expansion of trade with the Japanese was the work of C. D. (Nick) Carter, another one of those ever-appearing characters who with modest beginnings contributed significantly to the development of the company. Working as a sludge, or truck, technician in the United States, he was sent to Japan after the war where he showed a rare brilliance in negotiating. Incidentally, he earned the reputation of being the best-dressed man in any gathering. And he became a great collector of oriental objects.

Carter had a thorough understanding of Japanese manners and the way the Japanese government made decisions. His appreciation of Japanese character is clear in comments he advanced in conversation with Malcolm P. Murdock in November 1960, when Carter was asked to outline the qualifications desirable in an Ethyl man who would supervise the work in Japan. Although his comments were described as hurriedly written, they show a rare perception and wisdom in outlining desirable qualifications for the Ethyl representative in a joint enterprise, Mitsui-Ethyl. There are several such traits: (1) This man should have no prejudice as to race or religion, and indeed he should refuse to discuss such controversial subjects. (2) He should be both quiet and polite, because to the Japanese a loud voice is a sign of anger. (3) He should be so adept at negotiation that he would never take a position from which a compromise could not be developed, because Japanese business is based on compromise. (4) He should have infinite patience to discuss before deciding. (5) He should have both understanding and acceptance of the fact that in Japan certain things are different; these things may seem illogical but they ought to be accepted. (6) He should not be a heavy drinker or too interested in the fair sex. (7) As for the wife of the man, by way of background it should be noted that Japanese wives tend to stay at home and take care of their home and husbands. Japanese middle-aged women dress in quiet style and colors. The Japanese tend to resent an American wife who is a crusader and social climber. (8) A "too hardy or rough a character" is not well accepted. The back slapper is not welcome because the Japanese don't touch each other except when necessary. Indeed they are not prone to use first names unless this is insisted on, and even then probably they don't enjoy that familiarity. (9) The Ethyl man should be well versed in sales policies and be able to make decisions on his own, because he will be 7,000 miles from home. (10) The decision must be right or appear to be right every time, or else he will "lose face." Carter added that it would be helpful if a man showed calmness in times of crisis. The desired person probably should come from sales because the people in that group are more conditioned to handling delicate situations and at the same time to maintaining friendships. There would be a manufacturing man busy with the plant and training and he would come home after the Japanese had learned their lessons in manufacturing techniques.

As will be indicated later, Carter's knowledge of the Japanese situation meant that in the post-1962 period he would be called on for advice in various circumstances dealing with oriental affairs.

Research and Development

Ethyl could maintain its primacy in a competitive market only through a consistently aggressive program of research and development. It should be recalled that the original basic research division was in Detroit. In Baton Rouge there evolved certain research and development operations closely allied with the manufacturing division.

The first research quarters at Baton Rouge were primitive but cozy. The original laboratory consisted of one large room with a small room adjoining. The research people all worked together, and in an intimate kind of arrangement ate lunch at a table in the middle of the large room. During the lunch break some would play chess, some bridge, others penny-ante poker. Those poker players were not so venturesome as the term *penny-ante* might suggest. They used Louisiana tax tokens; the aluminum variety was worth a tenth of a cent, the brass ones half a cent. In its earliest form the small congenial group consisted of about fifteen laboratory people plus a dozen or so support engineers. The unit remained of limited size for several years.

In 1954 a new plan of organization gave more formal status to the Baton Rouge research group. In the division of responsibilities the Detroit Laboratories continued to be in charge of that research dealing with the automotive field. Baton Rouge carried forward the research and engineering on the remaining chemical problems. The physical facilities in both research centers were expanded. At Detroit new wings were put on the basic research building, the better to house engineering and chemical laboratories. At Baton Rouge the research group moved into larger quarters with about a dozen rooms. Even this housing proved inadequate, and immediately after World War II there was a new two-story addition that doubled laboratory facilities.

As for nomenclature, the original Baton Rouge research group was called the "technical development division of the manufacturing department." Subsequently it was given the title "research and engineering," then "research and development."

The development group at Baton Rouge operated with three basic objectives: First, to discover a cheaper way of producing tetraethyl lead, in particular to see whether a continuous process would be an improvement over the batch process, which had become the standard Ethyl procedure. Second, to see whether an antiknock better than tetraethyl lead could be discovered, this a continuation of the old pattern of defensive research. Third, to explore the possibility that some business other than antiknocks might be built on discoveries that the Ethyl scientists had already made.

The outcome of the investigation of batch versus continuous process was that every time the pilot plant operating a continuous process did well, a comparison with the batch process in the plant showed that there had been so many improvements in the batch process that the difference between the two was not significant enough to warrant capital outlay.

In the 1950s the research and development teams at Ethyl made notable advances in the antiknock field. They improved formulas for the tetraethyl lead compound; they created an allied compound, tetramethyl lead, with distinctive and useful qualities, as already mentioned in connection with foreign trade; and they discovered a novel antiknock additive, a straw-colored, stable organic compound of manganese that at the time seemed to be the most promising innovation of all. This last, known chemically as methyl cyclopentadienyl manganese tricarbonyl and temporarily in the market place as AK-33X, was announced late in June 1957, along with the report that tests in airplane engines showed a power gain of as much as 20 percent.

The prime use of the manganese compound, the first new antiknock with commercial possibilities discovered since the tetraethyl lead revelation of 1921, was as a booster for the tetraethyl lead compound, though the manganese compound was remarkably effective when added to gasoline as the sole antiknock. Indeed when injected into certain basic stocks it was twice as effective as tetraethyl lead on a weight basis. The patents obtained for AK-33X were 2,818,416 and 2,818,417. The manganese compound in later years was given major if momentary attention when tetraethyl lead came under severe attack.

The tetramethyl lead (TML), quite like the tetraethyl lead in composition and performance, is distinctive principally because of its volatility and its thermal stability.

New mixes, some involving the use of both tetraethyl lead and tetramethyl lead, offered to refiners seeking to satisfy the octane requirements of the newer automobile models, resulted in allied improvements such as removing engine deposits and reducing surface ignition. A widely accepted product called "motor plus" had as its innovative feature more ethylene dibromide. The tetraethyl lead and tetramethyl lead mixes went under the general category of MLA, meaning mixed lead alkyl formula.

More freedom was given the manufacturers when in 1959 the surgeon general approved an increase in the maximum allowed for tetraethyl lead from 3 cubic centimeters per gallon, which had been established in 1926, to 4 cubic centimeters.

Most conspicuous and least successful of the major attempts to move away from the "one-product" label was the effort to develop and market an agricultural chemical that went under the trade name "Lindane" (benzene hexachloride). The project from pilot plant to liquidation went on for about five years, 1948–53, and cost the company by its own reckoning over $4 million. Lindane left in its wake a research and development group slightly less self-confident but much wiser. The apt phrase given by one of the participants is that they all had *grown* a lot in the process, though he admits this was a very expensive learning technique.

The company entered the benzene hexachloride business in an understandable way. Apparently in examination of the volatilities of ethylene dibromide and ethylene dichloride, Bartholomew and his group saw that the volatility was different from that of tetraethyl lead. In working for what they called U.V. (uniform volatility), they were attempting to change the bromine and chlorine compound to something closer to tetraethyl lead, and in the process of doing that they came up with a compound very close to the agricultural chemical. In the refined operation of the pilot plant the results were termed "beautiful." But the Lindane factory never operated efficiently.

The writing-off of the whole deal was signaled at the meeting of the directors, November 2, 1954, when it was decided that the project was uneconomical and undesirable and that the assets should be disposed of. This was a fiasco even worse than the Ethyl Cleaner project.

Why had the Lindane project come a cropper? A composite answer, one developed from the testimony of several participants, adds up to about the following: first, the pilot plant program was inadequate; no one kept accurate records of materials used. One critic says there was absolutely no material balance at all. Thus the data from the pilot plant were not authentic. Next, much of the equipment in the commercial plant was quite different from that used in the pilot plant. Indeed, the design of the commercial plant was simply speculative rather than based on hard data from a good pilot plant operation. Also in retrospect, critics contend that in the commercial plant there was an attempt to develop a continuous process for making something that should have been made by a batch process offering the flexibility inherent in that process. Also, the salespeople discovered the hard way that selling just one product in the category of agricultural chemistry was too expensive; for economical distribution there should be a whole family of allied products.

There was apparently nothing wrong with the product itself, which was effective as a broad spectrum insecticide and readily destroyed a variety of pests; the problem was in production and marketing.

What was the impact of all this on the Ethyl Corporation? Did the Lindane misadventure and the earlier Ethyl Cleaner fiasco have anything to do with the reluctance of top management to accept much deviation from the one-product formula? The general opinion of those who lived through this period in the history of Ethyl seems to be that while these failures may have been mentioned from time to time, they were of no significance in the determination of management to preserve the "one-product" program largely intact. It has been suggested that while the Lindane episode was not a major factor in developments that eventually led to the sale of Ethyl, it was one of several minor items that convinced General Motors it was time to get out of its last joint venture.

As already suggested, there is general agreement that several important people *grew* tremendously in this experience. Participants are very specific about naming those who displayed greater ability and wisdom after this event. The experiment with benzene hexachloride not only meant a growth in personalities, but in a sense it provided a base for a research program initiated later on in what is generally called the agricultural chemical business. It seems to have been Bynum Turner who made the tough decision to give up the Lindane project.

Almost a year after the decisive meeting of the board of directors on November 2, 1954, a survey was set in motion and representatives of product development and of research and engineering were told to review the company's growth opportunities for the next decade. The members of the team undertaking that project interpreted their instructions to mean that, in addition to considering the natural growth of the tetraethyl lead business, they should think about "attractive offshoots which should be explored by Ethyl." The survey group was headed by Dr. Clarence M. Neher.

Neher, always known in the company as "Doc," was born in Twin Falls, Idaho, May 14, 1916, and received his higher education at Macalester College, which awarded him the A.B. degree in 1937, and at Purdue University, where he earned the M.S. in 1939 and his Ph.D. in 1941. In that same year 1941 he joined Ethyl, working in the research division. Of special importance in connection with the question of new products was his appointment as director of commercial development in 1957, a post that permitted him to exercise his imagination and enthusiasm, talents with which he is plentifully endowed.

In their report the study group included, among other items for development toward commercialization, the manganese project, already mentioned, and also the idea of a two-hour tetraethyl lead manufacturing cycle. They added that to strengthen the corporate base there should be an entry into "these natural offshoots of our present business," offshoots that included additives such as synthetic lubricants. The survey team looked with favor on polyvinyl chloride. The team presented its material in chart and diagram form, with a clear indication of the judgment of the group as to what were the *best* projects, those *borderline*, and those *poorest*.

Doc Neher's charts and diagrams provided him with reasoned arguments in the direction of expansion and diversification for many years, but immediate results were less than encouraging.

Rumors and a Growing Unhappiness

While the owners of Ethyl permitted a modest expansion into new products, their basic policy was to restrict the company almost exclusively to the field of antiknock additives or products closely allied thereto. This curbing of diverse production was peculiarly upsetting to a group of lively and ambitious scientists who felt they were being isolated from the "golden age" of the chemical industry, as that harvest time from the end of World War II to the early 1960s has been designated.

As the years went by, the researchers had become quite numerous. Although only a handful in the mid-1940s, the research unit rapidly expanded until in the early 1950s it numbered about 700.

These were bright people chosen from elite graduate schools and elsewhere who had been attracted to Ethyl not only by its liberal pay scale but also by its reputation for giving the researchers a large amount of freedom to experiment within a broad area of chemistry. In contrast with most of the chemical companies, Ethyl was thought of as benevolent and not always on the back of the laboratory people urging them to produce something of immediate commercial use. Charmed by the novel freedom offered in a corporate research laboratory, many of the young scientists enamored of their self-selected programs went through a season of almost lyric professional happiness.

Then came frustration. When this wide-open research did lead to something with commercial possibilities and with a promise of diversification in the Ethyl product line, usually some excuse was found by top management for putting the product aside and turning the researcher in other directions. Time and time again requests to move into pilot-plant and market-research phases were turned down. The evidence is overwhelming in this matter.

The main opposition to Ethyl's diversification into chemical ventures other than antiknocks came from Jersey; General Motors seemed not to care one way or the other, and thus the Jersey sentiment dominated. Jersey had its own chemical research group and the officials of that corporation did not think it prudent to encourage Ethyl to go ahead with the development of new commercial projects, the profits from which would come only 50 percent to Jersey. Why not encourage the same products in the Jersey laboratories, the profits from which would come 100 percent to Jersey?

The late Monroe Jackson Rathbone, head of Jersey Corporation during the period under review, said to this historian that the two main reasons for the sale of Ethyl were the fear of some antitrust action by the federal government and the impending conflict between Ethyl and Jersey research and development activities. "Well we didn't want [Ethyl] to move into new fields because of the direct conflict [with] our own. As far as we are concerned we weren't willing to have them branch out. This was actually the reason we eventually wanted to sell out, because we saw where we were going on a collision course. And if they [Ethyl researchers] went out broadly, well then, they immediately collided with Jersey's research, and we were researching in a most broad basis in the whole hydrocarbon field. So these are the two things that really influenced us very much."

One should not forget Rathbone's point that Jersey's objection to diversification in Ethyl was also based on the thought that if Ethyl developed and marketed products similar to those produced by Jersey, there was the risk of antitrust accusations.

Inevitably the question arises as to why Ethyl ever permitted such a large research group to exist and allowed the individuals free-ranging, but not commercial, research and development. The answer most often given is that such an arrangement was necessary to be certain that competent technical and professional people would always be on hand to insure a broad-gauge department. The budding scientists could not concentrate on anti-knocks with enduring enthusiasm, so went the official line.

The signals that Ethyl was going to remain primarily a one-product company came at various intervals over the years. There were earlier signals, as already suggested, but apparently the first major rebuff to those seeking diversification occurred in 1947, just before Webb relinquished his role as chief executive officer. Expansion-minded staff members wanted Ethyl to get into vinyl chloride, used in the making of plastics. The supporting research had been completed and a pilot plant had been successfully operated. Then to the dismay of Ethyl scientists the project was ordered discontinued. Jersey wanted no part of it. The 1947 veto sticks in the minds of many of those reminiscing about this period. As will be noted below, ten years later the project was revived, this time successfully. But old-time Ethyl people still bemoan that lost decade.

A notable denial came in 1951 and 1952, when it was evident that DuPont and Union Carbide would be required by the federal government to release their polyethylene licenses. Ethyl's search group proposed that a large polyethylene business, 50 million pounds or so a year, should be set up. This was turned down because of Jersey opposition.

There came a period of three or four years—approximately from 1954 to 1957—when many individuals in the research group developed a new enthusiasm for work with organometallics and became less attentive to diversification. Several events occurring about the same time contributed to the shift in mood: the failure of the Lindane project; the news of the Ziegler process for making tetraethyl lead, a procedure which appeared to threaten Ethyl's primacy in tetraethyl lead technology; and Ethyl's success in the creation of the manganese antiknock additive (MMT). The impact of these developments caused a major though temporary reorientation of interest in Ethyl's laboratories.

A close observer of this particular scene was Paul E. Weimer, who had joined Ethyl as a chemist in 1949 and before the sale to Albemarle became director of chemical research and development in Baton Rouge. Weimer was involved in the Lindane program. He says, "My wife still refers to this as the lost summer. I volunteered to take the twelve-hour night shift." And then he and a colleague were sent to Zurich, Switzerland, in 1954 to hear Dr. Karl Ziegler, a German professor, give his first public lecture on his new method of making tetraethyl lead. (It was a concept that, as will be explained more particularly in chapter 9, eventually led to Ethyl's major involvement in the aluminum alkyl business.)

The period of new enthusiasm for research surrounding organometallic chemistry ended with the realization that no dramatic breakthrough into a grander antiknock era was likely. The once promising leads fizzled and again key individuals turned their thoughts to diversification and suffered the frustration of trying to move into new fields.

A decisive disappointment came immediately after what otherwise might have been considered a break in the dike that had been holding back the development of new products. In 1957 when a revised vinyl chloride program was accepted by management and its owners, two officials had dinner with Frank Sergeys, a research scientist, and told him that this was to be the last of the major diversifications. Several of the more advanced scientists simply pulled up stakes and left the company. Among these were Paul McKim and Frank Sergeys in the Baton Rouge group. Apparently that announcement at the dinner party of 1957 was the event that pushed Sergeys into his resignation. He then went to work for W. R. Grace and Company, much later returning to Ethyl in a senior advisory role.

While several of the top-ranking scientists left, most remained; but morale was low. One of the most frustrated in the research

group was a young man named M. F. Gautreaux, whose irritation was no less than that of his seniors. Gautreaux, who eventually became head of research and development of Ethyl
Corporation of Virginia, was born January 17, 1930, in Nashville, Tennessee, the only child of Louisianians whom Gautreaux describes as "a couple of migrating Cajuns." His father,
who had little formal education, was in the lumber business where
he was quite successful, working his way up to the top, and the
top was in Nashville, where he had arrived just in time for his
company to go broke in the crash of 1929. Then the elder Gautreaux managed a grocery store in Old Hickory, Tennessee, a
chemical center right next to Dupontonia. Young "Bim" Gautreaux simply soaked up chemical language. As he says, "I guess
80 percent of my father's friends were chemists or chemical engineers." As he grew up Bim Gautreaux rode horses well enough
to participate in horse shows (his father had everything from a
sway-back mare to three-gaited and five-gaited horses). And young
Gautreaux played golf particularly well, scoring an impressive
sixty-nine (one under par) in a high school tournament. He attended high school in Nashville and subjected himself to the
discipline of editing the school paper for a couple of years. This
experience he considers great because in that assignment he learned
to write.

His father died as Bim was finishing high school. Young Gautreaux and his mother were left with very little, the family income being about $100 a month. In perspective Gautreaux says
that all in all he had great good fortune. Until he finished high
school he enjoyed the benefits of upper-middle-class living, the
country club, golf, horses, and that sort of thing. Then in a sudden turn of events he had to face up to some rough reality for
about five years. Gautreaux had long since determined that he
wanted to attend a good chemical engineering school and settled
on Louisiana State University because of its reputation in chemical engineering and because the costs were reasonable. He and
his mother bought a tiny trailer adjacent to the Louisiana State

University campus, and Gautreaux felt that he had the best of two worlds; he was at home and yet convenient to all college resources.

Circumstances required that he discipline himself and plan carefully. He had a rugged five years, not artificially created. He insists that if the situation had been contrived it would not have been as impressive. He had the good fortune to get a job in the school library, and he undertook some private tutoring, mostly in mathematics and chemistry. He doubled his family income with those side jobs. Furthermore he joined the ROTC, and for drill and summer camp received a small monthly stipend. He protests that he "was poor and didn't know it." He benefited by the sobering influence of the serious returning war veterans and by several great professors, including Jesse Coates and Bernard Pressburg. His college grade average was 3.9, and in 1950 he graduated magna cum laude with a B.S. degree in chemical engineering. His master's degree, obtained in 1951, was based on a thesis more creative than his later doctoral dissertation.

He came to Ethyl principally because of the influence of Paul McKim, whose name has been mentioned earlier in connection with the withdrawal of major scientists from the company. Gautreaux worked for Ethyl from 1951 to 1955, earning at the same time most of the additional hours he needed for doctoral course work. During these years he worked for a while on the Lindane program.

Gautreaux then decided that he wanted to return to university life, and he taught at Louisiana State University from 1955 to 1958. He received his doctorate and returned to Ethyl in 1958. It was then that he suffered the aforementioned frustration. He had developed a project, oxichlorination of ethylene to make ethylene chloride. Gautreaux explains: "It is the way you make vinyl chloride out of HCL instead of out of chlorine." He had worked diligently on the program. "We spent many an eighteen-hour day on that project. We got it completed and we brought it to the Jersey-GM board and *nothing* happened. The only person that I know of who was very bitterly disappointed about that, in fact downright angry, was myself. I was genuinely put out."

The unhappiness of Gautreaux and like-minded research people, an unhappiness characterized by Gautreaux as the "doldrums," coincided with the downswing of profits and severe cost-cutting measures everywhere. These were, as others had put it, indeed "critical times," a painful feature of which was the laying off a goodly number of workers.

This unhappiness radiating out from the research and development group was one of the several features that gradually persuaded Jersey and General Motors to dispose of their joint property, the Ethyl Corporation.

In 1958 discussion between Standard Oil Company of New Jersey and General Motors Corporation as to the desirability of making a change in the ownership of Ethyl became a matter of record. A representative of General Motors made inquiry of Jersey about the possibility of a change, and Jersey created an informal study committee to consider the question. The executive committee of Jersey heard a report from this study committee and then sent word to General Motors "that the company is not at the present time interested in taking the initiative to alter the ownership of Ethyl, but that in the event General Motors plans some action with respect to changing the ownership therein, the company would wish to reconsider the matter in the light of such proposed action of General Motors."

In response to this equivocal statement from Jersey, a spokesman for General Motors went a step further and affirmed the intention of his company to take some action to modify the ownership of Ethyl. Jersey eventually agreed that changes should take place.

Nowhere in the available records is there a definite and persuasive calendar of the owners' real reasons for their decision to sell Ethyl. On May 10, 1961, O. K. Taylor of Jersey, in considering the possibility of a public sale of Ethyl stock, addressed the question as to how the companies might best explain such a decision to sell. He came up with a halfhearted answer, "Antitrust considerations and 'elimination of an unrelated business' would seem to be the most cogent reasons we could muster, although the former could not be spelled out in the prospectus."

With the advantage of years for reflection, today one accepts Taylor's points as valid but incomplete. At the risk of oversimplification, it may be said that the major forces that pushed General Motors and Standard Oil of New Jersey to the point of sale were two: the fear of federal antitrust action and, more especially, the decline in Ethyl's profits. On a subordinate level Taylor's "elimination of an unrelated business" is quite acceptable, as are several other factors which might be briefly reviewed before a return to the major points.

Since the mid-1940s General Motors had pursued a policy of ending joint operations of any kind; a partly owned project should be either taken over entirely by General Motors or sold. Obviously, the chemical industry was now far from the mainstream of General Motors operations. As for Jersey, its management recognized that there was a certain liability in its ownership of Ethyl because Jersey's rival refining companies were not overenthusiastic about buying from a corporation owned 50 percent by Jersey. And, as already suggested, Jersey was discovering something contradictory about having both an energetic group of research and development chemists within its own organization and a parallel group in a corporation it half owned.

Returning, then, to the major issues: the threat of antitrust action by the Department of Justice was never overt, but the danger was easily recognized. This is a situation recalled with full clarity by the late Monroe Jackson Rathbone, then head of the Jersey corporation. As is well known, both General Motors and Jersey had suffered inquiry and litigation at the hands of the federal government.

Undoubtedly the most important of the factors encouraging the owners to dispose of Ethyl was the fact that profits had been declining since 1957, and private forecasts suggested further decline. Net profits for 1957 totaled $29,660,730; in 1961 they had dropped to $24,369,868. The earnings for 1962 were expected to be only $18,200,000. Ethyl's share of the North American sales dropped from 100 percent in 1947 to about 55 percent in 1960, and this despite intensive efforts by the sales people. In terms of pounds Ethyl sales had declined from 362 million in 1956 to 300 million in 1960; in a look ahead, the forecast for 1965 was 250 million.

Why this decline? By 1961 competition was coming not only from DuPont but from Houston Chemical, later acquired by PPG Industries. Nalco Chemical Company would soon enter the picture.

And as already stated, there were changes in the types and quantity of fuel needed in the new transportation pattern, changes that dampened the hopes of all antiknock producers. Note the increasing importance of the jet airplane, diesel trucks and buses, and smaller cars. Furthermore, there continued to be improvements in manufacturing techniques that permitted refiners, if they chose to subject themselves to extra costs, to step up the octane number appreciably without the use of tetraethyl lead. This last fact gave birth to the statement that Ethyl's greatest competition came from its own customers.

Although new energy was eventually put in foreign sales, Ethyl's non–United States market was threatened by several events. As early as 1955 Associated Ethyl appeared able to take care of its market needs through its own plants. As already noted, DuPont embarked on the venture of manufacturing tetraethyl lead jointly with the Mexican government, and Ethyl thereby was losing the south-of-the-border business which had amounted to about 10 million pounds per year.

If the owners wanted to change, what were the various options? An analysis of memorandums passed around within and between the two companies shows that these proposals were in the air: (1) General Motors to buy the Jersey shares; (2) Jersey to buy the General Motors shares; (3) the capital stock of Ethyl to be distributed by the two owners to their respective stockholders; (4) Ethyl Corporation to go public, all shares being sold in the open market; (5) Ethyl to be "mutualized," meaning the sale of Ethyl to its customers; (6) Ethyl to retain its basic form but diversify; (7) a third party to purchase the stock of either of the two owners; (8) a third party to purchase the stock owned by both of the two owners. Obviously the eighth alternative was the one finally settled on.

Neither General Motors nor Jersey was inclined to buy out the other; neither ever made the other a realistic offer. General Motors was reluctant to get into a business different from its major interest; Jersey, while tempted, was fearful of antitrust action. Furthermore it knew that if it achieved sole ownership of Ethyl there would undoubtedly be a loss of trade since some major oil companies, even then reluctant to funnel profits to Jersey by way of Ethyl, would shift their tetraethyl lead purchases to other manufacturers.

Gradually attention became centered on negotiations with third parties, who the owners hoped would be willing to pay a fair price. There were conversations with the major chemical companies, Union Carbide, Monsanto, Dow, and others, but offers from these, when they came, were well below what the owners considered adequate.

During 1961 extensive negotiations took place between the owners of Ethyl and representatives of the Hunt Oil Company of Texas, negotiations that set in motion a decisive series of events. An important intermediary was Walter Buchanan of Ebasco, the engineering consulting firm that several years earlier helped plan the expansion of the Albemarle properties at Roanoke Rapids.

Apparently it was in the first months of 1961 that Buchanan, an engineering graduate of Virginia Polytechnic Institute, heard of the new mood of the owners of Ethyl. Virginia-born of Scottish ancestry, Buchanan was widely traveled, broadly acquainted, and possessed of an inquiring mind and a forceful personality. Since 1954 he had been employed by Ebasco. Somehow alerted to the discussions between Jersey and General Motors, Buchanan in a discreet way talked with several Ethyl officials. He sensed certain uneasiness as they viewed their prospects.

Buchanan then approached the family of H. L. Hunt, the Texas oil magnate, first directing the information about Ethyl to Hunt's sons, W. Herbert and Nelson Bunker. Buchanan told them he thought they could buy Ethyl and was authorized to investigate further, which he did. Robert Herzog, William Perdue, and George Kirby, important Ethyl officials, went as far as they appropriately could in answering questions. Buchanan and the team of Ebasco investigators looked over fences, took photographs from the ground and air, examined all written data they could discover, and finally came up with an estimate of $200 million as the value of Ethyl. After a preliminary meeting with Leo D. Welch of Standard Oil of New Jersey, Buchanan arranged for Herbert Hunt and John Goodson, one of the financial officers from H. L. Hunt Company, to talk with representatives of General Motors and Jersey on Thursday morning, August 10, 1961. After introducing the parties one to another, Buchanan withdrew to leave the discussion up to the principals.

Herbert Hunt announced interest in buying Ethyl in order to diversify the Hunt holdings and asked several straight-forward questions as to number and location of plants. He was furnished with documents, including financial statements for the preceding five years. There were additional meetings. Finally H. L. Hunt himself came into the negotiations and presented a plan that in effect meant buying Ethyl Corporation using money borrowed from the owners. This proposal was coldly received by the owners, but potential buyers were scarce, and the owners were inclined to keep up negotiations with Hunt. Jersey representatives were returning to the idea of bargaining with General Motors in an attempt to persuade it to take over.

By the middle of December the elder Hunt had lost what interest he had. Apparently just before the Christmas holidays there was a Hunt family conference that proved to be the point of no return. On December 21, by way of terminating negotiations, H. L. Hunt telephoned Marion Boyer of Jersey, first using the word *temporarily* when referring to withdrawal from the bargaining table, but on questioning he defined the word to mean that

Jersey and General Motors should go ahead with any other plans they had.

If the representatives of the owners were somewhat disappointed, Buchanan was crushed. He and his aides had worked hard. The chance to have a major role in working out a multimillion dollar deal with its attendant rewards to himself and his company seemed to be disappearing. Sick at heart when reviewing the situation, he remembered a statement made by F. D. Gottwald some time earlier to the effect that he, Gottwald, was interested in chemical acquisitions. While Buchanan could not join his daughter and son-in-law in Richmond for Christmas Day, he decided he would make the visit a few days later and see if the Gottwalds were interested in acquiring Ethyl.

Buchanan and his wife ostensibly were celebrating the holidays with their daughter and son-in-law, Kathleen and Royal E. Cabell, Jr. This Cabell was the son of the man who was Albemarle's counsel for many years. At Buchanan's request the Cabells had invited the senior Gottwalds to come to the Cabell home for a social hour on the evening of the day the Buchanans arrived. Soon after the Gottwalds appeared at the Cabell house on Sleepy Hollow Road in the far west end of Richmond, Gottwald and Buchanan retreated into the library, where they were closeted for several hours during which time Buchanan unfolded to Gottwald the Ethyl situation as it had developed up to that time. Apparently this conversation took place Friday, December 29, 1961.

Part Three

ETHYL
OF
VIRGINIA

VII

Jonah Swallows
the Whale
1962

Gottwald's Decision to Buy

AFTER GOTTWALD was apprised of the breakdown of negotiations between the owners of Ethyl and the Hunts, he turned
the matter over in his mind, judging that this might be the major
purchase he had been seeking. And then at a family dinner Gottwald asked his sons if they would like to buy Ethyl. The question
was a revival of small talk initiated on a plane trip from Baton
Rouge to Richmond three and one-half years earlier. Both Bill
and Bruce said yes. At this dinner or soon thereafter Gottwald
underscored the absolute necessity for secrecy; otherwise the whole
effort would come to nothing. It was Mrs. F. D. Gottwald, Anne
Gottwald, who suggested the name Rachel to be used instead of
Ethyl. Thus Rachel became the code word, not only in family
conversation which might be overheard but even in the office of
Hunton and Williams when the principals were referring to Ethyl.

Gottwald's first move was to discover everything he could about
Ethyl Corporation, and this meant employment of Ebasco to
continue its investigation. In the process Buchanan received written
permission from the Hunts to use materials that earlier had been
accumulated by Ebasco. Subsequently, Albemarle reimbursed the
Hunts for payment they had made to Ebasco for the exploratory
study.

The more Gottwald studied the data, the more certain he was that here was the opportunity of a lifetime. He was especially impressed by the untapped potential in Ethyl's brilliant research group, eager to produce something to supplement their prime product. Gottwald himself was now all for diversification.

Did Gottwald realize that the sale of tetraethyl lead might continue its decline? The answer he gave was yes. He added, "Two things we knew: that the antiknock business was a good foundation for ten years anyway; and, secondly, that there couldn't possibly be anything but inflation in the American economy. The result is that we borrowed $200 million for a $200 million purchase. I don't hesitate to borrow money for something that is going to pay for it [self]."

Robert Herzog, who in those days had many discussions with the Gottwalds about the future, is certain that they were aware of the various factors that might depress sales. Floyd D. Gottwald, Jr., in recalling the days of negotiation said that the sellers of Ethyl of Delaware were open and honest about the lead problem. "I think they told us everything they knew about it at the time and we recognized the problems."

When recounting the events of 1962, Herzog uses a phrase that must not be lost: "He [F. D. Gottwald] may have had more faith in Ethyl than Ethyl had in itself." At times the senior Gottwald almost convinced himself that the trend in Ethyl's sales of tetraethyl lead would be turned around. In light of later events, it is curious that whatever pessimism existed about the future of tetraethyl lead was based mostly on factors other than the health issue. For several years there had been rumblings about air pollution (a topic to be reviewed in chapter 9). However, in the private memorandums and recorded remarks of the buyers and sellers one finds scarcely a hint of the coming attack on the additive as a health hazard.

When looking at Ethyl, Gottwald saw it not as a one-product company. He envisaged it as a diversified chemical empire. To quote Lewis F. Powell, Jr., "The one great optimist was Floyd Dewey Gottwald, Sr. He had the vision, imagination, and determination that made his dreams a reality. He not only believed the acquisition was feasible when no one else did; he also thought of Ethyl not as a static, ever shrinking tetraethyl lead company but as a base for a great chemical empire."

Negotiations with the Owners of Ethyl

The eleven months from December 30, 1961, to November 30, 1962, provided a drama that has been told many times, often under such a title as "Jonah Swallows the Whale." The late Monroe Jackson Rathbone, Jersey's president at the time of the purchase of Ethyl by Albemarle, invented another: "It was like a Mom and Pop grocery buying the A&P!" Extravagant language is appropriate, for the Gottwald team did borrow $200 million and did buy a company at least five times the size of Albemarle. There were key individuals who, working with F. D. Gottwald, made possible this coup that amazed both Main Street and Wall Street. These allies were essential in the success of the venture, though all acknowledged that Gottwald was the principal architect of the new structure; his unflagging optimism carried Albemarle's financial advisers and lawyers forward when affairs at times looked bleak.

Beyond the gathering of more facts about Ethyl, the first effort was to obtain an ally and intermediary in the highest financial circles of New York City. There may have been one or two small gestures elsewhere, but Gottwald's initial conversation of any importance was with an acquaintance at Chase Manhattan Bank.

This was John Bridgewood, Jr., vice president and trust officer, a splendid and competent gentleman of the old school, who almost went into a state of shock when the three Gottwalds spoke of borrowing a couple of hundred million dollars or some such sum. Bridgewood's first verbal reaction was "impossible, impossible." By the next day, however, he was encouraging the Gottwalds to do what they were about to do anyway after testing the waters at Chase Manhattan: to have a talk with the officers of Blyth and Company, the investment house that, as mentioned earlier, helped in the financing of the Dixie Queen in 1958 and even circulated a brochure entitled "A Study for Investors on Albemarle Paper Manufacturing Company." No cautious editor could quite blot out the bullish tone of the publication.

The relationship between Albemarle Paper Manufacturing Company and Blyth and Company is essentially the relationship between two men, F. D. Gottwald and James F. Miller. Their careers have something in common: modest beginnings and considerable advance in the financial and business world. Miller is an authentic American type. His grandmother rode in a covered wagon from Missouri to Oregon in the nineteenth century, and Miller started with Blyth as an office boy making $12.50 per week. His superiors soon saw that he was gifted with a nimble mind and an unflagging spirit.

When he moved from the West Coast to the New York office, a colleague urged him to become acquainted with F. D. Gottwald, saying, "I think he is a man who is going to do great things for his company." Miller liked Gottwald and he liked the convertible debentures being offered by Albemarle in 1958. Miller borrowed the money and bought $100,000 worth. Thus there was not only a professional but a personal interest in whatever was being presented by F. D. Gottwald.

All parties remember the day Gottwald first approached Miller about Ethyl. Miller had boundless energy and an imagination that blended with Gottwald's. And Miller had something Gottwald did not have: as a senior officer of Blyth, Miller had entree into the top business circles of the country. Albemarle was not only looking for an ally in its search for money but for an intermediary in the high priority assignment of approaching the owners of Ethyl to see whether they would sell.

That famous day when the three Gottwalds visited James Miller was quite cold. The Richmonders threw their coats on the chesterfield and warned Miller that when they finished telling him what they had in mind he would probably have them ejected from his office. Gottwald was armed with figures showing the

financial situation at Ethyl. According to Gottwald's recollection, "Miller never said a word while we were telling the story."

The more Miller studied the sheets given him by Gottwald,
the more he was convinced that it was quite possible to work out
the deal. As he recalls the conversation, he said, "I really honestly think something can be done from this base. You've got a
very interesting thing here. You've got a very substantial cash
flow, and when you have a cash flow of this magnitude you can
sometimes do interesting things. I'm willing to work on it."

In recalling those days, Gottwald gave full credit to Miller.
"Without Mr. Miller I am dead sure it could not have been done."
Then he added unexpectedly but quite truthfully, "But of course
without Mr. Gottwald I don't think it could have been done."

It is evident that Miller took the prime responsibility for Blyth's
share in the negotiations. However, he had as his allies several
vigorous personalities at Blyth, including Frank Mansell and Paul
Conley, each of whom eventually earned the top office at Blyth.
Protocol demanded that the then president of Blyth, George Leib,
be in general agreement with the enterprise. Thus there was a
luncheon and Leib's first reactions were all negative. Finally on
the elevator when going back to the office Gottwald said in effect,
"Mr. Leib, tell me if this is too big for you and we will go somewhere else." At that point Leib gave his consent. There is some
evidence that at the outset Leib may have seen Gottwald as
something of a promoter rather than a solid businessman. Leib
did call Marion Boyer, who was not only a Standard of New
Jersey officer but a director of Ethyl, in an attempt to prepare the
way for subsequent negotiations by Miller. Obviously the first
responsibility of Miller was to determine whether the owners of
Ethyl of Delaware, General Motors and Jersey, would sell to Albemarle and, if so, at what price.

Although the proper decencies were observed, courtesies exchanged, and friendships developed, the ensuing negotiations were
marketplace transactions, as they were intended to be. Each side
was careful not to give full exposure of its own position. The

owners of Ethyl avoided disclosing the depths of their pessimism, warning staff members not to summarize the company's dismal forecasts. On its side Albemarle was not revealing just how much it already knew about Ethyl and the pains it had expended to obtain a better view of Ethyl's resources, both actual and potential.

The darkest gloom hovered over Ethyl's management and the high officials of General Motors and Jersey early in 1962. The year just ended was the fifth consecutive year in which tetraethyl lead sales had declined. Direct competition was worse than it had been, and because of the increase in the octane level now being obtained by oil companies in their refining processes, there was a further slump in the amount of tetraethyl lead needed for gasoline.

Thursday morning, February 8, 1962, Miller approached the owners of Ethyl about a possible purchase of Ethyl, with the explanation that the plan was to merge Ethyl with Albemarle Paper or vice versa. It was probably at this time that the initial jockeying over price took place. Miller recalls that on being prompted by the owners he came up with a tentative offer of $135 million, which evoked such compliments as "good try" and the statement that Ethyl was worth at least $200 million. Each side was testing the other.

At the conclusion of the initial conference Miller was assured that the owners would reflect on the whole situation, but they somewhat bluntly indicated, so that Miller would entertain no false beliefs, that they felt no obligation even to call back. Negotiations between the owners and other possible buyers were being continued at the time of Miller's first visit. Dow Chemical, apparently in January, had suggested $150 million as a possible purchase price. Then, reviving earlier thoughts, Jersey was considering purchasing for $77 million the shares owned by General Motors. The General Motors response was to try to exert a bit of leverage on Jersey by noting Miller's offer. Jersey would not join in a serious consideration of Albemarle as a purchaser until it, Jersey, made another tender, this still in the neighborhood of $77 million. General Motors answered that the sum was unsatisfactory since Ethyl was worth about $200 million.

Some elements in the Ethyl management and owner groups were getting a bit panicky by March. One officer recommended a quick public sale because the earnings were continuing to decline.

With Miller on the doorsteps as it were, there was an energetic reanalysis of the whole situation. As late as March 21, 1962, Jersey and General Motors representatives again discussed several alternatives, including such variants as a sale to General Motors, a partial sale to Jersey, and the creation of a new chemical company. Jersey promised that it would give further consideration to buying or isolating the chemical business of Ethyl, and there were plans again to approach Dow. It was stated at that meeting on March 21 that if a public sale was seriously considered, it should be effected soon; that is, before Ethyl's earnings deteriorated much further. As for Miller, it was agreed that the Dow possibility should be settled before he would again be seen. It is clear that no favorable response came from Dow.

By the first part of April, General Motors and Jersey appeared to be in agreement that Albemarle was the best bet. Albemarle's small size might invite problems in raising all the money the owners wanted, but this very smallness made Albemarle an attractive buyer. As Monroe Jackson Rathbone, president of Jersey at the time of the sale, explained in conversation with the present author, Albemarle was the most "innocuous" of all potential buyers, and the whole affair would be absolutely clean; nobody could say that antitrust laws had been violated.

The beginning of constructive negotiations should be dated April 5, 1962, when Miller again met with representatives of General Motors and Jersey. Miller was given financial statements for 1957–61 and additional information, but he received no help when he asked the fair value of plant and equipment. He was told that this was his problem. After Miller left the April 5 meeting, an important simplification occurred. Jersey withdrew its offer to buy the General Motors stock. When the meeting was restricted to representatives of the two owners, there was some difference of opinion as to what the 1962 income would be, especially in light of action that might be necessary to meet the competition from Houston Chemical, which had only recently gone into the antiknock business.

Exactly a week after that significant April 5 meeting, that is, on April 12, an information session was held in Miller's office at Blyth and Company, Fourteenth and Wall streets, with representatives of the owners in attendance. Miller asked questions, some of these involving forecasting. The owners evaded by simply saying that this was a very difficult thing to do. Miller asked about key people who might leave Ethyl if management was changed, but the owners minimized this possibility. By the next day, April 13, various data were passed along to Miller dealing with book values, the six-year operating statement, a report on the Orangeburg activities, and a listing of products other than antiknocks headed by vinyl chloride that were being developed. By the last of May the two parties, the General Motors and Jersey group on the one hand and Albemarle on the other, were settling down to talk about dollars. A key meeting was scheduled for May 28, 1962. Before the arrival of Miller, Jersey and General Motors representatives spoke of the possibility of a public sale if the figures they had in mind proved too high for Miller, who had recently offered only $150 million. When Miller entered the meeting he was told that $150 million was not satisfactory; the owners would consider $180 million. Miller said that this figure did not frighten him and that he would think about it.

Despite these specifics, the Albemarle negotiations at this time had certainly not passed the point of no return. There was still discussion of the possibility of a new organization to be called Ethyl Chemical Company, having no representative from Jersey on its board. Some optimist thought he saw new interest expressed by Dow.

On May 31, 1962, Miller was given permission to talk with Bynum Turner, president of Ethyl. Miller was told that the appraisal of plant facilities was not available. An important point in the negotiations was reached when, on June 1, F. G. Donner of General Motors, recommended to his conegotiators acceptance of the Albemarle offer if it would be raised to $180 million with Jersey agreeing to purchase 50 percent of its tetraethyl lead requirements from Ethyl for a ten-year period.

Officials of the parent organizations concluded that it was about time to report directly to the Ethyl upper management what was going on. Accordingly, on June 13 Mangelsdorf of Jersey told Herzog of the information that had been given to Miller. Representatives of Ethyl were instructed that they could give oral forecasts but nothing in writing to Albemarle negotiators. A bit later a Jersey official wrote this memorandum: "Deal doing well— going into questions of future of lead additive business. I gave him no help on the question."

During the month of July a few ripples appeared on the surface, ripples that might have developed into waves rough enough to wreck plans to sell Ethyl to Albemarle. From Paris, Frank Howard suggested the sale of Ethyl, or a part of Ethyl, to the Octel group, once Associated Ethyl. He even spoke of tearing down two plants and reerecting them in Cologne. Also just about this time Edward Shea, former president of Ethyl, was reported as saying that he could have formed a purchase group if he had known that Jersey wanted to sell. Jersey's willingness to sell surprised Shea since he had been told several months earlier that Jersey wanted to *buy*.

Affairs were coming to a head. On August 1 at Gottwald's request there was a meeting of representatives from Albemarle, General Motors, and Jersey. Albemarle representatives offered to buy all shares of Ethyl stock based on a valuation of $181.4 million. At the same time they agreed that a cash dividend of $65.0 million representing earned surplus would go to General Motors and Jersey in advance of sale, making the sum due the owners at closing approximately $116.4 million. Accompanying these proposed terms was Albemarle's request that Jersey for five years buy from the new Ethyl at least 60 percent of the tetraethyl lead required by Jersey's operations in the United States and Canada.

According to several memorandums made at the time, the rule-of-thumb for figuring the sale price of Ethyl was book value plus $100 million. With relatively minor modifications the foregoing terms were embodied in the eventual and formal purchase agreement; by the time closing documents were prepared, the sum due the owners had been set at $116,366,264. And Jersey had agreed under a five-year arrangement to buy from the new Ethyl not less than 54 percent of the lead antiknock compound needed by Jersey's U.S. affiliate and a higher percentage needed by its Canadian, Venezuelan, and Aruban affiliates.

By September 7 George Russell, vice president of General Motors, was recommending to his finance committee that the sale to Albemarle be within the general framework of the August 1 proposals from Albemarle, and that General Motors accept subordinated notes as a fractional part of the purchase price. The board resolution approving the sale was dated September 19, 1962.

As negotiations with the Ethyl owners seemed to be progressing, Gottwald felt that he should give his directors formal notice by way of preparing them for possible definitive action. And he had to alert attorneys for assignments they might be asked to carry forward.

At the first news of the proposed venture the Albemarle directors could hardly believe what they were hearing. To quote Gottwald, "We had the most skeptical bunch of directors that ever was in kingdom come. They said, 'It is impossible for you to do anything like that.'" Never forgetting the rebuff he received when he made the Hummell-Ross proposition about twenty years earlier, Gottwald was determined that he would have no rejection this time, and planned carefully. Of course he had a board of his own choosing, but he was resolved that everything would go smoothly.

The first recorded statement to the board as a whole was made July 18, 1962. Gottwald briefed the meeting at length on negotiations that the officers of the company had conducted with the two Ethyl stockholders over the previous several months. Statistical exhibits were displayed on a large piece of high-gloss laminated blotting paper that showed the financial statements of both Ethyl and Albemarle for the previous several years, and a projection of future earnings and cash flow based on the data at hand. At this meeting board members were told of the continuing advice coming from Ebasco and from Blyth. A progress report was made on July 27, the emphasis being on the proposed bank loans. There was also a statement that definitive negotiations were planned for August 1. The board authorized continued negotiations. At the September 8 meeting the shift to a new financing was explained, the major lenders being three life insurance companies. At this time there was approval in principle, subject to later formal resolution.

By September it was necessary to bring attorneys into the negotiations. It will be recalled that in 1950 Royal E. Cabell, the main attorney for Albemarle, died, and Lewis F. Powell, Jr., had been engaged as counsel. He was a partner in Hunton and Williams, as the firm for convenience will hereafter be designated, though the abbreviated title was not officially adopted until 1976. He operated under the team concept, and by 1962 Lawrence E. Blanchard, Jr., and Joseph C. Carter, Jr., were his major colleagues. The team had been conditioned to Gottwald's sometimes unusual financing, a scrambling of sorts that would have shocked many legal firms in the country. During the summer of 1962 the Gottwalds and Joseph M. Lowry, treasurer and director, reported the possibility of purchasing Ethyl, but the lawyers were accustomed to such reports and were tempted to put this new plan in the category of those many proposals that had never worked out.

Early in September, Blanchard, who was vacationing at Virginia Beach, ran into F. D. Gottwald and learned that the Gottwalds were quite optimistic about the Ethyl situation and were planning serious meetings in the near future. Then Carter called Blanchard to explain that negotiations between Albemarle and the Ethyl owners were about to begin and that Blanchard should return to Richmond and prepare to go to New York on Monday, September 10.

The Halifax Conference

It was now necessary to bring buyer and seller together for formal confrontation. At this point in the negotiations Standard Oil of New Jersey took the lead as seller. For tax purposes Jersey officials wanted to conclude the agreement in Canada; therefore, representatives of Albemarle journeyed to Halifax for a meeting on September 12, 1962. Here was high drama seasoned with a pinch of comic opera.

The Albemarle team for the Halifax encounter consisted of the three Gottwalds, Lowry, and James F. Miller plus three lawyers from Hunton and Williams: Lewis F. Powell, Jr., officially chief; H. Brice Graves, a specialist in tax questions; and Lawrence E. Blanchard, Jr. Blanchard had been dropped from the list temporarily and sent home because two senior partners of a major New York firm were scheduled to go, and five lawyers seemed somewhat extravagant. However, the prestigious New York firm concluded that its members could not properly represent Albemarle in negotiations with Jersey, since from time to time Jersey had been a client of the firm. Blanchard, admittedly a bit downhearted on his departure from New York, immediately and happily returned from Richmond to make the trip to Halifax. As assignments were being rearranged it was thought that he would be doing most of the legal work in New York, and thus he should be present at that key meeting with the Jersey representatives in Canada.

At the Halifax meeting the Jersey representatives went through the formality of repeating an earlier understanding to the effect that Jersey would give consideration to a sale price of $100,000,000 in excess of book value, plus 1962 earnings up to the date of sale, less 1962 dividends up to that same date. As already indicated, the resultant sum eventually worked out to $116,366,264.

The chief negotiator for Jersey was H. W. ("Bud") Fisher, vice president. To quote Blanchard, "The meeting was one of the most amazing I have ever attended." Fisher with unexpected candor pointed out that Jersey and General Motors were now convinced that Albemarle had a good chance of raising the money. Fisher expressed great satisfaction from the fact that a sale to Albemarle would be free of any taint of violating antitrust laws. He added that, for the deal to go through, a rigid time schedule must be maintained. The arrangement was supposed to be concluded in two months, though he conceded the possibility of some small extension. Fisher also indicated that Jersey and General Motors each would be willing to take $10 million of subordinated notes as part of the purchase price.

Confronting the Jersey representatives in Halifax, Gottwald was at his persuasive best, modest but self-confident. He gratefully acknowledged the cooperative attitude of the sellers and assured all within hearing that he believed the deal could be closed within the time limits specified.

The Halifax meeting was notable not only for certifying the foreign locale of the negotiations between Albemarle and Jersey but also for originating colorful narratives soon translated into folklore. The Albemarle delegation could obtain only one room at the single first-class hotel, for there was a convention of Kiwanians, noisy but friendly people. In this room Albemarle's two senior negotiators, F. D. Gottwald and James F. Miller, were quartered. The rest went to Dartmouth, a seafaring town, where they found rooms at a hotel down on the waterfront. Many tales have flowed from this rather primitive structure with a rope fire escape and other amenities. A teasing group of Richmonders vowed that Lewis Powell never recovered from the indignities he suffered that night.

Fisher reported to the executive committee of the Jersey board that the Halifax meeting had resulted in an agreement in principle to a sale within the terms approved by the committee. Accordingly, the Jersey executive committee authorized the signing of whatever documents were necessary or desirable. Conversations parallel to those carried on in Nova Scotia were held with General Motors in mid-November and an equivalent understanding was reached, the way having been paved by the favorable resolutions of the finance committee in September.

Miracle in the Money Market

Fortunately for Gottwald he had a staff conditioned to the unusual. At the outset of negotiations, when Lowry was approached by Gottwald and asked if he would object to going into large-scale financing, maybe borrowing a couple of hundred million, Lowry simply shrugged his shoulders and in substance said, "No, it doesn't bother me; it's just adding three more zeroes." Floyd D. Gottwald, Jr., admits that when he first heard the negotiators refer to a sum "give or take a million dollars," the remark shook him up a bit. But the Albemarle group adapted quickly to the Wall Street way of doing business and at times even persuaded Wall Street to try the Albemarle way. Lowry put financial projections on some old kraft paper from the Hollywood Mill and carried the exhibit around Wall Street. When he pulled out those kraft paper exhibits, according to Joseph Carter, "those New Yorkers would look at him and laugh. They didn't know what they had run across. But the things almost hit it on the nose."

The team of financial negotiators consisted primarily of Gottwald, his two sons, Joseph Lowry, and James Miller, the latter assisted by two of his colleagues from Blyth and Company. As for Miller, he was the intermediary, or "buffer," as he describes his role. And in truth his imagination was a powerful asset. As for the Albemarle lawyers, after they returned to New York from Halifax they associated themselves with the Debevoise firm, then Debevoise, Plimpton, Lyons, and Gates, with which the Richmonders had become acquainted during the 1958 debenture financing when the Debevoise firm represented Northwestern Mutual and New England Mutual. In the Hunton and Williams team Blanchard was full-time in New York City. Powell operated largely in Richmond, where he had to assume not only responsibilities to Albemarle but to other clients. Joseph Carter, the "swing man" helping Blanchard in New York City and Powell in Richmond, worked on the loan and warrant agreements, and particularly on the charter amendments for Albemarle. In the middle of the whole operation it was realized that someone had to monitor the timing of the various steps and to work out minute details; thus John W. Riely joined the group.

The Richmond contingent, lawyers, financial negotiators and all, needed residential headquarters in New York, and Gottwald decided to take a post at the Waldorf. The rooms used most of the time were those in the Waldorf Towers, suite 42-H, consisting of a well-decorated living room, a dining room, three bedrooms each with twin beds, and what had been in former days a maid's room with a single bed. Incidentally, Lewis Powell first off chose the maid's room. Occasionally the group when out of the city released the suite, and when the men returned they sometimes had to spread around the hotel or in nearby hotels for a few days until they could become reestablished.

The typical routine of the Richmond group was a breakfast with the Gottwalds in their quarters, breakfast often dominated by creamed chipped beef, a favorite of some of the members. Occasionally the meal was punctuated by a serving of yogurt to Bill or Bruce Gottwald, a circumstance that provoked much teasing by the other people who complained of the disappearance of appetite. In the evening dinner at the Bull and Bear restaurant in the basement was the occasion for recital of the defeats or triumphs of the day. Pessimism outweighed optimism in many of the sessions. The dinners at the Bull and Bear became legendary among the waiters and bartenders.

September 12 is a convenient line of demarcation in outlining the total negotiations. As the time schedule in the Record Book indicates, a new phase of negotiations began on that date. "September 12—October 8, negotiations by Albemarle with the lenders and meetings with appraisal firms." In general, up to September 12 there were negotiations with owners as to the price. After September 12 there were negotiations with lenders as to amounts and conditions of the loans.

In planning its strategy of borrowing and in making its schedule, the Albemarle group began fully to understand the magnitude of what it had promised to accomplish before a deadline that was eventually set as November 30. There was an intensive, at times almost agonizing, period of two months and more. In truth it was a cliff-hanger almost to the end; not until two or three days before the zero hour did victory seem assured.

The typical lender saw the most conspicuous symbols of uncertainty to be three: the high ratio of long-term debt to assets, the declining earnings in the antiknock business, and the unknown quality of Gottwald as a master of large enterprises.

As for the ratio of long-term debt to assets, the Albemarle group, citing an impressive cash flow, exhibited careful plans for servicing the long-term debt under a realistic program of year-by-year funding. (To anticipate the story, it may be said here that these plans were carried out in excellent fashion, the ratio of long-term debt to capitalization declining from 82.2 percent to 17.8 percent in the period from November 30, 1962, to December 31, 1981). The downswing of earnings in the antiknock business might be reversed, said the spokesmen for Albemarle. However, the decisive rebuttal here was the proposed program of diversification. As for leadership in the planned merger, key officials in both companies would be retained. And Gottwald himself seemed to grow in stature as negotiations progressed. As will be noted below, the leading negotiator for the subordinated debentures was convinced that Gottwald was the best possible choice as chief executive officer of the new Ethyl.

In analyzing the financing of the Ethyl purchase, one should consider the affirmative factors in the general investment community in the autumn of 1962. To quote Bruce Gottwald, "We just had real fine timing. It came at a time when the financial institutions had a lot of money. It would be impossible to do it today under the same circumstances: a small equity buying a very large company."

Initial reactions from lenders blended astonishment with skepticism. When Lowry talked with Langmuir of Northwestern, Langmuir first exclaimed, "Why don't you go to Las Vegas and get it over with?" Then he became serious and agreed to lend $10 million. Eventually, as will be explained below, Northwestern wound up lending more than that.

At the Commonwealth Club in Richmond one day in the middle of the negotiations with the lenders, Lowry advanced to Gottwald a sale-and-lease-back plan that would limit the Albemarle loss to $10 million should the new enterprise fail. Northwestern was willing to go along with this idea, but Prudential, then being approached by Miller, said no. In the vernacular, "It's the whole ball of wax or nothing." From that time on, the job that had to be done was clear. A full $200 million must be borrowed. Nothing less than a company with proper working capital and proper payment of outstanding obligations would satisfy the lenders. The key lenders spelled out in legal form a proviso that every dollar of the $200 million would have to be raised or they would withdraw from the arrangement. (See Appendix D, "Long-Term Debt as of November 30, 1962, and Its Purposes.")

Miller and his allies early proposed a structure of borrowing to be made up of several layers of obligations. Essentially the risk capital was to be superimposed on prime obligations. As Miller explains it, "The pattern to me was a pattern where you can enlist the muscle that was available, namely, the commercial banks, the insurance companies, on whatever equity you had, and then a layer of venture capital money, so to speak, a mezzanine or whatever you choose to call it, of a subordinated security that had equity features. That in this particular case created some subordinated debentures with warrants." Essentially the money was borrowed on the assets of the company being bought.

The first plan was to obtain the bulk of the loan from commercial banks. This fell through, though in the process Gottwald developed a new appreciation of the decisive thinking of the country's great bankers. Three banks were to be approached: First National City Bank, Chase Manhattan, and Bank of America. As Gottwald recalled the circumstances, "I was always proud of our relations with the Bank of America. We met the representatives of the Bank of America, I did personally in New York, and we talked for one full day as to how we proposed to handle it. Then we had dinner that night, and he [the chief representative of the Bank of America] insisted on California wine. So he told me he would give an answer the next day, and that was whether or not he would go along with lending me $60 million. I thought that was pretty good, to review a subject and give an answer the next day. So by ten o'clock the next day I had the answer 'yes' from the Bank of America."

In the original plan either the three banks, or a group of banks which the three would head, would make a loan equal to two-thirds of the sum needed, the other third to be a subordinated debt representing money put up by other lenders. This bank plan was the program outlined in detail by Gottwald to his directors on July 27, 1962.

Then came a disappointing verdict from First National City Bank, though Chase Manhattan and the Bank of America seemed willing to go along. This is the way Gottwald remembered the ending of the bank plan: "Well, the chairman of the City Bank was in Europe at the time, and he, as best he could from a distance, tried to understand the deal. He finally cabled back to the bank in New York that $20 million was the most that they could go along with. And that broke up the deal with the banks."

Note that in the final pattern Chase Manhattan, which had made loans to Albemarle in previous years, did obligate itself to purchase $16 million of one- and two-year obligations at 5.5 percent. Looking back on this situation, and in particular remembering the embarrassment of Albemarle in the late 1930s because of short-term bank loans, the representatives of Albemarle later felt that it was a good thing that this bank consortium plan came apart.

Then by early September a major effort was directed at the insurance companies. Prudential was the lead company here. Prudential, Equitable, New York Life, and Northwestern worked out satisfactory arrangements for taking a total of $114 million in sixteen-year 5.75 percent senior notes. In the ultimate formula of financing, the ratio of senior notes to total borrowing was almost exactly the same as that specified in the earlier bank plan: two-thirds in the first instance, 65 percent in the final version.

Then came two categories of 5.5 percent notes: $16 million from Chase Manhattan and $20 million from General Motors and Jersey, the former owners. And finally there were the $50 million of subordinated notes with warrants with interest on the notes at 5.75 percent.

The interest rates of 5.5 percent and 5.75 percent seemed at the time to be quite high, and Gottwald said, "We were embarrassed to death that we had to pay 5.75 percent for the original money. Sure would like to get [that] today."

The most complicated and most interesting of all the financing was the sale of the $50 million of subordinated debentures with warrants allowing the purchase of class B common stock at $27.50 per share, eight shares for each $1,000 subordinated debenture. Events were to prove that $27.50 was an extremely favorable price. Just as Prudential was the lead insurance company, the U.S. Steel Pension Fund was the lead in negotiating the terms of the subordinated debentures with warrants. Other investors well knew the care exercised by the managers of U.S. Steel's Pension Fund and more readily agreed to go into the subordinated note purchase.

In the disposition of those subordinated notes, the Gottwalds agreed to an eventual rearrangement of common stock so as to abolish the distinction between voting and nonvoting categories and thus to reduce their own voting strength. Eventually F. D. Gottwald seemed quite reconciled to this change, which he said would have occurred anyway when the new Ethyl applied for listing on the New York Stock Exchange. The leader of those recommending this change was the representative of the U.S. Steel Pension Fund, John McMartin. In truth, in 1962 these two strong gentlemen were having a series of tempestuous sessions, though they grew to like and to respect each other very much. It was Blanchard who, remembering a family saying, described the meetings between these two as "when hickory meets blackgum." Fifteen years after the event McMartin in reminiscing said: "Mr. Gottwald and I had a series of negotiations. I hesitate to think what he thought of me, but I know what I thought of him. I thought this man is the greatest and I want him to continue to be at the helm of the Ethyl Corporation."

Academic institutions found these subordinated notes attractive, among them Stanford University, Wellesley College, Yale University, the University of California, and Wabash College. The Ford Foundation took $3 million worth and Teachers Insurance and Annuity Association subscribed for $1 million.

The borrowing was not only the decisive factor in effecting the purchase, but also it provided the pattern for Ethyl financing in the years to come. To quote Blanchard, "The truth of the matter is that the basic financial structure that was set at the time of the acquisition is still essentially the same financial organization that we have. Our debts have been extended and renewed and we have borrowed some more money, but basically the borrowings have been from the same group of four lenders who loaned the major part of the money at the time of the acquisition. That is a long time ago and those basic agreements have stood the test of time."

These months of negotiations were strenuous and, no doubt, all parties were affected by the tension of the period. F. D. Gottwald probably was the calmest and the most optimistic of all. Early in the negotiations for the $200 million Gottwald was forced into a reflective mood by the necessity of addressing the Newcomen Society dinner in Richmond on September 27, 1962. On that occasion he read a paper entitled "Albemarle, from Pines to Packaging: Seventy-Five Years of Paper-Making Progress, 1887–1962." Gottwald no doubt drew strength and determination from rethinking the history of Albemarle and its survival of many crises. In the course of his remarks he acknowledged the importance of his fellow workers, a gesture quite appropriate then and quite as appropriate later in considering the purchase of Ethyl.

The months of September, October, and November constituted a period of stress and uncertainty for all those negotiating on the Albemarle team; it was a razor-edge proposition to the very end. In periods of frustration Miller had to force himself to keep up his enthusiasm. "I remember seeing on the television the Oscar Awards in 1962, and I thought, gee, if anybody deserved an Oscar in 1962, I did."

As Lewis Powell well recalls, the period of final negotiations coincided with the Cuban missile crisis. It was not until October 28 that an agreement between Kennedy and Krushchev to end the crisis was announced. The tension in the atmosphere was particularly trying on those in New York far away from their families and wondering whether the Cuban difficulty would lead to World War III.

Not all was agony; there were amusing events that eased the tension a bit. During these critical final weeks a conversation occurred in a taxicab in New York which Gottwald always relished reporting:

> *Well, just a few days ahead of it [the actual signing], while we were having our toughest time selling the last of the debentures, we had had a very rough day of it. In going on back to the hotel in the taxi, Jim Miller was riding with me, and he said: "The one hundred fifty million dollars [mostly] insurance money, that's in our pocket, that's sure. But as for this fifty million dollars of subordinated debentures; we need that fifty million dollars." And then, all of a sudden, both of us went forward like this in the taxicab; I went off my seat and Miller caught himself, and the taxi driver said, "Excuse me, gentlemen, but you know a taxi driver can't close his ears, and I've just been listening to what you're saying. Our first stop is at the Waldorf. Are you gentlemen sure you can pay the fare?"*

A few days before the closing date Blyth regretfully announced to the Albemarle group its fear that not all of the notes would be sold by November 30. The first thought was to go back to old friends at Northwestern. At a meeting in Richmond in Lewis Powell's office on a Sunday, the Albemarle group asked Lowry to return to Northwestern, see Langmuir, and try to sell him another million dollars worth. Here is Lowry's version of the outcome: "So I got on a plane and went on out there the next day.

Didn't have an appointment or anything, and called up when I
got to maybe Pittsburgh or somewhere, and Langmuir said, 'Were
you coming out here, by gosh, without even having an appointment?' and I said, 'Well I was going to find you wherever you
were.' So after talking about it long enough he said he would take
the million."

Lowry returned to New York at dinnertime and joined the Ethyl
group in the Bull and Bear restaurant. He reported, "Langmuir
is going to call me as soon as he talks to his committee, but he
told me he would do it." Whereupon Gottwald said, "Well you
go sit by the telephone and don't move until you hear from
Langmuir." The Northwestern committee did accept Langmuir's
recommendation and agreed to take the extra million.

There still remained some of the subordinated debentures to
be taken. Blyth and the Gottwalds said that they themselves would
pick up what was left. In fact, a document was signed on November 29 by Blyth and the Gottwalds, who agreed to purchase the
remaining notes provided the sum did not exceed $3 million for
Blyth and $2 million for the Gottwalds. Actually the notes picked
up by these "insurers" were less than the specified limits. Blyth
and Company did take a million and a half, and the Gottwalds a
million, but the lawyers required that the notes be "put on the
shelf" and not be bought by the insiders until after several days
of trying to sell them to other private purchasers. And they were
sold out in just a few days.

In the Bull and Bear and elsewhere there had been much ban-
tering about Lowry's caution to his wife, Margaret, not to have
the kitchen painted until the $200 million effort was successfully
completed. Finally came the low-key phone call, "Margaret, you
can now have the kitchen painted." Indeed, the last dollar had
been subscribed. Incidentally a good many other things were
changed. Not only did Margaret Lowry get her kitchen painted,
but Joseph C. Carter said he never would have bought a house
on St. Andrews Lane if it had not been for the Ethyl deal.

Although the Albemarle group was only dimly aware of the
fact, at the time of the negotiations, back in the wings and ready

to help if need be, were General Motors and Jersey. The point is now quite clear, but it was less so then. General Motors and Jersey wanted the deal to go through, and evidence is available to indicate they would have gone much higher than the $10 million in purchase money obligations that each had already agreed to accept if such were necessary. General Motors and Jersey liked Albemarle as a buyer and certainly did not want to start over again. Furthermore, they would not want to lose the sizable amount of money they had already invested in the lawyers. Repeatedly representatives of the company gave Albemarle a good rating when inquiries were made: "This is a good little company," or words to that effect. Often the question would come from Jersey or General Motors to the Albemarle people, "How are you doing?" Just how far did General Motors and Jersey go in a sort of quiet guarantee program? Monroe Jackson Rathbone, president of Jersey, said to the present author that, as well as he could recall, Jersey and General Motors really guaranteed the banks that they would not lose anything if loans were made to Albemarle for the purchase of Ethyl. The present writer has found no evidence of a literal guarantee by General Motors or Jersey to banks or insurance companies lending money for the purchase of Ethyl, but at the mid-November meeting of General Motors representatives and Albemarle, George Russell of General Motors made a remarkably candid statement to the effect that General Motors and Jersey were putting themselves in a position so that if it were necessary they could step in and purchase the last several million dollars of notes themselves.

C. Raymond Hailey, the Ethyl controller in Nova Scotia for the closing with Jersey, was joined by an assistant treasurer of the Standard Oil of New Jersey and a somewhat mysterious companion. "The president of a bank in the Bahamas had come along representing Standard Oil of New Jersey. We didn't know what his role was except that he was a part of the Standard Oil of New Jersey contingent, until after the closing. He had been authorized by Jersey to buy these debentures if it looked like they [the unsold debentures] were going to prevent this closing."

In sum total there was in the background a friendly disposition on the part of the sellers, once they had made the agreement and laid down the calendar. But, as already noted, the money was raised without the necessity of asking the sellers to take more of the obligations than the total of $20 million which they originally assumed.

Spreading the News: Arrival of the Great Day

Despite the discretion of the Albemarle management, the mere physical activity of key personnel set Richmond tongues wagging long before there was any public announcement of plans to purchase Ethyl. Promises to the sellers held up any public announcements from Albemarle until September 18, 1962, when a letter was mailed to stockholders informing them of the negotiations in process.

Astonished reporters and editors looked on the transaction as the greatest "leverage" of this type ever seen on Wall Street. Here was a little company taking over a corporation many times its size, the multiplier depending on what index was employed as a measuring stick, profits, assets, or sales. "Jonah swallows the whale" was a favorite phrase used by journalists and commentators. The whale motif became a permanent part of the recollection of these events; at the fifteenth anniversary celebration the Gottwald sons presented to their father a beautiful Steuben glass whale.

News reporters pressed Gottwald for statements he was not then prepared to make. Characteristically he treasured his privacy and simply admitted that he was unhappy about being questioned and photographed. An occasional journalist took affront at Gottwald's silence; most of the accounts were factual and fair. A nondramatic and informative article appeared in the New York Times September 23, 1962, describing Gottwald as a rare man of determination and tenacity. "Persons familiar with Mr. Gottwald and Albemarle think that if he sees possibilities in the Ethyl deal and wants to go through with it, he will find a way."

The most talked-about essay was published in the December

lbemarle Paper Surprises Wall St.

pany Planning
cquire Concern
Times Its Size

y **LARRY GOULD**
al to The New York Times.

(MOND, Va., Sept. 22—
', an imaginative entre-
r named Edward B.
raised some Richmond
.pital and combined it
1e paper-making skill a
.med James Lishman had
d from his father in
d.

result was the Albe-
Paper Manufacturing
1y, with a subscribed
of $22,000 when it was
ed.

y, Albemarle has assets
925,252, but if negotia-
1nounced this week are
ful, the company may
) raise $200,000,000, about
mes the amount of cap-
*. Thaw raised to start
cern 75 years ago.

um-size Albemarle star-
1ancial circles when it
ced last Monday that it
gotiating with two giants
rican industry, the Stand-
l Company (New Jer-
1d General Motors Cor-
n, for purchase from
f the large Ethyl Corpo-

t. caused astonishment
e size of Ethyl in com-
with Albemarle. Based
·nings, Ethyl, a manu-
r of anti-knock additives
soline and other fuel
inds, is nearly 18 times
ze of Albemarle. Albe-
has never had earnings
·e than $2,500,000. In re-
ears, Ethyl's regular an-
ividends were more than
es that. Ethyl's sales ap-
·ly are several times those
remarle, being $44,284,-
he year ended March 31.
observers wondered
Albemarle manage the
Vas some of it concerned
more financial heft in-
but staying in the back-

F. D. Gottwald

ground? What will Albemarle
do with Ethyl if it is able to
put the deal through?

The man who could provide
the answers was keeping quiet.
He is F. D. Gottwald, president
of Albemarle, who is leading
the negotiations for the purchase and who apparently is
trying to raise the funds to
cover it.

Persons familiar with Mr.
Gottwald and Albemarle think
that if he sees possibilities in
the Ethyl deal and wants to go
through with it, he will find a
way. He usually does. One
knowledgeable Richmonder, discussing the proposed deal, said:
"It's going through."

Mr. Gottwald has been in-
volved in a couple of disputes
with the City of Richmond, one
over the building permit for
Albemarle's new $1,500,000 of-
fice building here.

The big, white, colonial-style
building was erected on a hill
overlooking the James River,
providing Mr. Gottwald a striking view of Albemarle's sprawl-
ing manufacturing facilities
along the river.

President Is Silent
About Proposal to
Buy Ethyl Corp.

This summer, Mr. Gottwald
and the city were involved in
another battle over company
plans to expand one of its Richmond plants. Involved was the
city charge for accepting in its
sewage system additional sewage from the plant.

Mr. Gottwald said negotiations had "collapsed," announced plans to close the
plant and furlough most of its
60 employes. He did so.

Problems Noted

In a letter to stockholders
Thursday, Mr. Gottwald said
the Ethyl negotiations were undertaken "with a view to enlarging and diversifying" the
company's business. He added
that management was not now
in a position to provide "more
specific information" about the
negotiations.

Mr. Gottwald has spent much
of his time in New York recently, working on the negotiations, being handled by
Blyth & Co.

Some reports say Albemarle
is seeking to raise $200,000,000
to finance the purchase, with
the Prudential Insurance Company of America one of three
insurance companies in on the
planning.

Financial observers in Richmond believe that Mr. Gottwald
sees a chance to fulfill a long
standing desire to expand Albemarle into plastics and polyethylene packaging through the
purchase of Ethyl.

Some shrewd Richmond in-
vestors are known to have had
their eyes on Albemarle for a
long time, and Mr. Gottwald is
believed to be one of the main
reasons.

Company Watched

The company's stock, which
had moved up sharply in recent
weeks, sold as high as $50 a
share the day following the announcement of the merger negotiations.

Mr. Gottwald joined the company in 1918 as an office clerk,
later served as export manager,
production manager, assistant
secretary, secretary and executive vice president, before becoming president in 1941.

When he took over as president, the company's sales were
$3,940,000 and its net worth
$2,350,000. In the latest fiscal
year, sales were $44,284,000 and
net worth was $25,024,000. The
company has about 2,000 stockholders and 2,300 employes.

In recent years Mr. Gott-
wald has carried out a vigorous expansion program at Albemarle building up existing
facilities, building new plants
and acquiring other companies.

About eight years ago, the
company set up a division for
research and development. This
unit now has between 25 and
30 scientists, engineers and
technicians. A company spokesman said research is devoted
to improvements in paper
quality, new processes, new finishes and coatings for containers and to chemicals.

At a stockholders meeting
here earlier this year, Mr. Gottwald said the company looked
for "vigorous growth" in many
areas based on future expectations. He conceded, however,
that the company's profit position had not improved in recent years, despite an investment of about $26,000,000 in
new property, plant and equipment.

He said one of the main
causes was intense competition
within the paper industry, and
indicated that one way out of
this situation would be to get
into new lines.

Albemarle operates plants in
Ohio, New York, Virginia, and
North Carolina.

Mr. Gottwald, 64 years old,
is known as a hard worker. He
still finds time, however for
fishing, boating and gardening. Until 10 years ago, he lived
in an older section of town,
Fulton, but then he moved into
the fashionable Windsor Farms
section. He is still active in
the Montrose Baptist Church
in his old neighborhood.

1, 1962, issue of *Forbes Business and Finance* under the heading "High Finance: Jonah and The Whale." The account began: "It was, unquestionably, one of the neatest leverage deals Wall Street has seen in many a year. It was pulled off, not by any of the Canyon financial whiz kids, but by a curmudgeonish Richmond, Virginia, businessman with a passion for anonymity and an obvious flair for high finance. The dealster: Floyd Dewey Gottwald . . . Jonah was swallowing a whale more than thirteen times his own size."

Gottwald's friends resented the tone of the essay, especially the use of the word *curmudgeonish* in describing Gottwald. Employees, acquaintances, and family members joined in refutation and cited gentler characteristics of Gottwald, which they insisted included patience, kindness, and generosity.

Later, in reviewing the whole financial transaction the *Christian Science Monitor*, February 16, 1963, headed its essay "Ethyl Deal Tops 'Gee Whiz' Yarns," underscoring the sensational movement of the Albemarle/Ethyl of Virginia stock prices. Before the month of September ended there had been some trading at $50 a share contrasted with a low of $18 earlier in the year. In October the $60 per share mark was reached; later stock was exchanged at a price slightly above that.

At the gyrations in the over-the-counter dealings, suspicious persons began inquiring as to possible manipulations by "insiders." However, agreement among those in the Albemarle group forbade any such trading, and there was never valid evidence of misbehavior. As Gottwald explained, "We had an understanding between us that not a damn one of us could purchase a share of stock or else the corporation and the individual would get in trouble. Aside from this was the fact that after each individual saw how his interest would increase, why he was satisfied with that rather than to try to get out and add more."

To the generality of Ethyl employees the news came as a thunderbolt. They had been hearing rumors of an impending sale for a long time and had developed calloused ears. Gossip became so rampant during the first half of 1962 that manage-

FORBES

BUSINESS & FINANCE

HIGH FINANCE

JONAH & THE WHALE

With no money down and as many as 20 years to pay, Albemarle Paper has gotten itself quite a deal in buying big Ethyl Corp.

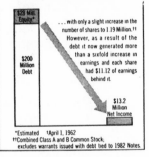

IT WAS, unquestionably, one of the neatest leverage deals Wall Street had seen in many a year. It was pulled off, not by any of the Canyon's financial whiz kids, but by a curmudgeonish Richmond, Va. businessman with a passion for anonymity and an obvious flair for high finance. The dealster: Floyd Dewey Gottwald.

Gottwald's little (fiscal 1961 earnings: $1.8 million) Albemarle Paper Mfg. Co.* was taking over the big Ethyl Corp. (1961 earnings: $24 million), the U.S.' biggest maker of antiknock compounds. It was doing so, moreover, with very little dilution of Albemarle's small (1 million common shares) equity. Jonah was swallowing a whale more than 13 times his own size.

Helping Albemarle pick up the tab were four insurance companies, a bank and several investment houses. Prudential Insurance Co. was putting up a large share of the $200-million purchase price in exchange for 16-year 5½% senior notes. The sellers: General Motors and Standard Oil of New Jersey, each of whom owned 50% of Ethyl.

The fiscal consequences of the merger would be explosive—to put it mildly. It would boost Albemarle's cash flow from $3.94 a common share to $18.04—even after allowing for exercise of 400,000 warrants issued as a sweetener to the investment house syndicate.

All in Favor. To be sure, neither Floyd Gottwald nor the Pru would say much about the acquisition last month. Gottwald simply presented his plan to shareholders, telling them

Floyd Gottwald

only what he had to. Stockholders quickly approved—the Gottwald family, after all, owns some 69% of the total common—54% of Class A and 15% of Class B.

Thus, much about the whole deal was unclear last month. But the basic arithmetic was intriguingly simple. Even after allowing for interest on the $200 million in debt, Albemarle would have earned something like $15.70 a share last year if the merger had been in effect—instead of the $1.46 it actually reported.

But there is even more to it than that. Ethyl's plant and equipment have been heavily depreciated over the years. Since Ethyl's plant, as part of Albemarle, the value of Ethyl's property can be written up to the full purchase price. So, next year (and in future years), the combined companies should be able to throw off some $15 million in tax-shelter cash from depreciation alone. The new amounts will be more than sufficient to meet interest payments and amortization on the loans.

Within the next five years, Albemarle should generate around $120 million in depreciation money and earnings to carry—and reduce—the big debt. After that, Albemarle could probably refinance its debt on more favorable terms and end up with per-share earnings that would pale anything it ever made before. Gottwald has also reported that there is a strong possibility he will be able to claim a sizable credit against Ethyl's income taxes from past years. And, even in the early years, the combined companies should be able to report a net profit of $11 or so a share, even after allowing for the heavy depreciation write-offs.

The Only Fly. The only fly in this potent ointment was of a business rather than a financial nature. What

does a small paper company do with a big chemical outfit? One rumor had it that Gottwald would make a plastic-paper substitute for bed linens. But there was no guarantee that he would, in fact, be able to combine his new oranges and apples.

Nor is it certain that Ethyl Corp. will have easy sledding over the next few years. Its basic patents on tetraethyl lead for gasoline ran out in 1947, and the company has lost much of its market to du Pont and other producers. Worse, the industry itself has lost 10% of its sales, exactly the amount it sold to the airplane market before the coming of jets, which don't use gasoline.

But Gottwald insists that the biggest declines for tetraethyl lead are in the past, and that Ethyl Corp. sales will now begin to grow with increased world-wide use of the automobile. In any case, with the kind of financial cushion the Gottwalds will have from their cash flow, they have plenty of leeway against financial reverses.

The Gottwald family has, in fact, already profited handsomely from the deal. Albemarle stock has climbed from $23.75 a share in July to $60 currently. That means a paper profit of some $9 million for the Gottwalds. It could be just the beginning.

*Albemarle Paper Mfg. Co. Traded over-the-counter. Recent price: 60. 1962 Range: 60–16. Dividend (fiscal 1961): 50c plus 5% stock. Indicated fiscal 1962: 50c. Earnings per share (fiscal 1961): $1.46. Total assets: $46.9 million.

ment distributed a notice dated June 29 protesting that "no change in the ownership of Ethyl Corporation is contemplated." The most pervasive word was that Jersey was to take over Ethyl. Shortly before he was given permission to say something to the employees about the impending sale, Bynum Turner was cornered at the meeting of the American Petroleum Institute in San Francisco. During a social hour in the Ethyl hospitality suite, a sales manager directly questioned Turner in front of a large group, "Bynum, our customers are asking us what's happening in Ethyl. And something is afoot. And are we going to be sold to N.J.?" Turner truthfully answered, "No."

At the official announcement the first startled question—and this was asked in a variety of ways, including a bit of profanity at times—"What in the dickens is the Albemarle Paper Manufacturing Company?" The formal notice of September 17, 1962, included a paragraph of reassurance. "If this transaction is consummated, the present Ethyl management will continue in active charge of the business and the company's operation will continue as now conducted. The management of Ethyl considers such an action as good for the company in that it will offer new opportunities for diversification and expansion." Naturally the general feeling among the rank-and-file was a combination of perplexity and apprehension. In an attempt to explain to its employees the reasons for selling Ethyl to Albemarle, company officials presented to middle management on September 18, 1962, a small catechism clearly marked "For Use In Oral Discussions with Employees Only." The first question was: "Why are our stockholders selling the company?" The answer was:

As General Motors states in its press release, it has for a long time been carrying out a program of disposing of its investments in partially owned companies. Its policy is to operate with wholly owned divisions or subsidiaries.

Jersey is expanding its domestic operations and it was probable that its ownership in Ethyl might become more of a handicap to Ethyl's sales of antiknocks. In general, no company likes

to buy from a competitor. Also, Jersey already has a very exten-
sive chemicals program and making Ethyl independent should
give Ethyl greater opportunity to develop its own line of new
chemicals.

The research and development people, after they found out
something about the plans of the Gottwalds, were delighted at
being unshackled and encouraged to go ahead with development
of new products.

The management group in Ethyl had been on the minds of
Gottwald and his coworkers ever since the purchase was first contemplated. Indeed, early in negotiations Miller asked Mangelsdorf of Jersey whether he felt the management of Ethyl would be
willing to come on over into the new Ethyl, and Mangelsdorf
gave an affirmative answer. In moments of cool appraisal the top
management knew that, if the company were to be sold, management had most to lose should the sale be made to a major
chemical company that had its own experienced senior officers.
Ethyl officials knew management had least to lose in a sale to a
small, and presumably less experienced, company.

Gottwald made proper advances to the senior officers of Ethyl
and on July 27, 1962, reported to his directors an important and
encouraging conversation with Bynum Turner, president of Ethyl,
during which they discussed "the desires of the Ethyl management with respect to compensation of top executives."

On September 8 Gottwald outlined to his board plans for
granting stock options to selected key personnel, and he explained the reasons for making this concession. It was the general
feeling of Gottwald that acceptance of the change by key people
must be insured by tact and by economic advantage. Accordingly, stock options were granted to a number of individuals in
the Ethyl management group, and there were either formal or
informal employment agreements with Turner, Kirby, Perdue,
Costello, and Murdock. Murdock was the last to agree, saying
finally that if the others did, he would. His comment was, "I
wouldn't want to be the skunk at the garden party."

Although the management of Ethyl realized that merging with Albemarle was the best choice of options before the company, it is not surprising that some of these officers, accustomed to being under the umbrella of two giant corporations, would experience moments of regret at the prospect of being owned by a small paper company down south. To some flippant souls it seemed as though the Ivy League was knuckling under to John Marshall High and VMI! And certainly the members of that management group, although experienced and valuable old hands, would have to adjust to a new group of forceful and strong-willed people. Especially sensitive was Turner, who though retaining the presidential title, would now have to share authority with the chairman of his board, F. D. Gottwald, who had a mind of his own.

The enabling resolutions had been passed by owners willing to sell and by purchasers willing to buy. Albemarle stockholders in Richmond had formally accepted the purchase plan on November 12, 1962. Five days later definitive agreements were signed by F. D. Gottwald of Albemarle and George Russell of General Motors in Elizabeth, New Jersey, and by Floyd D. Gottwald, Jr., of Albemarle and H. W. Fisher of Jersey in Halifax. There remained, however, the formal closing, which had to include the receipt of $200 million from the lenders in exchange for various notes and debentures, and the delivery to General Motors and Jersey of certified checks for amounts which had been agreed on in exchange for the stock. To the very last an air of uneasiness hovered over the Albemarle group as intricate legal documents were tendered by attorneys for the lenders. On the night before closing, lawyers for the lenders were still meeting with the Albemarle lawyers going over details which, if unsatisfactory, might jeopardize the whole deal.

On the morning of November 30 there was eager anticipation in the Gottwald camp as negotiations seemed concluded. It was typical of Gottwald to want his family as well as his business associates present for the closing, which was to take place on the twenty-third floor of the Chase Manhattan Bank Building, One Chase Manhattan Plaza. The dramatic nature of the final ceremony is perhaps best recalled in the words of Mrs. F. D. Gott-wald, "That really was a great day. It was one of the most interesting days I have ever lived in my life, and one of the most nervous, frightening days I have ever lived in my life. And one of the happiest days. It just kept your nerves frazzled." It is obvious that she is correct when she adds, "It was a very exciting day."

Everyone had to identify himself as he went into the big con-ference room where the last formalities were to take place. At the meeting there was one classic witticism that has become a per-manent part of the remembered pageantry. As Nancy Gottwald, Mrs. Bruce C. Gottwald, tells the story of the entrance of the Gottwald women, "Well it was the most thrilling thing, going in down there at the Chase Bank. They asked us when we went in, 'Do you represent the lenders?' And I said 'Oh, no, we are the spenders.' That just broke them up."

There was a well-earned thrill to all of this. Bruce Gottwald, in refreshing candor, says, "We were bug-eyed, with all those people coming and plopping down a check for a million or half a million." He recalls the off-hand remark of one bank represen-tative, who for the moment could not put his hand on a check for a million dollars worth of debentures. "Some guy popped up and said, 'It was in my in-basket this morning.' Just the idea of a million dollar check in somebody's in-basket! It was amazing."

The master of ceremonies, the presiding officer, was John W. Riely, member of the legal team from Hunton and Williams. Riely took authoritative command and by all reports carried out his assignment with style, plenty of "ruffles and flourishes," to quote one observer. He called to order the meeting, which con-sisted of some sixty or seventy-five people, and went through the procedure item by item, check by check.

It was necessary to synchronize operations in New York City with actions in Nova Scotia, where Raymond Hailey and Brice Graves, representing Albemarle, were dealing with representa-tives of Jersey, and with legal proceedings in Elizabeth, New Jer-sey, where Douglas Gottwald, recently elected assistant secretary for Albemarle, was closing with General Motors. Communication by telephone was readily and continuously maintained with the New Jersey group, but there was more trouble with the Canadian operators, who insisted on cutting off a silent line. Thus Brice Graves picked up a Gideon Bible and with proper reverence began reading Old Testament chapters for the most part loaded with genealogical "begats." In the words of F. D. Gottwald, "He was really serious reading that Bible. He was very respectful of the Bible." As Mrs. F. D. Gottwald recalls the situation, every once in a while someone would go over to the telephone and speak with Brice Graves and then come and say, "He is still begatting."

There were delays, interruptions, and stories of certified checks that were almost lost or mislaid. To quote Gottwald, "The delay was caused because some of the investors from the Pacific Coast that were buying the secondary debentures were coming in with the money on the morning of the closing, and that happened to be an extremely wet, muggy, foggy day. So here [we] are gathered together ready to close the deal and these gentlemen circulating in the air." But in fact they did come down and made the deposit on time.

James Miller recalls his misery as the clock ticked away, and ten minutes before the zero hour a promised check for $2.5 million had not arrived. As he tells the story, "We had to have that check. And I called over to the cashier at our office, which was only two blocks [away] and I said, 'Look, we are $2.5 million short, and the check isn't here yet, and we've got to have that check. Go down and get a certified check for $2.5 million payable to such and such and get it up here. We've got to have it here within ten minutes.' And he got it there within ten minutes. We were going to take the $2.5 million if the other people didn't. See what I mean?" The promised $2.5 million check came in with a couple of minutes to spare.

Especially dear to the heart of the raconteur is the story of a young lawyer who in preparation for the final closing dutifully picked up the check for $100 million that was to be delivered to General Motors at the closing in New Jersey, put it in his briefcase and went downstairs at the Chase Manhattan Bank. He noted that the driver of the black Cadillac limousine that General Motors had provided to take him to the closing had stepped out. Then the young lawyer put his briefcase in the car and wandered off just a few steps. Suddenly to his amazement, he saw the car being driven away as his own driver, who had circled the block, was approaching. The lawyer dashed after the car containing the briefcase and had visions of a legal career going down the drain! In the words of F. D. Gottwald, "So we had a demonstration of a marathon runner down Broad Street in Manhattan." The lawyer finally caught the wayward Cadillac at a stop light and all was saved, even a good story. (The reader should pay no attention to the party pooper who would ruin the cadence of a superb narrative by reminding that the payment to General Motors at the closing was not $100,000,000 but a certified check for $48,183,132 representing its half of the $116,366,264 sales price minus the $10,000,000 subordinated notes which it had agreed to accept.)

Later on it was discovered that the near misses were not confined to November 30, the actual day of the closing. One such near-miss occurred on the evening before. Fifty million dollars worth of debentures, now in negotiable form, were stored in a vault at the bank while the lawyers went out to dinner. Presumably the lawyers were in sole possession of the vault combination. They were shocked on their return to see the vault door wide open and a charwoman going about her usual business. Happily the debentures were still there.

The final check came in, the final document was signed, and the members of the Albemarle group, now Ethyl of Virginia, felt that they could enjoy themselves a bit. Bruce Gottwald indulged in the luxury of a dollar cigar from which his sinuses have not as yet recovered, he says! Incidentally, when he got rid of this lethal cylinder it landed in a construction site, and Lewis Powell who was accompanying him on this jaunt down the street, had a fear that conflagration would result. Happily the building remained intact and Powell survived to serve on the Supreme Court of the United States.

The entire group attended a cocktail party given by Hunton and Williams at the University Club. During the social hour there was reminiscing about the events of the previous six months. Then followed a big dinner, just the Albemarle group at the Four Seasons Restaurant. Participants remember little about the menu but several recall early morning headaches following that dinner.

The Ethyl of Delaware group was not left out of the celebrating. To quote Gottwald, "As for the Ethyl people, one of them said they were having a 'Thank God' party, and another said they were having a funeral. But they had a party that night. The lawyers had one, not the closing, but our New York lawyers. Gosh, there were more celebrations."

However, the official and formal dinner of the Ethyl of Delaware group occurred four days after the closing ceremonies. The banquet given at the Carlton House in New York City was perhaps less hilarious than the earlier Albemarle party. In truth it was a nostalgic meeting with substantial historical notes included on the printed menu. Officially it was a dinner given by General Motors and Standard Oil of New Jersey to honor the management directors of old Ethyl. The diners feasted well on a variety of wines, green turtle soup with sherry, filet of sole, and Grand Marnier. Five who were honored, the "management directors" of Ethyl—Turner, Kirby, Murdock, Costello, and Perdue—were by the time of the Carlton House banquet management directors of Ethyl of Virginia.

VIII

Expansion and Diversification

Transition to the New Organization

THE FORMAL CEREMONIES of November 30, 1962, marking the completion of the sale of Ethyl of Delaware and the rounding out of the $200 million financing coincident with that sale, were sandwiched between meetings of a board of directors that, during the day, changed its composition and created a new corporate organization. The board convened at 9:30 A.M. in the offices of the Chase Manhattan Bank, where the closing ceremonies were to be held, reconvened first at 11 A.M. at the same place, then at 3:30 P.M. in the offices of Ethyl Corporation at 100 Park Avenue.

At the beginning of the meeting the board of directors, now under the name of Ethyl Corporation of Virginia, the new designation of Albemarle Paper Manufacturing Company as of November 28, was in personnel pure Albemarle. The president and presiding officer was F. D. Gottwald, and the secretary Bruce C. Gottwald. The directors went through the formality of ratifying the purchase agreement whereby Ethyl of Virginia acquired Ethyl of Delaware. At this moment, if not earlier, Albemarle, now Ethyl of Virginia, was in the distinctive position of having two main subsidiaries, Ethyl of Delaware and Halifax Paper.

The merger of Ethyl of Virginia and Ethyl of Delaware was authorized in the following legal language: "RESOLVED, that Ethyl Corporation (formerly named Albemarle Paper Manufacturing

Company) merge, and it hereby does merge, into itself said Ethyl Corporation, and assumes all of its obligations."

The "corporate life line" was recognized by a description of the seal that contained the words "Incorporated February 15, 1887." (The impression seal abbreviates the date: "Feb. 15th, 1887.") In this manner the new corporation was certified as being in law that "body politic and corporate" established by Judge B. R. Wellford, Jr., of the Circuit Court of the City of Richmond, seventy-five years earlier.

K. F. Adams, B. W. Coale, H. W. Ellerson, Jr., C. H. Robertson, and H. K. Steen submitted their resignations to make way for new directors. A bylaw was enacted permitting the expansion of the board from thirteen to fifteen. Then a new board was established consisting of F. D. Gottwald, F. D. Gottwald, Jr., B. C. Gottwald, G. F. Kirby, Jr., W. R. Perdue, Jr., J. A. Costello, J. M. Lowry, M. P. Murdock, S. D. Fleet, F. A. Howard, R. T. Marsh, Jr., L. F. Powell, Jr., S. B. Scott, B. B. Turner, and E. L. Shea. Eight of the fifteen came from old Albemarle and seven from the Ethyl of Delaware group. The officers of the new corporation were: F. D. Gottwald, chairman; B. B. Turner, president; F. D. Gottwald, Jr., executive vice president; G. F. Kirby, executive vice president; W. R. Perdue, Jr., executive vice president and treasurer; J. A. Costello, vice president; J. M. Lowry, vice president; W. P. Murdock, vice president, B. C. Gottwald, vice president and secretary.

The Albemarle name was preserved by merging all paper operations into Halifax and then changing its name to Albemarle Paper Manufacturing Company, a wholly owned subsidiary of the new Ethyl Corporation.

What were the products and possessions of Ethyl of Virginia? In its paper branch it manufactured kraft, blotting, and filter paper and miscellaneous absorbent specialties. From its converting operations came multiwalled paper bags, shipping bags, folding boxes, and corrugated shipping containers. The newly acquired chemical operations produced principally tetraethyl lead, vinyl chloride monomer used in the manufacture of plastics, and a

First Board of Directors, Ethyl of Virginia. *Clockwise from left:* Lewis F. Powell, Jr., Bruce C. Gottwald, Joseph A. Costello, Malcolm P. Murdock, Robert T. Marsh, Jr., George F. Kirby, Bynum B. Turner, Floyd D. Gottwald, Floyd D. Gottwald, Jr., William R. Perdue, Jr., S. Douglas Fleet, Frank A. Howard, S. Buford Scott, Edward L. Shea, and Joseph M. Lowry few other chemicals. The chemical units were producing about 87 percent antiknocks and 13 percent other chemicals.

The physical properties in the paper division consisted of ten plants: the three paper mills in Richmond; two large paper mills plus a pulp mill in Roanoke Rapids, North Carolina; a multi-walled sack plant in Middletown, Ohio; a handle shopping bag plant in Walden, New York; a folding box plant in Richmond; and a corrugated shipping container plant in Richmond. In addition the corporation owned outright or had under lease over 200,000 acres of woodlands.

There were chemical manufacturing plants in Baton Rouge; Houston; Pittsburg, California; Orangeburg, South Carolina; and Sarnia, Ontario, Canada. An important research laboratory was located in Detroit. There were sales offices, testing laboratories, and minor establishments elsewhere.

Even before the ceremonies of November 30, 1962, the new corporation had employed an independent organization, the American Appraisal Company, to put a value on the various physical properties, this to produce authentic figures useful in computing allowable depreciation. The Internal Revenue Service contested the figures and thus began an argument that lasted a full sixteen years before being settled by compromise in 1978 just before the case was to go to court. A key individual in maintaining Ethyl's position throughout the years was Paul D. Cahill, manager of the tax department of old and new Ethyl.

Although the physical properties were important, the greatest asset of this new combination was its people. Gottwald had guided an energetic, imaginative staff. From Ethyl of Delaware had come a group of management and line individuals talented in an amazing way. Quality pervaded all sections of the company.

Gottwald himself within twelve months of the purchase had occasion publicly to comment on the staff that came with the purchase of Ethyl of Delaware. He could speak only in superlatives in addressing the Baton Rouge Chamber of Commerce on September 26, 1963. The effectiveness of his attribution of brilliance to the individuals who had moved into the new composite organization was amplified by his modesty in recounting the mistakes that he himself had made in old Albemarle.

As remarkable as borrowing $200 million for the purchase of Ethyl was the success of Gottwald in consolidating the two organizations in such a manner as to create a new corporate identity. It was an exercise in both firmness and diplomacy. Joseph C. Carter, Jr., a lawyer with Hunton and Williams, a man intimately associated with the creation of Ethyl of Virginia, and later an Ethyl director, gave high marks to Gottwald's initial moves. "One of the first things that impressed me was the way Mr. Gottwald took charge of the whole operation after the closing was over. There wasn't a bit of doubt about it." The first days were made more complex by the continued problem of rumor. As James E. Boudreau, a veteran employee who remained as director of public relations until his retirement in 1966, said, "The rumors were just as wild as anything you could get." Roger A. Moser, later senior vice president of research and development, recalls the false fears of a few people that the purchase by Albemarle was something of a raid and that the veteran Ethyl employees were going to be pawns in an exclusively financial game.

Gottwald displayed a strategic patience; necessary personnel changes were made gradually. He thought affirmatively all along, his official thesis being that there should be no difficulty in blending Albemarle and the old Ethyl Corporation because both were essentially chemical industries.

The answers to the question as to *when* the new regime was accepted by employees of old Ethyl range from "immediately after the purchase" to "three or four years thereafter." The speed of acceptance varied from division to division, and from individual to individual. One gentleman was perhaps not entirely facetious when, on being questioned as to how long the shakedown lasted, said, "We are even still shaking a bit now." No doubt the people most readily rejoicing in the new era were those who had been impatient with the restraints in the old regime. The frustrations of the research and development group already have been surveyed. Pronouncements by Gottwald as to his intention to expand and diversify soon were confirmed in directives and appropriations.

All in all, Gottwald and his colleagues did a remarkable job of bringing the talented people from old Ethyl into the new organization. In grooming individuals for the new era, Gottwald was patient. There was a willingness to try new techniques, a willingness that, as Moser said, would not have characterized men of lesser faith. To repeat the phrase used by Herzog, maybe Gottwald had more faith in the people from old Ethyl than they had in themselves. Certainly most of the former Albemarle group soon learned to be compatible with the people from old Ethyl and this was reciprocated.

It would be naive to think that everybody was totally happy with the new ownership. Inevitably nostalgic individuals looked with a touch of anguish at the shift of ownership from two of the greatest corporations in America to a small paper company headquartered in the onetime capital of the Confederacy.

Though the changes were gradual, there were at the outset two major facts that created a measure of uneasiness among some members of the old Ethyl group. First was the high ratio of long-term debt to assets characteristic of Ethyl of Virginia in its earliest days. As Murdock phrases it, there was shock at the concept of "being in debt up to your armpits." Because of the resources of the owners, the people of old Ethyl did not have to do sleight-of-hand tricks with the dollar. Second, the new owners concerned themselves with day-to-day operations more than did the former owners. The Gottwalds and their associates became active parts of management. They had no intention of simply holding latent power in a board that met monthly.

In this period of transition, Herzog emerged as a tactful and ingenious aid in the blending of old Ethyl and old Albemarle to make a new Ethyl. He was particularly helpful in getting the executive committee underway and became the first secretary of this important administrative arm.

During the years under survey, 1962–82, Ethyl's chief executive officer was F. D. Gottwald, and then Floyd D. Gottwald, Jr.

At the moment of the merger, November 30, 1962, Gottwald, as chairman of the board and heading the family owning over 50 percent of the voting shares, immediately assumed the prerogatives of chief executive officer. To be certain that the primacy in fact was reflected in the written statutes of the corporation, the board of directors passed a new bylaw in the summer of 1964 affirming the point that the chairman of the board was indeed chief executive officer. In an obvious attempt to release a fraction of his authority and responsibility, F. D. Gottwald, four years later—April 25, 1968—passed on to his older son, Floyd D. Gottwald, Jr., the chairmanship of the board. However, at the same time the elder Gottwald, in taking a new title as chairman of the executive committee, retained the position of chief executive officer. This particular arrangement lasted only two years. On January 22, 1970, he recommended to the directors that the chairman of the board be made chief executive officer of the corporation, saying that he believed such a move "would achieve a better distribution of responsibility and authority."

In the meantime the presidency, the chief operating office, was passed from Bynum Turner to George Kirby to Bruce Gottwald. It will be recalled that Turner, who had held the presidency of Ethyl of Delaware at the time of its purchase by Albemarle, was named to that same office in the original organization of Ethyl of Virginia. In June 1964 a spokesman for Ethyl Corporation announced that Turner, because of health reasons, had submitted his resignation in a letter dated May 28, 1964, and that on June 18, 1964, his resignation was accepted.

Dr. George Kirby was appointed to succeed Turner. Kirby, a native of Louisiana and a graduate of Louisiana College, B.S., and of Louisiana State University, M.S. and Ph.D., had joined Ethyl as a research chemist in 1940. At the time Albemarle bought Ethyl, Kirby was a director and vice president in charge of operations, overseeing manufacturing, engineering, and research and development departments. In the new organization he was director, executive vice president, and a member of the executive committee. Kirby's tenure as president lasted over five years; he

George F. Kirby

submitted a letter requesting that his resignation become effective December 31, 1969. He was accepting the executive vice presidency of Texas Eastern Transmission Corporation. Kirby remained on the board of Ethyl until his death in 1980. He was succeeded in the presidency by Bruce C. Gottwald, who had been serving as vice president and secretary.

During 1966 William R. Perdue, Jr., executive vice president and treasurer, stated that the proposed transfer of the finance department from New York City to Richmond presented insuperable personal and family difficulties, and therefore he tendered his resignation. The board, meeting on November 17, accepted with regret Perdue's resignation and in subsequent action at that same meeting elected Lawrence E. Blanchard, Jr., of Hunton and Williams to succeed Perdue as director, as a member of the executive committee, and as executive vice president of the corporation. Perdue's resignation was to become effective December 31, 1966, and Blanchard took office the next day. He came not as a laywer but as chief financial officer.

Blanchard recalls a candid statement from Gottwald when employment negotiations were being concluded. Blanchard said to Gottwald, "It sounds like this time you are asking me to work *with* you instead of *for* you. And I must say that makes a lot of difference." Gottwald agreed but added, "Just so long as you remember who is boss over here!" The new executive vice president had served Albemarle and then Ethyl of Virginia for many years, often in association with Lewis F. Powell, Jr. Blanchard had attended board meetings and was involved in several of Ethyl's more exciting projects, such as the Greek venture to be described in chapter 9. According to him, the consultation had been extensive and stimulating "a very great relationship." Thus when he moved into the company he was on familiar ground.

Not only the top management but the board of directors was changing. By 1982 none of the seven directors drawn in 1962 from the Ethyl of Delaware board remained. Turner and Perdue had resigned, Costello and Murdock had retired, and Howard, Kirby, and Shea had died.

The statement made by Ethyl management in the annual report for 1963 anticipates the events of the next years: "In the year ahead, we plan to continue the consolidation of the organization along divisional lines and to make further progress in expansion and diversification."

In a very real sense, Gottwald's announced program was fun-and-games. In his own words, association with the people of old Ethyl had been "a lot of fun." This phrase he used in that famous Chamber of Commerce speech in Baton Rouge September 26, 1963. He underscored the point by adding, "We have enjoyed every moment of it and I am sure we will continue to enjoy it."

Strategy of Acquisition

A program of diversification and expansion was in Gottwald's mind from the very moment he considered acquiring Ethyl. In public and in private statements, the point was made unmistakably clear. If he had his way, never again would the name Ethyl evoke the vision of a one-product company. He wanted diversification for both general reasons and, as he told his board, "in order to lessen our dependence on antiknock compound."

Such a philosophy gladdened the hearts of the research and development group. On the other hand the message of departure from the old way disturbed some of the old guard from Ethyl who had been brought up on the conviction that lead antiknocks represented about the greatest invention of the twentieth century. They were uncomfortable with the thought that management's attention might be turned away too much from the basis of company existence. This particular group, however, took heart from a speedy emphasis on foreign markets; and many of them adapted to chemical ventures allied in technology to the traditional antiknock operations.

A score of years later the result was a company quite different from what was essentially a tetraethyl lead–paper combination in 1962 with sales of about $240 million. Antiknock additives in 1981 represented only about 17 percent of the corporation's total sales. All the paper business had been sold. A diversified pattern of chemical production had emerged; plastics, aluminum, and coal became major enterprises. These several achievements constitute the heart of a fascinating story of maintaining a place in that prestigious list of America's top 500 corporations.

Obviously these were two routes to diversification and growth: (1) internal development and (2) acquisitions. The distinction becomes artificial when there is marked growth in the acquired company as a consequence of the application of techniques evolving from the internal operations of the basic corporation. To quote James M. Riddle, director, chemicals, for Ethyl S.A., "The initial growth and diversification was based on in-house technology and in-house capability. We got in the chlorinated solvent business because we had a wealth of chlorinated hydrocarbon technology which was developed in the process of learning [about] tetraethyl lead."

As for acquisitions, the concept was in the very bones of the new Ethyl management. From the time Gottwald persuaded Ellerson to buy Halifax, the search-and-buy technique was almost second nature to Gottwald. The acquisition of sundry paper–converting operations in the 1950s and the purchase of Ethyl of Delaware itself simply confirmed Gottwald's basic policies. There were dreams of gigantic acquisitions even before the Ethyl deal. Joseph Lowry recalls that perhaps as many as one or two hundred acquisitions were talked about. "As a matter of fact, it would have been a rare thing not to have at least a couple that we were considering all the time," to quote Lowry. When one saw Gottwald in his office communicating with the people at Hunton and Williams over the taxation problems that might be involved in an acquisition and observed Lowry and other financial officers telephoning Northwestern about financing, it all added up to a familiar picture.

The purchase of going concerns was made possible by an impressive cash flow from the basic enterprises, especially tetraethyl lead, and by an ingenious program of outside financing, mostly an outgrowth of the pattern of borrowing developed in 1962. Rarely did a suitable acquisition appear when the company had a thoroughly comfortable financial situation. To quote Bruce Gottwald, "It's never really been convenient. Mr. F. D. Gottwald, Sr.'s attitude has been that business is generally going to grow, and if we get an opportunity then we will find some way to make it work." Bruce Gottwald underscores the fact that none of the major acquisitions came at a time when the company really had the money on hand to make the purchase.

Through trial and error there evolved over the years certain principles in the game of acquisition, flexible yet usually considered basic guidelines for initial inquiry. Prominent among the negatives were: avoiding if possible joint enterprises; no competition with customers; no wasting time with projects too small. (As Gottwald often told his staff members, it takes just as much effort to swing a little deal as it does to swing a large deal.) The acquisition should be large enough to justify the necessary time and attention yet not so large as to jeopardize the existence or prosperity of the company if the facts did not agree with the prognosis of profit as the months rolled by. The formula of a medium-sized commitment would also apply to expansion within the already established units.

The ideal acquisition seemed to be something in which the corporation already had a measure of expertise and one in which the personnel of the company being sought could be persuaded that Ethyl was the best purchaser. This technique was explained carefully by Dr. Clarence Neher, a key figure in several acquisitions.

In connection with the goodwill of the key personnel of the company being taken over, it might be noted that with one possible exception there seems never to have been a "takeover" in the classical adversary sense. The exception was VCA, which had some peculiar characteristics. But even here the owners came out in good financial shape, and indeed some students of the VCA transaction think that perhaps the former owners may have outsmarted Ethyl in the deal.

It would be a mistake to think of the group having the responsibility for considering new acquisitions to have been restricted by narrow guidelines. As those involved recall, at the very beginning the situation was wide open, with the exception of banks and savings and loans associations, categories not eligible. Then there was a season after the development of specialty chemicals, aluminum, plastics, coal, oil, and gas when the tendency was to move principally in those areas already being developed. After careful examination one discovers that Ethyl was not so much in the chemical, aluminum, or any other business as much as it was in the *money* business. The possibility of profit from invested capital was always at the forefront in the minds of those making decisions. In the earliest days of Ethyl of Virginia, pronouncements were made that there was a continuous evaluation of the productivity of investments and when units were not profitable consideration would be given to divesting the company of these.

The highest officials of Ethyl have always been frank enough to say they are not certain what direction Ethyl would take in the future. Indeed, Floyd D. Gottwald, Jr., in conversation with the present writer several years ago indicated they simply didn't know what Ethyl would be getting into farther down the road. It seems as though the key word is *profitability*. The overall strategy is to make the sort of investments that will bring profit to the share-holders.

Like the fishermen from time immemorial, executives tell of "the big ones that got away." Perhaps the ones that got away— and some of those that got away may have been indigestible— were not quite so close to being hooked as they seem in retro-spect. If not, this is the way of sportsmen—and there was much of the sporting instinct in the planning by F. D. Gottwald and his allies.

In counting the ones that got away Gottwald remembered most painfully Anaconda Copper. Gottwald recalled that the financ-ing was arranged—some money was coming from Europe. And then, late in the day as it were, the American part of the financ-ing went to pieces. Ethyl was reminded of Rule U, which appar-ently prohibited the lending of funds by banks in the Federal Reserve System for the sort of purchase contemplated.

Liggett and Myers was looked at hungrily by the elder Gott-wald. By report the deal was of the quarter-billion-dollar variety. As Gottwald remembered it, the purchase would have been quite advantageous since the leaf inventory in storage itself possessed a value of almost the amount of money that the company would have cost. The move was opposed by certain interests in Dur-ham, including an endowment fund, and thus the whole thing was dropped. The proposal to buy the White Motor Corporation received the most publicity of all efforts that did not come to fruition. And there was even authorization by the board on March 26, 1970. However, because of a sudden drop in earnings, Ethyl officials were alarmed and gave up their efforts.

The negotiations with Associated Octel never passed the pre-liminary point, but during 1964–65 the matter was diligently in-vestigated by Ethyl representatives. The movement toward Octel had a certain historic validity because Octel was the new name for Associated Ethyl, the successor to Ethyl Export. There was consideration of many others including names as diverse as Doeskin, Bangor Punta, Calumet Industries, Lubrizol, and Ruberoid.

A word might be said here about the intensity of research and the breadth of knowledge in the groups studying acquisitions. Their approach represented an interdisciplinary exercise in various fields—chemistry, engineering, accounting, and economics—which would have warmed the heart of any graduate-business-school dean.

So important was the program of search-and-buy that the company's highest officials accorded it priority in time and thought, Floyd D. Gottwald, Jr., assuming special responsibilities. His role in the mechanism of acquisition was given formal recognition when he was designated "coordinator" by the executive committee at its meeting December 17, 1970. He and the senior officials working with him had the support of the office of financial relations, which studied possible new acquisitions as well as carrying forward its initial responsibility of answering inquiries from investors and their representatives, kindred assignments each involving study of financial data. This office took shape in 1969 when Lloyd B. Andrew, Jr., left his position as manager of VisQueen to become director of financial relations. Ian A. Nimmo in 1973 joined Andrew and became assistant director of financial relations. Nimmo's original job centered on acquisitions with something of a backup role in communicating with financial analysts. In the course of time, however, his work moved closer to investor relations. In a reshaping of the office in 1981, when Andrew became treasurer of the company and Nimmo director of investor relations, Robert A. Linn was brought into the acquisition process under the title of director of corporate business development. Linn had earned postgraduate degrees in chemistry, business administration, and law before joining Ethyl as patent attorney in 1961.

The acquisitions in the 1960s included VisQueen (plastics) in 1963, Bonnell (aluminum) in 1966, Oxford (paper) in 1967, and IMCO (plastics) in 1968. The pattern of acquisitions was much more extensive in the 1970s. Capitol Products (aluminum) was acquired in 1970, Flex Products (plastics) in 1973, Elk Horn Coal (energy) in 1973, VCA (plastics) in 1974, Edwin Cooper (lubricant additives) in 1975, Creative Dispenser Systems in 1977, Hardwicke Chemical (specialty chemicals) in 1978, and Massie Tool (plastics-related) in 1979. From the time of the merger of Ethyl of Delaware into Albemarle Paper Manufacturing Company to the end of the calendar year 1981, the company spent $396,369,000 for acquisitions. The sum includes approximately $124,000,000 paid for Oxford Paper Company, subsequently sold. The acquisitions allowed a magnificent pattern of increase in sales and operations profit. And yet Ethyl's diversification is a fact that sinks but slowly into the public consciousness. One reads a measure of surprise in the headlines in *Chemical Business* for September 22, 1980, "Ethyl Is No Longer a One-Product Company" and in the *New York Times* for August 15, 1981, "The Ethyl Corporation Is Diversifying to Alter Its One-Product Image."

Even a well-planned acquisition almost inevitably brings certain standard problems. Sometimes the company that is most attractive as a candidate for acquisition is one that has succeeded because of its self-identity and the vigor of the entrepreneurial spirit. Often these very qualities make merging with another company a bit more difficult. When a small company moves into a large corporation, there are trade-offs. At the top level there are greater capital resources and more technical assistance available; at the local level there is less freedom for making major decisions and making them quickly. In looking at the shift of decision-making, one observer has noted that in the long run probably fewer mistakes are made this way, but there is inevitably a price. The price sometimes is that a golden opportunity slips away because of delay. And the delay in turn can cause a decline in entrepreneurial enthusiasm. But on the whole the benefits of being a part of a large diversified company seem to outweigh the disadvantages.

In an acquisition it is sometimes necessary to get the people in the company being annexed to realize that they cannot continue as a self-contained operation, but that they are now in a division of a large company. In several instances it has taken positive action by top management to correct this situation. James H. Kirby, for many years controller of Ethyl Corporation, acknowledges that when a small company has a strong identity of its own, "You can't avoid conflict completely." He adds that he thinks Ethyl has done a tremendous job in reconciliation. Nothing of this nature has been 100 percent successful but great progress has been made. This problem, which might be called economic federalism, is not restricted to acquisitions but crops up in the established institution.

Plastics

Gottwald's dismay at the competition polyethylene film offered the paper industry had been a major factor in his resolve to guide Albemarle into new fields; therefore it is not at all surprising that he maintained a consistent interest in the plastics industry. Gottwald's first acquaintance with Ethyl of Delaware had come about because that corporation was a supplier of intermediates in the manufacture of plastics. To quote from the annual report of Ethyl of Virginia for the year ended March 31, 1963, the company is "a major producer of vinyl chloride monomer and has devoted considerable research to the development of polymers, basic materials in the manufacture of plastic products." An early act of the new corporation was to create a plastics division with Dr. Clarence Neher as head. It was quite natural that the first major acquisition of Ethyl of Virginia was a manufacturer of plastics.

The purchase of VisQueen was formally completed November 30, 1963, one year to the day after the creation of the new Ethyl Corporation. The opportunity came about because the Federal Trade Commission ordered Union Carbide Corporation to divest itself of three plastic film units, part of the Visking division which Union Carbide had bought in 1956. The federal regulatory agency saw the merging of Visking, an important producer of polyethylene film, and Union Carbide, likewise an important producer, as action contrary to the federal antitrust acts. The three units which had to be sold were located in Terre Haute, Indiana; Fremont, California; and Flemington, New Jersey.

The principal Ethyl representatives in negotiating with Union Carbide were Clarence Neher, Bruce Gottwald, E. Malcolm Harvey, and Warne. They were aided by Blanchard and Carter, from Hunton and Williams.

Ethyl's basic negotiating position was good. "I guess [there was] a list of twenty-five people who were in there trying to acquire and again we seemed to be an innocuous crowd," says Bruce Gottwald, remembering Rathbone's phrasing of Albemarle's position in the encounter of 1962. He adds, "We were about as clean as anybody [who could] buy it."

In the preliminary negotiations with Union Carbide, Harvey after many computations concluded that the Union Carbide people were wrong in their summaries of the profits made in the units under consideration. The Union Carbide negotiators said that Harvey simply did not know what he was talking about. Dr. Neher, constitutionally enthusiastic, was a bit upset at Harvey's presentation, and Bruce Gottwald later admitted that when Harvey said his piece, he, Bruce, felt like a little boy whose balloon had been pricked. However, the Union Carbide negotiators reviewed their computations and reported to the Ethyl negotiators that, after all, the young man was right. Thus the basis for negotiations was tilted a bit in the direction of Ethyl.

In reminiscing, Carter of Hunton and Williams recalls the negotiations with Union Carbide as among the most dramatic events in his association with Ethyl. He discovered a leverage technique that he describes as a "fascinating exercise." Every now and then during some rough spots in the negotiations, he would suggest that all parties go down to Washington. This ploy invariably worked, for the Union Carbide people were not at all enthusiastic about another review by the Federal Trade Commission, and concessions were made. The completed contract was approved by the Federal Trade Commission after some vacillation by that body, which at first feared a new combination in restraint of trade.

In this manner Ethyl moved into the position of being the world's leading producer of polyethylene film, its broad uses defined in Ethyl's annual report for 1963 as follows: "Polyethylene film is used in building construction, agriculture, industry, around the home and in modern packaging—in everything from weather balloons to transparent vegetable bags, from drapery material to painter's drop cloths."

Less impressive in performance was the Vypak Corporation, formed jointly by Ethyl and Solvay et Cie of Brussels in 1964 for the development of rigid polyvinyl chloride (PVC) bottles. It is said that the name "Vypak" was created by Dr. Neher's secretary who took liberties with the first letters of the two words vinyl packaging. The purpose of the arrangement was to combine Solvay's expertise in making blow-molded containers with Ethyl's knowledge of American markets and methods. The plant, erected in Rockaway, New Jersey, was equipped with machines that simply did not measure up to expectations. As the operation faltered, there was a tentative agreement drawn to sell Vypak to Solvay for $1.00, but ultimately Solvay's share of the business, including liabilities, was purchased for the sum of $1.00. After the installation of better machines, the Solvay unit in performance compared well with the other plants in the plastics division. In 1968 Vypak merged into Ethyl Corporation, and in the following year the operations of Vypak were passed over to IMCO, the acquisition of which will be described.

Following the Vypak misadventure, the next major excursion into plastics was the purchase of IMCO Container Company in 1968. Like the VisQueen addition, this was a consequence of antitrust action by the Federal Trade Commission. The stock of IMCO had been owned 50-50 by Rexall Drug and Chemical Company and El Paso Products Company. The Federal Trade Commission required Rexall to divest itself of IMCO, and El Paso was willing to sell. IMCO was a leading manufacturer of polyethylene bottles used in packaging toiletries, cosmetics, detergents, and other household chemical products. The purchase of IMCO provided entry into a market hitherto closed to the then existing line of PVC bottles produced by Ethyl.

Many companies were interested in acquiring IMCO, but Ethyl again appeared as one of the cleaner bidders in terms of any antitrust contamination. As Bruce Gottwald remarks in recalling the event, "So we did quite a courting job on them to encourage them to pick us as the candidate, and we were successful." IMCO was acquired July 31, 1968, at a cost of approximately $25 million.

The Plastics Group took on a new dimension, indeed a new character, when in 1974 Ethyl acquired VCA Corporation for about $90 million. The company, a diversified manufacturer of plastic and metal products, including aerosol valves and related dispensing devices, was originally known as Valve Corporation of America, but assumed the abbreviated title when the range of products extended far beyond aerosol valves. At the time of acquisition, VCA owned twenty-eight plants in nineteen different locations.

The company had been put together by a colorful man named Philip Sagarin. The nimble journalist Richard K. Weil, in an essay headed "Sagarin's Saga, Horatio Alger in Plastics," described Sagarin as a rags-to-riches character who played the part to the full. Sagarin had no conspicuous accomplishments until 1949, when he created an improvement in the aerosol valve. He managed to raise $1,000 to found the Valve Corporation of America.

Sagarin gathered under his supervision many smaller companies. While he had built up a large business by innovation and hard work, he had never disciplined its bigness. The company was loosely pulled together with a miniscule control staff. After the death of his wife, Sagarin did not seem to have his heart in the company. Yet pride in his creation did not readily permit him to sell out. First he looked for and thought he had found a Dutch group, Tyssen-Bornemeza, an outstanding industrial family that would help. Sagarin wanted outsiders who would put cash into the company but would remain in a minority position. Then came a period of confusion. Apparently some of Sagarin's management team wanted a new company to take over completely. At any rate there were varying prices per share set by Sagarin, and in the middle of the uncertainties Ethyl management successfully made a tender offer of $18.50 per share. The Tyssen people withdrew from the bidding. Technically there was a takeover, but in the long run Sagarin was quite satisfied with the money he received for his stock.

In a sense the purchase of VCA with its many small operations, sometimes called by the plastics people themselves a "nickel and dime business," changed the complexion of Ethyl. Furthermore, there was the immediate necessity for management reorganization. In the central office there were seven employees, including secretaries. According to Bruce Gottwald, "They had no idea what was going on in the business." So rapid was the move toward control by the new owners that the people at VCA felt as though they had been drenched by a bucket of cold water. Some of the formerly semi-independent operators simply could not adjust to the tight controls instituted by Ethyl.

In 1979, five years after the VCA purchase, Ethyl acquired Massie Tool and Mold, in St. Petersburg, Florida, organized in 1961. The Massie firm, which specialized in custom injection molds, mostly of the multicavity variety, owned 100 percent of the adjacent Modern Technical Molding, which made plastic parts.

There were other miscellaneous plastic additions, such as Flex Products Company, which made containers of clear plastic tubing used for packaging, bought in 1975.

Aluminum and Coal

Ethyl's entrance into the field of aluminum brought fond memories to F. D. Gottwald. He said, "Aluminum always has fascinated me. When I first went with Albemarle Paper and was in the export department I tried to trade paper for aluminum, particularly from the Swiss operation." And he added that to his astonishment not long ago an ancient goateed gentleman, associated with an aluminum company in Switerzland that was being approached by Ethyl in some licensing negotiation, recalled the original correspondence with Gottwald.

There were reasons more important than nostalgia for Ethyl's entry into aluminum. Here was an opportunity to expand and diversify, and this industry appeared ripe for the sort of integration that had proved highly profitable in the paper business. Furthermore the fact that about 10 million pounds of aluminum were bought annually for use in chemical operations at Houston was a persistent reminder of the metal. Gottwald thought it might be a good time, through acquisition of aluminum plants, to build up annual consumption to perhaps 100,000 tons, and with that base to push integration backward even to bauxite and primary aluminum production.

Important in planning to gain a position in the aluminum industry was Thomas M. Smylie, a Mississippian by birth, who received his B.S. degree in chemical engineering from Mississippi State University. After joining Ethyl in 1940 as a chemical engineer, he served in several divisions, including research, engineering, planning, and corporate marketing before becoming first head of Ethyl's aluminum division.

After aluminum was identified as a possible field of expansion, a group headed by Smylie undertook an orderly investigation. During the summer of 1965 Smylie and Malcolm Harvey presented to the executive committee a proposal for the purchase of the William L. Bonnell Company of Newnan, Georgia. The founder, William Bonnell, is described by Bruce Gottwald as "one of the real entrepreneurs in the aluminum extrusion industry, a giant of a man." Bonnell had died and his widow was trying to run this company. Ultimately, Mrs. Bonnell and Ethyl reached an agreement.

The purchase was completed on April 1, 1966, after Harvey had spent several months reviewing the books and actually managing the company. Gottwald recalled that the preferred stock issued to pay for Bonnell was retired after five years, and thus the business was entirely paid out in that length of time. After a brief interim arrangement, Harvey became president of Bonnell in August 1966. To quote Bruce Gottwald, "He, Mal Harvey, took over the company when it was earning $200,000 or $300,000 a year and turned it around to where it consistently earned over $1 million and sometimes over $3 million per year."

About four years after the purchase of Bonnell, Ethyl bought another aluminum company, Capitol Products Corporation of Mechanicsburg, Pennsylvania, a few miles west of Harrisburg. A controlling interest was acquired in 1969, the remaining shares early the following year. Mixing pig aluminum, scrap metal, and various alloys, Capitol Products made aluminum ingots, some of which were used in its own extrusion processes, the remainder sold to other extruders of aluminum. The specialty of Capitol Products was fabrication of aluminum frame doors and windows.

The story of Capitol Products down to the time it was purchased by Ethyl is largely the biography of one man, Eugene Gurkoff, onetime seller of shoes and venetian blinds. A self-educated man whose forefathers had emigrated from Russia, Gurkoff was another one of those Horatio Alger figures appearing in all corners of the Ethyl story. Planning was quite informal in those early days. "We used to make up budgets on the back of an envelope," said one of the old employees. The Capitol workers were in general a stable lot, many of them country people from scrub farms in Perry County.

The very traits that made Gurkoff a most efficient manager of local production—personal attention to daily details—contributed to his lack of success when he tried to expand into distant areas. Also he suffered with the aluminum industry as a whole in the 1950s and the early 1960s as the result of general over-expansion. By the mid-1960s affairs were improving. Then Gurkoff suffered a heart attack and decided that his assets simply had to be in more liquid condition.

Negotiations began with Ethyl in October 1969, and by November the basic agreement had been reached. Although Gurkoff was in a comfortable financial situation with $17 million or thereabouts that he and his family had received from Ethyl, he found himself somewhat depressed because, as he said, manipulating money was not quite as satisfying as manipulating machinery and people.

For several years after the purchase of Capitol Products there was the predictable problem of getting Capitol to move effectively into the Ethyl system. A close working relationship may be dated from the time George Thumlert, an experienced Capitol man whom Bruce Gottwald characterized as a "whiz bang," was put in charge as local manager, reporting directly to Harvey. In addition Ethyl brought in George L. Anton, an old-time Ethyl man who had departed the company for ten years and then returned. Anton, after a season with Oxford Paper, was placed in Mechanicsburg "to kind of bring along some of the Ethyl flavor," as he himself describes his initial role. After Thumlert left in 1980, Anton became vice president and general manager.

With the acquisition of Bonnell and of Capitol, there seemed to be enough of a captive market to justify a reconsideration of a large-scale integration backward toward, if not including, the bauxite mines. Repeatedly management reviewed, then rejected the program to build a reduction plant. Construction costs always seemed too great. Concessions for the mining of bauxite were obtained in Brazil along the Jari River, which flows into the Amazon. Ultimately these rights were sold, Ethyl Corporation taking a loss on the transaction.

Although the fully integrated aluminum operation from bauxite mines to the fabricated end-product has never been achieved, the periodic hopes and their fractional fulfillment had advantageous consequences quite apart from the profitable extruder business. The interest in aluminum led to substantial research and development programs that hold significant promise for the future.

With Smylie's illness and early retirement, Harvey took over the administration of all the aluminum operations, which included an expansion of Bonnell into a new aluminum extrusion plant near Carthage, Tennessee, completed in 1969, and the erection of an extrusion-fabrication plant in Kentland, Indiana, in 1972 under the direction of Capitol Products management.

Despite the cyclical nature of the aluminum industry as a whole, moving in cadence with the construction business, the aluminum division of Ethyl has been remarkably successful, the envy of its competitors. Today the aluminum division produces something approaching one-tenth of Ethyl's profits.

The aluminum ventures and the large plans which clung to them directed attention to a broad spectrum of energy sources. Waterpower in the west, the dams of the Tennessee Valley Authority, all had a place in the necessary game of imagination before the undertaking of big projects. And there was the conclusion, at least in Gottwald's mind, that coal reserves would now be a good investment.

Then along came Stuart Saunders, former railroad official, affiliated at the time with Wheat, First Securities of Richmond. Late in 1973 Saunders reported to Gottwald the availability of a large block of stock, about 25 percent, in the Elk Horn Coal Corporation owned by the Chessie System. Saunders had long been associated with Gottwald as a fellow director of the First and Merchants National Bank. Bruce Gottwald is frank enough to give chance and luck a large part of the credit for the Elk Horn purchase. In his words, there was not any "particular genius on our part; it was just darn lucky timing."

Elk Horn owns approximately 130,000 acres of coal lands in eastern Kentucky, most of which it leases to operators. At the time of the purchase about one-half of the total acreage was under contract. Elk Horn itself did no mining; it was owner, not operator. Ethyl bought the Chessie stock and additional shares sufficient to raise its holdings to over 95 percent by February 22, 1974. The total investment was approximately $25 million.

In terms of potential profit, Elk Horn was a handsome acquisition. In terms of administration, this was another matter. The quality of the coal proved to be, on the average, well above expectations. There was much low-sulphur, high-BTU coal, which put it in a classification superior to ordinary boiler quality. Some of it was labeled metallurgical grade. After the first investigations following the purchase, Gottwald said, "I haven't seen anything in my life like it." Exploratory drilling confirmed the estimates of large reserves, actually about twice as much as originally thought.

Partly offsetting the unexpected high quality of the coal were the unexpected numerous management and boundary problems confronting the new owners. For a proper understanding of this complex situation, one should remember the general history of the Cumberland Plateau, especially the wildly fluctuating price of coal and the effects of an uneven market on management philosophy and practice throughout the years.

C. Raymond Hailey suggests that the best introduction to the recent social history of the area in which Elk Horn is located is the book *Night Comes to the Cumberlands* by Harry Caudill. Caudill presents a bleak picture of past exploitation and inherited poverty. Until about 1974 even the operators, who might have owned equipment valued at thousands of dollars, had a life only a little bit better than the man smoking his pipe in the shanty down the hollow. Then in 1974, following the Arab oil embargo and skyrocketing prices for crude oil, came a sudden upsurge in coal prices. Individual operators made more money after taxes in one year than they had made in a lifetime.

The most immediate problem confronting Ethyl after the purchase of Elk Horn was the pattern of overlapping and conflicting lease claims. Frequently there were two or more "layers" of leases on the same piece of property—in one instance *four.*

This chaotic situation with regard to boundaries apparently originated in the loose and lax way of passing out leases when the coal business was in the doldrums, coal bringing at times only a bit above two dollars a ton. The owner wanted his royalty in a hurry; the operator was in even more haste for income that came from selling the coal. The game was to put the operator on as productive a piece of land as possible, and quickly move him somewhere else if the yield was low.

The landowner might say, "I put Joe on your land, but I'm going to give you some more over here. So we will straighten out the paper work as we go along." And then there would be delay or neglect in filing proper papers at the courthouse. This once friendly confusion became a serious matter when coal prices rose tenfold and there was a scramble for productive mines. By report another problem was that in some parts of the industry there was an outright under-the-table payment technique. Such maneuvers superimposed on carelessness resulted in a series of complex problems to be unscrambled.

Straightening out these boundary conflicts was no small task. Early in 1976 a change in Elk Horn administration was effected. Engineers and miscellaneous management people were borrowed from the parent company. Heading the operations by June was Raymond Hailey, who always seemed to gravitate toward trouble spots. Fresh from Oxford Paper Company's administration, an assignment that will be mentioned in a general review of the paper division, Hailey took over the management of Elk Horn and gave it prime attention until the coming of John D. Gottwald as general manager in December 1979, when Hailey divided his efforts between Elk Horn and the Plastics Group. With Hailey remaining as president of Elk Horn, John D. Gottwald, son of Floyd D. Gottwald, Jr., was named executive vice president and general manager of the coal company in 1980.

At the time of the acquisition by Ethyl, Elk Horn owned a subsidiary corporation named West Virginia Belt and Repair Company, which sold mill and mine supplies. In addition Elk Horn had one-sixth ownership of Kentucky River Coal Company, which, like Elk Horn, was a leasing and not an operating business. In a highly complex arrangement Ethyl sold its minority interest to the Kentucky River Coal Company for about $10 million. As F. D. Gottwald explained it, Ethyl had no business retaining an investment on which it had to pay a heavy income tax. The West Virginia Belt and Repair Company was sold by Ethyl in 1981.

Fitting into the pattern of Frank Howard's early fascination with the German experiments in hydrogenation of coal, Ethyl researchers undertook a continuing series of experiments in the area of coal chemistry. F. D. Gottwald spoke to his directors about the great possibilities in this sort of investigation. It takes no imagination to see that somebody was dreaming of the day when the fuel tanks of automobiles in America might be filled with a liquid originating in the Kentucky coal beds. Several years ago when he was being interviewed, Gottwald almost involuntarily let such a vision be revealed. First he referred to aluminum research and said, "It is so dog-gone exciting it makes you rise up in your seat." Then he added that when he turned his mind from aluminum to "what we are doing in chemicals from coal, why we get excited about that!"

Elk Horn as now operated should be classified as a superb investment. There is respectable current income. In 1979 the operating profit was $4.1 million, in 1981 about $10.6 million. Elk Horn could probably be sold for several times the original cost. However, John Gottwald's dream is to maintain the leasing that Elk Horn is now doing but also to develop new processing techniques. He envisages a subsidiary that would take care of some processing; and then this subsidiary would contract with operators for getting the coal out of the mines and for doing the processing. The processing might include a grinding to proper size and the treating of the coal to remove sulphur, thus enhancing its quality as steam coal.

Coal was not the only energy source sought by Ethyl. For the moment throwing aside the Gottwald antipathy toward joint enterprises, Ethyl shared with other corporations the cost of explorations for natural gas and petroleum in the North Sea. This venture began in the year 1966. Joining by way of its subsidiary Ethyl Netherlands, Ethyl Corporation, holding a one-sixth interest, became a member of the four-company group. (Ethyl's North Sea interests were sold in the spring of 1982). Natural gas wells in Louisiana and Arkansas owned by Ethyl currently supply a large part of the energy needs in the Baton Rouge plant. Natural gas was used in the very beginning of the manufacturing efforts in Baton Rouge, but in the 1960s and 1970s the development of this resource was undertaken with considerable vigor. At the beginning of 1982 Ethyl's reserves of oil and condensate were estimated to be about 1.9 million barrels, natural gas approximately 45.1 billion cubic feet. Most of these resources are in the United States, some in western Canada. Reflecting the growing importance of these resources, Ethyl created an Oil and Gas Division in 1968.

Expansion and Disappearance of Paper

At the time of the merger of Albemarle and Ethyl of Delaware, management had no idea of giving up the paper business with which the Gottwalds had been so intimately connected. Yet perhaps within that very consolidation and its attendant theme of diversification were factors that eventually led to the total disposition of the woodlands, pulp mills, paper mills, and converting operations. In the course of time those executives who determined company strategy were to find more interest and more profit in endeavors other than paper. The decision to surrender paper, however, came piecemeal and only after a period of trial with an enlarged program. Gottwald was openly defensive of papermaking as a sophisticated chemical enterprise, and in his Baton Rouge Chamber of Commerce speech of 1963 identified the merger as the joining of two chemical operations.

As the master papermaker, Gottwald gave advice to the industry when such was needed. In his address before the Kraft Paper Association in New York early in 1964, he urged the members to give up old processes and to modernize. Obviously Gottwald kept a large part of his attention focused on that subsidiary of the Ethyl Corporation entitled Albemarle Paper Manufacturing Company, in 1966 renamed simply Albermale Paper Company.

Superimposed on his interest in day-by-day operations of the paper business was Gottwald's interest, and indeed excitement, in plans for new processes. He had on the tip of his tongue a whole formula of innovative procedures that he was confident would, in the course of time, virtually revolutionize the industry and bring in major profits to Ethyl. Gottwald took particular interest in the paper-sizing projects, and reported that the processes were becoming more effective every day. On the subject of filler and blotting paper, he became almost ecstatic in his recital of the reduction of waste. He freely borrowed concepts from whatever other industries came under his observation. "So we have taken all they had developed in insulation board or building board and appropriated it for paper making."

Characteristically he urged the continuation of earlier efforts to make more effective use of hardwoods and waste such as sawdust. He now advocated the creation of a line of improved chemicals for the paper industry, and he encouraged paper research in Richmond, Roanoke Rapids, and Baton Rouge. "The goal we are working toward is a full line of paper-making chemicals," said Gottwald. He was proud of his paper research everywhere.

The most conspicuous evidence of the continuing interest in the paper industry was the purchase of Oxford Paper Company in 1967. The principal mill of Oxford Paper, maker of fine printing papers and allied quality products, was located in Rumford, Maine. There were two other mills, one in Lawrence, Massachusetts, and another in West Carrollton, Ohio. A special distinction of Oxford Paper was its contract with *National Geographic* magazine for supplying the paper used in the printing of that well-known periodical. Neither the Massachusetts nor the Ohio mill was an integrated organization; pulp had to be brought in from the outside. On the other hand the Rumford plant had its own pulp-making machines, and Oxford possessed over 300,000 acres of woodland in Maine and New Brunswick, Canada.

Oxford was owned by the Chisholm family, which for many years had exercised patriarchal and benevolent control over the basic operation in Rumford. The then head of the family was William ("Bill") Chisholm, a most polished gentleman who carried forward the tradition of management instituted by his father and his grandfather. Chisholm's senior thesis at Yale was *Benevolent Industrialism, Past and Present*, a theme symptomatic of a family philosophy. When the present researcher inquired of Chisholm as to the distinctive feature of Oxford, Chisholm protested that this was a difficult question, but attempted an answer: "Certainly the company had a great deal of consideration for people, customers as well as the Oxford people themselves."

Charlie Ferguson, who was reportedly the best superintendent Oxford ever had, and a man called "Mr. Oxford Paper," narrated the story of the interest and assistance of Bill Chisholm's father when in the old days Ferguson's wife needed open heart surgery. By the time Bill Chisholm came into full control the company did not have sufficient capital to do the things that management wanted to do.

The town of Rumford and the company called Oxford are as one. Oxford is Rumford's only major industry and traditionally there was a comfortable feeling when the people looked at Oxford management and remembered its inherited reluctance to interrupt the tenure which had been held by some families for generations. The community is a mixture of French Canadians, Prince Edward Islanders, some Poles and, of particular importance for the paper industry, a number of Scotsmen described as the major papermakers, men who could feel the stock and then give a crisp verdict. There were strong ties of kinship as well as friendship cutting across management-worker lines, and there was a certain insulation from the outside because of geography and climate.

Chisholm needed capital not only for improvement in existing operations but for building a plant in Upper Michigan. The deal with Ethyl was promoted by James F. Miller, who had played an important role in the purchase of Ethyl by Albemarle. Miller, when he moved to Blyth's New York office from the West Coast, had inherited the role of financial advisor to officials of Oxford Paper and had already assisted in some of their borrowing.

With Miller as intermediary and "finder," Ethyl management decided that Oxford would be a handsome complement to its existing paper operations. An analysis of Oxford assets showed that the merger would strengthen the Ethyl balance sheet, particularly in the category of equity versus debt. And the aquisition of Oxford with its bleached product would be a further move in the direction of diversification. The outcome was an exchange of Oxford stock for an issue of Ethyl preferred valued at about $124 million. The Ethyl board of directors on April 20, 1967, approved the Oxford merger in principle and, after a vote by stockholders, the merger became effective August 1, 1967. As a result of the merger, Chisholm became a member of Ethyl's executive committee and board, as well as executive vice president and divisional president.

At the beginning of the association with Oxford, F D. Gottwald, showed a great deal of enthusiasm for the new acquisition that featured bleached paper. To quote Gottwald, "When we first started out with Rumford, papermaking was my hobby as well as my forte and I traveled up there considerably." Someone in the Ethyl organization said with wry emphasis that it was a hardship on Oxford that the three top officials of Ethyl had been brought up in the paper business.

Unhappily, the purchase of Oxford coincided almost exactly with a drastic decline in paper prices, part of the cyclical pattern characteristic of the paper industry. The first result of the downswing of the paper industry in 1967 was the reappraisal of the older, not the newer, paper operations owned by Ethyl. In a move that surprised many individuals, Ethyl Corporation in October sold to Hoerner Waldorf Corporation for about $56 million substantially all the properties of Albemarle Paper Company, Interstate Bag, and Halifax Timber Company—in effect all the assets of the subsidiaries except the small paper operations in Richmond along the James River. For the moment these, with the familiar names of Hollywood, Riverside, Tredegar, and Brown's Island, were incorporated into a newly formed Ethyl subsidiary entitled James River Paper Company.

In explaining the sale to the directors on September 26, 1968, Gottwald emphasized three major points. (1) If the properties were retained there would be heavy capital requirements in order to expand operations in such a way as to create an adequate return; (2) the estimated rate of return on either the present or the possible additional capital investment in paper was less than that of the estimated return on other Ethyl operations; (3) the cash proceeds from the sale to Hoerner Waldorf would make possible an increased flexibility in planning for expansion elsewhere. Furthermore, the price was considered favorable.

In reminiscing about the decision to sell to Hoerner Waldorf, Gottwald said management feared that in the future the woodlands in the Virginia and North Carolina area would be inadequate for the proper operation of an integrated paper business; the plan was to purchase a paper mill in the Deep South.

Among the key individuals from the old Albemarle-Ethyl group who went along with the various properties to the Hoerner Waldorf company was Lebby Boinest, a skilled papermaker who earlier had moved from Roanoke Rapids to Richmond when the Consumer Bag Company was bought and he was needed as top official at that subsidiary. In 1969 when Kirkwood Adams retired as manager of the Roanoke Rapids operations, he was succeeded by Boinest.

Hoerner Waldorf, selective in its choice of Albemarle assets, did not need the Richmond riverfront operations. At the opening of the dove-hunting season in November 1968, two men sat in a cornfield in Goochland County with their guns empty of shells. Though they had dutifully dressed in outdoor clothing and had met at the appointed hour, they had lost all interest in the birds. Robert C. Williams and Richard C. Erickson, employed by Albemarle Paper Company, the Ethyl subsidiary, had heard of Hoerner Waldorf's acquisition of most of Albemarle's assets, and were trying to look into the future. Endowed with more than a dash of the entrepreneurial spirit, Williams had already begun to figure a way for a group of men from the papermaking and financial community to take over all, or part of, the properties that remained with Ethyl after the Hoerner Waldorf purchase. He was soon in alliance with Brenton S. Halsey, who, as already noted, had been transferred to the subsidiary, Interstate Bag Company, Inc.

Williams and Halsey, known today as cofounders of the new company, initiated negotiations for the purchase of the waterfront paper operations, not the full acreage. The primary arrangement, which involved the Hollywood and Riverside Mills and the adjacent saturating plant, was formally completed on April 25, 1969. James River Corporation dates its founding as an independent company from that particular moment. Two months later, June 21, 1969, the cast-coating operations—the business and the machinery, but not the real estate—were added to the original purchase.

The release of the properties to the new James River Corporation by Ethyl included whatever paper business was associated with Brown's Island and Tredegar, and also the transfer of the famous old trademarks, World, Vienna Moire, and Reliance, all in origin going back to the early days of Albemarle. In a sort of musical chairs maneuver, the Halsey-Williams group ended up with the name "James River Corporation."

The basic properties were sold to the Halsey-Williams group for about $1.5 million and the saturating plant for approximately $850,000. Soon Bruce C. Gottwald became a member of the James River board of directors. Oil filter and air filters for automobiles were major products manufactured by the James River Corporation. It is not surprising that Ethyl sold these units to its former employees. In its now emphatic ideas as to integrated operations, Ethyl would never have been happy with plants that had to buy pulp from other firms.

There is, of course, a kinship between Ethyl on the hill and James River down on Tredegar Street. James River has the original Albemarle property and until recently still operated the 1887 paper machine, though one must confess that new parts, major and minor, were required during the previous ninety-plus years. The date "1887" could be clearly seen on the framework until replacements were made in 1981.

Complex and even controversial is the story of the decision by Ethyl management to give up the idea of building an Oxford Paper plant in Michigan, a plant greatly desired by Chisholm and his aides. In reminiscing about these events, Chisholm explains that one of the reasons that Oxford management sought a firm with capital substantial enough for a merger was the hope for a large paper operation in Michigan. Ethyl management went no further than the promise to study the situation. As late as January 23, 1968, Ethyl's executive committee was considering the proposed plant in detail. Eventually, Ethyl management decided that $120 million, the estimated cost of the Michigan plant, was simply too much. Chisholm was unhappy about the decision, and this was only one of several disappointments. To put the matter simply, the Chisholm ideas and the Gottwald ideas of management were not the same.

In that tightly knit little community of Rumford there was subterranean resentment at the coming of the southern carpetbaggers, who with their efficiency squads would upset the ancient ways. The labor climate in Maine was different from that in Virginia and North Carolina. However, several leaders of the Oxford old guard conspicuously defended the proposed innovations in management and operations as necessary. Many procedures and some machines seemed obsolete to those seeking for improvement in the profit picture. Even the northern woodlands, with their slow growth compared with the southern pine, and some infestation, presented difficult problems.

By all reports the coming of Hailey into the management of Oxford Paper stabilized a difficult situation and brought profits to the point where the Oxford operation could present to the world a face attractive enough to bring in an outside buyer. On July 1, 1969, Hailey had left Hoerner Waldorf and returned to Ethyl as executive vice president of Oxford. In the spring of 1970 Hailey succeeded Chisholm as president of the Oxford Paper Division. A new cost-cutting approach was necessary and in the words of Andrew M. McBurney, an old-time Oxford man, "Ray went about it in a beautiful way, magnificent way. Tough but fair and he cut the work force back with the help of a lot of people."

After some difference of opinion within the Ethyl upper management group as to what price should be put on Oxford, the Rumford plant was sold in 1976 to Boise Cascade Corporation for approximately $90 million. The agreement in principle was

C. Raymond Hailey

announced February 19, 1976; the formal sale was dated April 26, 1976. The transaction was negotiated by James F. Miller, who had been the "finder" of Oxford in the first place.

At the time of the sale to Boise Cascade, Ethyl management said that the purchase money would strengthen the financial capabilities of Ethyl and permit it to concentrate on the chemical business. On the other hand, Ethyl management said that the sale would be a good acquisition for Boise Cascade, which had an organization to direct, and capital to spend, in modernizing the mill. Hugh Baird, a former Albemarle Paper treasurer, who in 1970 had taken over the position of controller of Oxford Paper Division, says, "Well, I thought this sale of Oxford was one of the few deals in which buyer and seller came out ahead." Baird's basic point of view is that Ethyl simply did not want to spend about a quarter of a billion dollars to make the mill automatic as should be done to put it in a competitive position. It was a matter of where one wanted to put his capital. In a moment of candid recollection Gottwald said, "Oxford Paper Company was in some respects our own fault in not thoroughly examining what we were buying."

The Oxford experience has been measured in various ways. There were several financial advantages offsetting much of the difference between purchase and sale price. Notably there was the receipt of $10 million in compensation for lands appropriated by Canadian authorities.

Any summation of the profit-or-loss question in the Oxford Paper venture should properly include the advantages to Ethyl of bringing into the Ethyl family individuals from the Oxford–*National Geographic* combination. Andrew McBurney was an important recruit. McBurney was born in Philadelphia in 1913. At Yale University he began his studies at the Sheffield Scientific School, but now vows that, as to engineering drafting, "I couldn't draw a straight line." According to his own gleeful report, his professor agreed that McBurney would be given a passing grade on the engineering drawing course if he would promise never, *never* to make a profession of engineering! After graduation from the Yale liberal arts program in 1936, he joined Oxford Paper, beginning by living in a lumber camp where he learned a great deal from his fellow workers, a mixed group of men some of whom did not speak English very well. To quote McBurney, "We didn't have beds; we lay on the boards with straw. So I had my start in the woods operation and worked all the way through the rest of the mill." In the mill he had the benefit of close supervision by Charlie Ferguson, "Mr. Oxford Paper."

After serving in the Pacific Theater from 1943 to 1946 with the Marine Corps, in which he earned the rank of captain, he returned to Oxford and in 1948 became eastern sales manager and a director of the company. In 1946 McBurney was elected executive vice president of Oxford. With the Ethyl-Oxford merger in August 1967, McBurney was elected to the Ethyl board of directors and has continued on the board ever since.

With the sale of Oxford, Ethyl (meaning that organization with a lifeline reaching back to 1887), was without paper manufacturing for the first time. At the moment of the disposition of the paper properties, however, Gottwald refused to look on these events as signaling a permanent departure from the paper business. He said that as for himself he never intended getting out of the paper business. In his mind there were special reasons for the sales. Emphasizing an earlier project, he said, "Our idea was to buy larger and more integrated operations farther south."

Insofar as the present writer knows, the nearest Gottwald ever came to a detailed summary of the reasons for disposal of the paper business once held by Ethyl was on August 1, 1977, when he was asked for such a statement. Said Gottwald: "We early in the game saw two things: one, that Roanoke Rapids was improperly located from the standpoint of the paper business as we expect it to be; and second that Roanoke Rapids together with the purchase of the Oxford Paper Company—the combination of the two—was a mistake. We wanted to go very largely into the paper business and every time we did that we ran into Federal Trade Commission regulations, or anyhow competition entered into the picture. So the best thing to do was sell out completely and start all over again. We still have in mind going into the paper business, but selling both of them was for the purpose of going into the paper business in a larger way."

When a visitor to his office soon after the disposition of Oxford asked him whether this was the first time he had been without a paper business, Gottwald replied, "Well, we have a difference of opinion within the company now. Some don't want to get back into the paper business, but the very fact that it is a replaceable raw material," and his voice at this point trailed off into a moment of silence. Then he began to talk in a nostalgic vein about the wonderful opportunities for new technology in paper, especially in the use of hardwoods. He spoke of a gum tree that could be cut off at the stump, and immediately a new tree would begin growing from that stump.

IX

Chemicals at Home and in Foreign Lands

"Get the Lead Out"

ETHYL'S PROGRAM OF diversification was made urgent by a two-pronged attack on tetraethyl lead as a gasoline additive: one by environmentalists, who alleged it to be a hazard to public health, and another by automobile manufacturers who, in attempting to meet emission standards adopted by federal authorities, developed a catalytic converter incompatible with the use of leaded gasoline. Ethyl Corporation took a stand from which it never retreated. Its basic position was that the use of lead antiknock compounds does not constitute a health hazard or a significant source of air pollution, and that this position is fully supported by over five decades of extensive research. Ethyl never denied that some lead came out of the tailpipes of automobiles using the tetraethyl lead additive, but contended that this lead was a very small part of the lead problem and an inconsequential fraction of the general pollution problem.

There were skirmishes and battles won and lost. Ethyl eventually lost in the courts by a five-to-four decision. The defeated, however, looked back on their efforts with pride. Ethyl's struggle to maintain the reputation of a product it considered a great contribution to American life is the subject of the first two sections of this chapter.

By way of review it should be recalled that soon after the discovery of tetraethyl lead as an effective antiknock additive to gasoline, manufacturers and governmental groups studied its acknowledged toxic qualities. The first investigations, which were conducted mainly by the U.S. Bureau of Mines, concentrated on the problem of automobile emissions. The verdict was favorable to the new additive. Then with the tragic deaths in 1924–25 attention was focused on the process of manufacture, mixing, and distribution. The result of this study, carried on principally under the supervision of Dr. Robert Kehoe, was the rigid application of safety measures that reduced the chance of fatalities in those areas. For the next twenty-five years Dr. Kehoe conducted for Ethyl elaborate research on the health aspects of lead and came to be generally recognized as the world's foremost expert on its toxic qualities.

In the 1950s there were new questions as to what comes out of the automobile tailpipe, these questions arising because of mid-century concern for the quality of the environment. In its origin the movement certainly seemed innocent enough. The advocacy of clean air as one phase of this environmental movement appealed of course to every breathing person. It attracted the attention of the Coordinating Research Council (CRC) made up of representatives from government and industry, including automobile makers, the petroleum industry, and CRC's suppliers. From the beginning of its formation in the pre–World War II days, Ethyl had been an active member.

When the problem of air pollution became a matter of public discussion, a division was set up within the CRC to cooperate with investigating groups. This general study was reinforced by Dr. Kehoe's desire to know more about automobile emissions, and a new company program was set up in 1950. Solid, documented research was carried on in Ethyl's Detroit laboratories following Dr. Kehoe's request, and the data were useful in bolstering the Ethyl reports to investigating bodies as events unfolded. In the words of a contemporary observer, the investigation known as Project 5OUI "stood the test of time."

George Kirby when president of Ethyl took a special interest in the investigations as to any possible hazard to public health as a result of gasoline being treated with lead additives. Important personalities involved in this pre–1970 period included Howard E. Hesselberg, Richard Scales, and Joseph Carter of Hunton and Williams. Although Dr. Kehoe was retired as medical director of the company in 1958, he was soon recalled for special services. A vigorous—one is tempted to say impassioned—advocate of his cause was Hesselberg. Born in Wisconsin, Hesselberg received the B.S. degree in mechanical engineering from the University of Missouri in 1940 and in that same year joined Ethyl. He was for a season engaged in a special program at the Detroit laboratories under Earl Bartholomew's supervision studying the advantages of higher compression. In Hesselberg's research he attempted to learn the fundamentals of knock and engaged in the on-going hunt for another effective antiknock compound. Save for a leave of four years when he served with the U.S. Army in World War II, he was with Ethyl from that time until his retirement in August 1981. In 1966 he was named coordinator, air conservation, in 1971 vice president, air conservation.

As Ethyl representative in the various activities of the CRC, Hesselberg became involved with California authorities trying to reduce air pollution. The Los Angeles area with its unique topography and congested freeways had a first-class smog problem and became the focal point of investigations. As a member of the CRC team, Hesselberg met with officials of the Los Angeles County Air Pollution Control District. He and his coworkers supplied the instruments for measuring air pollution, furnished headquarters in Ethyl's Los Angeles office for pioneering work on auto emissions, and aided the Los Angeles investigations in other ways. Hesselberg found helpful the results of the Ethyl program Project 5OUI started in 1950 to discover the nature and extent of lead that is emitted from tailpipes. Also useful were the data from the independent research group, Midwest Research Institute of Kansas City, which in 1956 had been employed by Ethyl to study the nature of photochemical smog. It was the conclusion of Midwest Research that lead did not enter into this reaction.

Dr. Kehoe, on April 30, 1956, in temperate and scholarly fashion addressed the California Club in Los Angeles, reassuring his audience in the matter of contamination of the air by lead compounds. A key figure in the critical approach was Dr. Clair Cameron Patterson, who had settled at the California Institute of Technology as research fellow in 1952. His earliest distinction was association with colleagues at the University of Chicago in developing methods for dating common rock minerals and determining the sequence of geological events.

It was no surprise that the refining industry was favorable to the lead antiknock compounds. The American Petroleum Institute, Division of Refining, meeting in Los Angeles on May 16, 1967, explained the high investment that would be required if the refiners had to install equipment to make up for the loss in octane numbers should lead be eliminated as an additive.

Ethyl's attempt to meet the challenge presented in California was not only by way of continued research and special testimony but through an effort to produce devices that would minimize exhaust problems. In the mid 1950s to cope with the California requirement, Ethyl developed an exhaust device that was approved by the Los Angeles authorities. In 1964, however, the major automobile manufacturers announced that their 1966 models would comply with the California standards in a way quite different from the exhaust devices; that is, their efforts would be concentrated on the intake system. This approach by the manufacturers appeared to eliminate the chance for a market for the Ethyl exhaust device at any time in the near future.

The clean-air movement in California spread to other parts of the land though in less vigorous form than on the west coast. To quote Hesselberg, "California was leading the pack in everything connected with air pollution and it was not long before we were having hearings in various parts of the country, and in fact the world." In his office files is a long list of cities, counties, and states where the Hesselberg group appeared to defend the use of lead in gasoline. Hesselberg himself was involved in nearly all of the local hearings, and sometimes two or more were going on simultaneously. Then Clarence A. ("Cap") Hall would head the defensive team.

Critics have said that Washington, D.C., was determined not to be outdone by Los Angeles. In a three-day symposium in Washington December 13–15, 1965, the U.S. Public Health Service Seminar examined the potential health hazards from all forms of environmental lead. Ethyl saw no adverse effects flowing from that particular meeting; the press releases underscored the economic hardships that would be caused by the disappearance of lead antiknocks.

Among the congressional committees set up was that headed by Senator Edmund Muskie of Maine and labeled the Air and Water Pollution Subcommittee of the Senate Public Works Committee. Dr. Kehoe testified at the Muskie Committee hearing in 1966. In the opinion of the late Richard Scales, Kehoe had the fate of the company in his hands; if he had wavered the company would have been faced with disaster. "He was the key man in that whole thing; he bought us time," said Scales. The Muskie committee planned to hear about air pollution and to give consideration to the sources of lead in the atmosphere. At the end of the testimony before the Muskie group, Kirby, president of Ethyl, reported to the board that overall the results of the proceedings were satisfactory from the company's viewpoint, a judgment with which Joseph Carter, who had been present throughout the entire hearings, agreed. In general there was no undue emphasis given to the company's product and no adverse publicity with regard to the additive.

Although the various investigations tended at times to be critical of tetraethyl lead, officials of Ethyl looked on the developments up to the end of 1969 as of second- or third-rate importance.

When George Kirby, late in 1969, submitted his resignation as president of Ethyl to become head of Texas Eastern Transmission, the Ethyl executive committee parceled out the various functions Kirby had performed. Bruce Gottwald was elected president and assumed basic high-level responsibilities, but in the president's office, as organized at that time, there were odds and ends that on review by the executive committee seemed more appropriate elsewhere.

As the members of the executive committee looked at the Detroit-based air conservation group that upheld Ethyl's point of view in the miscellaneous skirmishes over lead, the discussion slipped into a jesting mood, and there were moments of inspired levity. As Blanchard recalls the circumstances, "They jokingly said that nothing was going on, and even Larry ought to be able to handle nothing." In this offhand, casual manner Blanchard, in effect, was appointed general in a war that was to endure even as this volume is completed. The very day the air conservation group was put under Blanchard's jurisdiction was the beginning of what has been called "the environmental decade."

Blanchard enjoyed two full weeks of relative calm on the lead front before the storm broke. Edward N. Cole, who had been president of General Motors since 1967, announced in Detroit at a meeting of the Society of Automotive Engineers on January 14, 1970, that to achieve the desired air quality in the engine exhaust as scheduled by federal regulations General Motors planned to install a catalytic converter. And he added that since leaded gasoline was incompatible with the platinum catalyst, leaded gasoline would have to be phased down or out.

Although Cole in his speech never actually used the phrase "get the lead out," headline writers summarized his statement in that unforgettable line. The cryptic imperative, drawn from the forepart of a somewhat inelegant folk saying, caught the fancy of the public.

The statement by General Motors was a bombshell, striking the automotive and allied industries without warning. Here was General Motors, which had fathered the additive, calling for its demise! And it struck some people as incongruous—not to use a harsher word—for General Motors to sell half of what was essentially a lead additive firm for many millions and then to advocate annihilation of the lead antiknock business.

The automobile manufacturers in general seemed willing to follow the General Motors advocacy of unleaded gasoline. The oil companies and the makers of tetraethyl lead saw the move as "passing the buck" to the petroleum industry, which would have to spend billions of dollars in remodeling refineries to produce the high-octane gasoline ordinarily required by that generation of automobiles. Both alarm and bitterness characterized the Ethyl camp.

Cole, a smart, hard-hitting executive, was the epitome of the forceful and confident character of the company he headed. He was simply soaked in the General Motors tradition; even his bachelor's degree came from the General Motors Technical School, an institution that had earned academic accreditation. The antilead stance was no personal whimsey of Cole, it might be said. Apparently the General Motors research group concluded that the catalytic converter route was the only possible way to meet the scheduled federal clean air regulations.

This was a time for soul-searching and stock-taking at Ethyl. Almost coincident with the General Motors statement, a statement only slightly modified in the ensuing months, there was in various sections of the country a quickened move for governmental restrictions on tetraethyl lead itself, which was accused of being a public health hazard. The year 1970 saw the celebration of Earth Day and other clamorous public demonstrations. After reviewing all factors, Ethyl management decided that it was fully justified in speaking out for this additive, which had saved billions of dollars for the American economy and helped make possible the modern automobile. There had to be alternatives to Cole's catalyst that was incompatible with leaded gasoline. And again Ethyl management reviewed all data available and was convinced that the exhaust from automobiles using gasoline treated with tetraethyl lead made only an inconsequential addition to the contaminants in the atmosphere.

The Ethyl air conservation group was made up principally of Scales, Hesselberg, and Hall, aided by the Hunton and Williams team composed of Joseph C. Carter, Jr., John J. Adams, and soon David F. Peters. Blanchard took the lead in direct confrontation with major critics.

Almost immediately after the Cole announcement, Blanchard was tugged at from all sides. At the time he was scheduled to speak in California in March 1970, he was simultaneously asked to appear before congressional committees. The meeting in California was called by then Governor Ronald Reagan, who invited—reluctant participants used the word *summoned*—the automobile manufacturing concerns, the oil refining companies, and the makers of tetraethyl lead to a two-day meeting in Sacramento. On the morning of March 4, 1970, Reagan opened the meeting, and then came the keynote address given by Cole. The chairman was Dr. A. J. Haagen-Smit, sometimes known as the "Father of Smog," a dedicated man, head of the California Air Resources Board (CARB) that sponsored the hearings. The California Air Resources Board has been described as a forerunner of the U.S. Environmental Protection Agency (EPA).

When it came time for Blanchard to speak, he gave a hard-hitting defense of tetraethyl lead and a clear statement in opposition to the program presented by General Motors. The forceful address by Ethyl's representatives earned accolades for the speaker and a new prestige for Ethyl in the petrochemical industry. Though the speech today may seem aggressive, even intemperate, it was in fact a compromise between the understandably furious statements of F. D. Gottwald and the compromising mood of some of the Detroit group, which insisted that General Motors was an old and helpful friend who should not be antagonized.

In the various encounters between Ethyl and General Motors, Blanchard, in a combination of complaint and wry humor, reminded one and all that General Motors was disavowing the products of its own offspring. He made the point by referring to the popular song "A Boy Named Sue" and by adding that he, Blanchard, was just "A Boy Named Ethyl." Said Blanchard, "I feel like the boy named Sue; my father named me Ethyl, but even Sue's father in the song never disowned him."

Some prankster found one of Cole's pictures and faked his autograph adding the words "To my friend, Larry." Then on the back of the picture was this doggerel:

I want my friend Larry to know
That when I say lead must go
The reason for all this flack
Is just to get Muskie off my back.

The message of the "poem" is that some observers thought Cole was trying to get Senator Muskie to point his finger at the oil companies instead of at the automobile companies. According to his critics, Cole in effect was saying, "If only the oil companies would give us the right kind of gasoline we can clean up this mess."

In Washington there were both House and Senate committee hearings on the question of clean air, and the lead question came up early in 1970. In the House of Representatives Paul G. Rogers of Florida headed the Subcommittee on Public Health and Welfare of the Committee on Interstate and Foreign Commerce. In the Senate there was the Subcommittee on Water and Air Pollution of the Committee on Public Works headed by Senator Muskie. The burden of the Ethyl testimony was to refute a simplified approach that insisted getting the lead out would pretty well clean up the air. Blanchard defined his job as trying "to show the regulatory authorities how complex it was to get the lead out" and how dependent the world was on this near-magic ingredient that enabled refineries to pick up at a small cost six or eight octane numbers that otherwise would cost billions of dollars.

A Virginia senator and a Virginia congressman saw to it that Ethyl received a fair hearing. It was the good luck of the Ethyl team to have Representative David Satterfield III, from Richmond, as a high-ranking member of the environmental subcommittee of the House, the Rogers committee. Senator William B. Spong from Portsmouth was on the Muskie committee.

The hearings were essentially on the bill that eventually became the Clean Air Act of 1970 designed to regulate not only automobiles but many other possible sources of pollution. Obviously one of the key issues was what to do about lead in gasoline. There was pervasive use of the phrase "gasoline additive," but it was always lead which people had in mind.

As already indicated, the efforts of Satterfield, Spong, and others enabled the Ethyl group in general to receive a fair hearing in the sense that it was given a large amount of time. The hearings and the testimony in Blanchard's words were "heated and lengthy." In summarizing the situation Blanchard says, "I think it is fair to say that we made great progress in convincing the legislature that the matter was infinitely more complicated than they had realized." The economic cost if lead were eliminated was underscored.

The final result was the Clean Air Act of 1970, which permitted the Environmental Protection Agency, after the hearing of medical and scientific evidence to determine whether any fuel additives would endanger the public health, to phase down or out any particular fuel additive.

About the same time a few mild victories were being obtained in congressional hearings, the Council on Environmental Quality, a group headed by Russell Train, advised the president to sponsor legislation levying a tax on leaded gasoline equal to 500 percent of the price of the product. Such a tax, of course, would annihilate the manufacturers of tetraethyl lead. It was simply another approach to "getting the lead out." To fight on a fairly intelligent level as to regulations was one thing, but this direct attack was something else. Blanchard in effect moved to Washington to prepare for battle before Representative Wilbur A. Mills and the House Ways and Means Committee, the group that would hear this "revenue" proposal.

Joining in the debate were the health and environmental agencies headed by Russell Train, a former staff adviser to that very Ways and Means Committee. Paul Rogers of Florida urged the Ways and Means Committee to adopt this proposal that would eliminate tetraethyl lead.

Blanchard probably made the best speech of his career at this hearing in September 1970. In his words, "It was just one of

those great days that you have occasionally. You could just tell
that your argument was being well received." The comment made
by Wilbur Mills from the bench was a very warm tribute; he
noted that he had finally found some good in governmental expenditures because Blanchard had cited the report from the Bureau of Mines that indicated the great advantages of lead. "Sure
enough the proposal was as much as dead that day," recalls Blanchard. The environmental people tried to manage for further
hearings, but the proposal never got out of the Ways and Means
Committee after that final day of testimony.

While the foregoing events were taking place in Washington
in 1970, there was considerable activity in the various states. When
Hesselberg was asked what events in his business lifetime he felt
best about, he said he would start off with the defeat of the Schabarum bill in 1970 in California and then work on up to the
great two-to-one court decision, which will be treated later. The
Schabarum bill had interesting origins: Peter ("Pete") Schabarum
was an All-American football player at the University of California, Berkeley, and then a professional halfback with the San
Francisco 49ers. He moved into politics, was elected to the California Assembly, and introduced the Schabarum bill to restrict
the use of lead in gasoline in California. He explained that the
two reasons he introduced this bill were to protect the catalytic
converter and to counter the ill effects of tetraethyl lead. There
was considerable struggle and the bill was defeated in the summer of 1970. After the failure of that bill the California Air Resources Board decided that the Schabarum proposals could best
be put into effect by having a series of hearings after which the
CARB would set lead levels. The contest in California ended
only after the U.S. Supreme Court in 1976 refused to hear the
appeal from the five-to-four circuit court decision. Hesselberg
was present at most of the California hearings during all those
years.

At the very end of the exhausting year 1970 an interview by
Agis Salpukas was published in the *New York Times* on Decem-

ber 27, 1970, reporting the point of view of the officers of Ethyl Corporation. They were described as being caught between the environmental movement and the auto industry, but they thought they had a good chance of coming out of the two-front war with only small injury. Management reminded the interviewer that even if leaded gasoline did not have a future in America, diversification and foreign trade would sustain the company; the foreign automobile users were not as hysterical as the Americans.

The sudden changeover of General Motors created bewilderment and hurt. The hurt was aggravated, said Blanchard, as he watched the image of Ethyl change from being "the *good guy* that made engines run smoother to the *villain* that must be eliminated if the nation wants to clean up its air."

The year 1970 ended with the Environmental Protection Agency being given by statute the authority to regulate fuel additives. But it could regulate only after listening to scientific and medical evidence. For the next five years Ethyl and its allies testified before the EPA. As will be noted more particularly below, all this eventually culminated in EPA regulations that Ethyl contested in the courts and ultimately lost in the courts.

EPA v. Ethyl

Ethyl's opposition to the act giving the EPA authority to reduce and abolish gasoline additives was, then, unsuccessful; the act was signed by President Richard M. Nixon in December 1970. The makers of tetraethyl lead, however, were to be given another chance to present their argument, this to carry out the proviso that EPA rules could be issued only after that regulatory agency had heard additional scientific and medical testimony.

The EPA gave notice on February 22, 1972, of its proposed phasedown of lead, and then scheduled public hearings in Washington, D.C., Dallas, and Los Angeles. The notice of February 22, often referred to as the "first health document," explained that the plan was to require the introduction of nonleaded gasoline by July 1, 1974, and to phase down the lead content of other gasolines to reach 1.25 grams per gallon by 1977, a reduction of 60 percent.

The oil companies, the manufacturers of the lead additives, environmentalists, and other interested people testified at the scheduled hearings. No doubt there were persons of good conscience and deep convictions on both sides of the controversy. As the hearings went on, however, and the documents issued by the EPA were studied, Ethyl representatives saw that, as administrative law was developing, the EPA assumed the role of both adversary and judge. This situation was clearly revealed in the hearings of May 2–4, 1972, in Los Angeles. At the earlier hearings in Washington and Dallas, Ethyl representatives attended and listened, but, as Blanchard recalls, "We concluded that where the most flack would come would be in Los Angeles, because that had been the state where lead had been so violently attacked, and that was where we expected the most environmentalists to gather. We concluded that it was important for Ethyl to stand up and be counted in the Lion's Den." Thus Ethyl representatives decided to wait and to testify in Los Angeles, where they drew a fortunate place in the proceedings; they were the last to testify. The testimony on May 4, 1972, was, to use Blanchard's phrase, "Ethyl's greatest moment."

The EPA staff seemed to realize that Ethyl's presentation would be the most difficult to rebut. In what was apparently the regular procedure, the EPA staff asked Ethyl representatives to file their testimony one day in advance. Naturally the EPA staff wanted no surprises. Ethyl's maneuver was to file a speech and to explain that Blanchard was still working on what he was to say; therefore there would be changes. The speech given on the fourth included references to documents which indicated that the EPA reports were based on data favorable to the antilead cause and were not judicious surveys of all the evidence before the staff members. Especially devastating to the reputation of the EPA was the demonstration of the fact that one or two important pieces of evidence, in particular the reports of Dr. Carl Shy which had been mentioned in a footnote in the first health document, presented results contrary to the contention of the EPA.

At the beginning of the hearings on May 4, Blanchard handed in his testimony and, to quote him, "I could see them flipping through it and all the way back to back, and I could hear them lean over to the other one saying, 'My God, he's gotten the Shy document.' So here they knew good and well that this document was in existence, knew how damaging it was, but they had never referred to its conclusion." The Ethyl presentation was essentially a joint effort by Blanchard and Hesselberg. Hesselberg gave supplementary material and answered questions.

At the conclusion of Blanchard's testimony, he made several requests. First he asked that the requirement that lead-free fuel be available by July 1, 1974, be postponed. He indicated that if the 1975 emission standards were postponed, clearly the unleaded fuel requirements should be postponed. Second, as for the proposed regulation requiring a phasedown of lead in regular and premium gasoline, he said, "There is absolutely no health justification for such a regulation." He argued that cars equipped with the catalytic converters and using lead-free gasoline would multiply to the extent that lead emissions would be reduced at least 40 percent by 1980. Third, he claimed that leaded gasoline had been made a "lead herring" because somehow it had been unfairly associated with the eating of old lead-based paint by children. Fourth, since some authorities still felt that a measure of control was needed despite all the evidence showing no health hazard that could be blamed on lead emissions, he advocated the use of practical lead traps that had been developed to reduce the particulate emissions, including that minute amount of lead. Such a device would control from 60 to 90 percent of lead emissions, and it would be less expensive for the nation than the approach proposed by the automakers. His concluding remarks also referred to a factor which became more important in the succeeding years; that is, the waste of crude oil because of new methods that would be required to obtain high octane gasoline if lead could not be used.

The Ethyl testimony lasted about an hour, followed by two hours of cross-examination by members of the panel and their experts. As a result of the hearings it was generally conceded that the first health document was in deep trouble. Lead companies other than Ethyl had presented their own damaging testimony. Subsequently the EPA issued a document in the *Federal Register* explaining that the EPA was reexamining its stand and was soliciting further information from the scientific community. The EPA officials were going back to the drawing board to see whether they could write another health document, one that would take care of the objections and complaints evoked by the first one.

During the year 1972 F. D. Gottwald, though admitting that the regulations proposed in February constituted a severe blow, seemed to be in a rather calm mood. He felt that the five years or so before the full impact of the phasedown was sufficient time for the company to develop earnings from sources other than tetraethyl lead.

On December 27, 1972, the EPA announced the "finalization," to quote from the annual Ethyl report, of regulations making available lead-free gasoline by July 1, 1974. Also on December 27, 1972, the EPA issued a new proposal dealing with the lead in the gasoline for cars already in existence. These regulations would require reduction of lead in gasoline from the average of that time, about 2.25 grams per gallon, to 1.25 grams by January 1, 1978; this proposal represented a one-year delay from the previously proposed deadline. Also in this report there was a revealing concession by EPA administrators, who in effect said that a serious controversy existed among government medical experts as to whether there was any evidence of a health hazard in leaded gasoline. Because of this announced difference of opinion, the EPA administrator asked for sixty more days of public comments, comments especially from the scientific community.

For Ethyl and other manufacturers of tetraethyl lead to maintain authentic arguments, it was necessary to see all relevant data. Although Ethyl had requested and received numerous documents from the EPA relating to the problem of regulating the lead in gasoline, the EPA had identified and withheld certain papers that Ethyl considered important. Believing that the EPA was withholding from the public and from interested corporations certain materials unfavorable to the antilead posture, Ethyl on September 1, 1972, sued the EPA under the Freedom of Information Act and sought access to this material. It was the first such court action under the Freedom of Information Act, which had been on the books since 1966. On November 20, 1972, Judge Robert R. Merhige, Jr., of the U.S. District Court for the Eastern District of Virginia ruled in favor of Ethyl; the ruling was sustained by the United States Circuit Court of Appeals for the Fourth District. In the meantime, in November 1972 Ethyl had initiated a second suit and on May 4, 1973, this also was settled in Ethyl's favor. However, in July 1973 there was a compromise between Ethyl and the EPA that in effect meant the EPA was agreeing to make available all the documents needed by Ethyl, and the EPA would not further appeal the two cases.

During these years of hearings and litigation, Ethyl attempted to develop engines that, using gasoline containing tetraethyl lead, would meet any commonsense emission standards. Among the results was the lean reactor system, consisting of a special manifold and unique carburetor operated on a very lean fuel-air ratio. Other lean-burn systems were developed by the automobile companies, notably Chrysler, with its electronic control of ignition firing, and Honda's CVCC. To those efforts Ethyl added what is termed an advanced lean-burn concept called the turbulent flow system that, according to Ethyl engineers, reduced emissions to levels below the standards set in all states except California, which had its own stricter limits. A distinctive feature was a new intake manifold using standard carburetors. In the late 1960s and 1970s there was notable work by Bartholomew and his protégé Fred Marsee, who became an expert in lean-burn technology. Marsee supervised the converting of the Australian Cortina to Ethyl's lean-burn system for road testing in Australia.

Did the lean-burn approach receive a good and fair examination by the automobile companies? As M. F. Gautreaux remarks, there was the NIH factor, meaning "not invented here." More important was the fact that the EPA was in general control and its approach at that time was endorsement of the catalytic converter. Gautreaux feels that EPA's position deterred the automobile people from any significant efforts at examining alternatives to the catalyst built of "noble" metal and incompatible with lead.

The EPA, after issuing the second health document, decided not to have public hearings, a decision perhaps made because of the difficulties encountered in the California hearings. But EPA did call for comments from the scientific community. Many holes were poked in this second document although it represented an entire change of approach. Then, since the EPA seemed to be in a state of disarray on the matter of evidence sufficient to issue regulations, an environmental group sued the EPA in the Court of Appeals in Washington to force it to issue rules in thirty days. The court agreed and told the EPA it had to do something in the specified thirty days. And no one in opposition was given a chance to comment on these rules that were based largely on the second health document. It was those rules forced out of the EPA that were now contested in the court by Ethyl and other manufacturers of lead additives.

The key point in the appeal from the EPA was based on the charge that the EPA had not proved the case against lead medically or scientifically; the EPA simply had not developed proper bases for determining the public health consequences of using leaded gasoline.

It was Monday, December 23, 1974, that the Federal Appeals Court set aside the ruling of the EPA that would have required the oil companies to reduce the lead in gasoline after the first of the year. The court voted two-to-one in favor of Ethyl and the other lead additive companies and against the EPA, which had been promoting a four-year program to phase down lead in gasoline. For the moment the court did not give reasons for the decision but said that the opinions would be presented later. The ruling left intact the order that there must be unleaded gasoline offered by service stations, but it did strike at the phasedown requirements.

In its issue for December 30, 1974, *Barron's* published an essay entitled "Knock at Bureaucracy," underscoring the economic benefits of retaining tetraethyl lead. It added in condemnation of the EPA, "The Company [Ethyl] charges—and the record plainly indicates—that EPA, in seeking to mandate a reduction in the lead content of gasoline, has acted in irrational, unscientific, and arbitrary fashion. It had relied heavily on documents which seem to support its claims and ignored others which effectively refuted them. It has misquoted and distorted, to the point where, as noted, its peers in the scientific community angrily rejected its findings. It has sought to suppress contrary opinion in its own ranks."

There was a season of euphoria at Ethyl. Blanchard, executive vice president and leader in the industry's fight against the antilead standard, said, "I keep thinking that I'm going to wake up and find it all just a dream." The euphoria was short-lived. The EPA asked for a full court review, and in March 1976 the nineman court divided five-to-four sustaining the EPA.

Blanchard, in his irritation with the ruling, said, "The whole proceeding against an industry that has made invaluable contributions to the American economy for more than fifty years is the worst example of fanaticism since the New England witch hunts in the Seventeenth Century." He added that, in the whole period of fifty years, "no person has ever been found having an identifiable toxic effect from the amount of lead in the atmosphere today." Ethyl management announced plans for an appeal to the United States Supreme Court. The Supreme Court review was requested by Ethyl, DuPont, PPG, and Nalco as well as by the National Petroleum Refiners Association and four oil companies. All had argued that the lead additives permitted refiners to obtain from 5 to 6 percent more gasoline from the same amount of crude oil. The Supreme Court of the United States on June 14, 1976, refused to issue the requested *writ of certiorari* and therefore let stand the five-to-four decision. The effect of all this was to uphold the 1972 regulations issued by the EPA.

A spokesman for Ethyl Corporation indicated disappointment but the company did not waver in its position. To repeat a theme already advanced, responsible company officials were proud of the stand of Ethyl Corporation and believed that the four justices in the five-to-four decision were correct in their analysis of the weaknesses of the EPA argument. The contention of the majority of that court that the EPA was justified in making a decision based on imperfect evidence because of the potential health risk involved seemed to some onlookers to be contrary to traditional standards of American justice.

The statement that no proof was needed rankled the spirits of many individuals. An editorial in the *Richmond Times-Dispatch* of Sunday, March 29, 1976, said, "In an opinion with profoundly disturbing implications, a federal court in Washington has ruled that the Environmental Protection Agency does not have to prove that a product is a public hazard in order to prohibit its use. Merely the apparent likelihood that the product is dangerous, said the court, is sufficient."

After the Supreme Court refused to hear the appeal, F. D. Gottwald took a philosophical stance and said that a decision favorable to Ethyl would have been only a paper victory because Congress would probably have passed a firmer law that would have held up in the courts.

For a time the management of Ethyl felt that it had an additive that might partly fill the gap created by the decline in tetraethyl lead sales consequent on the unfavorable rulings of EPA. This was a manganese-based additive. First developed in the 1950s as a stimulating supplement to the basic tetraethyl lead additive, it was discovered to be an effective creator of high octane numbers on its own. The entire output of the Orangeburg plant making this manganese additive was sold way ahead of production, and an expansion in Baton Rouge for large-scale production was planned. Construction was even initiated. However, the EPA soon modified its earlier tolerant attitude toward the manganese additive, which accordingly went the way of tetramethyl lead and tetraethyl lead. It is still being used in some leaded gasolines and at the time of this writing Ethyl is reviewing with the EPA the possibility of putting small amounts in unleaded gasoline as is done in Canada.

Although bulletin boards at Ethyl headquarters bravely carry the slogan "Lead is Not Dead," even the most sanguine admit that the antiknock business is in declining health. Domestic sales dropped from 368 million pounds in 1964 to about one-third of that in 1981. Perhaps the most dramatic evidence of the erosion of the market was the shutdown of the antiknock facility in Houston, June 30, 1980, at a cost of $13.2 million, a sum that comes to about $6.8 million when taxes are considered.

In addition to limiting the use of lead in gasoline, the EPA administered regulations designed to clean up the air, soil, and water. In conforming to these rules and in carrying out its own program to avoid pollution, Ethyl Corporation now spends on an average between $25 and $30 million per year.

In historical perspective Ethyl might be classified as a pioneer in the area of general safety and control of hazardous chemicals. Following the tragedies of 1924–25 there were rigidly disciplined procedures that set a pattern for both old and new Ethyl. Certain phases of company regulations to inhibit contamination were even more severe than those promoted by the EPA. The better to carry out company and governmental regulations, a department of toxicology and industrial hygiene was formed with Dr. Gary L. Ter Haar as director. A corporate environmental affairs group with Donald E. Park as director was established in 1980 to see that there was a compliance with all applicable environmental rules. Several cases involving the disposition of chemical wastes are still in the courts, conspicuously that entitled *U.S.* v. *Petro Processors of Louisiana, Inc. et al.*; summation should be delayed until all arguments have been heard and final verdicts rendered.

The experience with congressional committees in the "environmental decade" underscored the fact that Ethyl needed to maintain and strengthen a Washington organization that could promptly present its point of view to legislators and administrators when such was needed.

Ethyl's Washington office was opened in March 1965 and was first staffed by Dr. Davis M. Batson of the commercial development section on a part-time basis. After the beginning of the intense lead debate in the 1970s, Blanchard assigned him to Washington full-time. In January 1980 Lt. Gen. Jeffrey G. Smith, who had retired from the U.S. Army in 1979, became director of governmental relations for Ethyl and in that capacity heads Ethyl's office in Washington. General Smith, a Texan by birth, holds the B.S. degree in civil engineering from Virginia Military Institute, the M.S. degree from the Johns Hopkins University, and the M.A. degree from George Washington University. General Smith earned numerous decorations in his extensive military career. Dr. Batson continued to serve as associate director of governmental relations.

Several years ago a college student asked Floyd D. Gottwald, Jr., about Ethyl's lobbying activities. His reply was, "The thing we try to do is set the record straight." And he added that if legislators are not properly informed only one side of a story is written into law.

Specialty and High-Technology Chemicals

Despite the erosion of the market for its prime product, Ethyl achieved an impressive overall growth in sales and profits. There were two main avenues of expansion: first, by acquiring other companies, and second by development of internal technology. The first method is illustrated by the history of the Plastics and Aluminum groups. On the other hand most of the progress in chemicals was internal, based on methods developed by Ethyl's own researchers and engineers. Of course the dividing line between the two methods is blurred because progress in the units acquired, though primarily based on their own technology, was reinforced by expertise from Ethyl's research and development department.

It would be difficult to imagine a corporation more research-oriented than Ethyl. Ethyl of Delaware was founded as a result of laboratory research that discovered the antiknock qualities of tetraethyl lead. Continuing research to improve the product, to make production more economical, and to discover alternatives to tetraethyl lead disciplined the group of scientists ready to break out of the old restrictions and enter into novel areas under encouragement from the new administration.

Leaders in the new Ethyl management were willing to underwrite longtime research. In the words of Dr. Joseph E. Faggan of the Detroit laboratories, "They are very generous in giving us all the tools that we need to really do our research." F. D. Gottwald's interest in research was reflected in his close relationship with Gautreaux, who eventually became senior vice president and head of the research and development department.

Blanchard in a speech to the Specialized Chemicals Exposition in New York in 1979 identified Ethyl in the following words: "Contrary to what people think, Ethyl really is best classified as a specialty chemical company." He explained that when Ethyl of Virginia was formed it would have been rather easy to expand in the area of commodity chemicals and considerable effort was expended in examining that opportunity. The outcome of the study was the belief that Ethyl could not develop a distinctive position in the mass production of commodity-type chemicals that could flow rather readily from the technology involved in making tetraethyl lead. Therefore the company would move into what is broadly called specialty chemicals. In seeking a definition of specialty chemicals one recalls the remark of Ian A. Nimmo, whose task as director of investor relations often has been to interpret Ethyl policies to financial analysts: "The notion of what is a specialty and what is a commodity is defined by any twenty scribes on the subject in twenty different ways." According to Nimmo, the generally accepted definition in the trade is that specialty chemicals are those sold on the basis of *performance characteris-*

tics they provide in the user's process as opposed to the products sold by their chemical identity. In other words, specialty chemicals are marketed because of the functions they serve, not because of the products they are. At this point in his explanation Nimmo adds with a touch of the dramatic which comes only to the total believer, "It [the creation of the specialty chemical] is unique but quite often not unique in its chemistry but unique in its applications know-how. It is the black art of the tradesman who has learned the secrets which quite often set the successful specialty company apart from the nonsuccessful one; not a series of patents but a series of know-hows about the customer and the requirements of the customer."

Blanchard expanded this definition to include "special technology chemicals." These are products sold to specialty chemical markets and are based on improved manufacturing processes growing out of unique technology.

In Blanchard's judgment four areas of the Ethyl product line are particularly interesting as specialties. "They are Edwin Cooper lube additives, our line of antioxidants, our specialty PVC (polyvinyl chloride) resins and compounds, and our specialty polyethylene film."

Lube additives make it possible for the lubricants used in the crankcase, in transmissions, and in gears to satisfy the modern requirements for improved performance, such as extended mileage, longer intervals between changing oil, and lower viscosities for cold weather performance.

The second category mentioned by Blanchard is the chemicals used in antioxidants. They are sold "to manufacturers of rubber, plastic, fibers, fuels, lubricants and adhesives to resist oxidative degradation of the customer's finished product. Ethyl's antioxidants are based on the company's unique orthoalkylation technology and fall into the classification of hindered phenolics."

PVC resins, the third area, are sold sometimes but not always on a commodity basis by Ethyl. The emulsion resins are marketed in a very particular area; they are sold for battery separators and obviously they must be impervious to battery acids. The market is not only domestic, with Delco one of Ethyl's largest customers, but worldwide.

The fourth subdivision as organized by Blanchard is polyethylene films. Since the purchase of VisQueen its approach has been more in the direction of specialty products with less emphasis on the commodity-type film. Here the specialties include disposable diapers, shrink packaging, and other products. The company's taffeta films, very sophisticated polyethylene films that feel like cloth, are used in the outer sheet of diapers, although there are newer products that are marketed as liners.

Many of the products fitting Blanchard's definition of "specialty technology chemicals" are based on Ethyl researchers' work with aluminum alkyls. The catalyst nature of these products was discovered by Dr. Karl Ziegler in West Germany in the 1950s. Initially, Ethyl was looking for an alternate process in the production of lead antiknocks. Out of this work came a new class of commercial chemicals—orthoalkylated anilines and phenols—which found applications as intermediates for herbicides, antioxidants, fungicides, and pharmaceuticals. Development of this technology also led to Ethyl's current position in synthetic primary alcohols and alpha olefins, both of which have applications as intermediates for biodegradable detergents and plasticizers. Aluminum alkyls continue to be used as catalysts in plastics and synthetic rubber.

Although the aluminum alkyl procedure was never used commercially in the production of lead, those alkyls are, to quote Blanchard, "important catalysts for making polyethylene, polypropylene, polybutadiene and other rubber polymers. We've now gone on to include this same type of technology in manganese and tin. We call this group organometallics instead of just aluminum alkyls. Ethyl is the leader worldwide in these products and makes them in Belgium and Canada as well as at two locations in the United States." Here he is referring to plants in Houston and Orangeburg.

The first major development of a new plant after Albemarle acquired Ethyl was the construction of a larger linear alcohol plant in Houston. The linear alcohol process had evolved from the aluminum alkyl technology just mentioned. Blanchard explains: "It's a process for chain-growing ethylene to a linear, even-carbon alcohol from C_4 to C_{20}, again starting with aluminum alkyls and ethylene." This was a major undertaking and a major risk. Blanchard recalls that when word leaked out that he was thinking about leaving the practice of law to join Ethyl, a couple of friends came to see him to tell him what a mistake he was making—"that obviously I didn't know any chemistry, and this alcohol plant was going to be an absolute disaster, and it was going to be such a horrible financial and psychological problem when we wrote it off that I was making a big mistake. What I explained to them was that they may well have known more about chemistry and manufacturing than I did, but I sure knew more about Mr. Gottwald than they did. Ethyl might have gone bankrupt absorbing perpetual start-up costs on that alcohol plant, but I was absolutely confident Mr. Gottwald would never write it off." The company survived that period and the technology learned in this venture was useful in other specialty lines.

There was a contract between Ethyl and Procter and Gamble Company for the production and sale of these alcohols. The partnership with Procter and Gamble resulted not only in the sale of specialty alcohols to the soap manufacturer, but also in the revelation by Procter and Gamble of its future needs for detergent intermediates. Such information permitted Ethyl's development of manufacturing capabilities for production of certain of these chemicals. One such need arose from the attempt to cope with new government rules against phosphates in washing powders. This story should be presented in two parts: the development of the product NTA (sodium nitrilotriacetate), a substitute for phosphates in the manufacture of detergents; then after NTA was, in effect, banned by a federal agency, the production of zeolite A, another substitute for phosphates, was begun with more favorable reaction from federal authorities.

In 1970 an agreement was worked out with Procter and Gamble

for Ethyl to build a plant for the manufacture of NTA. The product of the plant was designed for sale to Procter and Gamble and to other purchasers. There were admittedly certain risks in the capital expenditures; however, it was felt that this was a move in the right direction of diversification. Procter and Gamble guaranteed most of the appropriation, but since Ethyl was not going to restrict the sale of the product from the new plant solely to Procter and Gamble, Ethyl took ultimate responsibility for a fraction of the costs. Then at meetings on December 17–18, 1970—Nimmo calls the second day "Black Friday in Washington"—federal authorities surprised soap manufacturers by announcing that NTA could be a health hazard to humans. The chief governmental representatives confronting the soap manufacturers were Surgeon General Jesse L. Steinfeld and EPA director William D. Ruckelshaus. In the judgment of Ethyl scientists the technical data on which the verdict was given were preliminary, fragmentary, and far removed from reality. Gautreaux, who felt that federal officials had acted "precipitously and arbitrarily," said that under the conditions of the experiments relied on by government representatives even orange juice would have flunked the test.

The detergent producers were divided in approach, offering no united front in response to the attack against NTA. In any event Procter and Gamble felt it had to give up NTA. Ethyl proceeded to cancel all its construction contracts and to take down that part of the plant which had been completed. Procter and Gamble honored its contracts to the letter and reimbursed Ethyl for most of its expenditures in a minimum of time and with a minimum of negotiations.

About a decade later the EPA seemed to indicate that it had been wrong. Note the following from an article in *Chemical and Engineering News*, January 11, 1982: "However, after exhaustive tests the Environmental Protection Agency in 1980 gave the compound at least a lukewarm bill of health, declaring that, at least for the time being, it saw no reason to regulate NTA." In

1978 Ethyl was involved with Procter and Gamble again and built a plant in Houston to manufacture zeolite A, another substitute for phosphates.

Parenthetically, it might be indicated here that Ethyl learned to cope with the governmental restraints of the day. Indeed governmental regulations in paradoxical fashion occasionally worked to the advantage of the company. In his report to stockholders of May 5, 1977, Bruce Gottwald remarked that many of the new products such as the company's insecticides that had replaced DDT were due in part to the ecological movement. In this same report he stated that Ethyl's biodegradable detergent ingredient that had replaced phosphates was moving ahead, and he also referred to meeting the attack on flourocarbons by substituting hand-activated pumps that were proving to be quite satisfactory.

After several false or partial efforts in the direction of acquiring pharmaceuticals, Ethyl established its position as supplier of intermediates to that industry. In a special category is the manufacture for McNeil Pharmaceutical (McNeilab, Inc.) at the plant in Sarnia of a major ingredient in Tolectin, a widely used antiarthritic drug. There are two small chapters in the history of Ethyl's attempts to move more directly into the finished product: first, the incomplete development of a drug known in the company as 702, which initially promised to be useful in lowering cholesterol; second, the acquisition of a minority interest in the common stock of Cooper Laboratories and the eventual disposition of these shares.

In 1965 the board of directors of Ethyl was informed of the discovery of the aforesaid drug useful in lowering cholesterol in the human body. This material at that time was undergoing limited clinical tests in the laboratories of A. H. Robins Company. In the following year there was talk about licensing 702, but further development and clinical testing required more capital than seemed warranted and the project was dropped.

With a view to outright purchase of an ongoing pharmaceutical company, an Ethyl team made serious study of the industry in the early 1970s. After a long period of investigation, Ethyl in

1974 bought 837,328 shares, a 12.5 percent interest in Cooper Laboratories, for $7.50 per share. Floyd D. Gottwald, Jr., thought this a unique opportunity to get into the drug industry on a large scale. Cooper Laboratories was well received by the medical profession and employed a large number of detail men in dermatology, internal medicine, and opthalmology. Cooper had a particularly strong position in the manufacture of toothbrushes.

Disappointment with the progress at Cooper Laboratories prompted Ethyl to sell the stock on June 20, 1977, for cash at $13.75 per share. The Cooper Laboratories venture was a good learning experience for Ethyl management; it confirmed what company officials already knew about the limited power of the minority stockholder. Furthermore there was a comfortable gain on the sale of the shares of Cooper Laboratories.

Domestic chemical plants spread beyond the old centers of Baton Rouge, Houston, and Orangeburg. The nucleus of an important new area was established when Ethyl began extracting bromine from salt wells in Columbia County, Arkansas, near the town of Magnolia. Ethyl was initially attracted to Columbia County because of the saltwater in the so-called Smackover Formation. Since the creation of Ethyl of Virginia in 1962, F. D. Gottwald had been encouraging his staff to find some source of bromine other than seawater. After extensive investigations at home and abroad the Arkansas location was chosen in 1969. Initially the operation was a joint venture with Great Lakes Chemical Company. The plant was constructed to produce ethylene dibromide using the bromine extracted from the brine in the local salt wells. Opening the Arkansas plant meant the closing of the joint venture with Dow Chemical in Freeport, Texas, which under the name of Ethyl-Dow had been extracting bromine from seawater since 1937. The new joint operation with Great Lakes ended in 1974 when Ethyl acquired full ownership.

Over the years, with the decline in sales of the Ethyl antiknock additive for reasons already outlined, the production of ethylene dibromide declined. The Magnolia complex, however, continued to grow. There was added the manufacture of other bromine

Alcohols plant at Houston

chemicals, and some which are in no wise related to bromine technology but are located in Magnolia simply because of favorable manufacturing experience in that community. In 1976 a CBN plant (chlorobutyronitrile) was established to manufacture an intermediate used in agricultural herbicides. The next year an ADMA plant (alkyldimethylamines) began manufacturing an intermediate used in various products including corrosion inhibitors, foam boosters, and germicides. In 1978 there were two new plants, one making DECTP (diethylchlorothiophosphate), an intermediate used in agricultural pesticides, the other manufacturing Pyrochek, a flame retardant. The latter subsequently discontinued operation. In 1980 a calcium bromide plant was put in operation to manufacture what was known as "a completion fluid" useful in the oil and gas industry. All in all, the capital investments in the vicinity of Magnolia totaled approximately $50 million with a labor force now numbering about 187.

The story of the Edwin Cooper Division of Burmah Oil Company provides a natural bridge between two topics, specialty and high-technology chemicals on the one hand and foreign operations on the other. As already suggested, Edwin Cooper products are perfect examples of specialty chemicals. The purchase of Edwin Cooper was a significant venture in the area of acquiring and developing chemical enterprises abroad.

Ethyl bought the British-based Edwin Cooper from Burmah Oil Company, in July 1975 for about $46 million. The purchase made possible the offering of a full line of lubricant additives, complementing the gasoline additives, Ethyl's original product. In the words of Bruce Gottwald at the time, "Of course, the fit is just beautiful!"

Long before the acquisition of Edwin Cooper, Ethyl had spent millions of dollars attempting to develop a full line of lubricant additives. Successful efforts in marketing required a combination of four, five, or six additives, each performing a special service, which would be put together in one package, as it were, to be added to lubricating oil and gear lubricants. Only in this way could the individual chemicals in a compatible mix be successfully sold to the refiners producing the lubricants.

It was a difficult business to enter. At one time Ethyl, in an attempt to broaden its line of oil additives, had tried and failed to obtain a license from Lubrizol, the company that dominated the field of lubricant additives. The possibility of buying Lubrizol had been discussed, but nothing came of gestures in that direction. In pressing its research for a more complete line, Ethyl found that it was encroaching on an area claimed by a customer on the basis of earlier patents. To keep the peace, Ethyl backed away. As Bruce Gottwald recalls in referring to the field of lubricant additives, "We just never found a way to research our way into it."

Then came the chance to buy Edwin Cooper. With headquarters in Bracknell, Berkshire, England, Edwin Cooper owned plants and laboratories in that country and in the United States. The most important American operations were a laboratory in St. Louis and a plant in Sauget, Illinois, near St. Louis, both of which had previously been owned and operated by Monsanto Company, from which most of the U.S. personnel had come. Dr. Clarence Neher was told by friends in Edwin Cooper that the owner of Edwin Cooper, the once mighty Burmah Oil Company, was facing financial difficulties. Key individuals in Edwin Cooper wanted to see the business taken over by a respectable firm able to supply capital and direction.

Many of the administrative problems in Edwin Cooper had been caused by its complex structure, a half dozen or more different corporations entwined. As Frederick Warne observed in looking back on these days, "Well, it was a very interesting project from a lawyer's point of view. It was a very complicated deal, and really a great challenge." Warne and Allen Goolsby, a lawyer who worked closely with Joseph Carter at Hunton and Williams, went to England for the negotiations. Carter, who devoted much time to this problem, remained in America. The acquisition had to be effected in such a way as not to invalidate Burmah's setup of bits and pieces that had been developed with tax burdens in mind, and at the same time to create an organization that would offer Ethyl all proper tax advantages and write-offs. As Fred Warne recalls the situation, there were so many exhibits that the attachments to the contract started with A and went past Z through OO.

There were closings in Belgium, Australia, and Singapore simultaneous with that in London. The people in London sat around for hours waiting for a letter from the Bank of England that had to be received before the deal could legally be closed. A few Ethyl representatives wondered whether there would be last-minute opposition from the Labour Government. There had been some talk of nationalization, but the American principals never did take seriously such suspicions.

According to report, Blanchard, who was in London for the closing, wanted a celebration to mark the end of negotiations. He was quoted as saying, "Well, these guys are certainly going to become one of our biggest customers, so we may as well do this thing right." Therefore a big luncheon was planned as a postscript to the closing. Although the release from the Bank of England had not come by lunchtime, the Ethyl hosts held the luncheon anyway. Finally the letter did come by 4:50 p.m. The official closing did not take place until about twenty-five minutes after five, for the letter had to be reviewed in detail. There was then the telephone call to New York City with instructions to transfer the funds, and fortunately with the difference in time the U.S. banks were open. As partial payment Ethyl deposited $34.6 million in the Morgan Guaranty Trust Company in New York City. James A. Hancock, managing director of Edwin Cooper in the Burmah era, became president of Edwin Cooper, the Ethyl subsidiary. He was later succeeded by Ray Wilkins, who had been serving as head of Ethyl's pipe and polymer divisions in the Plastics Group.

Plants and Sales Abroad

To compensate for the decline in the domestic consumption of tetraethyl lead, Ethyl looked with hope not only to general diversification and expansion at home but especially to the foreign sale of the antiknocks and other chemicals. Overseas customers were supplied with products from American operations and from the several plants abroad. At the time of the acquisition in 1962, Ethyl was operating only one plant outside U.S. boundaries, the tetraethyl lead plant in Canada. In the score of years under consideration, Ethyl built or acquired chemical plants in Greece, England, and Belgium, a story to be treated in the following pages. An ill-fated attempt to create a partnership operation in Japan will also be reviewed. Foreign sales accounted for 15 percent of total sales in 1964 and 25 percent in 1981. The dollar value of these sales rose in the years indicated from $40 million to $433 million.

Direct export was encouraged by the improved delivery systems characteristic of Ethyl Corporation. In its first year of operation, Ethyl of Virginia created a new International Division headed by A. B. Horn, Jr., and having as its vice president C. A.

("Nick") Carter. The global interests of Ethyl can only be appreciated by conversations with Julian Frey, Horn, and other leaders in the foreign operation. Even the most casual glance at company files shows concern with markets over the world. Foreign operations brought enlarged responsibilities to management. The company now developed a sensitivity to international politics and gave close attention to problems of currency exchange. While some of this concern was not new in kind, as will be recalled in any review of the history of Albemarle and old Ethyl, it was new in degree. Always in the background was the competition, especially that offered by Associated Octel, an offshoot of export operations of Ethyl of Delaware.

As explained in an earlier chapter, a plant was built in 1956 in the Chemical Valley near Sarnia, Ontario, Canada, primarily to supply tetraethyl lead to Canadian refiners. It was the special status of the Canadian operations which caused the listing of Ethyl's long-term debt on November 30, 1962, as $207,361,074 instead of the $200 million that otherwise would have appeared in the records. Ethyl of Delaware had guaranteed the loan obtained from three Canadian banks by its subsidiary in the building of the plant near Sarnia.

At the time of the merger in 1962 the name of the Canadian operation was Ethyl Corporation of Canada and the chief local officer Allen C. Tully. On July 1, 1969, he was succeeded by Kenneth A. Freberg, whose original employment by Ethyl came about in a way novel in the annals of American business history. Near the end of his terminal year at the University of Washington, Freberg was approached by a friend who asked a favor. Would Freberg be good enough first thing in the morning to meet with interviewers from a company called Ethyl, and then brief him as to the general approach of the interviewers so that he, the friend, would be prepared for his 11 A.M. appointment? "Certainly," said Freberg. He would do this favor for a friend. Easy and utterly relaxed since he had nothing to lose, Freberg had his interview and dutifully reported to the friend. As the reader has already guessed, Freberg, not his friend, received the phone call and the job offer!

Freberg has always been sensitive to the nationalistic mood in Canada. Indeed the construction of the plant in Canada was a concession to this very nationalistic inclination, and the operation is identified in many ways with the "Buy Canadian" concept. Ethyl Corporation applied for and obtained listing on the Toronto Stock Exchange in 1974, making shares in Ethyl readily available to Canadian investors.

In Canada the restrictions on lead are less severe than in United States. It seems easier to present a point of view to people in high places in the Canadian government. Freberg says, "They're very polite, they'll sure listen, and now I really feel the atmosphere has changed." In his efforts to give the facts to the proper Canadian officials, Freberg has had much help from "Cap" Hall stationed in the nearby Detroit offices.

By virtue of its acquisition policy, Ethyl soon owned plastic manufacturing plants in the neighborhood of Toronto. The supervision of these units is apart from the administration of the chemical complex near Sarnia. The local manager of the plastics operations reports directly to the plastics administration in the United States.

About the time Albemarle bought Ethyl of Delaware, Esso approached Ethyl about building a plant in Thessaloniki, Greece. The Greeks were attempting to become more industrialized and were offering certain concessions to foreign investors contingent on investment of a specified size. For Esso to get the concessions to build a refining complex near Thessaloniki, it was required to bring into Greece about $200 million worth of investments, and thus Esso was encouraging Ethyl to build a plant in the complex thereby fulfilling part of the conditions laid down by the Greek government. The proposed plant fitted in with the ambition of new Ethyl to get into the Common Market, Greece at that time being an associate member of this European economic consortium. There were tariff barriers existing in other European countries, but only a very modest tariff was levied when goods moved from Greece into the Common Market areas.

The eventual agreement with Esso included a most important sales contract permitting Ethyl to sell antiknock compounds to Esso in Europe and other parts of the world. The sales agreement involved not only the product of the Greek plant but also materials to be shipped from the United States. This sales contract enabled the International Division of Ethyl to set up a network of terminals and to establish a new sales organization with headquarters in Brussels in 1964. It was the hope of Ethyl officials that the Esso business would be a base for contracts with other refineries in Europe and elsewhere in the world.

In developing these new distribution channels for the International Division and especially in an effort to obtain a royal decree in Greece, Ethyl representatives spent much time in Europe during 1963 and 1964. Leading the negotiating team was A. B. Horn, heading the International Division, assisted by Blanchard, who at that time was still with Hunton and Williams, and by Frederick P. Warne, inside counsel. A royal decree that spelled out the rights of the company including the repatriation of capital and profit was the equivalent of a charter. After many months of negotiations, this important document was finally signed by governmental ministers and the king of Greece. It became effective August 11, 1964. A minimum investment of $6 million was required of Ethyl, but the original plant cost more than twice that. Some of the basic equipment of the new plant was that moved from California after the closing of the tetraethyl lead operation there. The Greek enterprise was designed not only for the manufacture of antiknock compounds but also for the production of vinyl chloride monomer.

The plant in Greece was substantially completed in 1966 and was in full operation the following year. The dedicatory exercises were organized around a dinner in Athens on August 8, 1967, and ceremonies in Thessaloniki on August 10, ceremonies attended by the king. The members of the Ethyl executive committee, their wives, and a sprinkling of children made the trip to

F. D. Gottwald and the King of Greece

Greece and participants called the venture great and glorious. The Greek monarch was most gracious and charmed the American delegation.

Despite the subsequent exiling of the king, the original agreements have been maintained by the succeeding regimes. Good relations have existed with the Greek government, though there have been local critics who complained that Pier Number Five, on the harborfront and used by Ethyl, was too near the center of Thessaloniki. One reason for the generally amiable relations with the Greek government—no matter what party is in power—is the fact that Ethyl Hellas Chemical Company is one of the largest dollar exporters from Greece.

The major event in the oriental story was the erection of a tetraethyl lead plant in Japan, jointly owned by Ethyl and several Japanese companies, but never actually put in commercial operation. In this particular venture, the principal Japanese company was Toyo Sota, part of the great Mitsui operation. Toyo Sota, which owned a tetraethyl lead-making process obviously inferior to the Ethyl method, had obtained from the Japanese government exclusive rights to the building of an antiknock plant in Japan. Ethyl's clever sales director in the Far East, Nick Carter, introduced in an earlier chapter, had been using what influence he could muster to insure that Ethyl would participate in any plant to be built. Eventually the minister of trade and industry encouraged Toyo Sota to move toward a partnership with Ethyl.

Certainly as early as January 1961 there was a serious discussion between officials of Ethyl of Delaware and the Mitsui Chemical Industry Company in Tokyo regarding the possibility of the erection of a tetraethyl lead plant. A report of the proposed project was published in the English edition of *Japan Chemical*. In the early negotiations Ethyl was uneasy because, to develop a firm estimate as to the cost, Ethyl feared that it would be required to reveal more about its processes than it was willing to do at that time. On their part, the Japanese were attempting to expand the talks to include consideration of the production of aluminum alkyls and other chemicals. Ethyl management, however, was unenthusiastic about expanding the talks and felt that negotiations should be restricted to the proposed tetraethyl lead plant. Carter was taking the major responsibility for on-the-ground conversations with the Japanese in these early negotiations.

An agreement between Ethyl and Toyo Sota as to procedures and ownership was concluded in 1965, but only after extended negotiations in the United States and Japan. To round out the basic agreement, various Ethyl officials joined Carter in Japan, among them Harvey, fresh from the VisQueen negotiations; Horn, head of the International Division; Warne, inside counsel for Ethyl; and Mr. and Mrs. F. D. Gottwald. The Ethyl team wanted to review the economics of the situation before concluding these negotiations with the Japanese.

There was one evening of entertainment never forgotten by the American contingent. The hosts in this instance were not representatives of Toyo Sota but a group of Japanese interested in a technical process involving the chain-growth of ethylene. The host, a talented Japanese who could play a thirteen-string instrument, was persuaded by one of his Japanese colleagues to entertain the group, and after some conversation a skit or a little play involving the Samurai, a drama that was supposed to go along with the playing of the instrument, was agreed upon. Volunteers were sought, and since Harvey was the youngst member of the American team he was chosen as a "volunteer." He was taken backstage and dressed in elaborate Japanese gear. He disappeared for so long that Gottwald professed to believe Harvey might have been kidnapped! Actually Harvey was rehearsing; this was the reason for the delay. Harvey's equipment was by all reports ancient and beautiful. In Harvey's reminiscing words, "Well, we went on stage and we had a ball of a time. Mrs. Gottwald always asks me if I'm still dancing."

There was a lot of difference between the spirit of the entertainment of that evening and the actual negotiations with Toyo Sota. Negotiating the details of the 1965 agreement in principle consumed much time of various Ethyl executives for several years. A more definitive agreement was signed in March 1967, but thereafter many other problems developed. There was continued debate between the Japanese and the Americans on the subject of export sales for Japan and over special deals which the Japanese wanted but which Ethyl felt were quite unwise. The plant location chosen by the Japanese caused great uneasiness in the Ethyl group. Although there were certain advantages in terms of availability of utilities, the real problem seemed to be that the new plant was being put in a corner of Japan inconvenient to both raw materials and markets. Ethyl refused to participate in the next step of borrowing money until the various differences could be resolved. The Japanese partners, however, proceeded to build the plant anyhow, they being individually obligated on the debt.

The final blow came when the Japanese government precipitously put a severe limit on the use of lead antiknock compounds in gasoline. A political group using clearly flawed data contended that the use of tetraethyl lead was poisoning large portions of the population of Tokyo. The press picked up the cry and the government officials capitulated in short order. While privately they recognized the invalidity of the data, they concluded that their political opponents were too strong to resist.

The severe restrictions on the use of lead antiknocks in Japan meant that the almost completed plant could never be profitable, and the resultant financial burden rested on the Japanese. In 1971, in a series of negotiations conducted primarily by Horn and Floyd D. Gottwald, Jr., a deal was worked out whereby the plant would never be operated. Ethyl agreed to buy most of the equipment (at a severe discount) in hopes that it could be used as spare parts for its plant in Greece, which was substantially identical. Furthermore Ethyl agreed to certain commission arrangements with its Japanese partners for all lead antiknocks sold by them in Japan.

The opposition to the use of tetraethyl lead in Japan following the government's declaration was such that today approximately 95 percent of the gasoline sold in Japan is unleaded.

A colorful personality removed himself from active participation in the oriental negotiations when Nick Carter retired from the company October 31, 1968, accepting the role of consultant for a limited period of time. The consulting agreement contained effusive comments on the value of Carter's services to Ethyl. As already observed, Carter had an amazing career and earned considerable fame as a collector of art objects. In the Art Museum at Princeton University there is a display of Chinese bronzes identified as purchased from the collection of Chester Dale and Dolly Carter between 1964 and 1966. Carter died in 1980.

Several of Ethyl's European activities were organized in or near Brussels. As already mentioned, as a result of the Esso agreement that brought Ethyl to Thessaloniki, marketing groups were set up in Brussels in 1964.

A manufacturing complex took shape at Feluy, near Brussels, beginning with the construction of an aluminum alkyls facility costing $11 million and dedicated in September 1976. Then Ethyl management decided to shift the Edwin Cooper production of oil additives from England to the Continent and proceeded to

Plant at Feluy, Belgium

build adjacent to the aluminum alkyls plant at Feluy a facility costing approximately $24 million. Construction began in 1978; the completed plant was dedicated in June 1980.

The third unit at Feluy, estimated to cost about $20 million, was designed to manufacture orthoalkylated intermediates for herbicides and other agricultural chemicals. The new plant began operations during the second quarter of 1982.

All manufacturing activities at Feluy—aluminum alkyls and orthoalkylated intermediates as well as the lubricant additives—are under the management of the Edwin Cooper Division. Although the manufacture of Edwin Cooper oil additives was moved from England to Belgium, administrative, marketing, accounting, and research groups remain in England. Indeed for a while the Edwin Cooper plant in Sauget, Illinois, across the Mississippi from St. Louis, reported to English headquarters. Soon, however, Edwin Cooper took the form of two divisions: (1) Edwin Cooper, U.S., responsible for marketing and distribution in the United States, Latin America, and the Far East, and (2) Edwin Cooper, U.K., with similar responsibilities in Europe, the Middle East, and Africa. Ray Wilkins, president of Edwin Cooper since the retirement of J. A. Hancock, has his headquarters in St. Louis. B. B. Abrahamson, managing director of Edwin Cooper, U.K., reports to him.

"Ethyl Is People"

Management never forgot the tragic loss of life caused by ignorance or carelessness in the manufacture of tetraethyl lead compounds in 1924–25, coincident with the founding of the Ethyl Gasoline Corporation. The survival of the company hinged on the success of Dr. Kehoe and his fellow workers in instituting a program of safety in the manufacture and distribution of antiknock compounds. It is no exaggeration to say that concern for the health of the individual worker in any area where he or she might be exposed to hazardous substances is and has been a notable characteristic of Ethyl. Simply telling workers about the necessity for care has never been considered enough; the point must be incessantly repeated in both formal injunction and tailgate conferences, as the on-the-job instructions are called. There is careful monitoring of work places by the medical department and the toxicology and industrial hygiene department to be certain that exposure to toxic substances, noise, and other harmful agents remain at safe levels. Safety measures include special clothing and decontamination procedures in work areas that might involve exposure to lead.

In the words of Wallace F. Armstrong, retired vice president, manufacturing, referring to tetraethyl lead: "We were dealing with an extremely toxic material; it was difficult to produce; it was hazardous to handle and it required extreme care in the production, handling, and marketing. Ethyl took that responsibility seriously and set up safeguards which are still in use today. And those safeguards were so well prepared and so well ingrained into the every day operating procedures of the company that it has been as safe as any other industrial chemical on the market today." Outright fatalities in Ethyl's manufacturing of tetraethyl lead because of its toxic qualities have been rare since the early tragedies. The worst industrial accident—and this was unrelated to exposure to tetraethyl lead—occurred March 2, 1961, when the lead alkyl process "Wash House A" in the Baton Rouge plant exploded killing four people; three of these were plant employees and one a contract engineer.

Major elements of Ethyl's labor policy in the post–1962 period flowed directly from what might be described as the "second phase" of labor practices by Ethyl of Delaware when competition forced cost-cutting and thus required a reexamination of labor relations.

James Gill summarizes the current situation in these words: "I think that our labor policy today is a progressive labor policy. We are up-to-date and we have a good balance. The company is not weighted toward antiunionism and aggressively fighting the union on every move, but on the other hand I also think that we are far from pushovers. We are willing regularly to take matters to arbitration, and we are willing to take a strike if the issues are there. So I think it is a good balance." The word *balance* is frequently used in the summation of Ethyl's labor policy.

Stephen Rodi gives the following capsule version of his philosophy: "In my view management has to manage; it can't let labor manage. But at the same time management has to treat its employees, its labor, well because they are very, very valuable, and an essential asset. But you are not treating them well when you permit them to manage because this is not their function."

F. D. Gottwald was philosophical in his long view of unionization; he believed that unions could be useful instruments for dealing with workers. He contended that the biggest problem with unions comes from the rule of plantwide seniority, which, in his opinion, sometimes meant that a man not fully capable can demand the right to operate an advanced machine. "I really believe in seniority, but seniority can go so far that it wrecks a plant." Bruce Gottwald appears to be optimistic about the future role of the unions in this country, but he and other members of Ethyl's management group were quite pessimistic about trends in England under the Labour Party.

Many of the operations at Ethyl are unionized. It should be noted that the Pittsburg, California, plant, which was not long to survive the post–1962 period, became unionized immediately after the acquisition of Ethyl of Delaware by Albemarle. According to the workers in the plant, they liked the plant management, but never having heard of Albemarle they were uncertain so as to what might happen in the future, and they thought that they needed the union for protection. As already indicated, the plant went out of business in 1964.

New dimensions in labor-management relations were created by expansion and acquisition. Each plant purchased had its own labor tradition and the workers their own ideas as to what was valuable in making arrangements with management. Rodi says, "You must, when you are dealing with people, know their traditions. You will find that they have some little minor customs that [are] very important." To illustrate he refers to Mardi Gras as a tremendously tender subject in one area, Louisiana, but with little or no significance in other locations.

Reflections on the Houston strike of 1975 provoked in F. D. Gottwald a characteristic pattern of innovative thinking. The plant was kept open, run by about 200 supervisory people, whereas during normal operations there were approximately 500 workers.

Although the management people handled unaccustomed tasks, they actually increased production. It is true, however, that at the same time they postponed sundry maintenance tasks. In recounting the stepped-up output during the strike, Gottwald advanced theories which come very close to the idea of profit-sharing with operators. He realized that in practice he could not fully follow up on this thesis, but he continued to turn it over in his mind: "If we divided half of the benefit to us to the men themselves, it would be a glorious situation. And that would be a way of determining just what does efficient labor service mean to a corporation." According to Rodi, in the settlement of the Houston strike, which lasted 131 days, "We actually managed to gain back a lot of labor flexibility."

Management instructs those staff members involved in employment and promotion to follow the guidelines without regard to age, race, sex, creed, color, or national origin. As to employment, A. B. Horn, Jr., who has been charged with running the Petroleum Chemicals Group, says that the only question in hiring people is whether they can do the job. "The thing I'd like to leave with you: Honest to God, we do not consider a man's nationality, birth or anything when we consider an appointment. We don't really care about how he gets along with people. *Can he produce?* We move Greeks into Brussels, we move Americans in at the bottom level to learn the business and [then] go somewhere else." It might be noted here that in general the personnel policy in foreign lands is to use nationals as much as possible. According to Bruce Gottwald, "It is just good business to have competent people from their own nations who know their own way around and do their own job."

All manuals in personnel underscore the point that the company prefers promotions from within the organization. If it seems necessary to bring in an outsider, the decision should be made only after a careful review of all present employees who might possibly be qualified.

To recruit, train, assign, and promote constitutes a first-class challenge to top management. In the words of the late F. D.

Gottwald, "Personnel management is the biggest problem of all." It was obvious to any observer that he characteristically was surrounded by talented staff. He readily acknowledged that the problem of selecting individuals and promoting them is not easy. He was most emphatic in encouraging promotions from within the company. On his staff he wanted practical-minded people, but such a point of view did not require that an individual be immediately productive. Indeed, Gottwald was famous for his willingness to support long-time research efforts. He explained that sometimes a very brilliant person is in the wrong spot but when shifted about proves to be extremely worthwhile.

Under the head of helping individuals mature, Gottwald asserted that from time to time he silently watched some of his staff members make mistakes, this under the belief that they would learn better after commiting errors than if they were simply warned by him. How does one test to see whether they are capable? This question was presented to Gottwald one day by Buford Scott, Sr., when the two were coming out of a meeting. Gottwald had asked, "Is young Buford any good?" In answer, Scott asked another question, "How can you tell?" Whereupon Gottwald replied—and Buford, Jr., vows that he is quoting Gottwald directly—"Give him more responsibility than he can handle, and you will find out right quickly."

As for relations with employees in office and plant, Gottwald said that the worker wants "a reasonable friendship. And certainly he has got to be convinced that he's being treated right insofar as pay is concerned." He acknowledged that being recognized as an individual is important for the worker's morale. Then he added, "But the second best thing is never overrule a subordinate. If you do, the employees will completely lose confidence in him. If he is wrong and you have to make a change, get the opposing parties together and reason the thing out and let him [the supervisor or foreman] make the change, not you."

Here one must return to the well-worn saying "Ethyl is people." In the words of James Kirby, "The other things are peripheral. The corporate structure and other things are interesting, but are all sort of props for the show." The 14,500 people employed by the company make that organization what it is. And it is now one of America's foremost corporations.

One of the Prestigious "Fortune 500"

What were the results of the agressive management of Ethyl Corporation by 1982, a year which marked the ninety-fifth anniversary of the founding of Albemarle Paper Manufacturing Company and the twentieth anniversary of the chartering of Ethyl of Virginia?

Ethyl had become a diversified, modern corporation with plants and distribution bases in the four corners of the globe. Shedding the one-product image, Ethyl was now, in management's self-description, a "diversified, high-technology producer of performance chemicals for the petroleum industry, specialty chemicals, plastics and aluminum products. Also, the company has developing interests in oil, gas and coal. Ethyl also owns First Colony Life Insurance Company."

From the beginning of its corporate existence the new Ethyl was ranked in that prestigious group the "Fortune 500," a label meaning that it was one of the largest publicly-owned industrial corporations in the United States. In 1963 *Fortune* magazine rated Ethyl as 275th in sales on the basis of something less than a full year of operations following the merger in 1962. In 1964 the rank was 247th. The typical ranking throughout the years has been in the 200s. For 1980 Ethyl's position was number 208 and for 1981 it was 214.

In journalistic vernacular, Ethyl became a "billion-dollar corporation" when its annual sales reached and passed that zero-cluttered mark in 1976. Unfortunately for writers, there is no rhythmic equivalent for the one and three quarters billion dollar sales figure reached and passed in 1981, the last full calendar year covered by this study.

Even after one discounts the inflated dollar, the growth of sales, earnings, and dividends is impressive. In the nineteen calendar years under review, 1963–81 inclusive, annual sales rose from $227 million to $1,757 million, a sevenfold-plus increase; assets rose from $205 million to $1,262 million, a sixfold increase; net earnings rose from $16 million to $90 million per year, a five-fold-plus increase; earnings per share of common stock rose from $0.65 to $4.56; and dividends per share of common stock rose from $0.055 to $1.50 (1963 per share figures adjusted to reflect stock splits). At the same time the ratio of long-term debt to capitalization was reduced from 82.2 percent to 17.8 percent. The fluctuation in the statistics and in their portrayal in the attached graphs prove that corporations are not islands; Ethyl has always been part of the national and even the world economy, affected by the general expansion and contraction of business.

The ratio of dividends to earnings is always on the mind of the stockholders. Traditionally the ratio has been modest. Several years ago Floyd D. Gottwald, Jr., said, "Our dividends have always been very small," adding that the company has been trying to get the rate up. In fact the company has succeeded in raising dividends, until they are now in the respectable range of a 30 percent payout. The company likes to have the cash on hand to finance a considerable fraction of its development and thus not be at the mercy of moneylenders for all expenditures.

The impressive growth of Ethyl is probably best seen in the three accompanying graphs: (1) equity per common share, (2) net income, and (3) sales subdivided on a basis of particular products. See the revealing table in Appendix C on which the last-named graph is based.

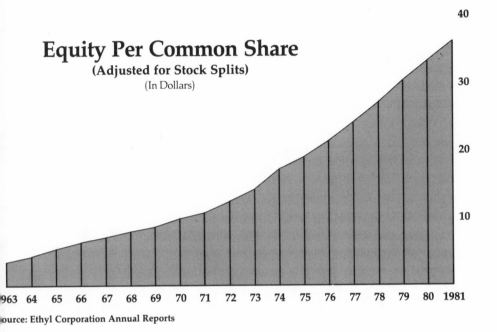

Equity Per Common Share
(Adjusted for Stock Splits)
(In Dollars)

Source: Ethyl Corporation Annual Reports

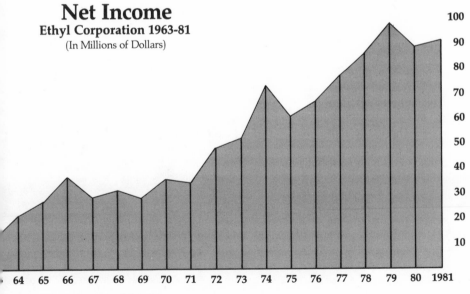

Net Income
Ethyl Corporation 1963-81
(In Millions of Dollars)

Source: Ethyl Corporation Annual Reports

Net Sales by Industry Segment

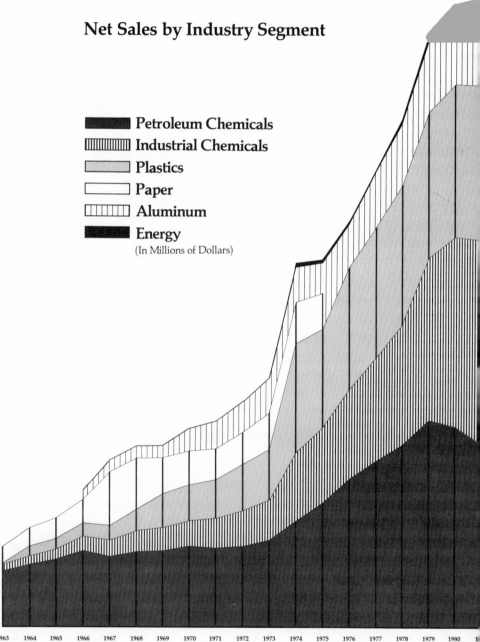

Petroleum Chemicals
Industrial Chemicals
Plastics
Paper
Aluminum
Energy
(In Millions of Dollars)

1963 1964 1965 1966 1967 1968 1969 1970 1971 1972 1973 1974 1975 1976 1977 1978 1979 1980

Source: Ethyl Corporation Annual Reports

Part Four

GOTTWALD

X

The Management of a
Billion-Dollar Corporation

Nurturing the Corporate Image

ETHYL MANAGEMENT KNEW that the company was good, more than simply good, even great. But how could this fact be best presented to Ethyl's several publics? In a sense everyone connected with the company, consciously or unconsciously, shares in creating an impression—senior management and sales people in particular. Yet a more structured effort was required for maximum effectiveness. The program of explaining what the company is and does was put principally in the hands of four departments—corporate communications, investor relations, advertising and sales promotion, and corporate community relations. To insure that company personnel are kept abreast of developments, Ethyl provides orientation programs for the newly employed and in-house publications for all hands.

At the time of the formation of Ethyl of Virginia, the director of public relations was James E. Boudreau, a graduate of the U.S. Military Academy, who had headed public relations in Ethyl of Delaware since 1951. Boudreau had joined the sales division in 1930. At the time of his retirement in 1966 Boudreau was vice president of public relations and advertising. Public relations and advertising had been separate staff departments until Boudreau's eventual title covered both areas.

For a brief period the vice presidency of public relations and advertising was held by L. L. Huxtable, who soon retired because of ill health. In 1967 Charles H. Zeanah, at the time director of community relations for both Baton Rouge and Houston, was named director of corporate public relations. Public relations and advertising again became separate units reporting directly to George Kirby, president. In 1977 corporate public relations was subdivided into two departments: corporate community relations headed by Zeanah and corporate communications directed by A. Prescott Rowe, a graduate of Washington and Lee University with a B.A. in journalism. Before coming to Ethyl in 1970 as corporate public relations representative, Rowe had held various appointments in his field, the most significant being director of information services for Central Virginia Educational Television Corporation in Richmond.

Ethyl in its several locations is careful to fulfill its civic obligations in community fund drives, blood bank campaigns, and programs sponsored by chambers of commerce. The company has been active in the area of both local and national philanthropy. The fellowship and scholarship program as established by Ethyl of Delaware was changed to a system of unrestricted grants to university departments in which Ethyl has an interest. The money may be used for equipment, grants to students, or any other purposes the college or university may elect. Furthermore, under the matching-gifts program, Ethyl will give to colleges and universities money equal to that contributed by its employees.

At the time of the acquisition of Ethyl of Delaware by Albemarle, the director of advertising was Russell B. Weston, whose distinctive personality has been mentioned in the summary of media campaigns in the 1950s. Weston retired in 1963, moved to Vermont and enjoyed the happy experience of living next to a golf course in a house dating back to the Revolutionary War. At Ethyl he was succeeded by James B. Lonergan, who in 1974 was followed by Gordon E. Saxon.

Saxon, director of advertising and sales promotion, was graduated from the University of Michigan with a B.S. degree in aeronautical engineering. Since joining the company in 1951 he has served in a variety of engineering, marketing, and advertising posts.

In the early 1960s there was a considerable change in advertising policy, principally a reflection of a new emphasis on diversification. Some deviation from the old approach could be seen even before the acquisition of Ethyl by Albemarle. First, most of the energetic campaigns in support of the petroleum industry were phased out and turned over to the American Petroleum Institute for its use. With the expiration of Ethyl's patents and the appearance of competition in the production of tetraethyl lead, the oil refiners objected to putting the Ethyl sign on the gasoline pumps, a characteristic of the earlier period. After all, the refiners might have bought the antiknock compound from DuPont, Nalco, or PPG.

In the new era there was less emphasis on the broad corporate image in advertisements and more emphasis given specific products produced by various divisions. Basically that philosophy continues to this day. Advertising became very specific, and instead of buying space in such general magazines as *The Reader's Digest* and in effect saying to the reader, "Look, Ethyl makes a lot of different things," the company is now going into publications such as *Beverage World* and other specialized journals and saying, for example, that Ethyl now has a Molded Products Division that makes caps for soft drink bottles.

There was an understandable desire by Ethyl management to inform the general public of the emergence of the company as one of America's most dynamic corporations and one well diversified. To one segment of society, the investing public, Ethyl made a special appeal. After the acquisition of Ethyl of Delaware by Albemarle in 1962 and the wide distribution of stock in the newly named corporation Ethyl of Virginia, the financial analysts naturally showed increased interest in Ethyl. Some analysts seemed unable to erase from their minds the old one-product picture of Ethyl, and the stock was selling well below what the company considered its true value.

The needs of the analysts were handled on an "as requested basis" by the financial vice president Perdue and later by Blanchard. But this service began taking too much of Blanchard's time. Accordingly, Lloyd B. Andrew, Jr., was brought to Richmond in 1969 from VisQueen and made director of financial relations with primary responsibility for providing information to the investing community. Andrew had joined Ethyl in 1951 partly to escape the dismal carbon black in a west Texas plant where he was employed. At Ethyl he moved from process engineering to "speculative estimating" and then to "definitive estimating," assignments which, combined with his experiences as general manager of the VisQueen division, well prepared him to undertake financial analyses.

At first Andrew, as director of financial relations, continued with the established pattern of being *available* if there were inquiries. In the early 1970s a somewhat more regular pattern developed. Floyd D. Gottwald, Jr., Bruce Gottwald, and sometimes Bim Gautreaux went out on occasion. Prescott Rowe, in the department then called corporate public relations, and Andrew shared in helping the Ethyl emissaries prepare for their excursions. But competitors were getting ahead of Ethyl in obtaining attention, and conviction was growing that Ethyl should be more aggressive in its relationship with the analysts.

In reviewing the situation, Blanchard insisted that a multiplicity of people simply could not maintain consistency in presentation to the analysts; explanation primarily was Andrew's job. To assist Andrew in his important assignment, Ian A. Nimmo came to Richmond from Baton Rouge in 1973 with the title assistant director of financial relations. After graduation from Georgia Tech with a B.S. in chemical engineering and an M.S. in industrial management, he had joined Ethyl in 1963. As the months went by, he and Andrew worked so closely together that there was no observable variance in their explanations to the financial community.

Ethyl invited a group of financial analysts to attend a two-day field trip centering in Houston, February 9–11, 1976. Judged by the reaction of those in attendance, the meeting was a marked success. As Andrew summarized the session, "In my opinion, what we got most out of this is an awareness of the analysts that Ethyl is a heck of a lot more than a lead antiknock company, and that Ethyl is literally loaded with people that know their business and are capable managers. And they were overwhelmed." Representatives of financial houses could be seen slipping out of meetings to telephone buy orders to their home offices. In the week of the Houston meeting, February 9–13, Ethyl stock rose over ten points, closing at 33 on February 9 and 43½ on February 13. The rise continued, but at a slower pace, reaching the year's high of 49¼ on March 1, about 20 points above the low of 29½ on January 12. (It should be noted that these were prices before the two-for-one stock split in 1977.) Subsequently there were meetings of analysts in Orangeburg in 1977, in Houston for the second time in 1979, and in Williamsburg in 1981. All were considered useful, but none topped the first Houston gathering in immediate results.

A Strong Executive Committee, Hallmark of Ethyl Management

Like other corporations, Ethyl is equipped with directors responsible to the stockholders and a management responsible to the directors. Not quite so obvious is the unusual distribution of authority and responsibility within the usual framework. If there is a hallmark of Ethyl management, it is strong control exercised by the executive committee.

In the usual pattern of corporations, the stockholders, owners of the company, receive dividends and financial reports quarterly, and at least once a year they meet to hear summary reports and to vote on sundry matters, especially the election of directors.

It will be recalled that at the time Albemarle purchased Ethyl of Delaware there were two classes of common stock: A, with full voting rights, and B, with limited voting rights. Ownership of the majority of the common-stock-A by Gottwald and his family had resulted in a control that permitted Gottwald to carry out his own ideas of diversification and expansion. However, at the time when major funds were borrowed to enable Albemarle to purchase Ethyl of Delaware in 1962, the Albemarle group agreed to a plan for the abolition of the distinction between A and B stock. The merging of A and B common stock took place June 22, 1965, in a formal act of reclassification. From that time on all shares of common stock were of equal voting strength. By virtue of this reclassification the F. D. Gottwald family ownership of voting stock was reduced from approximately 53 percent to about 13 percent.

The listing on the New York Stock Exchange and the Pacific Coast Stock Exchange in 1965, and a listing on the Toronto Exchange nine years later, made possible a wider distribution of stock ownership. There were three stock splits in the period under review: a two-for-one in 1963, a three-for-one in 1964, and a two-for-one in 1977. Increasing dividends, a fact already mentioned, made the stock more attractive to the investor who, in addition to his concern with capital growth, wanted a regular and respectable quarterly income.

Because of growing attendance, which caused city fire marshals to worry about exits, the annual meeting of stockholders was moved out of Building No. 1 on Gamble's Hill, first to a hotel ballroom and then to the auditorium in the conveniently nearby Federal Reserve Building, several floors of which Ethyl now occupies. The crowd, principally a combination of employees who had benefited by the savings plan that permitted automatic purchase of company stock, a group of downtown brokers, and a miscellaneous collection of small stockholders interested in the public appearance of a management usually very retiring (and also interested in the souvenir plastic bags or colorful glasses for old fashioneds or for orange juice) gathered promptly. Present also were newspaper reporters and a security analyst or two, though most of these preferred special visits to the company at a time when they might ask more extensive and detailed questions.

A typical meeting was an orderly affair with a minimum of

excitement. There has always been special interest in what might be said about the future, and in those days when F. D. Gottwald took the lead the audience was amused at his extemporaneous comments that seemed to alarm some members of the executive committee.

Like the management of other corporations Ethyl executives were secretly a bit edgy before the meetings since they never knew when some would-be exhibitionist might claim the floor in an attempt to create a soapbox out of the lectern. The nearest thing to such an invasion occurred in 1971 when a student at one of the Virginia colleges purchased a lone share of Ethyl stock and claimed in a letter to management the privilege of moving for a series of reforms. In full compliance with all rules of the Securities and Exchange Commission, management printed the proposals and circulated them to stockholders well ahead of time. But the student never even showed up for the meeting.

In the years under review there was at no time any real worry about basic control because management before the beginning of every annual meeting had in its pocket proxies guaranteeing a continuation of announced policies.

Though the procedures were modified a bit after F. D. Gottwald chose not to take the platform, a standard formula for many years was for each member of the executive committee to make a report on matters in his special area of responsibility.

Gottwald said that he saw some virtue in annual meetings. He referred to the criticism received every now and then on these occasions as "eye openers." Points were touched on never thought of before. Yet he believed that over half of the criticism was "just wish-wash" statements by people disgruntled in general and their comments simply had to be taken in stride.

At the typical meeting the most significant legal action is to vote for the directors nominated by management. The number of directors in the corporation has fluctuated from fifteen, the original size established in November 1962, to as many as twenty. At the end of the calendar year 1981 there were nineteen. In general there is a combination of people from three areas: (1)

management, (2) outsiders, and (3) finally, in a gray area, two or three from the banking, brokerage, and legal communities, all doing business with Ethyl Corporation. The announced intention of bringing in more outsiders occurred in 1963, when Gottwald expressed a desire for two new persons on the board, not connected with the corporation. These two were Irwin H. Will, then chairman of the board of Virginia Electric and Power Company, and E. Claiborne Robins, then president of the A. H. Robins Company, who were unanimously elected.

It is obvious that the board is made up of friendly, cooperative people. If one wants historical justification for this commonsense arrangement, he might review the history of Albemarle in the 1940s. And yet it must be made clear that, according to testimony presented to this researcher time and time again, the directors should not be described as of the rubber stamp variety. It is simply not made up of a group of yes-men. F. D. Gottwald once said, "We have elected directors that have a will and a mind of their own." The foregoing statement should not obscure Gottwald's conviction that management itself should exercise decisive leadership in the company. Management consults with, informs, and seeks the support of the directors.

Probably one reason for a relatively smooth-running board is the fact that the members are given a detailed briefing ahead of time about matters scheduled to be brought up. And the directors might be invited to make preliminary comments. Director James Miller says, "It's a good, diversified board." The board appoints special committees, the most important of which is the executive committee. The executive committee by all accounts runs the company.

As already indicated, there are many who describe Gottwald's ingenuity in melding the Albemarle and the Ethyl people and policies quite as remarkable as the raising of $200 million for the purchase of Ethyl of Delaware by Albemarle. Immediately after the acquisition Gottwald had as his prime responsibility the creation of an administrative structure which would bring together for efficient operation the paper and chemical businesses and would respond to his own plans for diversification and expansion. Thus there evolved a strong executive committee and a system of budgeting and follow-up controls that have become a distinctive feature of Ethyl. He was groping for an administrative body distinct from the operating committee inherited from old Ethyl, a new one that would reconcile the best features of centralization and local management.

The general outline of the new executive unit was drawn up by F. D. Gottwald slightly less than a year after Ethyl of Virginia was formed. At the meeting of the board on November 21, 1963, Gottwald presented a memorandum outlining the functions and procedures of the executive committee in its dual capacity as a committee of the board and as the top management committee of the company. Gottwald's memorandum was referred to Lewis F. Powell, Jr., for legal guidance as to the distinction between board-level actions and operating matters.

Many corporations have executive committees, but the situation at Ethyl is distinctive because of the power exercised by that committee. There is a charter, or list of empowerments, twice modified, but the essential elements remain. The dual functions of the executive committee are clearly outlined—it is to operate as a committee of the board *and* as top management committee. Since the new executive committee took full form, the minutes always have indicated whether it is sitting as a management committee or as a committee acting for the board. Apparently the most significant point is that the executive committee does have the power to act for the board of directors in virtually all areas between the meetings of the board.

The composition and number of members of the executive committee has varied over the two decades under review. The membership was either five or six. By 1969 the executive committee consisted of six members: the three Gottwalds, Blanchard, Chisholm, and Kirby.

With Kirby's resignation and Chisholm's withdrawal, Robert Herzog, the former secretary of the group, on December 23, 1969, was put on the committee, and Arthur W. Helwig was

Executive Committee, 1969–82. Left to right: Robert Herzog,
Floyd D. Gottwald, Jr., F. D. Gottwald, Bruce C. Gottwald,
and Lawrence E. Blanchard, Jr.

made secretary. For the period of the 1970s and into the 1980s the three Gottwalds, Blanchard, and Herzog constituted the committee. By special rule, Gautreaux is privileged to attend all meetings as an advisor. Helwig, in addition to being secretary of the executive committee, is vice president in charge of corporate planning.

Arthur W. Helwig's diversified experience had prepared him for the complex assignment that was now his. Graduating in chemical engineering from the Missouri School of Mines (now the University of Missouri at Rolla), which awarded him the B.S. degree, and from the University of Illinois, where he earned the M.S. degree, he joined Ethyl in 1952 as a chemical process engineer. Subsequently he filled various managerial positions that involved both technical services and a study of the economic bases of the company. Probably the high point of his first decade with the company was his successful appearance before the directors in 1960 to explain why the price of the tetraethyl lead additive should be lowered. He worked closely with Herzog and Gautreaux in many assignments, which moved from lead forecasting to long-range planning. As director of planning and profit improvement in the new Ethyl beginning in 1964, he was more and more involved with the executive committee and sat through many meetings, especially in the late 1960s. Thus he was the logical choice to fill the vacancy when Herzog left the secretaryship to become one of the five members of the executive committee.

In the committee a wide range of information is brought together. Bruce Gottwald feels that there are fewer mistakes made when not one but several people review all the factors involved. How does the executive committee go about making its decisions? As Hailey observes, consensus in large measure seems to be reached on the basis of the trust which the group has in the individual who is presenting the problem before that committee. Nimmo points out that a distinctive feature of Ethyl's arrangement as he understands it is the degree to which various levels of people are exposed to individuals in top management or to the executive committee in particular. He feels that not only the general manager but the man with the day-to-day responsibility is often able to present his views to those in authority. All in all it is quite certain that the major decisions are made in the executive committee, and this seems an effective arrangement, according to the directors. To quote Miller, "I think it a very sensible way to run a company and this is where the major decisions are made. They are not made in the board room. The board room certainly so far as the outside director is concerned is supposed to be there for the purpose of keeping a watchful eye on the company, not to make the business decisions."

When the executive committee is acting for the full board, the matter is reviewed at the next meeting of the directors and certified. The whole arrangement seems to work rather well. Apparently there has been no appreciable conflict between the executive committee and the board. The report of the executive committee to the board is always presented with a united front, no matter what point of view might have been presented at the earlier meeting of the executive committee. As Herzog wisely remarks, in the executive committee one cannot say that everybody has an equal vote because certain officers have responsibilities to the company obviously greater than some of the others. The executive committee has the advantage, as Herzog notes, of being a forum where ideas are exchanged and tried out; one reason it works is that when discussions get too long somebody is there who can remedy the situation. "There is a chief executive officer and he does have something to say about when to cut the discussion off." Someone has said that the votes in the executive committee are not counted, they are *weighed*.

The budget committee is in a sense a subcommittee of the executive committee. As indicated earlier, F. D. Gottwald viewed the budget process as one of the important characteristics of the company. The budget committee and the executive committee carefully review the performance projections in progress reports periodically compared with agreed-on objectives.

Note the importance of the budget director in his reports to the executive committee. As Benjamin D. Harrison, first budget director of the new corporation, says, there is "a classic control situation." Harrison carried out his duties as an industrial engineer, not simply as a financial man; his job was to look at the corporation from a performance standpoint. When Harrison retired in 1975 he was succeeded as budget director by Paul E. Weimer, formerly director of chemical research.

To use a phrase enunciated by Bruce Gottwald, "We require a very disciplined budget procedure." He feels that this financial system is quite flexible and can operate whether the manufacturing unit is 500, 1,000 or 10,000 miles away. He is convinced that Ethyl's financial system, which includes control of manpower as well as money, is the real strength of the company. This "disciplined budget procedure" fits in with Bruce Gottwald's idea of decentralized day-by-day operation and centralized control of money and manpower.

In Bruce Gottwald's judgment, this system of a carefully controlled budget procedure permits a great deal of individual elbow room, allowing the local manager to be as innovative as he wants to be. Bruce Gottwald notes, however, that sometimes it is very difficult to get the management of a new acquisition to understand what corporate headquarters is trying to do. "And once we are able to talk to the people and they can see the logical way you are controlling manpower, once they understand what you are trying to do, it's not wet blanket any more. I think the wet blanket theory comes from edicts that are passed down from some far-off headquarters, without the reason for the edicts coming along too."

Of course various agencies and divisions of the corporation are called on for information and support in the decision-making process, which obviously is the major responsibility of the executive committee. Most consistently relied on are the finance and law departments, which by their very nature are in intimate alliance. Witness the fact that Ethyl's two chief financial officers in the era under review, Perdue and Blanchard, were lawyers by education and by initial professional experience.

When Ethyl of Virginia was created, Perdue, chief financial officer, held the title of executive vice president and treasurer. The director of finance was Frank J. McNally, a native New Yorker, who had special training in both law and accounting, and experience with the Securities and Exchange Commission before coming to Ethyl in 1946. McNally's first assignment was house counsel for Ethyl Specialties Corporation, a subsidiary marketing the famous Ethyl Cleaner. With Perdue's resignation in 1967, McNally was elected treasurer; he became vice president in 1977. Both the treasurer and the controller, James Kirby, reported to Blanchard, who succeeded Perdue as chief financial officer. McNally's extracurricular activities over the years include championship tennis, and, after his removal to the warmer climate in Richmond, the growing of prize-winning camellias and poinsettias.

An important subdivision of the finance department is taxation, headed by Paul Cahill, a man trained in the classics before enrolling in New York University Law School, where he earned not only the usual Bachelor of Laws degree but also the Master of Laws in taxation. McNally, who retired in 1981, was succeeded as treasurer by Lloyd Andrew. In addition to his new duties, Andrew continued to pay close attention to acquisitions and investor relations.

When Frederick P. Warne retired as general counsel in 1979, he was succeded by E. Whitehead Elmore, a native of Lawrenceville, Virginia, and a graduate of the University of Virginia, who came to Ethyl by way of Hunton and Williams. In 1980 he was elected secretary of the corporation, thus continuing Ethyl's policy of combining the role of general counsel and corporate secretary.

Hunton and Williams's service as outside counsel is the continuation of a relationship initiated in the days of old Albemarle when Gottwald approached Powell after the death of Royal E. Cabell. The indispensable role of Powell and his colleagues has been traced in the foregoing pages. With Blanchard's move from Hunton and Williams to Ethyl in 1967 and Powell's appointment as an associate justice of the U.S. Supreme Court in 1972, Joseph C. Carter, Jr., became the senior member of the outside counsel group. Carter's relationship with Ethyl took on an added dimension when he was elected a board member in 1980. The better to serve Ethyl and other clients, Hunton and Williams established an office in Washington, the first partner in that office being John Adams, who assumed this position in 1968. Ethyl employs local counsel, domestic and foreign, when the situation so warrants.

Any summation of the activities of the law department is avowedly subjective and incomplete. Observers would agree that the most interesting as well as the most important of the law cases are those involving the lead controversy. Dramatic and colorful is the long, drawn-out case of *David Balter* v. *Ethyl Corporation,* which probably is as important in the history of journalism as in the history of litigation. Ethyl was accused of "malicious interference" designed to destroy a man's business and in a jury trial was fined $1,020,450. On appeal the verdict was overturned and in 1981 this reversal was in effect sustained by both the Florida Supreme Court of Appeals and the Supreme Court of the United States. As already noted, several domestic cases involving chemical waste are in adjudication and any estimate at this time would be premature. In 1978–79 employees of Ethyl Hellas in Thessaloniki, Greece, were charged with negligence resulting in an alleged lead-related illness of 35 port workers. A higher Greek court dropped the case, in effect overturning a verdict unfavorable to Ethyl rendered by the local courts of Thessaloniki. Ethyl's part in enforcing the Freedom of Information Act has been summarized as one feature of the lead controversy. An important chapter in the evolution of the "law of capture" was written by Ethyl attorneys in their attempt to obtain a definition of rights in the Arkansas brine fields. Here the question was of *flow*, not static substance such as coal. The litigation, though resulting in varying judgments, brought about clarifying interpretation of old laws and the writing of new statutes.

Understanding the next two subdivisions of the chapter can

best be insured by hearing a story that comes out of Canada. Blanchard, Bruce Gottwald, Floyd D. Gottwald, Jr., and Herzog were at the Canadian plant, but F. D. Gottwald was absent. Some problem came up that needed prompt settlement, at least the local manager thought so, and he suggested that since four-fifths of the committee were there they might go ahead. One member of the four—perhaps it was Bruce Gottwald—said, in effect, yes, but the quorum is the other fifth.

Forces That Shaped F. D. Gottwald

The decisive personality in the creation and development of the present Ethyl Corporation obviously was Floyd Dewey Gottwald. Many called him a business genius; certainly his successes were remarkable. What were the forces that made him what he was? Acknowledging the inadequacy of his statement, the present author offers the not-very-novel thesis that Gottwald was a product of his distinctive heritage and his early disciplined environment, obviously one shading into the other.

Like most Americans, F. D. Gottwald had a mixed Old World ancestry. His maternal great-grandfather, William Bottoms, was born in England; his paternal grandfather, August Gottwald, was born in Prussian Silesia. As this observer interprets the Gottwald family heritage, the most enduring influence came by way of the Freyfogle-Gottwald lineage. There were two strong characters in this line who were foremost in shaping the family tradition: first, Christian Freyfogle; second, Louisa Freyfogle Gottwald, Christian's great niece and F. D. Gottwald's grandmother.

It is an intriguing fact that the company-owned acreage near Ethyl's headquarters buildings includes the lot on which the Christian Freyfogle cottage, fronting the Kanawha Canal towpath, stood until it was destroyed by the great fire of April 1865. And this now bare lot within a few years after that fire passed to Christian Freyfogle's great niece, Louisa Freyfogle Gottwald, by way of Jacob Freyfogle, Louisa's father.

The founder of the Freyfogle connection in Virginia was

Christian Freyfogle. A professional soldier, he was born in the year 1777 in the Grand Duchy of Baden. After serving in both the French and Austrian armies, he crossed the Atlantic and on March 4, 1812, in Philadelphia enrolled in the U.S. Marine Corps. His enlistment papers indicate that he was six feet one inch in height, of light complexion with blue eyes, brown hair, "apparently of sound constitution" with neither rupture nor "ulcers." He served throughout the War of 1812 and was honorably discharged on March 4, 1817. He came to Richmond, enlisted in the Public Guard, and married.

Of an economical disposition, he and his wife, Mary Bowne, somehow managed to set up a shop and to accumulate profit from their mercantile enterprise sufficient to make an important purchase: a lot and a brick dwelling on the south side of the Kanawha Canal, adjacent to the Virginia Manufactory of Arms.

As the years went by he acquired the symbols of prosperity; he purchased a carriage and a domestic servant with her two children. In September 1839 Christian Freyfogle's twenty-two-year-old nephew, Jacob Freyfogle, joined him in the New World. Christian, however, had only a few months to enjoy the company of his only blood-relation in his adopted country. Christian Freyfogle died and was interred in Shockoe Cemetery on March 8, 1840.

Under the terms of his will, the house and lot on which he resided went to his wife Mary during her lifetime, the adjoining tenement to adopted daughter Ophelia at her majority. At the death of Mary, her real estate was to descend to nephew Jacob.

No living person is qualified to give a categorical estimate of the tall, blue-eyed German who renounced the Old World to join the New. In the light of subsequent events one guesses that the most significant act of his life was to persuade his nephew to join him in Richmond. Christian Freyfogle, soldier-merchant, was tough, authoritarian, acquisitive in the best sense of the word, but at one and the same time he was imaginative, patient in the long view, venturesome, militantly loyal to both new country and old family. Above everything else, he could break out of circumstances that kept lesser men in the bondage of their birth. He left a permanent impression, avuncular rather than fatherly though it may have been, which meant that his traits, either fractionally or fully, would reappear from time to time in future generations. It was a legacy more enduring than the solid brick house along the towpath of the Kanawha Canal.

Like his uncle, Jacob Freyfogle was a native of the Grand Duchy of Baden. He developed the habit of buying real estate in and around Richmond, using profits from the grocery business in which he engaged. Perhaps his most conspicuous position in the German-speaking community derived from his role in the founding and development of the German Lutheran Church, organized in 1843.

Jacob Freyfogle's second wife was German-born Caroline Rebman (or Rebmann), who came from Boblingen, a few miles southwest of Stuttgart. One of the children of this marriage was Louisa, born in 1855. She was one of the strong personalities shaping the Freyfogle-Gottwald family character.

During the Civil War, Jacob Freyfogle served in the home guard. The fire of April 1865 that consumed large portions of the city destroyed the buildings on that choice piece of property Jacob Freyfogle had inherited from his uncle, the lot that today is part of Ethyl's property. This loss was merely an introduction to a series of misfortunes that beset Jacob's declining years. There was illness, the scattering of the four children born to him and Caroline, and an apparent breakup of his marriage to a young Englishwoman, Jacob's third wife. He was living alone when he died, on December 15, 1872.

At the time of Jacob Freyfogle's death, Louisa, the youngest child, aged seventeen, was part of the household of Anton Staude, where for several years she had helped with the domestic chores. She was something of a ward of the family, who worshiped alongside the Freyfogles in the German Lutheran Church. Staude ran a public house of sorts, which blended the character of the early American inn and the German biergarten.

In October 1871 Staude had bought property adjacent to the

James River wharves on Rocketts Street, where he could profit from a new business immediately across the river in Chesterfield County, the stonecutting operations of Andrews, Ordway, and Green. The firm was recruiting skilled craftsmen, mostly from Germany, England, Scotland, and Ireland. And these workers in granite had extra money to spend; by contemporary standards they were, at least for the moment, blue-collar aristocrats.

The granite-cutting enterprise was based on a contract to "cut, dress, and box" the enormous blocks of first-quality "Westham" or "James River" granite, which were then to be shipped by water and precisely placed in the exterior walls of what was then called the State, War, and Navy Department Building in Washington, now referred to as the Old Executive Office Building. It took skilled craftsmen, working with hand-powered hammer and chisel, to carry out the intricate designs and specifications laid down by the representatives of the federal government.

Among the stonecutters employed by Ordway was August Gottwald, born in the village of Streigau, Prussia, in March 1840. Trained in the craft of stonecutting, a characteristic art in the town of his birth known even today for its granite quarries, he entered the employ of the Ordway firm late in 1872. It was natural for a lonely man, far from his place of birth and trying to speak a new language, to seek out people of German origin or German cultural heritage. August Gottwald found a comfortable atmosphere when being served meat and drink in the Staude establishment, which seemed like a piece of the old country. And it was only a few minutes by skiff from the cutting sheds across the river.

Written records do not show how the thirty-three-year-old bachelor and the recently orphaned teenager, Louisa, carried on their courtship. Written records do show that on July 3, 1873, a license to wed was issued to August Gottwald, "stonecutter," and to Louisa Freyfogle, and that the ceremony took place later that day at the German Lutheran Church, the pastor, Charles Sholz, performing the service.

August and Louisa Gottwald were active members of this congregation in which her father had played important roles. The couple saw to it that each of their four children went through the formal ceremony of christening, or baptism.

August and Louisa Gottwald first set up housekeeping in the 800 block of West Broad Street. In the liquidation of a trusteeship established by Jacob Freyfogle, Louisa received that lot on which Christian Freyfogle had lived. There is an enduring tradition that somebody somehow made off with a goodly portion of Louisa Gottwald's rightful legacy.

While Louisa Gottwald's relatives appeared to be prospering, August and Louisa were falling upon hard times. It was a condition brought on, at least in part, by August Gottwald's declining health. He had become a victim of his own vocation, contracting silicosis, the characteristic ailment of a stonecutter. He and his wife sold the property they occupied on West Broad Street and moved to the country. August Gottwald's health continued to decline and he died at home, 11 P.M., January 19, 1886.

The widow proved to be endowed with a spirit of heroic dimensions. She did not easily give up, but the farm was a losing proposition, and by 1890 she decided she should sell out and move back to Richmond, where there might be more economic opportunities for herself and her children. Then came a blow. Her title to the farm was questioned because of awkward phrasing in August's will. Considerable legal maneuvering was necessary to provide for sale under a clear title and to make acceptable to the court investment of the proceeds in a residence in the city. Settled down in her new house on Lewis Street in the eastern section of Richmond, Louisa Gottwald suffered another tragedy. Son August, Jr., or "Gus" as he was called, became paralyzed and could use neither arms nor legs.

Her descendants remember Louisa Gottwald as a sturdy, uncomplaining person. They picture her as a small woman, with hair pulled back from her face, a quiet, sometimes whimsical matriarch, who taught German songs to those grandchildren willing to learn and handed out peppermints often enough to make a permanent impression on the younger generation. More than anything else she was a woman of fortitude and determination. And she was a private sort of person. She had some of the characteristics of her uncle, Christian Freyfogle, the stout soldier. A few of her own traits may have passed into the more impressionable grandchildren who came around her.

The oldest of the four children of August and Louisa Gottwald was William Henry, a man of medium size, with no extra weight on him. He was "physically tough," as one of his children phrased it, and had that tanned, weathered look of a man who welcomed the outdoors, as in fact he did. He had blue eyes, one of which he lost in middle age as a result of an accident at the American Locomotive Company, Richmond Works, where he was employed as a machinist.

In the rise and fall of the economy the locomotive works would shut down for months at a time. Thus William Gottwald had to turn his hand to other endeavors. For a time he became a woodworker and was employed by the Richmond Cedar Works. Mostly because he needed supplementary income for support of his family, and partly because he simply liked activities out of doors, he became adept at gardening, hunting, fishing, and trapping. He often set his lines in the James and his traps in Boar Swamp east of Seven Pines.

In 1897 at the age of twenty-three he married Mary Alma Bottoms. Temporarily, William and his bride lived with his mother, Louisa Gottwald, but soon they bought property next door. It was there, on Lewis Street, at 626 and 628, that the children of William Henry and Mary Alma Gottwald were born and brought up, not far from Gillie's Creek and the James River. Of the children, four reached adulthood: Floyd Dewey, Russell Lee, Milton Linwood, and William Douglas.

The first child of William Henry and Mary Alma Gottwald was born May 22, 1898, only three weeks after the surrender of the Spanish fleet to Admiral Dewey at Manila Bay. It seemed only proper that this national triumph be celebrated by the inclusion of "Dewey" in the infant's name. "Floyd" was a family name which the mother liked; "Dewey" was the father's choice. In the compromise, "Floyd Dewey," the mother's victory seemed to be only temporary, for family and early friends called him "Dewey." Later in life acquaintances who claimed first-name privileges, the Rotarians for example, called him "Floyd." So far as is known, Dewey Gottwald never had a nickname in his youth, perhaps an indication of the seriousness with which the senior son approached life around him.

Dewey Gottwald's youth was basically home- and work-centered. Family life was organized around the dinner table. The father, a great conversationalist, would describe everything that went on that day at the American Locomotive Company. In later years, Dewey Gottwald recalled that "the boys who were going to school put in their two cents' worth, and I added my five cents' worth."

The mother, Mary Alma, usually sat silent. She was a very quiet sort, "a beautifully motherly woman," as her oldest son described her, who had her own formula for bringing up children. At times she knowingly watched them make mistakes, believing that they learned their lesson better by experience than by incessant reprimand. As he was growing up, Dewey Gottwald at times sought dinner-table advice, and considered the mixture of his father's freely spoken words and his mother's more reluctant phrases solid wisdom. "I always thought they were superior to any other adviser or any other influence I had."

As the oldest of the children in a family where the official breadwinner was sometimes out of work and never highly paid, Dewey Gottwald early assumed special responsibilities; he was thought of by the younger children as belonging to a generation different from theirs. Dewey matured under forced draft, as it were, and sought what work he could get before and after school hours and during summer recess.

His first regular full-time job was summer employment at the age of twelve, when he began working for the firm of P. H. Mayo and Brothers, manufacturers of plug, smoking, and cigarette tobacco. In the huge, spreadout, four-story brick factory he was employed for three summers, principally on the second floor. He remembered his first wages: $4.08 per week, including overtime.

His main assignment was to assist with the application of the various flavorings, or "casings" as they were called, to the leaves as they came up from the floor below, and then to help ship the pressed tobacco from department to department.

Fortunately for the boy, the manager of the plant at that time was the alert and perceptive John Green Hayes, a gentleman with a beard that nicely covered a facial scar. Hayes was helpful and sympathetic then, and many years later, as noted in a previous chapter, supported Gottwald in his early efforts as president of Albemarle. On his daily visits to the packing machine where Dewey Gottwald was working, Hayes recognized solid, grim determination when he saw it and registered his confidence in the boy by making him sole trustee of the brandy used for flavoring.

Though life was principally school and work, Dewey Gottwald did find time to savor the normal activities of his age group. He learned to swim in the river; he made long trips over the nearby Civil War battlefields, picking up minnie balls by the bushel (or so the amount seemed in retrospect); and he played baseball. The husky teenager proved to be one of those young men who are naturally well coordinated on the baseball diamond, being especially agile at first base. In fact, his batting and fielding earned him a place on one of those local "semipro" teams that abounded in the cities and towns all over the country at that time. He left the team after five games because his father would not allow him to travel out of town.

In 1912 Dewey Gottwald completed Nicholson Graded School and entered John Marshall High School, which, according to nostalgic recollections of teachers and students, was then in its golden age. Teachers fired the ambition and curiosity of the pupils, and from the student body came a distinguished group of business and professional leaders. Impatient for tools immediately useful in the marketplace, Dewey Gottwald elected a curriculum labeled "Short Commercial," which, in addition to basic subjects such as English, history, and mathematics, included shorthand, typing, and practical bookkeeping.

Among his memorable teachers were Arthur W. James, whose

enthusiastic delivery and frequent human-interest stories enlivened his history classes, and Miss Charlotte K. Wheeler, English teacher, who would always ask, "Do you believe what's written?" In this manner she invited independent thinking, and encouraged a tendency to cautious skepticism, which remained part of Dewey Gottwald's intellectual baggage throughout his life. He judged the shorthand classes, "phonography," taught by Miss L. R. Angel, as priceless, perhaps the most useful course he ever had. In later years his business associates were intrigued and even confounded by his strange marks on scratchpads and reports.

In a subterranean sort of way, the adolescents at John Marshall High School, which drew students from all corners of the city, had their own brand of provincialism, or sectionalism, or worse. For example, the boys from Fulton were discouraged from joining the regular high-school baseball team. In turn, the Fulton boys vowed they would not play even if asked, since *their* brand of baseball was so much superior to that of the clique of soft guys who had cornered control of the team.

In the spring of 1915, as his last year of high school was drawing to a close, Dewey Gottwald began looking for a permanent position, one with a chance for advancement. His high school principal, James C. Harwood, heard of a vacancy in the treasurer's office of the Richmond, Fredericksburg and Potomac Railroad Company and recommended that Gottwald apply. He had conversation with David Kemper Kellogg, treasurer. Although someone else was hired at that time, future events proved the ambitious seventeen-year-old had made a lasting impression on Kellogg.

Then Gottwald discovered that the firm of Woodward and Son, wholesale lumber dealers with yard and office south of the James River, had an opening that would be available only if he immediately began work. Jobs were scarce; therefore he accepted, even though this meant an incomplete school year. And thus he became stenographer and clerk for Woodward and Son, holding this position for a year and a half.

Stewart Woodward, manager of the lumber company, was a

most economical man, directing the young clerk to slit all incoming envelopes to create a supply of memorandum paper. On the other hand, he was not a hard taskmaster. Gottwald improved his time by learning to inspect lumber and to classify it by variety and grade.

Upset by a minor difference with Stewart Woodward, Gottwald reapplied to Kellogg, treasurer of the railroad company. Kellogg looked at the young man, now a bit older and more experienced than at the time of the first interview, and said, "It just happens . . . " In this way F. D. Gottwald in November 1916 began working in the treasurer's office quite sure that one day he would be president of the railroad.

Under the accounting designation of "clerk" attached to the treasurer's office, Gottwald performed various stenographic, clerical, and financial duties during his two years with the railroad. Officials tested the new clerk's integrity in a variety of ways during the early months of his employment. In the office at 823 East Main Street, Gottwald gave direct help to the paymaster and assistant treasurer. Also, fortunately for the young man, he continued to work with David K. Kellogg.

Kellogg was clerk of the session of the Ginter Park Presbyterian Church. This conscientious gentleman took great pride in the accuracy and neatness of his typed minutes. As he reported to the session on April 4, 1918, he turned the typing over to his "stenographer, F. D. Gottwald." The resulting pages (which may still be examined in the archives of the Union Theological Seminary) brought compliments from the Presbytery when Kellogg submitted his records for review.

With the outbreak of World War I, many men not ages twenty-one to thirty-one, the group being drafted, felt that they ought to volunteer. Among these was young Gottwald, who was turned down by the recruiting officer because of the German origin of his name. The president of the railroad, William H. White, attempted to intervene in Gottwald's favor, and argued that if names were a test of loyalty the recruiting officer should remember the origin of "Dewey," but to no avail. Such prejudice against those of German name and descent was not an isolated event. With understatement a historian of the German Lutheran Church in Richmond wrote that the "excited prejudice of the time made the war years an unhappy period for the congregation."

When the federal government took over the railroads as a wartime measure in 1918, it required an analysis of salaries and wages extending back for many years, a study in which Gottwald, now assistant paymaster, shared. It was an investigation that alarmed Gottwald, for he saw what he considered a snaillike pace in promotions. He liked the work he was doing, and he had no real complaint about his wages at that time. (He had begun at $60 per month and was raised to $95 by September 1918.) He decided to talk it over with Kellogg.

When Gottwald went to Kellogg and asked about chances for promotion, Kellogg responded fully and frankly. Advancement would come very slowly; as a matter of fact, Gottwald was "waiting for a dead man's shoes." (Gottwald never forgot the phrase used by Kellogg.) Kellogg added in all candor that if the young man was dissatisfied with such a prospect, Kellogg would aid in the search for employment elsewhere. Kellogg said he had a friend and a fellow church member, Arthur F. Robertson, secretary-treasurer of Albemarle Paper Manufacturing Company, to whom Gottwald should talk.

This conversation with Kellogg was considered by Gottwald the turning point in his career. Even in his later years Gottwald always referred to Kellogg in affectionate terms because of his guidance: "I always loved him very much for that."

Kellogg himself arranged for the critical interview, which was held in the office of the Albemarle Paper Manufacturing Company. Arthur Robertson talked with Gottwald and introduced him to H. Watkins Ellerson, the president. Gottwald was offered a clerkship, which he accepted.

The middle of November 1918 was an exciting time for a twenty-year-old man burning with ambition. Armistice Day, a departure from friends in the R.F.&P. treasurer's office, the beginning of a new job with the paper company, all in less than a

Floyd Dewey Gottwald, about 1918

week. Gottwald began working with Albemarle Paper Manufacturing Company on November 15, 1918.

Several of his friends thought him extremely foolish to leave the railroad, where he had a secure position. One well-meaning acquaintance went so far as to take his argument to Gottwald's girlfriend, Annie Ruth Cobb, in an attempt to persuade Gottwald that he was making a cardinal mistake. But Gottwald insisted that he knew what he was doing. One day he would be president of Albemarle, so he said.

The young lady of the neighborhood Gottwald was courting, Annie Ruth Cobb, was the only child of Mr. and Mrs. David A. Cobb. (Later she preferred to be called "Anne"; for uniformity the single name will be used in the following pages.) Anne's major energies, outside of school, were devoted to the activities of the Fulton Baptist Church, at the southeast corner of Fulton and Nicholson streets. Although she taught Sunday School and worked with other young people's groups, her most conspicuous service was in the program of music, having been trained by Ernest Cosby, director of All Saints boys choir, and by Alton Howell, once organist at the First Baptist Church. She started singing in the choir at the age of fourteen, became organist at sixteen, and later added choir directing to her other church responsibilities.

Anne Cobb and Floyd Dewey Gottwald first met squarely in the middle of Fulton Street as she was leaving church. Gottwald began to attend Fulton Baptist Church mostly to be near Anne. Perhaps his interest in this church also resulted from the influence of his grandmother, Louisa Gottwald, who was having doubts about the theology in the German Lutheran Church and was inclined to total immersion in the Baptist manner. (She eventually joined the Fulton Baptist Church by baptism on April 21, 1920.) Floyd Dewey Gottwald was received into the Fulton Baptist Church some time during the year 1916 and soon began teaching a Sunday School class, his first lesson being organized around the verse "In the year King Uzziah died . . . " (Isaiah 6:1). In 1918 he was chosen assistant secretary and treasurer of the congregation.

Whether in church or out Gottwald did not neglect his courtship. When, during the summer season, the Cobbs sent Anne to visit her grandparents on their farm in Cumberland County, Dewey Gottwald sometimes followed. And he ingratiated himself with Anne's grandfather by helping with the tobacco crop, even donning protective sleeves and engaging in the messy business of *suckering*.

On November 17, 1919, almost exactly a year after Gottwald started working for Albemarle, he and Anne were married, the officiating minister being W. Thornburn Clark, pastor of the Fulton Baptist Church.

Like other bridegrooms Gottwald resolved to make life more bountiful for his bride. Anne Gottwald recalls an evening stroll with her husband soon after their marriage. "I remember one night we were walking in front of Miller and Rhoads store looking in the windows, and I was admiring the clothes. Of course we hadn't done anything other than just live, as most young people did then. And I said, 'Do you think I'll ever need a beautiful evening dress like that?' He said, 'Of course you're going to have beautiful evening dresses like that.' I looked at him and smiled, and thought, 'That's real nice of him to feel that way about me, but I just wonder'." She adds that she lived to see fulfillment of every promise he ever made to her. Dewey Gottwald's resolution to improve his family's economic status was one of the several forces impelling him toward achievements rarely seen in the economic life of America.

From the moment Dewey Gottwald entered the employment of Albemarle Paper Manufacturing Company his biography becomes part of the corporate history already surveyed. For more than sixty years he shaped the company and, quite as important, the company shaped him. The result was a distinctive corporation and a personality sui generis.

A Closer Look at a "Very Private Person"

What are those characteristics that made F. D. Gottwald so different from other men as to be classified a business genius? Perhaps the points most frequently emphasized by longtime colleagues are: first, his unusual imagination; second, his singleness of purpose; and third, a feature that flows naturally from the second point, his willingness to work long and hard.

If only one trait could be listed by his contemporaries it would be Gottwald's imagination, the fact that he was a man of tomorrow. Gottwald was always thinking about what came next. He had an inquiring mind, a rapidly running mind, and a mind that encompassed possibilities most other people could not see. And he blended with his imagination a great amount of optimism. Perhaps the word *courage* should be repeated here. Once he clearly saw his way, he was willing to stake everything on that transaction. To put the matter in a domestic setting, Gottwald was known in his family as one who never admitted that anything is impossible.

He was devoted to his business; the subject simply absorbed him almost one hundred percent. It was his life, it was his hobby, and he loved it. Surely it was something of a game with him. There is persuasive evidence that Gottwald was always thinking about his work. Once when Robert Herzog, executive vice president, asked Gottwald what he did with those reports he took home, Gottwald answered, "I put them under my bed and if at night I wake up I reach under and I read reports so that I don't waste that time."

Indeed Gottwald had a mind too comprehending and retentive for the comfort of any staff member who presented a project with even *one* weak place in his proposal. As an officer ruefully observed, you knew it was going to happen, you just *knew* it. Sure enough when you went in for oral explanation your typed proposal was open at page 47, just where your reasoning was most vulnerable. It happened practically every time.

Gottwald's mind was not only retentive but it quickly adjusted to new situations. When something unusual came up he could, with considerable coolness, shift his plans. "I marvel at that," says his daughter-in-law, Mrs. Floyd D. Gottwald, Jr. In the Albemarle days Gottwald repeatedly would come to the plant and merely stand, apparently watching those machines running. But his mind was tuned to the whirling cogs and rollers.

Gottwald could become quite excited when talking about the future of American industry in general and his own company in particular. Answering a question as to whether we have now reached the limits of industrial chemistry, he emphatically said that "we haven't begun to reach [the limits] yet."

Gottwald mixed outright forcefulness in business dealings with conspicuous modesty in social gatherings. Thus he was a puzzle to many. The influence he radiated came from personality, not from an overpowering physique, for he was of only average height, five feet seven and three-quarter inches. Not infrequently he complained of a weight problem, particularly after a vacation! With some success he coped with this situation by omitting his midday meal or by reducing his lunch menu to soup and crackers. His eyes were blue-gray and his firm mouth in the midst of a somewhat roundish face gave more than a hint of the fact that he was a very private person. As he grew older his facial features more and more resembled his father's.

According to Larry Weekley, writing in *Commonwealth Magazine*, January 1963, an unidentified Albemarle executive estimated Gottwald in these words: "He's the boss around here and nobody ever forgets it. He runs the place, period. At the same time, he is a kind and considerate man. He is one of the most retiring people I know. Believe it or not, he's shy."

In truth Gottwald was not given to much small talk. This reticence, an enduring part of his nature, was sometimes misunderstood to his own disadvantage. Strangers on occasion misinterpreted silence to mean disinterest, outright disapproval, or surliness. Witness the stir caused by the use of the word *curmudgeonish* in a description of Gottwald in the *Forbes* article at the time of the 1962 acquisition of Ethyl of Delaware by Albemarle. Such charges angered his friends, who cite countless instances of warmth and helpfulness. Senior staff members remember sharing rides with him on the way to work and stopping by the Stumble Inn on Main Street for doughnuts, coffee, and lively talk.

One judges that Gottwald in making major decisions preferred objective information over direct advice. He was known to check one informant against another, this to insure accuracy, a precautionary maneuver not always comfortable for his staff. He did not suffer dissent gladly. In a word, to repeat a point contemporaries made with emphasis, he was indeed "the boss."

Though human levity seemed foreign to Gottwald's personality most of the time, it emerged on special occasions such as the annual meeting of the stockholders and during relaxed days while he walked down Virginia Beach inviting friends to a social gathering at the Gottwald summer home. In 1965 Conrad Lemon, business editor of the *Richmond Times-Dispatch*, noted that the annual meeting of stockholders was entertained by F. D. Gottwald. While he is not a performer in the conventional sense, his performance "has all the effects of a well-staged theatrical production. He lifts the spirits of the audience, draws its members into spontaneous and jovial conversation and sends them on their way with a smile on their lips." It was this reporter who insisted that Gottwald was not "retiring or stuffy. He's anything but that. It's just that he's a busy man who seeks no publicity."

Often in private conversation Gottwald exhibited a humor ranging all the way from his story of Parson Jones and his fox hunting, given in a dialect and with mimicry, to the display of a solemn-looking tongue-in-cheek version of the "laws of science" featuring Murphy's and allied verities.

Although Gottwald read all the time, he was not given to composition. He rarely wrote letters. Friends of long standing vow that they have in their files no more than one or two written communications from him. And he said, "I never file anything, just put it on my desk 'til it's no good." In truth he had a retentive mind stored with facts that he could pull out when necessary. His contemporaries have remarked that Gottwald never stopped learning.

He held firm ideas as to education, emphasizing the practical. However, when the argument reached specific cases, he accepted as valid more of the traditional liberal arts courses than his original position might have suggested, allowing the virtues of the basic sciences and admitting his own interest in history, in biography especially. He confessed even to the reading of poetry, and applauded Charles W. Eliot's "five-foot shelf" of classics. Furthermore, as has been noted in the narrative of Albemarle in the 1920s, while still a young man he developed a working knowledge of three Romance languages.

A questioner ventured to suggest to Gottwald that probably a regular full-length college course would not have made him one bit more successful as a businessman. In quick response Gottwald denied this assumption and said that certainly he would have been better off, and would have been a more effective person.

Gottwald never made public the extent of his personal support of educational institutions and the amount of corporate giving which may be credited to his influence. Certainly these contributions were considerable. Among the known beneficiaries of his interests were Virginia Military Institute, the University of Richmond, the College of William and Mary, and the Virginia Foundation for Independent Colleges. For Virginia Military Institute, from which both sons graduated, he had the warmest regard. Gottwald served the University of Richmond as a trustee and trustee emeritus. Valuing his own experience with William and Mary by way of a year's chemistry course in its Richmond Division, Gottwald developed a lively interest in the School of Business Administration at the college in Williamsburg.

Anne Gottwald's answer to a question about her husband's hobbies in essence confirms his devotion to business. "Work came first, second, third. He worked all his life, and worked very hard." And she adds, "He never felt that he had time for anything but work."

Although Gottwald occasionally indulged in several outdoor sports, they never captured him quite as they have other men. In his more active days he occasionally went hunting, often at his hunting club, the Wright's Island Game Association, in the company of his close friend the late Dr. Webster P. Barnes, surgeon. From time to time Gottwald went fishing, both freshwater and saltwater. In early life he played an acceptable game of golf.

In a different category was his interest in "Snowden," his farm in Goochland, on which he had a house named "Clover Hill," and where he carried on experimental work with swine. Partly because a branch of the James River and the Kanawha Canal ran through the property, he began the study of canals in general.

There were semihobbies allied with his work. In a sense the building of that great headquarters structure on Gamble's Hill was a hobby. And he commissioned a handsome portrait of the first master of Gamble's Hill, Colonel Robert Gamble, which hangs in Ethyl's board room. He began to purchase choice books on Richmond history and planned to keep them handy in an impressive breakfront in the board room.

One may trace a series of events which persuaded Gottwald to

Restored Tredegar Gun Foundry

take an active part in the preservation and restoration of elements in the historic Tredegar Ironworks, bought in 1957. When the folding box board plans failed, Gottwald considered the proper disposition of the historic remnants. He said, "And it was only after that fell through that we decided that it was not necessary for us to hold them [for business purposes], not only unnecessary, but it wasn't exactly fair."

In the early 1970s plans became more specific. In 1971 Gottwald was inquiring as to which buildings were of historic interest. The great flood of 1972, a result of tropical storm Agnes, caused the roof of the Tredegar gun foundry to collapse, and the city inspector said that the roof should come down. This prompted further thinking. After hearing reports of additional research, Gottwald presented to the board meeting December 28, 1972, the first phase of a program of restoration. The board approved and five years later there were ceremonies marking the completion of the rebuilding of the historic gun foundry, a model for students interested in nineteenth-century industrial technology and architecture.

The restoration program, carried on under the watchful eyes of F. D. Gottwald, was supervised by Roy E. Johnson, a graduate of Virginia Polytechnic Institute, who joined Albemarle in 1940 and, save for service in the U.S. Navy during World War II, has been with the company ever since.

In the field of aesthetics Gottwald was more sensitive than he admitted. Here the outsider must tread softly. Gottwald was quite affected by some of the glories of nature, and in rare moments expressed his joy in watching such phenomena as the waves at the beach coming and going and ever-changing.

Gottwald's church always was a major point of concern. Even in the trying period that marked the conclusion of Ellerson's presidency of Albemarle and Gottwald's assumption of the leadership of the corporation, Gottwald and his wife exercised a decisive and cohesive influence on the congregation of the Fulton Baptist Church, which sold its old building and became the Montrose Baptist congregation in a new structure. During the transitional years when the worshipers used a schoolhouse, Mrs. Gottwald was important in holding the young people together. Gottwald himself was chairman of the building committee and appropriately presided at the dedicatory exercises in 1945. Some time after moving from the eastern part of the city to Windsor Farms in the West End, Gottwald transferred his membership from the Montrose Baptist Church to the more convenient First Baptist Church at the corner of Monument Avenue and the Boulevard.

Gottwald's business life can be understood only within the context of his family, for Gottwald was a very intense family man. It is the verdict of the sons and the daughters-in-law that Gottwald and his wife were absolutely devoted to each other. As Libby, Mrs. Floyd D. Gottwald, Jr., observes: "Mom and Pop discussed everything. I think when he came in he sat down and they discussed the day, what he did, what she did. And she was always pretty well informed as to what went on."

Family members agree that nothing made Gottwald happier than having all generations around him and his wife. His supreme moments were at Virginia Beach in the huge dining room, where he sat at one end of the table and Anne Gottwald at the other, with the intervening space filled by the younger generation. Then he was in his glory. Incidentally, in his more active days Gottwald enjoyed puttering around the Virginia Beach house. Nancy, wife of Bruce Gottwald, says: "I told Pop that if they ever made a statue of him, they would put an oil can in his hand because his happiest moments were going around at Virginia Beach fixing things."

Although Gottwald professed to keep activities other than his work at a minimum, as a responsible member of the community he shared in a number of civic enterprises. For varying periods of time he served on the Richmond School Board, the Richmond-Petersburg Turnpike Authority, the board of directors of the First and Merchants National Bank, and the board of directors of the Metropolitan Richmond Chamber of Commerce.

Gottwald was a member of the Commonwealth Club, the Country Club of Virginia, and the Princess Anne Country Club of Virginia Beach. His interest in the past was suggested by his membership in the Virginia Historical Society and his frequent attendance at the Antiques Forum in Williamsburg. Gottwald was a member of the Collectors Circle of the Virginia Museum of Fine Arts. As a young man he joined the Masons, and in the 1940s he was a member of the Rotary Club of Richmond.

Gottwald's abilities were recognized in a variety of ways. On October 23, 1964, at its annual convention the National Management Association meeting in St. Louis named him "Management Man of the Year." In 1965 the University of Richmond awarded him the honorary degree of Doctor of Commercial Science. On November 11, 1977, Virginia Military Institute bestowed on Gottwald its "Distinguished Service Award." In that same year the College of William and Mary named him and his older son, Floyd D. Gottwald, Jr., the recipients of the Medal-

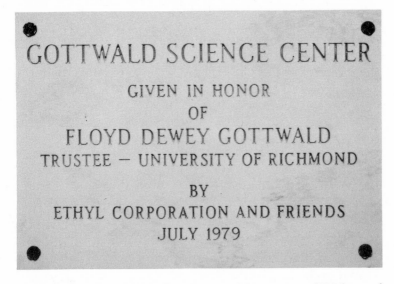

GOTTWALD SCIENCE CENTER

GIVEN IN HONOR
OF
FLOYD DEWEY GOTTWALD
TRUSTEE — UNIVERSITY OF RICHMOND

BY
ETHYL CORPORATION AND FRIENDS
JULY 1979

Tablet in Gottwald Science Center, University of Richmond

lion Award given by the School of Business Administration. The year 1979 saw the naming by the University of Richmond of the Gottwald Science Center. Also in 1979 there was established at the College of William and Mary the Floyd Dewey Gottwald Professorship of Business Administration.

Inevitably one reaches for the larger meaning in the career of such a man as F. D. Gottwald. Was there conscious and formal development of a stewardship theory such as is embodied in the "God's gold" phrase used by John D. Rockefeller? Perhaps not, but Gottwald felt that a corollary to the doctrine of free enterprise is the basic imperative of responsiblity to society. Once in an offhand way he said that "the population of the United States is increasing, even though moderately, and it is the obligation, I think, of business people to constantly increase employment."

An observer of more than ordinary perception ventured his opinion that Gottwald's willingness to yield control to others as the years went by was as remarkable as his creative judgments in building the company. It is an axiom that strong men surrender power reluctantly. One can only guess the exact time—and the possible pain—of withdrawal from being the boss to being a lieutenant, of sorts, but certainly as a practical matter the transition was completed by the mid or late 1970s. Of course such a maneuver was made easier by the fact that the two chief officers were sons who had been in training for many years.

The Chairman and the President

F. D. Gottwald maintained that he never tried to persuade his sons to join the company he headed. This disavowal of pressure on Bill and Bruce is confirmed by statements of both. As Bill says, "I don't think I ever got any indoctrination at all." Of course his father would come home and talk a little bit about some particular problem, but it was all very low key. "In fact it was so subtle that it wasn't even noticeable," according to Bill. As indicated in an earlier chapter, F. D. Gottwald saw to it that once the sons were employed they worked diligently and were exposed to a variety of company experiences, including service as corporate secretary. Gottwald always felt that this office was an extremely valuable training experience. Obviously, it has not been easy to live up to the expectations of a man like F. D. Gottwald. However, as a member of the family has said, the sons have never been heard to complain about their role.

Of course when the three Gottwalds came to a consensus they represented a majority of the executive committee, and the executive committee runs the company. When the question is raised as to how the three Gottwalds reached agreement, there is never any answer that an outsider can understand. As Nancy Gottwald says, "They just must have had a feeling about things, an empathy one with the other. It's just always amazed me. I'll say, 'How in the world do you know such and such?' [And then referring to Bruce] He'll say, 'I just know.'"

Floyd Dewey Gottwald, Jr., elected chairman of the board in 1968 and chief executive officer in 1970, was born in Richmond on July 29, 1922. Bill, as he was known to family and friends from his enjoyment of the childhood song "Billy Boy," had the normal boyhood experiences of his neighborhood, including act-

Floyd D. Gottwald, Jr.

ing out the Tarzan fantasies of youth in the wooded lot on Government Road. As a young boy he would sometimes travel to the mill with his father, who thought he would be there about fifteen minutes but would remain for a couple of hours. In that time Bill would wander about the plant and talk to the people whom he learned to know. That friendship survived the years and even when Bill was in higher office some of the older workers would call on him from time to time.

Partly inspired by a pictorial history of World War I that he discovered in the attic, and partly because of a favorable tuition-and-board policy, he entered Virginia Military Institute on graduation from John Marshall High School. As Anne Gottwald, Bill's mother, recalls, these were years of the depression, but later on Bill did not remember that the times were hard; it all seemed a matter of course to him. With reference to going to VMI, Bill says that he was a bit interested in the military, not the regular army as a career, but perhaps the reserves, and he thought it might be interesting. "I just had the feeling that we were going to have World War II, and I just felt like it might be a good idea to be a little bit prepared."

On graduation from VMI with a B.S. degree in chemistry in 1943, he entered the army as a cavalryman and trained at Fort Riley, Kansas. When he completed officer candidate school, he was sent to a horse regiment stationed in Texas on the Rio Grande at Rio Grande City, and he thinks it was probably the last horse outfit in the United States. His group was sent overseas to the China-India-Burma Theater, with all the cavalry equipment, but once overseas the soldiers were dismounted and trained as infantrymen. In the CIB Theater, they trained in India for approximately six months and then went into Burma, where they remained for about the same length of time.

His outfit had a brief encounter with the Japanese on the Burma Road during which he suffered a shoulder wound, which resulted in a temporary absence from active duty, the award of the Purple Heart decoration, and a permanent tendency to arthritic pain in the joint near where the bullet entered. According to the family, Bill's letter written home announcing his wound was typical of his gift for understatement. According to his wife Libby it was something like this: "I don't want Mother to be upset, but something I did not plan on happened today." Then he reported his wound. As Libby says, "That has always struck me as being just like Bill. Very calm." After the Burma Road episode his group went into China, where it engaged in military police duty until the end of the war.

Back home Bill Gottwald married Elisabeth ("Libby") Shelton of Charlottesville on March 22, 1947, after a reacquaintance of about ten months. They first knew each other when he came home for weekends and vacations during his VMI days, and they dated when he was briefly stationed at nearby Fort Lee before going to officer candidate school at Fort Riley. Earlier she had come to Richmond from Charlottesville on invitation to work in the credit office of a department store, then had been employed as a receptionist by dentists allied with the Medical College of Virginia. This last was a job for which she had been specifically trained in business school.

Bill Gottwald completed a course in business administration at the University of Richmond mainly if not entirely consisting of evening classes. He received a master of science degree in business administration in 1951. After receipt of that degree he taught courses in the evening school for two years, enjoying this experience. According to his wife Libby, "I always felt that he was getting a great deal of satisfaction out of it. I would help him with his grading papers and do things like that."

Libby Gottwald, who was in charge of domestic bookkeeping, persuaded him soon after their marriage to give up a horse with an appetite too expensive for their budget at the time. When the couple settled down on Chamberlayne Avenue, the good ladies of the neighborhood shook their heads as they saw the other young husbands go to work in crisp collars and flannel suits while Bill, being given fundamental jobs in the plant, went dressed for the occasion in khaki pants and shirt. "Too bad," they said about young Mrs. Gottwald, "married to the only man in the neighborhood who's never going to get ahead in business." Bill had started working at the chemistry laboratory where he had been employed during previous summers.

As Bill went over the plant there was at times some self-consciousness because he had the inevitable, and, to him at the time, unenviable, label "the boss's son." Bill moved from the position of laboratory chemist to superintendent of the waterproofing department and then was advanced to production manager, secretary, and vice president of Albemarle Paper. At the time Albemarle and Ethyl merged to become Ethyl of Virginia in 1962, Floyd D. Gottwald, Jr., was elected executive vice president and director. He was vice chairman of the board from 1964 to 1968; he became chairman of the board in 1968, and chief executive officer in 1970.

According to Libby Gottwald, her husband is "a perpetual student." She adds, "He is interested in everything. His principal reading matter is technical literature, but he does like mystery stories and CIA narratives."

As for ideas on education, he complains of the uselessness of many courses, asserting that the physics to which he was exposed "just never tied to anything." He adds, "I don't think the curriculum in the average high school when I was going—it may be changed now—and in college is practical enough. A lot of college graduates have no practical knowledge of anything."

Despite this criticism of the typical college curriculum, Floyd D. Gottwald, Jr., gives both personal and financial assistance to a number of institutions of higher learning, especially those he attended. He serves as president of the board of trustees of the VMI Foundation and as a trustee of the University of Richmond. The esteem he and his wife have for Washington and Lee University, from which two of their sons graduated, is revealed in the announcement that the university has named the gallery exhibiting the paintings of Louise Herreshoff Reeves the Gottwald Gallery in honor of Elisabeth Shelton Gottwald.

At one period Bill Gottwald made a special effort to learn French. He did not study that language in college though he did undertake Spanish and German courses. First he and Libby enrolled in a French class but discovered that Bill's business commitments did not permit regular attendance. Then Bill resorted to using lessons on a tape recorder. He explains his interest in French by saying, "Well we do a pretty fair amount of business overseas, and I have always felt that it was bad that we always have to conduct it in English. I think, next to English, that French is the most generally used language."

Floyd D. Gottwald, Jr., holds directorships in many companies, including CSX Corporation and Reid-Provident Laboratories. He is also a director of the American Petroleum Institute, the National Association of Manufacturers, the Chemical Manufacturers Association, and the National Petroleum Council.

Both Bill and Libby Gottwald are active members of the River Road Church, Baptist. A former deacon, he now serves on the church administrative board. She is a past member of that board.

As for hobbies, he gives priority to fishing and hunting. He says, "I used to hunt but I haven't done too much lately. Went on one trip to Africa. And it was nice, but I don't have an awful lot of desire to go back." He notes with more enthusiasm a hunting trip to Canada that was more of a camping than a hunting trip. He is an award-winning fisherman. He is more fond of saltwater than freshwater fishing, and says that fishing is very good at Virginia Beach, just as good as it is in Florida, maybe a little better.

Bill Gottwald has loved horses all of his life. Libby Gottwald speaks of his ribbons and adds, "He is a beautiful rider. He rode in many of the shows at the Deep Run Hunt Club. He was going to horse shows all the time." His interest in automobiles, both domestic and foreign varieties, is allied with his business concerns. Several years ago he enrolled in a course for automobile mechanics in the Richmond Technical Center on Westwood Avenue.

The Bill Gottwalds now have a handsome house, "Herndon," near River Road and overlooking the James River. Libby describes with enthusiasm the scenes of nature about her. "To tell the truth, there is very little I would find any more pleasure in than the surroundings that I find myself in every day, with my bluebirds flitting around, the deer coming up to graze." She often sees deer at 6 P.M. as they graze and she sees them in the morning. "One morning at the fence I just couldn't believe it, there

were eight just lying in the sun." She adds that being at Herndon is just like being in the country.

Although Libby Gottwald usually prefers her suburban residence to foreign lands, her trip to Japan in August 1980 for the christening and launching of the *Libby G*, the first ship in the corporate fleet that Ethyl owned, was a memorable and happy event. As sponsor and godmother she recited the phrase, "I name you Libby G," and swung a razor sharp chrome plated hatchet, which severed a rope and triggered a mechanism for breaking a champagne bottle over the bow. As the ship slid down the ways to the water there were fireworks and the release of 200 doves, all creating an impressive spectacle. The *Libby G*, built at a cost of $15.4 million, is 383.9 feet in length—as long as a football field plus end zones—has a capacity of 6,700 metric tons of antiknock compound, and a cruising speed of about 15 knots per hour. The ship presented a crisp and pleasing appearance, with funnel markings in Ethyl colors—a wide yellow stripe with narrower black stripes above and below the yellow stripe. The celebration of the day included a brief address by Floyd D. Gottwald, Jr., and additional remarks by Libby Gottwald, who returned to the United States commending the friendliness, precision, and neatness of the Japanese.

Bill and Libby Gottwald have three sons: the oldest William Michael, next James Tyler, the youngest John David. As already explained, John David is manager of the Ethyl subsidiary, Elk Horn Coal Corporation. He has recently been joined in this division by William Michael, who was trained as an M.D. The middle son, James Tyler, lives on a farm in Goochland County and is involved with real estate, construction, and allied enterprises.

Bruce Cobb Gottwald was born on Government Road in Richmond, Virginia, on September 28, 1933. Eleven years younger than Bill, Bruce has accepted his juniority with good grace. His role as a third member of the Gottwald triumvirate has called for hard work and adaptability.

Though a quiet and modest boy, he had a venturesome spirit; at an early age he would explore Richmond by way of the streetcars. John Marshall High School with its variety of personalities was something of a revelation to him. Bruce's reaction was to grow in spirit and to develop a gift of getting along with all types of people. His experiences were broadened when he and his older brother took trips with their parents to conventions of papermakers. By all reports Bruce was a dutiful son who gave his parents little trouble.

In an educational sense Bruce Gottwald for years followed in his older brother's footsteps. After Bruce graduated from John Marshall High School, a family crisis seemed in the offing when it appeared that Bruce might attend some college *other than* Virginia Military Institute. With proper persuasion from Bill, Bruce entered VMI and survived that famous "rat year," though he claims that Bill, to be certain Bruce would not waver in his final decision to attend VMI, had given no fraternal warning of what to expect. Bruce bridged his moments of discouragement by looking at some of the cadets who had gone through the first year and saying to himself, "If those so-and-sos can do it, I know that I can." And he did.

Perhaps Bruce Gottwald's major educational influence in terms of personalities was Colonel Herbert E. ("Butch") Ritchey. To quote Bruce, "He would just quietly take you to pieces if you weren't prepared for his class. And after the first three weeks in there I decided that maybe studying was a whole lot better than taking this abuse." In responding to academic challenges, Bruce developed a concept of *planning* that he highly values today. After graduating in 1954 from VMI, he enrolled for postgraduate study at the University of Virginia and at the Institute of Paper Chemistry, Appleton, Wisconsin.

Bruce Gottwald married Nancy Hays of Hope, Arkansas, on December 22, 1956. She first became acquainted with Virginia when, as a young girl, she visited in Washington, D.C., her uncle George Lloyd Spencer, then U.S. senator from Arkansas. Nancy always felt that this uncle and his wife were, in a sense, second parents. The Spencers had no children of their own. While on a Washington visit Nancy in her own words, "just fell in love with it [Virginia] then."

Nancy Gottwald was born in Little Rock, Arkansas. The family moved to Hope, Arkansas, under encouragement from Senator Spencer. She enrolled in Randolph-Macon Woman's College in Lynchburg, Virginia. Her acquaintance with Bruce came about because she dated his roommate for two years.

After graduating in 1955, she taught for one year in Louisiana, living in New Orleans next door to a medical fraternity. At La-Fitte, to which she commuted daily, she taught the third grade, though "from November until March half of my class was gone trapping." Friends persuaded her to come to Duke University, where she obtained a place in the Master of Arts in Teaching (MAT) program, a relatively new venture at that institution. During the MAT program, which began in a summer session, she wrote Bruce explaining her return to the Atlantic seaboard. Affairs moved ahead rapidly; between the summer session and the fall term she and Bruce drove to Arkansas to see her parents. She departed the MAT program at Halloween. As already indicated, she and Bruce were married three days before Christmas 1956.

Bruce C. Gottwald

In that same year Bruce had begun his first full-time work at Albemarle. He undertook in 1959 to manage an Albemarle division, Randolph Paper Box, where, according to him, he earned his first ulcer. There was considerable frustration in that highly competitive field and he never had the opportunity to build the new paper mill on Brown's Island that he hoped to construct. He was made assistant secretary of Albemarle in 1960.

Bruce was enthusiastic about the acquisition of Ethyl from the very beginning of negotiations although he was frankly bewildered at the thought of raising the necessary money. He joined with Bill in saying yes very promptly at that family gathering when the possibility of acquisition was presented by his father. As negotiations went on, he was honestly astounded at the size of the sums of money involved. Bruce's frankness in narrative is a constant characteristic of his reminiscing. Nancy's spontaneous quip at the beginning of the closing ceremonies—the story of the *spenders* rather than the *lenders*—neatly matches the light touch offered by Bruce.

At the time of the merger in 1962 Bruce was elected director, vice president, and secretary; he became president in 1970. In the general distribution of responsibility among the three Gottwalds, Bruce took for a time special care of the Plastics Group and engaged in nightly telephone conversations with Dr. Neher. Bruce's duties carry him to Baton Rouge almost every Monday, and sometimes he must spend Monday night in Baton Rouge. As a good family man he insists that arrangements be made so that he does not have to be away from home as a usual thing more than one night a week.

Bruce has a number of interests outside of his business. During the administration of Governor John N. Dalton, Bruce Gottwald served as chairman of the Virginia Governor's Advisory Board on Industrial Development. He is currently on the board of governors of the Virginia Council on Economic Education. His directorships include the James River Corporation and Virginia Electric and Power Company.

For a period of time he served as trustee of the Presbyterian School of Christian Education. Both Nancy and Bruce Gottwald have been elected for terms as deacons in the First Presbyterian Church. Bruce Gottwald was formerly on the Randolph-Macon Women's College Board. It is acknowledged, however, that although he has a concern for higher education in general, his principal affections go to St. Christopher's School in Richmond and Virginia Military Institute in Lexington.

A major interest is the Virginia Museum of Fine Arts, where he serves as trustee. In this concern he has the active support of his wife Nancy, who is a member of the Museum Council.

Bruce Gottwald has the talent of excellent recall when reviewing events of the past. Furthermore, in a natural way he indulges in the raconteur's sure-fire device of laughing at himself a bit in his recollections—he may cheerfully report his own discomfort at Colonel Ritchey's harassment that persuaded him to study; he merrily confesses the near-lethal effect of his dollar cigar purchased in a period of ecstasy after the closing of the deal in November 1962; he recounts in good humor Bill's neglect to give proper warning about the agonies of the rat year at VMI.

The Bruce Gottwalds have three sons: Bruce Cobb, Jr., Mark Hays, and Thomas Edward. In a recent interview the last-named, who is a favorite with sports columnists because of his football achievements at VMI, confirmed the thesis that the Gottwald family does not believe in persuading the new generation to enter the Ethyl work force. To illustrate the fact that his father lets the sons find their own way, Thomas Edward ("Teddy") Gottwald said, "I have two brothers. One [Bruce, Jr.] works at Ethyl, the other, Mark, is at cooking school in Baltimore. He wants to be a chef. I think he'll be a good one. So does my father. He's supported us all in every decision we've ever made."

To conclude a review of F. D. Gottwald and his family, it seems appropriate to quote Lewis F. Powell, Jr., associate justice of the Supreme Court of the United States. After stating that F. D. Gottwald, Sr., "is the most remarkable business man I ever served as a lawyer," he adds: "This family, and the corporate history in which the family has been so intimately involved, reflect much that is both typical and admirable in the American free enterprise system. I wish there were more F. D. Gottwalds—and more families like the Gottwald family—among younger generations who now question the values of achievement and success in commercial enterprise. The real meaning of the story of Albemarle/Ethyl, apart from what it has meant personally to the Gottwald family, is the creation of a great multinational corporation that provides thousands of jobs and many needed products. This notable contribution to our country, and indeed to a broader society, has resulted not from any inherited wealth, but solely from intelligence, imagination, willingness to assume large risks and work hard, and an indefatigable will to achieve and build something worthwhile. These are qualities I greatly admire."

Epilogue, Prologue: First Colony Life Insurance Company

ON JANUARY 20, 1982, Ethyl Corporation and First Colony Life Insurance Company of Lynchburg, Virginia, jointly announced agreement for Ethyl to purchase all the stock of First Colony at a cost of approximately $270 million. The arrangement was subject to approval by directors and stockholders of both companies and by the appropriate regulatory agencies. Consent was soon given by all the necessary parties. Especially notable was the overwhelming approval in the two stockholders' meetings held May 14, 1982. By virtue of these votes the purchase of First Colony was officially concluded.

Organized in 1955, First Colony, one of the fastest growing insurance companies in America, needed additional capital to satisfy reserve requirements for expansion. For several months it had been searching for a suitable partner, one that would supply capital but would let First Colony keep its own identity and go ahead with its program of growth. *Fortune* magazine, February 22, 1982, reported the arrangement in these colorful words: "Clinging to traditional businesses has never been a failing of the Gottwalds of Richmond, Virginia. In two decades the company they effectively controlled, Ethyl Corp., has jumped like a pogo-stick rider from paper to antiknock compounds to chemicals, boosting sales 36-fold to $1.8 billion in 1981. Ethyl may now be boarding a rocket by paying $270 million to acquire First Colony Life, whose insurance in force has grown 100-fold in 17 years." The growth rate of First Colony has indeed been impressive. During the last ten years net income has grown at a rate of about 18 percent and over the past five years about 24 percent. Life Insurance in force during that past five-year period has increased from $2.5 billion to $10.8 billion.

First Colony does business in forty-nine states, and in New York through a wholly owned subsidiary. One of the company's distinctive features is that it operates through general agents, who, in turn, deal with licensed insurance brokers numbering about 25,000. The sales approach of First Colony differs from the or-dinary procedure of having agents that sell directly to clients.

First Colony discovered that its operating expenses were dra-matically reduced when it stopped training full-time career agents and utilized brokers and agents who would take on the specialty offerings of First Colony as a side line.

The dynamic leader of First Colony is George T. Stewart III, a gentleman with a big physique, an even larger imagination, long cigars, and joy in working. In 1966 he came to Lynchburg from New York, where he had been serving with Blyth and Com-pany as vice president and specialist in life insurance company investments.

A clue to the success of First Colony Life is the fact that it has been innovative and has boldly offered policies that old-line companies would not write. An early specialty was the so-called impaired risk life insurance policy. This was the insurance of people who, because of their poor health, were usually consid-ered bad risks. After studying the improving life expectancy of those individuals, First Colony management was convinced that these could be handled with advantage to both company and client. This judgment was correct and the specialization proved extremely profitable. First Colony developed other innovative plans, including impaired-risk annuities, and adapted its policies to compete successfully in a variety of unorthodox markets.

Though the purchase of First Colony Life Insurance Company is Ethyl's first acquisition in the area of financial management, it is in many respects a continuation of the traditional themes of diversification and innovation. The novel specialized insurance packages that are at the center of First Colony's growth are in a sense the counterparts in insurance of the specialty chemicals coming from Ethyl plants. It will be recalled that the specialty chemicals in general are tailor-made compounds created to fill particular needs.

An important asset is First Colony's ownership of real estate in Los Angeles. From this property over 300 million barrels of oil have been produced since initial development in 1924. While it is anticipated that oil will continue to be pumped from this property for a number of years, the location of the land is such that it is prime acreage for commercial and residential development. Adjacent to the oil-bearing acreage is property already utilized commercially. It is hardly necessary to point out that these oil wells fit in with Ethyl's recent emphasis on energy resources.

An important aspect of the purchase of First Colony stock by Ethyl is the fact that First Colony is a business neighbor and that there is intimate acquaintance with the history and the people of First Colony. It was in the office of Lewis Powell, Ethyl director and counsel, at that time with Hunton and Williams, that the First Colony charter was written. For several years Blanchard was a director, and he was on the committee that persuaded Stewart to leave Blyth and Company to join First Colony.

Obviously, the most important single factor in Ethyl's offer to purchase First Colony was the conviction that this investment in the long run would be profitable for Ethyl's stockholders. To put the purchase in proper perspective, one must remember that when the aggressive program of acquisition was instituted in the 1960s, instructions to those looking for acquisitions were to consider any business that looked good except banks and savings and loan companies. Never has Ethyl management claimed it has achieved the ultimate and final mixture of businesses in its diversification. Repeatedly at annual meetings there was the assurance to stockholders that when operations became inefficient they would be cut off, and when profitable opportunities were discovered these would be added if possible.

Several years ago when the present writer presented to Floyd D. Gottwald, Jr., the question of the ideal mix of business, Gottwald said that he simply did not know what might be down the road. In January 1982, according to Bill Gottwald, when looking around for something profitable the company officials discovered that First Colony was head and shoulders above all other alternatives. The official statement of the company included the assurance that although this acquisition obviously represented a departure from the traditional lines of business, "We would emphasize, nevertheless, that we intend for Ethyl to continue as a strong specialty chemical producer, pursuing our long-term corporate objectives." Management believes it has resources to support both the First Colony acquisition and other businesses. Ethyl's management estimates that the ratio of long-term debt to capitalization would be increased only to about 30 percent. From the point of view of the historian, looking at various clues over the years, it appears that Ethyl in the purchase of First Colony is in no way renouncing its chemical business and other commitments, but is clarifying the fact that Ethyl is primarily in the *money* business.

To this observer the investment in First Colony Life Insurance Company seems to be the beginning of a new chapter in the history of Albemarle / Ethyl. For the first time the company considers financial management as a product to be sold. However, old ideas still apply—diversification, innovation, and profit being among them. This current move might be seen as preparation for the centennial celebration a scant five years down the road.

Floyd Dewey Gottwald, the leading character in the foregoing pages, died in Richmond, Saturday, July 31, 1982, after serving his company longer than any person in its history.

Appendixes

A Note on Sources

Acknowledgments

Index

Board of Directors, December 1982. Clockwise from left: George T. Stewart III, James F. Miller, Melvin M. Payne, A. B. Horn, Jr., M. F. Gautreaux, Robert Herzog, Lawrence E. Blanchard, Jr., Bruce C. Gottwald, Floyd D. Gottwald, Jr., Joseph M. Lowry, John N. Dalton, Prime F. Osborn III,

Appendix A

Directors of Ethyl Corporation, 1962–1982

BLANCHARD, LAWRENCE E., JR. Born 1921, Lumberton, N.C.
Joined Ethyl 1967 as executive vice president. Vice chairman of the board since 1980. Director Ethyl since 1967.

CARTER, JOSEPH C., JR. Born 1927, Mayfield, Ky. Partner,
Hunton and Williams. Director Ethyl since 1981.

CHISHOLM, WILLIAM H. Born 1917, New York City. Joined Ethyl
1967 as executive vice president and president of Oxford
Paper Division. Resigned 1970. Director Ethyl 1967–71.

COSTELLO, JOSEPH H. Born 1900, Scranton, Pa. Joined Ethyl
1928 as field representative, sales department. Retired as vice
president 1966. Director Ethyl (Del.)/Ethyl 1952–70.

DALTON, JOHN N. Born 1931, Emporia, Va. Governor of Virginia 1978–82. Now partner McGuire, Woods, and Battle.
Director Ethyl since 1982.

FLEET, S. DOUGLAS Born 1907, Glen Allen, Va. Joined Albemarle 1925 as office boy. Retired 1965 as vice president.
Director Albemarle/Ethyl since 1948.

GAUTREAUX, M. F. Born 1930, Nashville, Tenn. With Ethyl
(Del.) 1951–55, then returned 1958 as head of engineering
and mathematical sciences, research and development.
Currently senior vice president. Director Ethyl since 1972.

GILL, JAMES M. Born 1922, Ruston, La. Joined Ethyl (Del.)
1948 as chemical engineer, manufacturing. Currently senior vice president, chemicals group. Director Ethyl since
1970.

GOTTWALD, BRUCE C. Born 1933, Richmond, Va. Joined Albemarle 1956 as chemist. Currently president and chief operating officer. Director Albemarle/Ethyl since 1962.

GOTTWALD, FLOYD D.   Born 1898, Richmond, Va. Joined Albemarle in 1918 as office clerk. Director Albemarle/Ethyl 1937–82. President Albemarle 1941–62; chairman Ethyl 1962–68. Vice chairman of the board at the time of his death, 1982.

GOTTWALD, FLOYD D., JR.   Born 1922, Richmond, Va. Joined Albemarle 1943 as chemist. Currently chairman of the board, chief executive officer, and chairman of the executive committee. Director Albemarle/Ethyl since 1956.

HERZOG, ROBERT   Born 1918, New York City. Joined Ethyl (Del.) 1940 as chemical engineer, manufacturing. Currently executive vice president. Director Ethyl since 1970.

HORN, A. B., JR.   Born 1923, Corsicana, Tex. Joined Ethyl (Del.) 1949 in manufacturing, technical services, research and development. Currently senior vice president, petroleum chemicals group. Director Ethyl since 1972.

HOWARD, FRANK A.   Born 1890, Danville, Ill. President Standard Oil Development Company, vice president Standard Oil of New Jersey. Director Ethyl (Del.)/Ethyl 1924–64. Died 1964.

KIRBY, GEORGE F.   Born 1916, Cheneyville, La. Joined Ethyl (Del.) 1940 as research chemist. Resigned 1969 as president of Ethyl. Director Ethyl (Del.)/Ethyl 1957–80. Died 1980.

LACY, ANDRE B.   Born 1939, Indianapolis, Ind. President Lacy Diversified Industries, Inc. Director Ethyl since 1981.

LOWRY, JOSEPH M.   Born 1908, Richmond, Va. Joined Albemarle 1947 as controller. Retired 1974 as senior vice president of Ethyl. Director Albemarle/Ethyl since 1951.

McBURNEY, ANDREW M.   Born 1913, Philadelphia, Pa. With Oxford Paper 1936–76. Currently consultant Boise Cascade Corporation. Director Ethyl since 1967.

McKNEW, THOMAS M.   Born 1896, Washington, D.C. Advisory chairman of the board, National Geographic Society. Director Ethyl 1967–72.

MARSH, ROBERT T., JR. Born 1901, Ridge Spring, S.C. Former chairman of the board, First and Merchants National Bank. Director Albemarle/Ethyl 1959–81. Died 1981.

MILLER, JAMES F. Born 1905, Portland, Oreg. Advisory director, Blyth Eastman Paine Webber, Inc. Director Ethyl since 1973.

MURDOCK, MALCOLM P. Born 1905, Melrose, Mass. Joined Ethyl (Del.) 1933 as field representative. Retired as senior vice president 1969. Director Ethyl (Del.)/Ethyl 1952–72.

MURRILL, PAUL W. Born 1934, St. Louis, Mo. Served Ethyl 1981–82 as senior vice president, research and development. Director Ethyl 1981–82.

NEHER, CLARENCE M. Born 1916, Twin Falls, Idaho. Joined Ethyl (Del.) 1941 as chemist, development section. Retired 1981 as senior vice president, plastics. Director Ethyl 1970–82.

OSBORN, PRIME F., III Born 1915, Greensboro, Ala. Chairman and chief executive officer, CSX Corporation. Director Ethyl since 1976.

PAYNE, MELVIN M. Born 1911, Washington, D.C. Chairman of the board, National Geographic Society. Director Ethyl since 1972.

PERDUE, WILLIAM R., JR. Born 1913, Macon, Ga. Joined Ethyl (Del.) 1950 as general counsel. Resigned Ethyl 1966 as executive vice president and treasurer. Director Ethyl (Del.)/Ethyl 1955–66.

POWELL, LEWIS F., JR. Born 1907, Suffolk, Va. Director Albemarle/Ethyl 1953–72 while partner Hunton, Williams, Gay, Powell and Gibson. Resigned directorship 1972 when appointed associate justice U.S. Supreme Court.

RICE, W. THOMAS Born 1912, Hague, Va. Former chairman and chief executive officer, Seaboard Coast Line Industries, Inc. Director Ethyl 1967–76.

ROBINS, E. CLAIBORNE Born 1910, Richmond, Va. Chairman of the board, A. H. Robins Company. Director Ethyl 1962–72.

SCOTT, S. BUFORD   Born 1933, Richmond, Va. Chairman of
the board, Scott and Stringfellow, Inc. Director Albemarle/
Ethyl since 1959.
SHEA, EDWARD L.   Born 1892, Nashua, N.H. President of Ethyl
(Del.) 1947–56. Director Ethyl (Del.)/Ethyl 1947–63. Died
1963.
STEWART, GEORGE T., III   Born 1924, New York City. Presi-
dent, First Colony Life Insurance Company. Director Ethyl
since 1982.
TURNER, B. B.   Born 1910, Angleton, Tex. Joined Ethyl (Del.)
1946 as assistant plant manager, Baton Rouge. Resigned 1964
as president, Ethyl. Director Ethyl (Del.)/Ethyl 1952–64.
Died 1979.
WILL, ERWIN H.   Born 1900, Richmond, Va. Former chairman of the board, Virginia Electric and Power Company.
Director Ethyl 1963–81. Currently honorary director.

NOTE: *Albemarle* means Albemarle Paper Manufacturing Company before its merger with Ethyl of Delaware; *Ethyl* means Ethyl
of Virginia constituted in 1962; *Ethyl (Del.)* means the original
Ethyl Gasoline Corporation chartered in 1924, name changed
to Ethyl Corporation in 1942.

Appendix B

Ethyl Plants and Their Products
(From 1981 Annual Report)

CHEMICALS

Plants:
Baton Rouge, La.
Elgin, S.C.
Feluy, Belgium
Houston, Tex.
Magnolia, Ark.
Orangeburg, S.C.
Sarnia, Ont., Canada
Sayreville, N.J.

Products:
Alkyl dimethyl amines
Alum
Aluminum alkyl catalysts
Antioxidants
Bromine and bromine chemicals
Chlorinated and brominated
    hydrocarbons
Chlorinated solvents
Detergent intermediates
    alpha olefins
    linear primary alcohols
    zeolite A
Flame retardants
Fungicide intermediates
Germicide intermediates
Herbicide intermediates
Insecticide intermediates
Modifiers for reaction injection
    molded polyurethane
Monomers
    alpha olefins

vinyl bromide
vinyl chloride
Oil well chemicals
Pharmaceutical intermediates
Plasticizer intermediates
    alpha olefins
    linear primary alcohols
Sodium
Special organometallics

PETROLEUM FUEL
ADDITIVES

Plants:
Baton Rouge, La.
Orangeburg, S.C.
Sarnia, Ont., Canada
Thessaloniki, Greece

Products:
Antioxidants
Combustion Improvers for
    fuel oil
Corrosion/rust inhibitors
Diesel additive packages
Diesel fuel ignition improvers
Distillant fuel antistatic additive
Gasoline antiknock compounds
Gasoline detergents, de-icers,
    corrosion inhibitors
Oil-soluble dyes

LUBRICANT ADDITIVES

Plants:
Feluy, Belgium

Sauget, Ill.

Products:
Ashless dispersants/detergents
Corrosion/rust inhibitors
Hydraulic, turbine, and gear oil
    additives
Marine alkaline agents
Metal deactivators
Metal working oil concentrates
    and bases
Metallic detergents
Oxidation inhibitors
Poly alpha olefins
Pour point depressants
Tackiness agents
Viscosity index improvers

PLASTICS, IMCO
CONTAINER

Plants:
Belvidere, N.J.
Carlstadt, N.J.
Goleta, Calif.
Harrisonburg, Va.
Jeffersonville, Ind.
Kansas City, Mo. (2)
La Mirada, Calif.
Lewistown, Pa.
Louisville, Ky.
Minneapolis, Minn.
Mississauga, Ontario, Canada
Pittsfield, Mass.
Vandalia, Ill.

Products:
Bottles and containers
    (polyethylene,
    polypropylene, polyvinyl
    chloride and polyethylene
    terephthalate with
    decorating by heat transfer,
    transfer, hot stamp and silk
    screen)
Extruded polyester and cellulosic
    shapes
Oriented bottles and containers

PLASTICS, VISQUEEN FILM

Plants:
Carbondale, Pa.

Flemington, N.J.
Fremont, Calif.
LaGrange, Ga.
Manchester, Iowa
New Bern, N.C.

Products:
Films (embossed, structured and
    specialty) for agricultural and
    disposable product
    applications
Films (shrink or stretch) for
    industrial and consumer
    packaging applications

PLASTICS, MOLDED

Plants:
Alsip, Ill.
Bedford Heights, Ohio
Brooklyn Heights, Ohio
Chicago, Ill. (2)
Excelsior Springs, Mo.
Garrettsville, Ohio
LaGrange, Ky.
Pittsfield, Mass. (2)
Pomona, Calif.
St. Petersburg, Fla. (2)
South Grafton, Mass.

Products:
Custom-designed plastic molded
    parts for automobiles and
    engineering applications
Decorating services for injection
    molded plastics
Injection molded powder boxes,
    compacts, soap boxes, talc
    containers, deodorant sticks,
    lip balm dispensers, and jars
Injection molded closures, plugs
    and fitments for rigid
    containers and glass, plastic,
    and metal products
Mold and mold bases

PLASTICS, POLYMER

Plants:
Baton Rouge, La.
Delaware City, Del.
Gallman, Miss.
Tiptonville, Tenn.

Products:
Polyvinyl chloride resins and
   PVC compounds

SPECIALTY PACKAGING

Plants:
Bridgeport, Conn.
Erie, Pa.
North Riverside, Ill.
Scarborough, Ont., Canada
Waterbury, Conn.

Products:
Aerosol valves for bottle
   packaging
Custom metal packaging
   components
Decorating services for metal
   container products
Drawn and extruded dentifrice
   tubes
Mechanical spray pumps for
   packaging of fragrances,

personal and household
   products
Metal container closures

ALUMINUM

Plants:
Carthage, Tenn.
Kentland, Ind.
Mechanicsburg, Pa.
Newnan, Ga.

Products:
Aluminum windows and doors
Decorated aluminum products
   for the floor-covering and
   home-building industries
Extruded aluminum shapes in a
   variety of painted and
   anodized finishes for high-
   rise buildings, windows and
   doors, store fronts, boats,
   swimming pools, trucks, and
   trailers

Appendix C

Net Income and Sales

Table 1: Albemarle Paper Manufacturing Company 1934–62

Year Ending March 31	Net Income	Year Ending March 31	Net Income
1934	$111,722	1949	$ 269,331
1935	138,722	1950	92,706(Loss)
1936	209,437	1951	1,043,096
1937	253,696	1952	1,094,368
1938	296,246	1953	642,110
1939	21,731	1954	616,659
1940	74,997	1955	669,219
1941	68,008(Loss)	1956	1,608,255
1942	656,599	1957	2,305,840
1943	114,558(Loss)	1958	1,921,007
1944	134,788	1959	2,133,300
1945	125,625	1960	2,139,049
1946	142,987	1961	2,434,619
1947	557,367	1962	1,762,266
1948	758,888		

SOURCES: 1934–41, *Moody's Industrials,* 1941; 1942–49, Albemarle *Annual Reports;* 1950, Report of A. M. Pullen and Company, Auditors; 1951–62, Albemarle *Annual Reports.*
NOTE: Although the ending of the fiscal year varies from March 26 to April 3, it has become customary in statistical tables to list each year as ending March 31.

Table 2: Ethyl (Delaware) 1924–62

Year	Net income	Year	Net income
1924	$ 72,524(Loss)	1944	$12,853,987
1925	1,348,253(Loss)	1945	12,674,924
1926	1,211,927(Loss)	1946	8,561,425
1927	99,425(Loss)	1947	10,140,290
1928	1,586,929	1948	15,337,541
1929	5,262,909	1949	19,256,039
1930	6,863,661	1950	26,384,209
1931	7,583,965	1951	16,164,249
1932	3,758,133	1952	18,123,325
1933	5,822,409	1953	21,019,845
1934	8,699,139	1954	26,901,658
1935	8,725,982	1955	26,971,995
1936	9,431,597	1956	29,487,324
1937	11,386,505	1957	29,660,730
1938	12,240,918	1958	25,155,617
1939	18,691,603	1959	27,806,556
1940	20,508,046	1960	24,066,167
1941	19,167,289	1961	24,369,868
1942	9,767,153	1962	18,200,000[*]
1943	11,805,852		

SOURCES: Ethyl Corporation, "Annual Financial Statements" for the years 1924–61.
NOTE: Common stock dividends from December 26, 1929, through September 11, 1962, totaled $461,761,239.02. In addition a special dividend equal to earned surplus was authorized by the Ethyl directors October 26, 1962. This special dividend amounted to approximately $65,000,000.
[*]Estimate based on various memorandums passed among representatives of the sellers in the 1962 negotiations with Albemarle.

Table 3: Ethyl Corporation 1963–81

Year	Net Income
1963	$16,427,000
1964	21,059,000
1965	27,989,000
1966	37,306,000
1967	29,662,000
1968	31,502,000
1969	29,524,000
1970	37,066,000
1971	34,764,000
1972	49,130,000
1973	52,699,000
1974	73,750,000
1975	60,471,000
1976	67,998,000
1977	77,793,000
1978	82,698,000
1979	97,515,000
1980	89,682,000
1981	90,891,000

SOURCE: Ethyl Corporation, *Annual Reports*

Table 4: Ethyl Corporation: Sales by products, 1963–81

Year	Petroleum Chemicals	Industrial Chemicals	Plastics
1963	$157,122,000	$ 18,309,000	$ 2,211,c
1964	173,001,000	25,389,000	28,856,c
1965	189,504,000	29,855,000	29,955,c
1966	213,112,000	40,009,000	37,702,c
1967	199,310,000	45,030,000	40,111,c
1968	210,807,000	57,688,000	63,034,c
1969	213,840,000	65,157,000	95,461,c
1970	229,119,000	69,668,000	102,748,c
1971	222,166,000	82,556,000	111,038,c
1972	225,993,000	100,120,000	132,108,c
1973	243,624,000	109,180,000	146,323,c
1974	298,218,000	189,216,000	306,076,c
1975	349,079,000	209,722,000	275,659,c
1976	417,129,000	245,757,000	345,737,c
1977	463,736,000	287,960,000	364,839,c
1978	509,799,000	334,230,000	391,804,c
1979	577,644,000	455,372,000	408,737,c
1980	560,542,000	529,777,000	427,090,c
1981	512,382,000	570,058,000	433,050,c

SOURCE: Ethyl Corporation, *Annual Reports*

thyl Corporation: Sales by products, 1963–81

Paper	Aluminum	Energy	Total
,912,000	—	—	$ 226,554,000
,232,000	—	—	277,478,000
,697,000	—	—	305,011,000
,433,000	$25,922,000	—	384,178,000
,845,000	32,642,000	—	468,938,000
,020,000	34,523,000	—	509,072,000
,783,000	37,061,000	—	509,302,000
,283,000	63,038,000	—	556,856,000
,666,000	75,632,000	—	577,058,000
,185,000	85,193,000	—	631,599,000
,957,000	97,918,000	—	699,002,000
,099,000	100,234,000	$10,716,000	1,019,559,000
,118,000	86,719,000	8,923,000	1,029,220,000
	120,274,000	6,515,000	1,135,412,000
	156,142,000	9,410,000	1,282,087,000
	172,960,000	13,658,000	1,422,451,000
	198,961,000	16,263,000	1,657,977,000
	200,676,000	22,542,000	1,740,627,000
	208,583,000	33,122,000	1,757,195,000

Appendix D

Long-Term Debt as of November 30, 1962, and Its Purposes

Summary of Long-Term Debt

5½% Bank Loan, due $8,000,000 annually 1963–64 $16,000,000
    The Chase Manhattan Bank

5¾% Senior Notes, due $8,000,000 annually 1965–78   114,000,000
    The Prudential Insurance Company of America
The Equitable Life Assurance Society
The Northwestern Mutual Life Insurance Company
New York Life Insurance Company

5¾% Subordinated Notes, due annually to 1967   20,000,000
(Amounts of required annual payments based on earnings)
General Motors Corporation
Standard Oil Company (New Jersey)

5¾% Subordinated Notes with Warrants, due 1979–82   50,000,000
    Privately placed with various investors   _____

    Total new debt incurred $200,000,000

Debt Assumed:
3⅜% Guaranteed Notes, due 1963–70   7,361,074
Three Canadian banks
This debt owed by the Canadian subsidiary and guaranteed by the parent company

    Total debt November 30, 1962 $207,361,074

Items for Which Debt Was Incurred
Paid to General Motors and Standard Oil Company
    (N.J.) $116,366,264

Payment of bank loan assumed on purchase of chemi-
cal business   43,000,000
Payment of Albemarle Mortgage debt   13,000,000
Increase in working capital   27,633,736

    Total new debt $200,000,000

Debt of Canadian subsidiary assumed on purchase of
chemical business   7,361,074

    Total debt November 30, 1962 $207,361,074

*Cost of Assets Acquired in the Purchase of Ethyl of Dela-
ware*
Amount paid for stock $116,366,264
Liabilities assumed   73,585,552

    Total cost $189,951,816

SOURCE: Ethyl Corporation, *Annual Report for Year
Ended March 31, 1963*, p. 8.

Note on Sources

Oral Sources

This history of Ethyl Corporation rests primarily on interviews with the following people who gave me the benefit of their recollections and observations. Each name is followed by a partial identification and the location of the interview. No distinction is made between past and current status of the individual named.

John J. Adams, Washington office of Hunton and Williams, Richmond; Kirkwood F. Adams, Albemarle and Halifax Paper, Roanoke Rapids, N.C.; William E. Adams, Detroit laboratories, Detroit; Lloyd B. Andrew, vice president and treasurer, Richmond; George L. Anton, Capitol Products, Mechanicsburg, Pa.; Wallace F. Armstrong, vice president, manufacturing, Baton Rouge; Carolyn Wilde Bache (Mrs. Cyrus McCormick), Albemarle office secretary before World War I, Richmond; Hugh H. Baird, Albemarle controller, Richmond; Lawrence E. Blanchard, Jr., vice chairman, director, Richmond; M. Lebby Boinest, Jr., Halifax Paper, Roanoke Rapids, N.C.; Wilmer Kuck Borden (Mrs. Edwin B., III), friend of the Webb family, Winston-Salem, N.C.; Robert I. Boswell, son of early president of Albemarle, Richmond; James E. Boudreau, public relations, Southbury, Conn.; Thomas A. Boyd, early antiknock researcher, Detroit; Walter A. Buchanan, Ebasco representative, Richmond.

Royal E. Cabell, Jr., son of the longtime Albemarle attorney, Richmond; Paul D. Cahill, tax section, Richmond; Joseph C. Carter, Hunton and Williams, Ethyl director, Richmond; William H. Chisholm, Oxford Paper, New York City; Charles E. Colvin, purchasing and traffic, Baton Rouge; Walter A. Cosgrove, employee relations, Richmond.

Charles Davey, N.C. State University, Raleigh; Louise Edwards Duke (Mrs. Floyd M.), Albemarle office secretary, Richmond; Mrs. Frances Thompson Ellerson (Mrs. H. Watkins, Jr.), Richmond; Richard C. Erickson, James River Paper Company, Richmond; Joseph E. Faggan, Detroit laboratories, Detroit; Charles Ferguson, Oxford Paper, Rumford, Maine; S. Douglas Fleet, vice president, director, Richmond; Kenneth A. Freberg, Ethyl Canada, Inc., Sarnia, Ont., Canada; Burr J. French, technical writer, Detroit; Julian J. Frey, Ethyl International, Sarasota, Fla.; M. F. Gautreaux, senior vice president, director, Baton Rouge; Harold J. Gibson, Detroit laboratories, Detroit; James M. Gill, senior vice president, director, Baton Rouge; Anne Cobb Gottwald (Mrs. F. D.), Richmond; Bruce C. Gottwald, president, director, Richmond; Elisabeth S. Gottwald (Mrs. Floyd D., Jr.), Richmond; Floyd Dewey Gottwald, chairman, director, Richmond; Floyd Dewey Gottwald, Jr., chairman, director, Richmond; John D. Gottwald, Elk Horn Coal Corporation, Richmond; Nancy Hays Gottwald (Mrs. Bruce C.), Richmond; W. Douglas Gottwald, assistant secretary, Richmond.

C. Raymond Hailey, senior vice president, Richmond; Benjamin D. Harrison, budget director, Richmond; E. Malcolm Harvey, vice president, aluminum, Newnan, Ga.; Louise Kersey Haywood (Mrs. Lue Raymond, Sr.), August Gottwald's granddaughter, Chesapeake, Va.; Arthur W. Helwig, vice president, corporate planning, Richmond; Robert Herzog, executive vice president, director, Baton Rouge; Howard E. Hesselberg, vice president, air conservation, Detroit; Julian G. Hofmann, Halifax Paper, Roanoke Rapids, N.C.; Fred D. Hogan, Ethyl-Greylock, Pittsfield, Mass.; A. B. Horn, Jr., senior vice president, director, Baton Rouge; James A. Inge, Brown's Island and Hollywood Mills, Richmond; Mary Ellerson Jamerson (Mrs. Osmond T.), daughter of H. Watkins Ellerson, Richmond; Arthur W. James, John Marshall High School teacher, Richmond; Robert A. Kehoe, medical authority on lead, Cincinnati; Virginia King (Mrs. James W.), Ethyl nurse, Richmond; George F. Kirby, president, director, Richmond; James H. Kirby, vice president, accounting, Richmond; John C. Klock, manager of administration, Baton Rouge; Margaret A. Knowles, granddaughter of August Gottwald (joint interview with William K. Knowles, Jr.), Richmond; John C. Lane, technical writer (joint interview with Burr J. French), Detroit; Willis Lankenau, advertising, Richmond.

Lionel E. Lester, assistant manager, Orangeburg, S.C.; Louise Kellogg Lorraine (Mrs. Alfred L.) , daughter of David Kemper Kellogg, Richmond; Joseph M. Lowry, senior vice president, director, Richmond; David W. Lundy, Marland Mold, Pittsfield, Mass.; Andrew M. McBurney, Oxford Paper, Ethyl director, Richmond; Frank J. McNally, vice president and treasurer, Richmond; Jean Kersey Martin (Mrs. W. J.), great-granddaughter of August Gottwald, Richmond; James F. Miller, Blyth and Company, director Ethyl, New York City; George M. Modlin, Chancellor, University of Richmond; Roger A. Moser, senior vice president, research and development, Baton Rouge; Malcolm P.

Murdock, senior vice president, director, Santa Barbara, Calif.; Andrew Nance, Webb's caretaker and driver, New Bern, N.C.; Clarence M. Neher, senior vice president, director, Baton Rouge and Richmond; Ian A. Nimmo, director of investor relations, Richmond; William R. Perdue, Jr., executive vice president, director, New York City; David F. Peters, Hunton and Williams, Richmond; Lewis F. Powell, Jr., Hunton and Williams, Ethyl director, Richmond; Monroe J. Rathbone, Standard Oil of New Jersey, Baton Rouge; James M. Riddle, director of chemicals, Ethyl S.A., Baton Rouge; John W. Riely, Hunton and Williams, Richmond; Stephen B. Rodi, vice president, employee relations, Baton Rouge; Mattie Sandifer, office secretary, Orangeburg, S.C.; Isabel Coale Souder (Mrs. Holt), daughter of Basil Coale, Richmond; Gordon E. Saxon, director of advertising, Richmond.

Richard Scales, vice president, Naples, Fla.; S. Buford Scott, Scott and Stringfellow, Ethyl director, Richmond; James H. Scott, Scott and Stringfellow, Richmond; John H. Shiriff, Ethyl Canada, Inc., Sarnia, Ont.; Mary Shipman Short (Mrs. Albert B.), Albemarle office secretary, Richmond; Frances H. Stakes (Mrs. A. Gary), librarian, Webb Memorial Library, Morehead City, N.C.; William C. Strader, Baton Rouge plant, Baton Rouge; Grace W. Taylor (Mrs. Joseph Clarence), Earle Webb's niece, Morehead City, N.C.; Paul L. Thomason, VCA, Pittsfield, Mass.; George S. Thumlert, Capitol Products, Mechanicsburg, Pa.; Bennett H. Wall, historian, New Orleans; Thomas Elliott Wannamaker, founder Wannamaker Chemical Company, Orangeburg, S.C.; Frederick P. Warne, general counsel, Richmond; Paul E. Weimer, budget director, Richmond; J. Harvie Wilkinson, Jr., United Virginia Bank, Richmond; Erwin H. Will, honorary director, Richmond; Frederick P. Wilmer, Albemarle engineer, Richmond; James E. Wintermeyer, finance director, Ethyl Hellas, Thessaloniki, Greece, and Richmond; Charles H. Zeanah, corporate community relations, Richmond.

The typical person interviewed freely shared thoughts and memories which, in their composite form, give to this history whatever vitality it possesses. The result might be classified as oral history if that phrase is loosely defined. Perhaps I strayed from the best textbook procedures in assuring those interviewed that the resultant tapes and transcriptions would be used only in the specific Ethyl history project and would not be available for general research purposes. Such an understanding seemed appropriate for best results.

This sort of information gathering was undertaken from stark necessity; today's historian dealing with the immediate past does not have at hand the great collections of letters on which writers of yesterday depended for intimate details. The telephone, its sophisticated electronic cousins, and jet airplanes provide speedy and usually unrecorded communication.

As indicated in the preface, I have a new respect for mankind's memory of events in the considerable past. Although the investigator should not expect from those being interviewed total accuracy in chronology, there is full compensation in the recollection of colorful circumstances. The taped interview offers a special reward in "the bounty of the gleaning"—that is, listening to the recording many months after an interview is much more revealing than hearing the words the first time. The enrichment of the context by subsequent conversations with others, or by the examination of written records not available at the time of the interview, makes meaningful remarks once put aside as inconsequential. Most likely the supposedly insignificant points would never have been recorded in the old-fashioned, longhand scribbled notes developed by an interviewer desperately trying to concentrate on what at the moment he considered important.

Interviews with 90 percent of the people listed above were recorded on tape and then transcribed. As for the others, the interviewer depended on handwritten notes. Several of the people named above were interviewed in the company of one or two of their colleagues; more numerous than those involved in joint interviews were the people subjected to several interviews. The extreme example is F. D. Gottwald, who was a special target of my inquiry. He generously gave me no less than 27 formal appointments, which resulted in about an equal number of hours of taped interviews. Also there were numerous brief question-and-answer periods in his office. A note as to tape transcriptions: for the comfort of the reader's eyes, elliptical marks have been eliminated.

My cabinet of tapes holds three recordings in the making of which I had no part but which I found useful: the two speeches made by F. D. Gottwald, in Baton Rouge, September 26, 1963; the comments made by Floyd D. Gottwald, Jr., in a closed circuit interview with Professor William H. Warren's class at the College of William and Mary, December 12, 1974; and the reminiscing remarks made in New York City at the Waldorf-Astoria, November 30, 1977, in celebration of the fifteenth anniversary of the purchase of Ethyl of Delaware by Albemarle Paper.

In addition to the face-to-face encounters, I benefited by several important telephone conversations, notably talks with Rosalie Hanes Rice (Mrs. Jonas), of Winston-Salem, N.C., a friend of the Webb family; Leonore B. Schaefer (Mrs. John H.), widow of the onetime vice president and director of Ethyl of Delaware, Clarence A. Hall of the Detroit

laboratories regarding the lead controversy; and Frank J. Sergeys, a retired scientist, a man who knew firsthand the frustrations of the Ethyl
laboratories in the 1950s. In telephone conversations and correspondence Margaret Moser of the Allegheny College Library gave helpful
information regarding the first public exhibition of selections from Ethyl's collection of Petroleum Americana, January 1959.

Of course, added to the somewhat formal interviews indicated above
were dozens of shorter conversations with individuals having information important in the writing of this history.

Printed and Manuscript Sources

An underpinning of hard facts is provided by an unbroken set of directors' and stockholders' minutes, which, while often painfully brief and
frequently lacking in supporting documents, offer an invaluable calendar of corporate actions. Save for the annual report of 1950—a void
remedied by an auditor's statement—printed annual reports of Albemarle operations from 1942 to 1962 are available. Typed annual financial statements for Ethyl of Delaware are in the company files. Printed
annual reports of Ethyl of Virginia are readily obtained. Invaluable are
the legal "Record Books," those documents accumulated and bound as
acquisitions and major loans were developed.

In addition to the bibliographical credits that appear in the text and
the interviews, company minutes, annual reports, record books, and
reference material mentioned above, there are particular books, essays,
and manuscripts important enough to require citation.

Albemarle

As for Richmond, an authentic guide is Virginius Dabney's *Richmond:
The Story of a City* (Garden City, N.Y., 1976). Michael Chesson, in
his well-written volume *Richmond after the War, 1865-1890* (Richmond, 1981) provides a good, general background for the founding of
Albemarle, but he is not as assured of Richmond's forward-looking attitude as were the journalists of that era. Of first-rate importance are
the city directories, tax records, wills, deeds, and cemetery records.
Richmond Newspapers, Inc., made available a collection of clippings
organized by subject matter. The Division of Vital Records and Health
Statistics, Commonwealth of Virginia, furnished helpful information
in several instances.

A useful introduction to Richmond's paper manufacturing is the essay "The Story of Papermaking in Richmond, Virginia," *Superior Facts,*

published by Papermakers Chemical Corporation and Associates, no. 10 (Richmond Number, April 1929). Most revealing for its comments on papermaking in Richmond is *The City on the James, Richmond, Virginia,* edited by Andrew Morrison, (Richmond, 1893). Less specific but nevertheless useful is a Chamber of Commerce publication entitled *Richmond, Virginia: The City on the James* (Richmond: George W. Englehardt, 1902–3). For the physical layout of the papermaking industry and other manufacturing enterprises in Richmond, note particularly the insurance map *Richmond and Manchester, Virginia,* issued by Sanborn Map and Publishng Co. (New York, 1886).

As already noted, the story of Albemarle Paper Manufacturing Company is summarized in an address entitled "Albemarle: From Pines to Packaging," given by F. D. Gottwald before the Newcomen Society, which met in Richmond September 27, 1962. Happily, several handwritten journals and ledgers from Albemarle's first score of years offer precise details and descriptive items that bring life to the statistics, the records of purchases, and payrolls. Especially valuable to the historian of Albemarle are Journal "A," which covers the period from May 10, 1887, to April 1, 1891, and Ledger "A," covering approximately the same period.

The story of Thaw is clarified in part by an examination of the Chesterfield and Bedford County records. Correspondence between H. Watkins Ellerson and E. B. Thaw in the year 1912, when Ellerson was fretting over the water contracts with Richmond and Allegheny's successor, the Chesapeake and Ohio, throws light on the construction of Hollywood Mill and on early contractual agreements made by Albemarle. Letters between C.P.A. Burgwyn and A. B. Tower in 1887 and 1888 provide an important supplement to Thaw's recollections.

The Isle of Wight County records reveal something of James F. Chalmers and his background. The relationship between Chalmers and Thomas F. Flournoy, Jr., and the loan of $9,500 are explained in the City of Richmond Deed Book 233B, pp. 278–79. As for W. E. Dibrell, there are in the Virginia Historical Society several of his manuscripts dealing with the history of his family. Illuminating letters from his great-nephew, Louis N. Dibrell, Jr., to the present author are in private files.

The story of James Lishman is given briefly in the survey of the Albemarle Paper Manufacturing Company in Morrison's *City on the James,* already cited. Lishman's personal appearance and habits are clarified in correspondence with two of his grandchildren, Mrs. Kenneth MacPherson of Leroy, N.Y., and James Dennis Wootton of Lancashire, England. The real estate records in Richmond and the city directories are also helpful in filling out this story.

Notes on important directors may be discovered in the book entitled *A Century of Service: A History of the First and Merchants National Bank, 1865–1965*, by Frances Leigh Williams (Richmond, 1965) and in *A Narrative Report of the Century 1848–1948 as It Dealt with the Davenport Insurance Company* (Richmond, 1948). Also there is a 48-page document in the Virginia Historical Society entitled "Notes on the Davenport Family," compiled by Beverly Fleet (Richmond, 1948).

Early as well as later generations of the Ellerson family are mentioned in William Bolling Blanton's *The Making of a Downtown Church: The History of the Second Presbyterian Church, 1845–1945* (Richmond, 1945). With regard to H. Watkins Ellerson, the interview with Mary Ellerson Jamerson (Mrs. Osmond T.) is extremely important. Douglas Fleet, Frederick P. Wilmer, and Kirkwood Adams all have vivid recollections of Ellerson. In the manuscript collection of the Virginia Historical Society are several letters exchanged by Ellerson and his cousin William T. Reed. There is a good factual sketch of Henry Watkins Ellerson in the *National Cyclopaedia of American Biography*, III, 484–85. Glen Roy, the Ellerson home, stands intact. Ellerson's death was reported in the *News Leader* on May 7, 1941, and an editorial appeared in that same journal on May 9, 1941. Ellerson's burial record is in Hollywood Cemetery Register IV, folio 167, interment on May 8, 1941.

The relations between Albemarle and the Chesapeake Corporation are illuminated in the well-written volume by Alonzo Thomas Dill entitled *Chesapeake, Pioneer Papermaker: A History of the Company and Its Community* (Charlottesville, Va., 1968). Dill offers helpful biographical sketches of directors common to Albemarle and Chesapeake. The author courteously provided me with excerpts from an oral history interview with Ellis Olsson conducted by Elwood R. Maunder of the Forest History Foundation, Inc., February 18, 1959.

The amazing codicil to McSwain's will is dated October 15, 1945, and attached to the basic document signed March 15, 1944. McSwain lived only a few days after that codicil was signed. The will was probated November 5, 1945.

The accumulation of Albemarle shares by F. D. Gottwald, Sr., can be traced in the records of the corporation and in a letter from Wachovia Bank and Trust Company, Raleigh branch, under date of August 26, 1947. The story of the Hofmann Forest is best explained in the publication entitled *The Hofmann Forest: A History of the North Carolina Forestry Foundation*, compiled by William D. Miller (N.C. State University, 1970). Also helpful are the recollections of Dr. Julian G. Hofmann, son of the Hofmann for whom the forest is named. For the

Tredegar story see the 43-page memorandum regarding the history and significance of Tredegar Iron Works prepared by Roy E. Johnson and addressed to the American Society of Mechanical Engineers. Albemarle research in the 1950s is explained in a conversation with, and a memorandum from, Brenton S. Halsey. The pamphlet on Gamble's Hill was written by Vera Palmer and entitled *Gamble's Hill: A Rebirth of an Elegant Richmond* (Richmond, 1962).

Ethyl of Delaware

I used with appreciation sections of Williams Haynes's *American Chemical Industry*, 6 vols. (New York, 1945–54). Chapter 24 of vol. 4, with the subtitle "The Merger Era," is headed "Petroleum and Tetraethyl Lead."

As for Ethyl (Delaware), an important guide is offered in the so-called Green Book entitled "Historical Summary: Ethyl Corporation, 1923–48," dated July 1, 1951. There were plans to continue the story to 1962, and additional paragraphs were drafted, this in 1975, but the extended document was never put together. This pioneer effort by Thom Yates has been a handy reference tool for many years. All of those interested in the history of Ethyl of Delaware are indebted to Thom Yates.

In a class by themselves are the writings of T. A. Boyd, who recorded with care the research of Kettering and his group in a company document entitled *The Early History of Ethyl Gasoline*. The bound volume, which runs slightly over 400 pages, is identified as Report OC-83 Project No. 11–3 issued by the Research Laboratories Division of General Motors Corporation, Detroit, Michigan. Boyd's *Professional Amateur: The Biography of Charles Franklin Kettering* (New York, 1957) is of special merit since it was written by a man intimately associated with his subject. If there is a fault in Boyd's writings, it is his tendency to minimize his own importance in the discovery and development of the antiknock additive. Boyd courteously shared in a round-table discussion of early days when the present author was in Detroit. Charles H. Zeanah's account of Kettering's dramatic statement in Houston as to the future importance of solar energy may be found in the Introduction to *Ethyl Digest* 1977.

As for Midgley, the most intimate account is that given orally by the late Richard Scales. Various letters to and from Midgley are in the correspondence now filed in the Detroit research laboratories. (Copies of several important letters were supplied by the Detroit staff.) A good sketch of Midgley may be found in *DAB*. The pamphlet entitled "The Thomas Midgley Award: A Memorial to an Inventive Genius," published by the Detroit section of the American Chemical Society in cooperation with the Ethyl Corporation, gives a cheerful estimate of the man. Among Midgley's writings which should be mentioned is an article, "How We Found Ethyl Gas," in the *Motor Magazine*, Annual Number, January 1925.

The developments in Dow Chemical, often in alliance with Ethyl, are treated in Don Whitehead's *The Dow Story: The History of the Dow Chemical Company* (New York, 1968). With regard to Standard Oil, note the volume *The Resurgent Years: History of Standard Oil Company (New Jersey) 1917–1929*, by George Sweet Gibb and Evelyn H. Knowlton. See also *New Horizons: History of Standard Oil Company (New Jersey) 1927–1950*, by Henrietta M. Larson, Evelyn H. Knowlton, and Charles S. Popple (New York, 1971). For an illuminating account of the man who was president of Standard Oil of New Jersey from 1917 to 1937, see *Teagle of Jersey Standard*, by Bennett H. Wall and George S. Gibb (New Orleans, 1974). The discovery of the effectiveness of tetraethyl lead as an antiknock is traced in an interesting pamphlet entitled *The Trail of the Arbutus*, dated August 29, 1951.

An analysis of the longtime meaning of tetraethyl lead is in the article by John A. Moore entitled "Gasoline Has Come a Long Way and TEL Helped Make It Happen," *Oil Daily*, March 25, 1977.

Useful information regarding James T. Grady was furnished by Paul E. Palmer, curator of Columbia University, Columbiana Collection, New York City.

Kehoe's development of safe procedures for handling tetraethyl lead is well illustrated by a letter he wrote to Webb dated Cincinnati, November 9, 1925.

Webb's personality has been summarized in interviews with a number of people that knew him: Mrs. Grace Taylor, Mrs. Borden, Mrs. Schaefer, Mrs. Rice, Andrew Nance, and Paul Weimer among others. Clippings indicating certain features of Webb's life and career have been supplied by the Webb Memorial Library, Morehead City, N.C. Webb's letter to Dean Wannamaker of Duke University regarding the death of Earle Webb, Jr., is preserved in the Duke University Archives from which came other valuable data on Webb. Entries in the census returns of 1880 and 1900 for Carteret County give revealing information about the Webb family.

A handsome summary of the operation of Ethyl Corporation in the 1930s is provided by a 244-page document entitled "Economic Basis for General Excess Profits Tax Relief for Ethyl Corporation, New York, N.Y.," by Thomas N. Beckman, professor of business organization, Ohio State University, March 1950.

The suit against DuPont to force it to give up its ownership of shares in General Motors produced two briefs of considerable importance as a source of information about the Ethyl Corporation: United States District Court, Northern District of Illinois, Eastern Division — United States of America, Plaintiff, vs. E. I. DuPont de Nemours and Company et al., Defendants — Civil Action No. 49 C 1971 "Trial Brief for Defendants" (Twentieth Century Press), and "Plaintiff's Trial Brief" (Scheffer Press).

Earl Bartholomew's career can best be traced in his numerous essays and lectures treating the relationship between engines and fuels. Perhaps the most reflective and autobiographical of his statements is the Horning Memorial Lecture, "Four Decades of Engine-Fuel Technology Forecast Future Advances," presented before the Society of Automotive Engineers November 2, 1966.

A concise and authentic biographical sketch of S. D. Heron is in the section entitled "About the Author" in Heron's History of the Aircraft Piston Engine: A Brief Outline, published by Ethyl Corporation in 1961.

As for Krieger, much of his career is explained in a collection of papers received from his sister, Mrs. Frank Curtis Weaver, of Hopewell, Va. The book Food for America's Future, published in 1960 by McGraw-Hill for Ethyl Corporation, was prepared under the editorial supervision of George Krieger.

As for foreign sales, there is a memorandum entitled "Introduction of Antiknocks in Germany," by Wolfgang W. Ellissen, who gave credit to Dr. Inge Wilkie for the notes on which the memorandum is based. The essay includes developments as late as the 1960s. The copy used by the present author was addressed to A. S. Hawkes, to whom I am indebted for this and other favors. The Ellissen document is a valuable treatise.

The trade relations between Americans and Germans are discussed in the reprint from the December 1962 issue of the Western Political Quarterly, "American Business and Germany, 1930–1941," by Gabriel Kolko (Bobbs-Merrill Reprint Series in American History). The Borkin book is entitled The Crime and Punishment of I. G. Farben (New York, 1978).

I Kept No Diary, by F. R. (Rod) Banks, issued by Airlife Publications in England in 1978, gives a good picture of antiknocks in Europe in the 1930s and 1940s.

The key evidence as to the British agreement is in the minutes of the Ethyl coordination committee April 30, 1937. Here, Webb reported on the British prewar strategy with regard to tetraethyl lead. In the same report he referred to the contract with the French government.

The story of Nick Carter in the Orient calls for a novelist rather than a historian. A description of the Carter Collection and its origin is given in a handsomely illustrated volume entitled *Chinese Bronzes from the Collection of Chester Dale and Dolly Carter* (Ascona, Switzerland, 1978).

The suit against the Ethyl Corporation for allegedly violating the Sherman Anti-Trust Act by its licensing system was appealed to the Supreme Court, which affirmed the verdict of guilty given by the U.S. District Court for the southern district of New York (Ethyl Gasoline Corp. *v.* U.S., 309 U.S., 436, 1940).

Ethyl of Virginia

The purchase of Ethyl of Delaware by Albemarle is described in corporate minutes, the record book, and in reminiscences of the three Gottwalds, Miller, Powell, Riely, Lowry, Carter, Blanchard, and many others. Of particular value is Blanchard's essay on this subject prepared for the volume planned to cover the recent history of Hunton and Williams. Blanchard's basic memorandum is dated August 1974; Lewis Powell's addendum is dated July 3, 1975.

Of prime importance in providing behind-the-scene details are documents from the files of Jersey and General Motors obtained by Ethyl for use in the dispute with the Internal Revenue Service over the valuations of properties acquired from Ethyl of Delaware in 1962.

Kehoe's comments before the California Club in Los Angeles, April 30, 1956, are summarized in a paper entitled "The Behavior of Lead in the Human Organism in Relation to Modern Community Life." Probably the most thorough of the various essays about Robert Kehoe is that by Irene R. Campbell called "The House That Robert A. Kehoe Built," in *Archives of Environmental Health* 13 (August 1966): 143–51. It is in this essay (p. 145n) that reference is made to Dr. Alice Hamilton's approval of the new precautions in the distribution of the tetraethyl lead additive. There is an informative and lively introduction of Kehoe by T. Lyle Hazlett before the Association of Industrial Physicians and Surgeons on the occasion of the presentation to Kehoe of the Knudsen Award, April 5, 1949.

Harry M. Caudill, in addition to the volume *Night Comes to the Cumberlands* (Boston, 1962), cited in the text, has written a most revealing essay entitled "The Strange Career of John C. C. Mayo," *Fil-*

son Club History Quarterly 56 (1982): 258–89, wherein the founding and early years of Elk Horn Coal Corporation are discussed.

Although not cited article by article, these several company periodicals were major sources of information: *Ethyl News*, 1934–67; *Ethyl Bulletin Board*, 1941–62; *Ethyl Reporter*, 1963–80; *Ethyl Magazine*, 1968–70; *Ethyl Digest*, 1971–77; *Ethyl Intercom*, since 1980. A notable series of full-page interviews appeared in the *Ethyl Reporter* 1976–79.

Gottwald

The history of the Gottwald-Freyfogle family of Richmond is built on several written records in addition to the facts and family traditions passed along orally to the present writer by F. D. Gottwald, W. Douglas Gottwald, Mrs. Haywood, Miss Knowles, Mrs. Martin, and Miss Elsie McClintic. Among the written records are the following items of importance.

The so-called size roll giving the physical characteristics of Christian Freyfogle, is in the National Archives, Record Group no. 127, Records of the United States Marine Corps, Size Roll page 99, 1812. Christian Freyfogle's testimony before a special committee as reported in *Journal-Documents, Virginia House of Delegates*, 1832–33, Document no. 81, p. 15. Christian Freyfogle's marriage record, Henrico County Records at Large (Marriages) 1815–53, p. 20. Christian Freyfogle's key purchase of real estate in City of Richmond, Hustings Deeds, vol. 22, p. 296, April 19, 1924. Christian Freyfogle's will in Henrico County Wills, vol. 10, p. 573. Christian Freyfogle's burial in the official Shockoe Cemetery records in Range 6, Section 2, Quarter Section 1, Range of Graves 1, Grave 1. Also noted in Bohman Rudd, ed., *Shockoe Hill Cemetery, Richmond, Virginia*, Register of Interments, vol. 1, p. 20.

Jacob Freyfogle's naturalization petition is recorded in Henrico County Court Minutes, 1842–43, p. 41, March 7, 1842. Jacob Freyfogle's trust agreement may be found in Henrico County Deed Books, vol. 56, page 121, reel 27 in microfilm version. Jacob Freyfogle's home guard record can be found in the Compiled Service Records of Confederate Soldiers Who Served in Organizations from Virginia, Microcopy 324, roll No. 364, the originals in National Archives. The role of Jacob Freyfogle in the German Lutheran Church (in this period officially known as St. John's German Evangelical Lutheran Church) is outlined in the records available in the church office and in the Virginia Historical Society. In the translation of these and other German-language documents I received valuable assistance from Mrs. Lee C. Sheppard.

The marriage of Jacob Freyfogle and Caroline Rebman is mentioned in Henrico County Deed Books, no. 51, p. 453. Jacob Freyfogle's interment is recorded in *Shockoe Cemetery Records*, vol. 3, 1871–1955, p. 373, line 4.

August Gottwald's listing in the Ordway payrolls may be found in the National Archives, Record Group no. 217; U.S. General Accounting; Records of the 1st Auditor of the Treasury Department; Miscellaneous Treasury Accounts; A/C 188, 478, voucher 647, subvoucher 10, payroll no. 217. There are other listings. The marriage of August Gottwald and Louisa Freyfogle is recorded in Register of Licenses and Marriages, Hustings Court, City of Richmond, 1853–77, vol. 1, p. 238. And Evangelical Lutheran Church, Church Record: 1865–97, p. 138. August Gottwald's death is noted in the church records: 1865–97, St. John's Evangelical Lutheran Church, p. 344, and in *Richmond Dispatch*, Thursday, January 21, 1886. The suit to clear up the title to the Henrico County property is described as Suit in Equity, Gottwald *v.* Gottwald and others. The case was decided by the Circuit Court of Henrico County, March 23, 1891.

With permission of F. D. Gottwald the author examined Gottwald's academic records: Nicholson Graded School, John Marshall High School (both now in the Virginia State Library), and the College of William and Mary, Richmond Division (now deposited with Virginia Commonwealth University), showing grades made in his chemistry course. The R.F.&P. payroll records were, at the time of this investigation, in the company archives on Broad Street in Richmond.

The statement by Thomas Edward ("Teddy") Gottwald as to his freedom of professional choice is drawn from an interview by John Markon, *Richmond Times-Dispatch*, November 19, 1982.

First Colony

The purchase of the insurance company in 1982 is well described in reports and press releases issued by Ethyl and First Colony, and in the periodicals of the day, especially the *Richmond Times-Dispatch*, the *Richmond News Leader*, and the Lynchburg *Daily Advance*. Quoted in the text is a vibrant statement as to the significance of the First Colony acquisition drawn from an article "Joining Agility and Innovation" in *Fortune* February 22, 1982. An excellent background essay is Gary Robertson's "Once Tiny First Colony Now a Giant Company," *Richmond Times-Dispatch*, December 13, 1981.

Acknowledgments

In the typical research venture, access to printed and manuscript sources hinges on the goodwill of those quiet heroes the librarians and archivists. I am grateful to these preservers and purveyors of the word, especially to the staffs at the Virginia Historical Society, Boatwright Memorial Library of the University of Richmond, the Richmond Public Library, the Valentine Museum, the National Archives, and the Virginia State Library. I have been especially demanding of Conley L. Edwards, my former graduate student, now with the last-named repository, and I give thanks to him for his careful services, far beyond the call of his profession. Bennett H. Wall, now completing a volume in the *History of Standard Oil Company (New Jersey)* series, not only supplied useful materials drawn from his own research but also offered practical advice on the writing of business history.

A host of Ethyl staff members, past and present, gave me aid and comfort. Arthur W. Helwig, vice president of the corporation and secretary of the executive committee, bore up well under many telephone calls and interviews made in my attempts to bring into focus otherwise formless events and strange terms. Ian A. Nimmo, director of investor relations, answered repeated and naive questions about chemical engineering as well as inquiries concerning the process of making acquisitions. F. Case Whittemore of the law department patiently explained important litigation and certain matters of legal procedure. Robert A. Linn, director of corporate business development, gave helpful comments on two widely separated topics: the significance of the purchase of First Colony Life and the importance of Earl Bartholomew in the area of research. Benjamin D. Harrison, former budget director, was one of the first to introduce me to the history of Ethyl of Delaware and provided guidelines for subsequent investigations. In many a lunch hour Roy E. Johnson, Richmond properties manager, spoke not only of old Albemarle but attempted to educate me in the mystery of papermaking in the past. The assistant secretary of the corporation, W. Douglas

Gottwald, Jr., suffered without complaint repeated interruptions when I needed records in the company vault or storage cabinets.

As indicated elsewhere, the old guard of Albemarle—Fleet, Lowry, Kirkwood Adams, Boinest, and Hailey—reviewed many episodes and circumstances in the history of the original paper company. Because of the nature of the management of Ethyl, there were extensive conferences with members of the executive committee. I trust that in the text proper recognition has been given to the testimony of Robert Herzog, Lawrence E. Blanchard, Jr., Bruce C. Gottwald, Floyd D. Gottwald, Jr., and F. D. Gottwald.

In recognizing conspicuous assistance I must cite the corporate communications department, which for many months had to bear with my presence and my inquiries. I am grateful to the director, A. Prescott Rowe, and to his staff: Robert P. Buford IV and Raymond F. Kozakewicz. This volume is better as a result of professional criticism available at the University Press of Virginia. The book was further improved by the careful scrutiny and constructive suggestions of Edward C. Peple, professor of English emeritus, University of Richmond. For more than three years I have benefited by the loyal and efficient service of my secretary, Lois F. Shaw (Mrs. Irwin V.), to whom I offer my thanks.

I now record my gratitude to certain longtime and trusted friends who repeatedly gave me hope and renewed strength by their words of wisdom. I refer especially to Clarence J. Robinson of Alexandria and to the late Joseph E. Nettles of Richmond.

While I am not certain as to what I have done to the history of Ethyl, I am quite aware of what it has done to me. In the course of the investigations I have profited by acquaintance with dozens of talented people. More than ever, I recognize the importance in our national life of vigorous entrepreneurs who have taken risks and created great institutions. As is always the case with historical research, there have been seasons of drudgery, but the exhilarating episodes more than compensated for the periods of drabness.

In concluding this book I claim the personal privilege of saluting the teachers who have appeared from time to time in the testimony of those being interviewed. In employing its people, Ethyl has captured not only the individual whose name appears on the rolls but all those personalities who made that individual what he is. Already I have briefly touched on the subject of the enduring influence of successful teachers. This topic, however, warrants a postscript paragraph. There is more confirming evidence than can be put in the text.

Paul D. Cahill tells of the forceful teachers at St. Peter's College in Jersey City, among them being Father Johnson, a true Victorian who knew eight languages, including Anglo-Saxon, and Father Chetwood, who made Shakespeare come alive. James M. Riddle, brought up in Bentonville, Arkansas, reports that he and his peers were captivated by several great teachers, among them Ruth ("Ma") Barker, "a very professional old-line teacher, a real educator [who] had a dramatic influence on our class." Ma Barker announced that all members of Riddle's class were going to college. She was just about right: fifty-one of fifty-five who graduated from high school did just that, making their marks in the arts, sciences, and other useful areas. When Riddle went to the University of Arkansas he was confronted by a brilliant teacher of mathematics, Professor Bernard H. Gundlach, a German who had come to this country with Wernher von Braun. In Riddle's words, "There is not a doubt in my mind that had it not been for that one college professor I would not be working with Ethyl Corporation today." These instances might be multiplied. I now take the immodest liberty of referring to my own experience. I suppose that whenever I attempt to link subject and predicate in any sentence I am responding to imperatives given by a train of masterful teachers, ranging from Ada Joyce Foster in the first grade to William Kenneth Boyd in the Duke University Graduate School. I am grateful to you, ladies and gentlemen of the classroom. Monotonously didactic, I remind my colleagues in school and college of the awesome responsibilities they bear.

I end this volume with thanks to my wife, Evelyn Bristow Robert, for her patience and good humor in the face of strange schedules and my appropriation of any flat surface in our house. When space for books and papers ran out in study and library, I even confiscated the dining room table for a season! Trained in history by great professors, including Maude Howlett Woodfin at Westhampton College, University of Richmond, and Carl Becker in the graduate program at Cornell University, she has displayed sympathy and understanding throughout my efforts to picture Ethyl Corporation and the people who made it.

Richmond, Virginia   JOSEPH C. ROBERT

Index

Picture Credits

Illustrations are drawn from Ethyl files unless otherwise indicated. Endpaper — front, basic drawing from Beloit Iron Works; frontispiece, painting by Albert Murray; page 4, courtesy of Valentine Museum; page 6, courtesy of Virginia State Library; page 11, courtesy of Mrs. Kenneth MacPherson; page 13, courtesy of Mrs. Robert I. Boswell; page 16, *Men of Mark in Virginia*, vol. 4 (1908); pages 22-23, courtesy of Valentine Museum; page 30, courtesy of Mrs. H. Watkins Ellerson, Jr.; page 33, courtesy of Mrs. W. Holt Souder; page 49, courtesy of North Carolina Division of Archives and History; page 71, based on drawing by Roy E. Johnson; page 82, Dementi-Foster Collection; page 87, photograph by Lewis Longest, 1982; page 94, courtesy of Cadillac Motor Car Division, General Motors Corporation; page 109, courtesy of General Motors Research Laboratories; page 243, *New York Times*, September 23,1962 ©1962 by the New York Times Company, reprinted by permission; page 245, reprinted by permission of *Forbes* magazine, ©Forbes Inc., 1962; page 318, photograph by O. Winston Link, 1965; page 367, Dementi-Foster Collection.